SOUL EATER

9

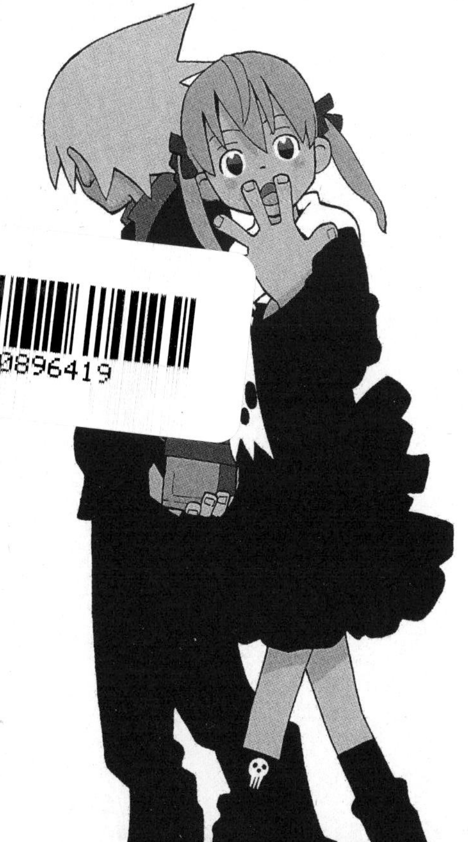

ATSUSHI OHKUBO

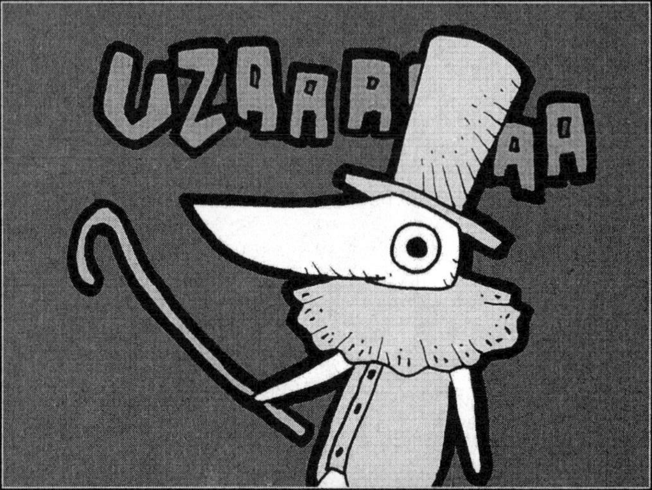
UZAAAAAAA
UZAAAAAAA: ANNOYING AS HELL

SOUL EATER

vol. 9

by ATSUSHI OHKUBO

DUKES BLAZE, SOUL IGNITE

SOUL EATER 9

VS

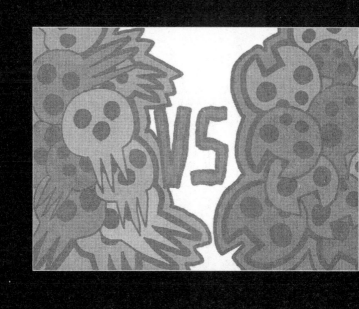

CONTENTS

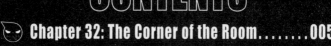

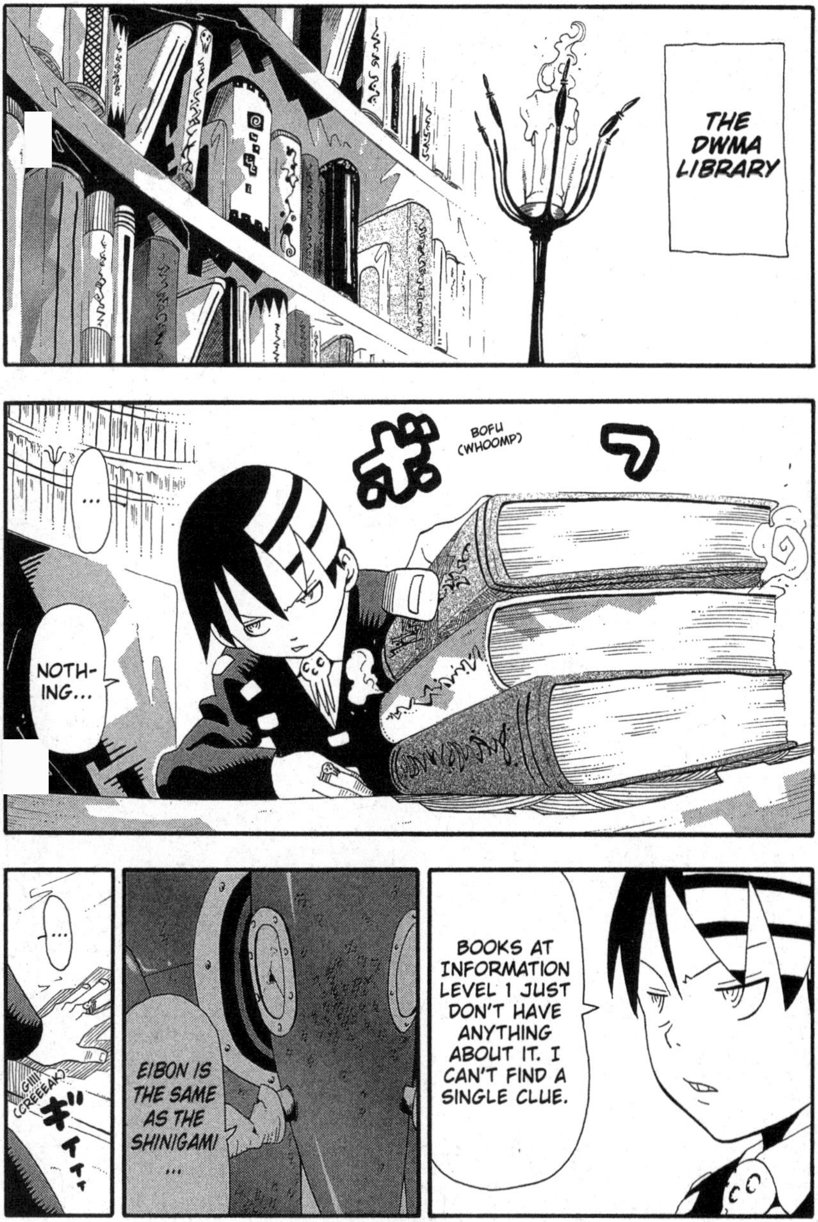
THE DWMA LIBRARY
BOFU (WHOOMP)
...
NOTH-ING...
BOOKS AT INFORMATION LEVEL 1 JUST DON'T HAVE ANYTHING ABOUT IT. I CAN'T FIND A SINGLE CLUE.
EIBON IS THE SAME AS THE SHINIGAMI ...
...
GIIII (CREEEAK)

WHO THE HELL IS THIS "EIBON"...?

SOUL EATER

CHAPTER 32: THE CORNER OF THE ROOM

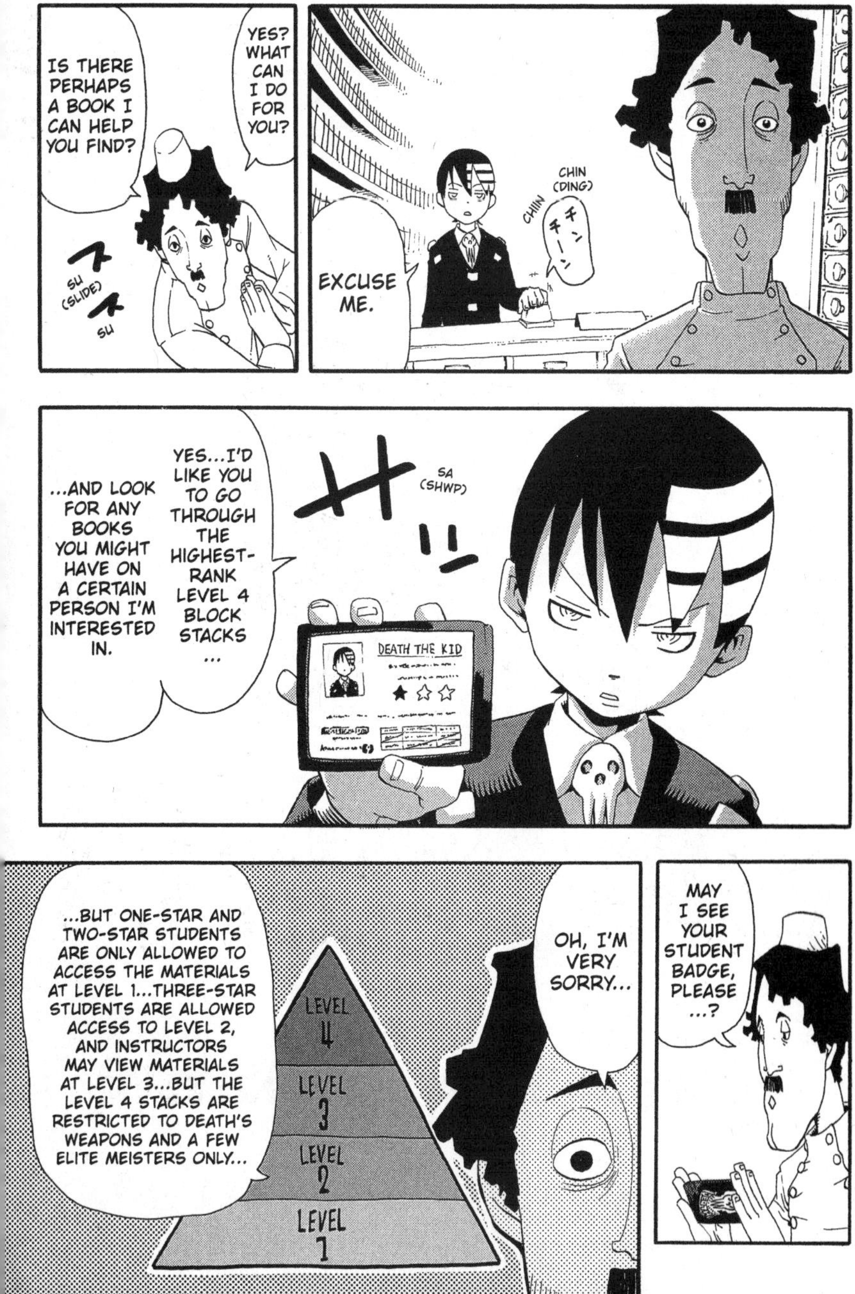
CHIN (DING)
CHIN
EXCUSE ME.
YES? WHAT CAN I DO FOR YOU?
IS THERE PERHAPS A BOOK I CAN HELP YOU FIND?
SU (SLIDE)
SU
SA (SHWP)
DEATH THE KID
YES...I'D LIKE YOU TO GO THROUGH THE HIGHEST-RANK LEVEL 4 BLOCK STACKS ...
...AND LOOK FOR ANY BOOKS YOU MIGHT HAVE ON A CERTAIN PERSON I'M INTERESTED IN.
MAY I SEE YOUR STUDENT BADGE, PLEASE ...?
OH, I'M VERY SORRY...
...BUT ONE-STAR AND TWO-STAR STUDENTS ARE ONLY ALLOWED TO ACCESS THE MATERIALS AT LEVEL 1...THREE-STAR STUDENTS ARE ALLOWED ACCESS TO LEVEL 2, AND INSTRUCTORS MAY VIEW MATERIALS AT LEVEL 3...BUT THE LEVEL 4 STACKS ARE RESTRICTED TO DEATH'S WEAPONS AND A FEW ELITE MEISTERS ONLY...
LEVEL 4
LEVEL 3
LEVEL 2
LEVEL 1

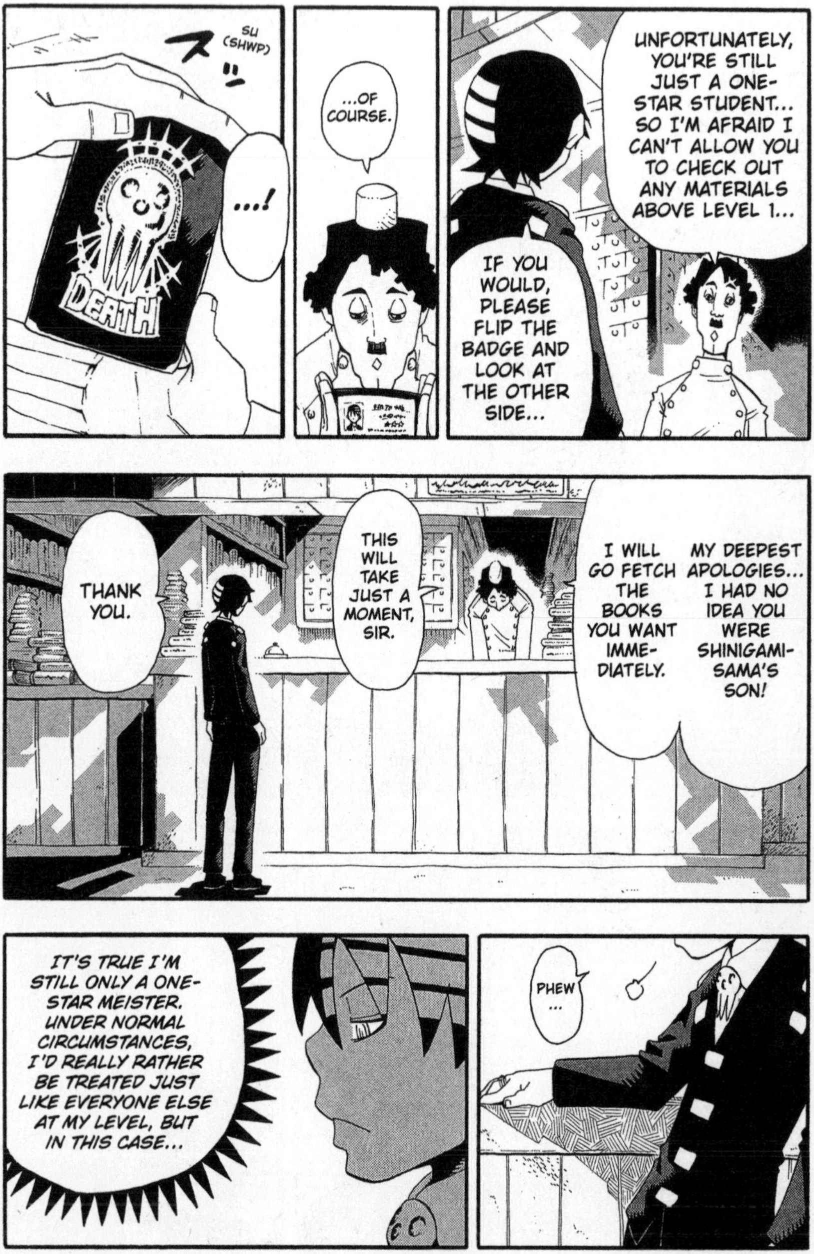
UNFORTUNATELY, YOU'RE STILL JUST A ONE-STAR STUDENT... SO I'M AFRAID I CAN'T ALLOW YOU TO CHECK OUT ANY MATERIALS ABOVE LEVEL 1...
IF YOU WOULD, PLEASE FLIP THE BADGE AND LOOK AT THE OTHER SIDE...
...OF COURSE.
SU (SHWP)
...!
DEATH
MY DEEPEST APOLOGIES... I HAD NO IDEA YOU WERE SHINIGAMI-SAMA'S SON!
I WILL GO FETCH THE BOOKS YOU WANT IMMEDIATELY.
THIS WILL TAKE JUST A MOMENT, SIR.
THANK YOU.
PHEW...
IT'S TRUE I'M STILL ONLY A ONE-STAR MEISTER. UNDER NORMAL CIRCUMSTANCES, I'D REALLY RATHER BE TREATED JUST LIKE EVERYONE ELSE AT MY LEVEL, BUT IN THIS CASE...

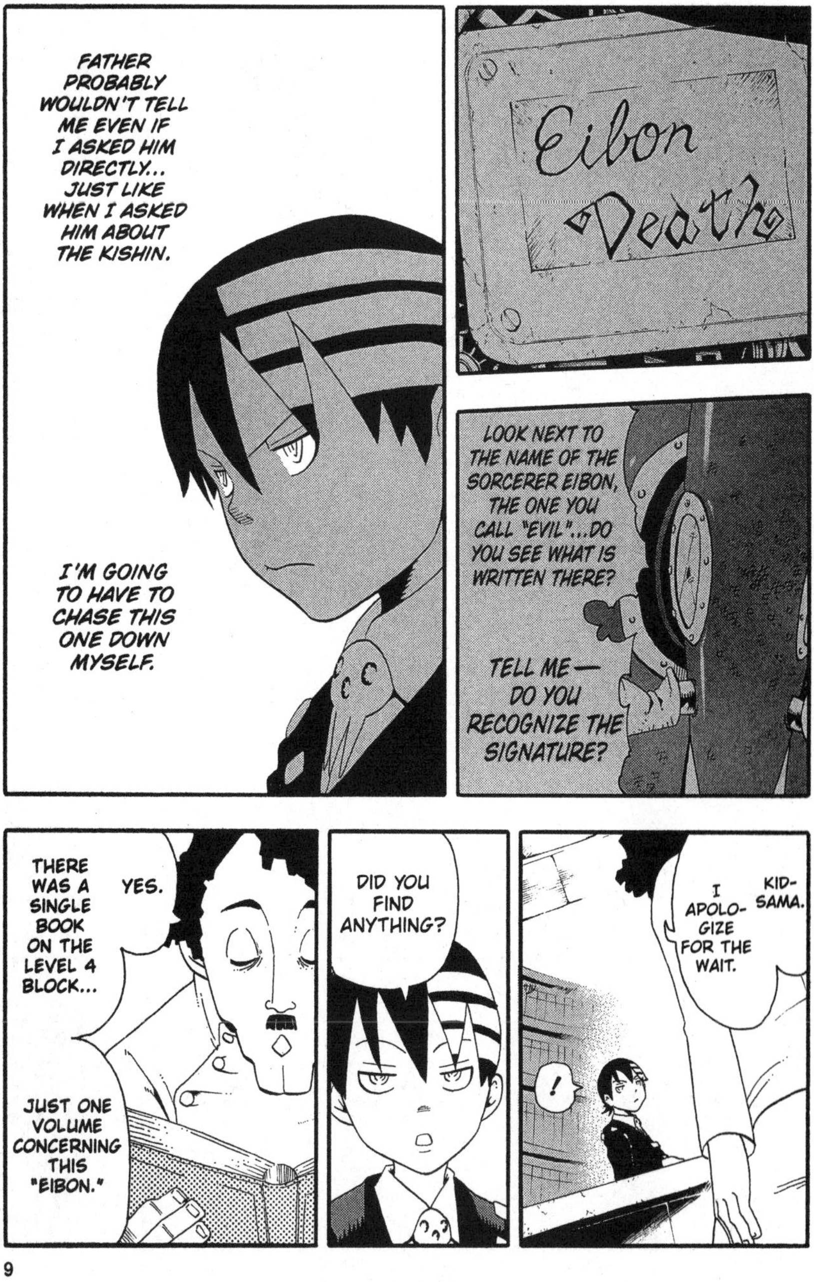
Eibon
Death
LOOK NEXT TO THE NAME OF THE SORCERER EIBON, THE ONE YOU CALL "EVIL"...DO YOU SEE WHAT IS WRITTEN THERE?
TELL ME— DO YOU RECOGNIZE THE SIGNATURE?
FATHER PROBABLY WOULDN'T TELL ME EVEN IF I ASKED HIM DIRECTLY... JUST LIKE WHEN I ASKED HIM ABOUT THE KISHIN.
I'M GOING TO HAVE TO CHASE THIS ONE DOWN MYSELF.
KID-SAMA.
I APOLO-GIZE FOR THE WAIT.
!
DID YOU FIND ANYTHING?
YES.
THERE WAS A SINGLE BOOK ON THE LEVEL 4 BLOCK...
JUST ONE VOLUME CONCERNING THIS "EIBON."

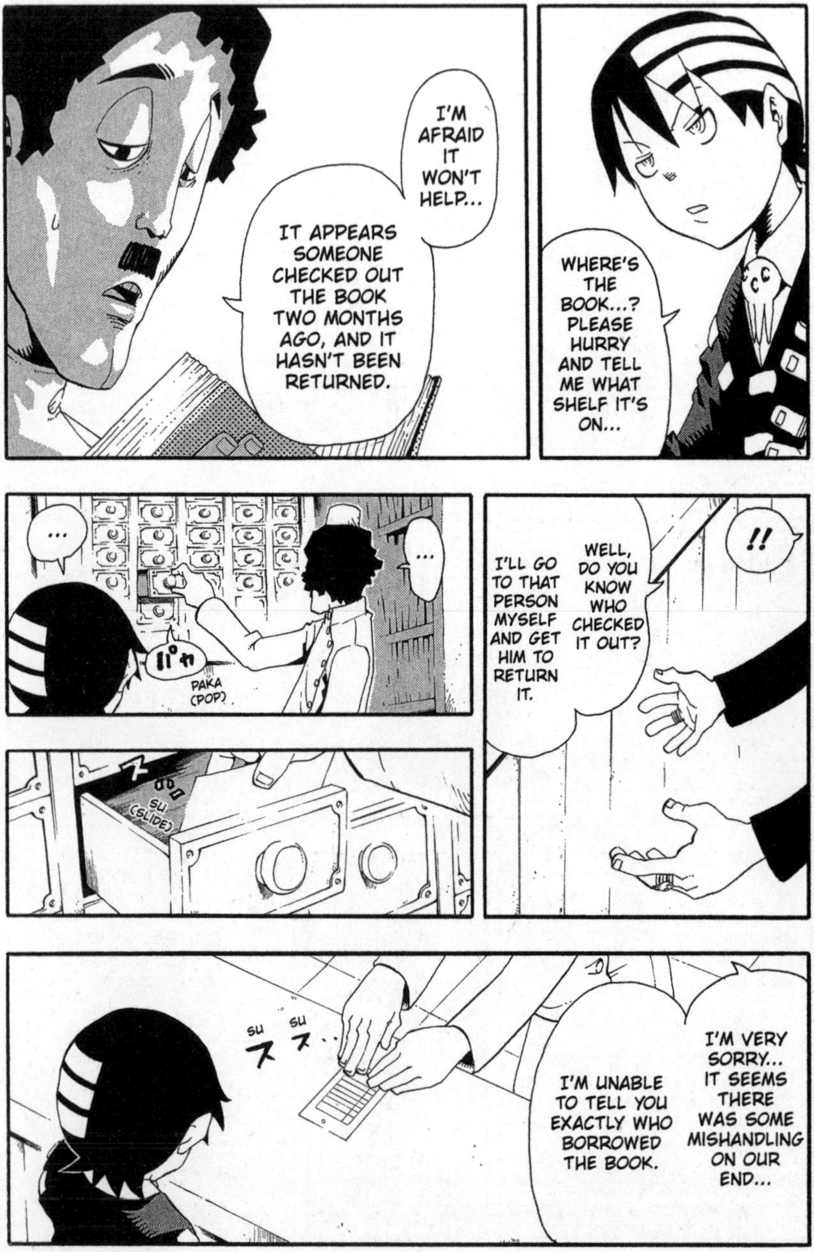
WHERE'S THE BOOK...? PLEASE HURRY AND TELL ME WHAT SHELF IT'S ON...
I'M AFRAID IT WON'T HELP...
IT APPEARS SOMEONE CHECKED OUT THE BOOK TWO MONTHS AGO, AND IT HASN'T BEEN RETURNED.
!!
WELL, DO YOU KNOW WHO CHECKED IT OUT?
I'LL GO TO THAT PERSON MYSELF AND GET HIM TO RETURN IT.
...
...
PAKA (POP)
SU (SLIDE)
I'M VERY SORRY... IT SEEMS THERE WAS SOME MISHANDLING ON OUR END...
I'M UNABLE TO TELL YOU EXACTLY WHO BORROWED THE BOOK.
SU
SU

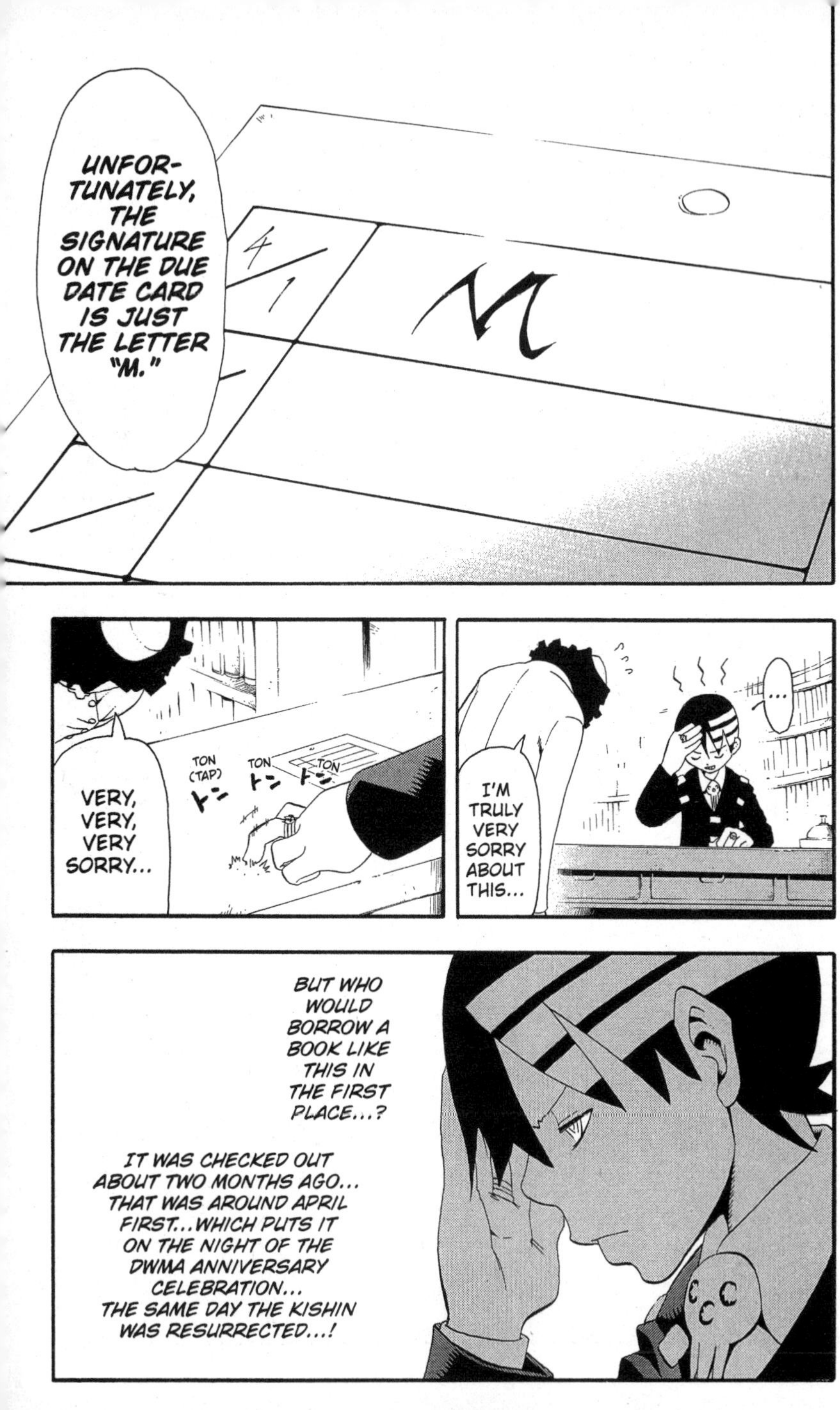
UNFORTUNATELY, THE SIGNATURE ON THE DUE DATE CARD IS JUST THE LETTER "M."
...
I'M TRULY VERY SORRY ABOUT THIS...
TON (TAP) トン
TON トン
TON トン
VERY, VERY, VERY SORRY...
BUT WHO WOULD BORROW A BOOK LIKE THIS IN THE FIRST PLACE...?
IT WAS CHECKED OUT ABOUT TWO MONTHS AGO... THAT WAS AROUND APRIL FIRST...WHICH PUTS IT ON THE NIGHT OF THE DWMA ANNIVERSARY CELEBRATION... THE SAME DAY THE KISHIN WAS RESURRECTED...!

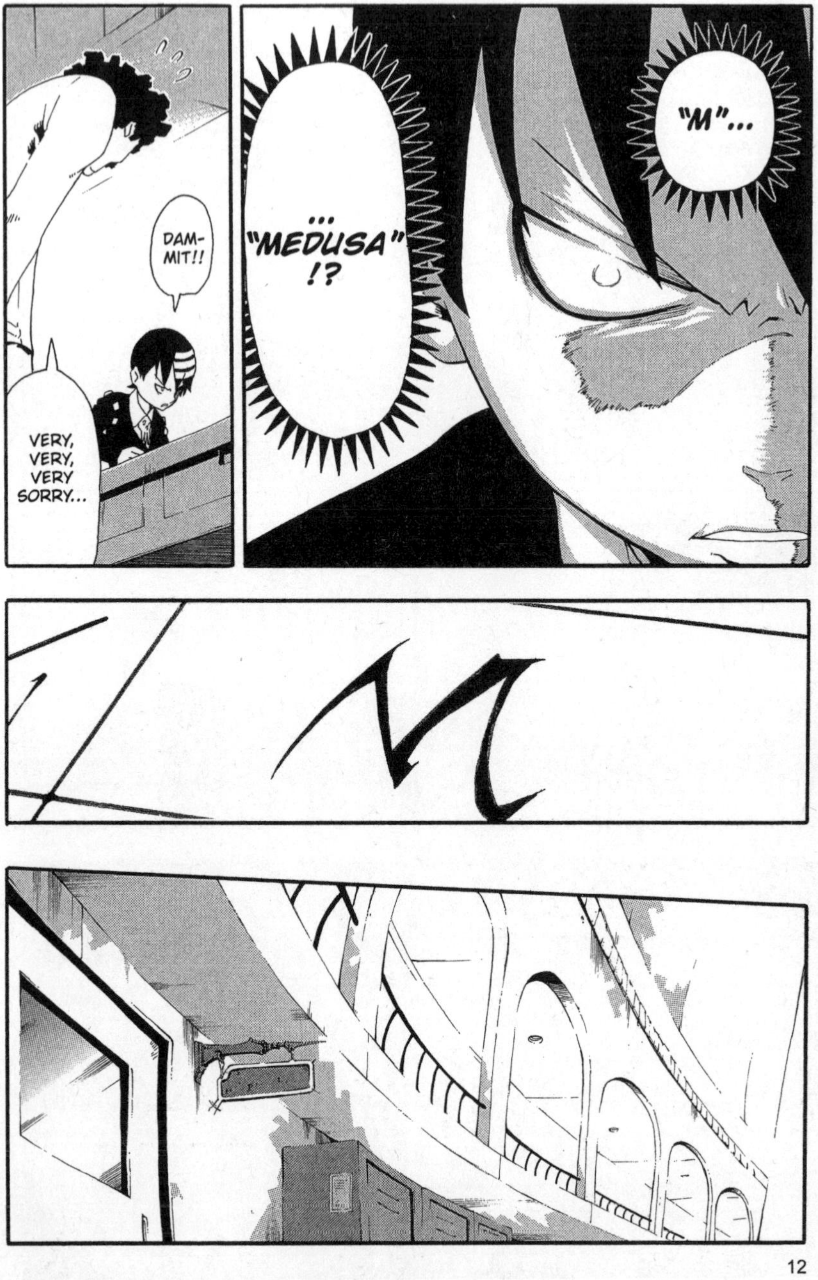
"M"...
..."MEDUSA"!?
DAM-MIT!!
VERY, VERY, VERY SORRY...

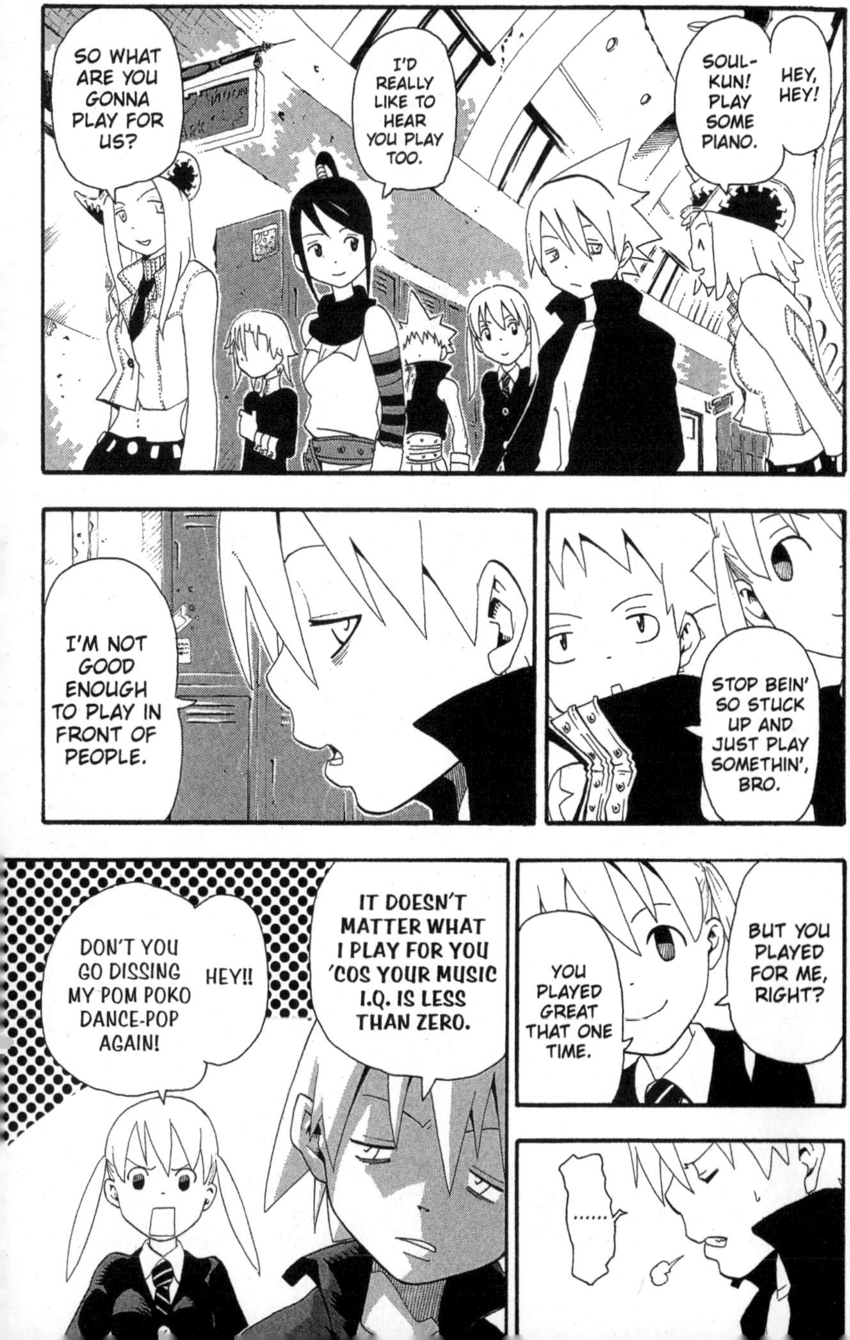
HEY, HEY!
SOUL-KUN! PLAY SOME PIANO.
I'D REALLY LIKE TO HEAR YOU PLAY TOO.
SO WHAT ARE YOU GONNA PLAY FOR US?
STOP BEIN' SO STUCK UP AND JUST PLAY SOMETHIN', BRO.
I'M NOT GOOD ENOUGH TO PLAY IN FRONT OF PEOPLE.
BUT YOU PLAYED FOR ME, RIGHT?
YOU PLAYED GREAT THAT ONE TIME.
......
IT DOESN'T MATTER WHAT I PLAY FOR YOU 'COS YOUR MUSIC I.Q. IS LESS THAN ZERO.
HEY!!
DON'T YOU GO DISSING MY POM POKO DANCE-POP AGAIN!

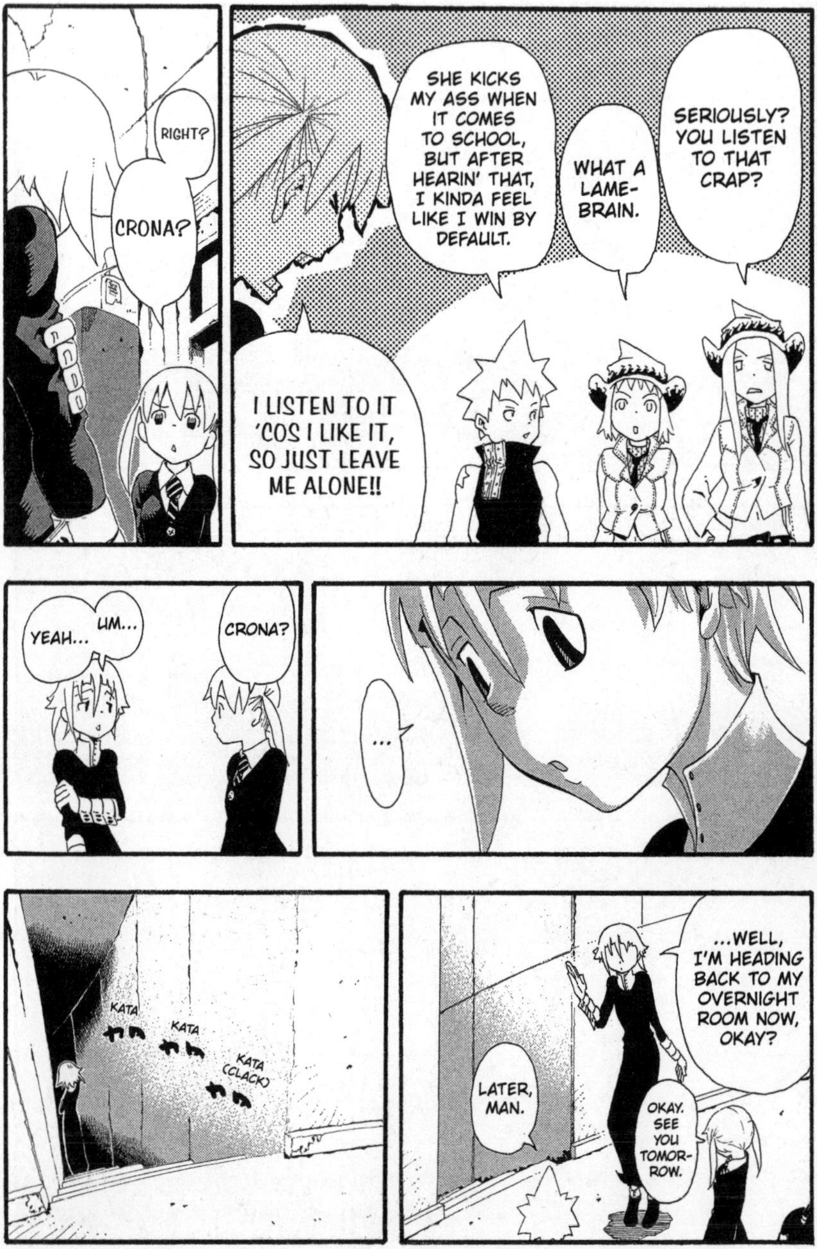
SERIOUSLY? YOU LISTEN TO THAT CRAP?
WHAT A LAME-BRAIN.
SHE KICKS MY ASS WHEN IT COMES TO SCHOOL, BUT AFTER HEARIN' THAT, I KINDA FEEL LIKE I WIN BY DEFAULT.
I LISTEN TO IT 'COS I LIKE IT, SO JUST LEAVE ME ALONE!!
RIGHT?
CRONA?
...
CRONA?
YEAH... UM...
...WELL, I'M HEADING BACK TO MY OVERNIGHT ROOM NOW, OKAY?
LATER, MAN.
OKAY. SEE YOU TOMORROW.
KATA
KATA
KATA (CLACK)

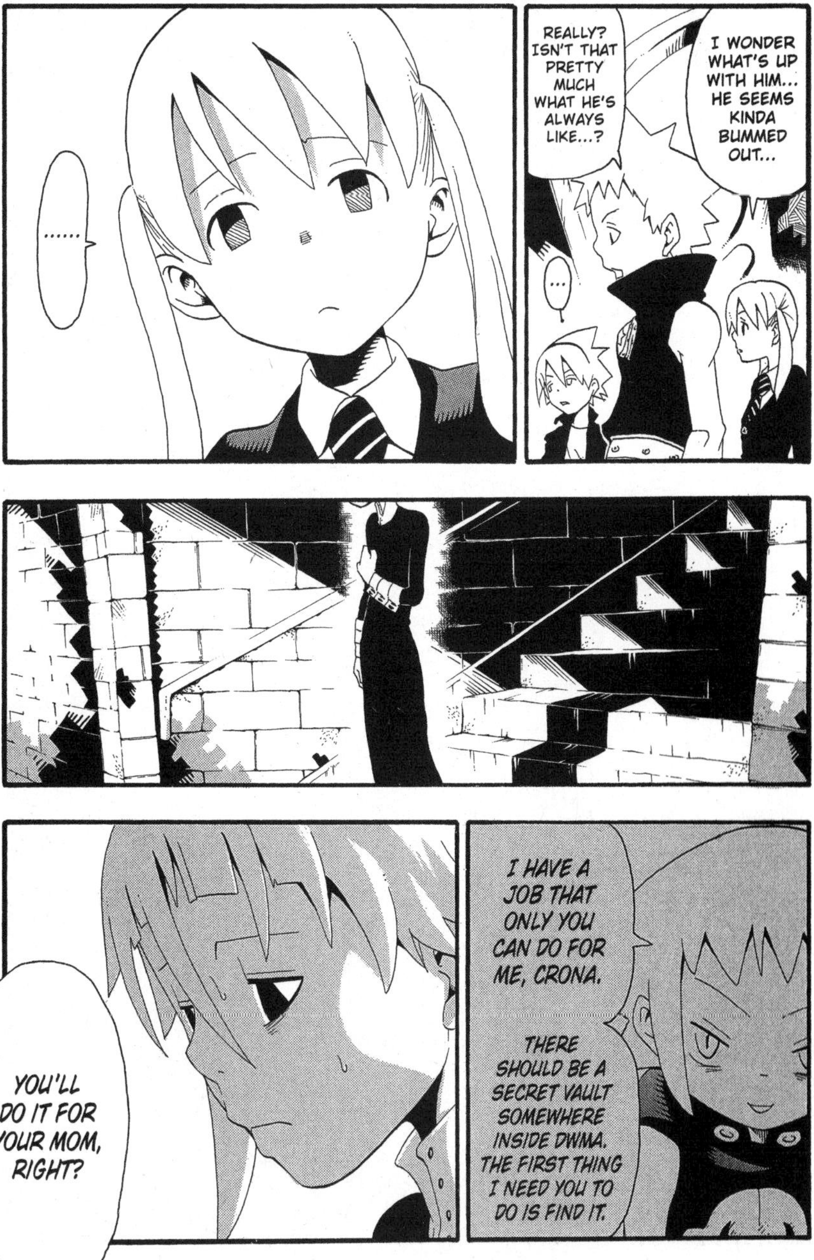
I WONDER WHAT'S UP WITH HIM... HE SEEMS KINDA BUMMED OUT...
REALLY? ISN'T THAT PRETTY MUCH WHAT HE'S ALWAYS LIKE...?
...
......
I HAVE A JOB THAT ONLY YOU CAN DO FOR ME, CRONA.
THERE SHOULD BE A SECRET VAULT SOMEWHERE INSIDE DWMA. THE FIRST THING I NEED YOU TO DO IS FIND IT.
YOU'LL DO IT FOR YOUR MOM, RIGHT?

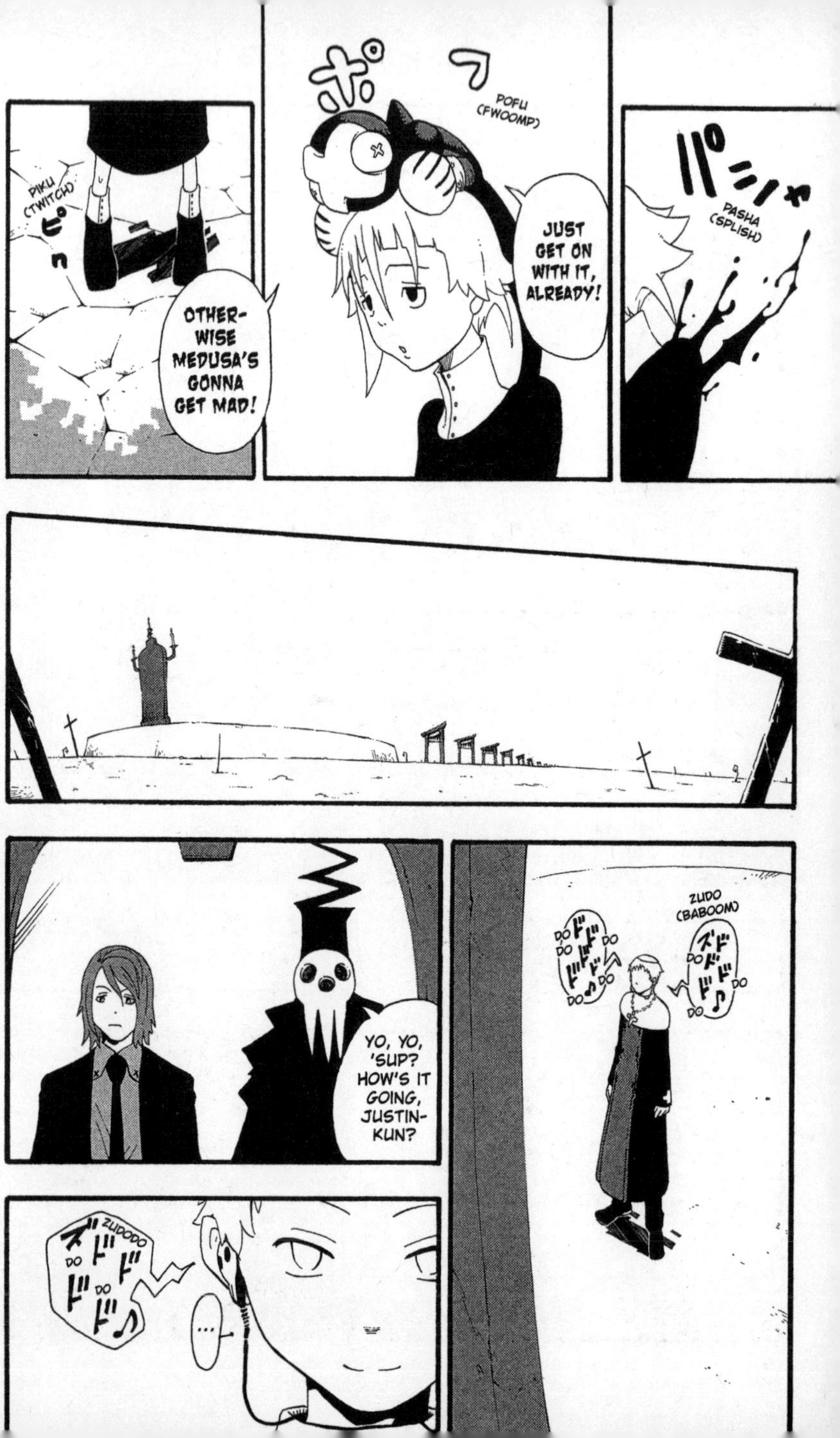
PASHA (SPLISH)
POFU (FWOOMP)
JUST GET ON WITH IT, ALREADY!
PIKU (TWITCH)
OTHER-WISE MEDUSA'S GONNA GET MAD!
ZUDO (BABOOM)
DO DO DO DO DO
DO DO DO DO
YO, YO, 'SUP? HOW'S IT GOING, JUSTIN-KUN?
ZUDODO
DO DO
...

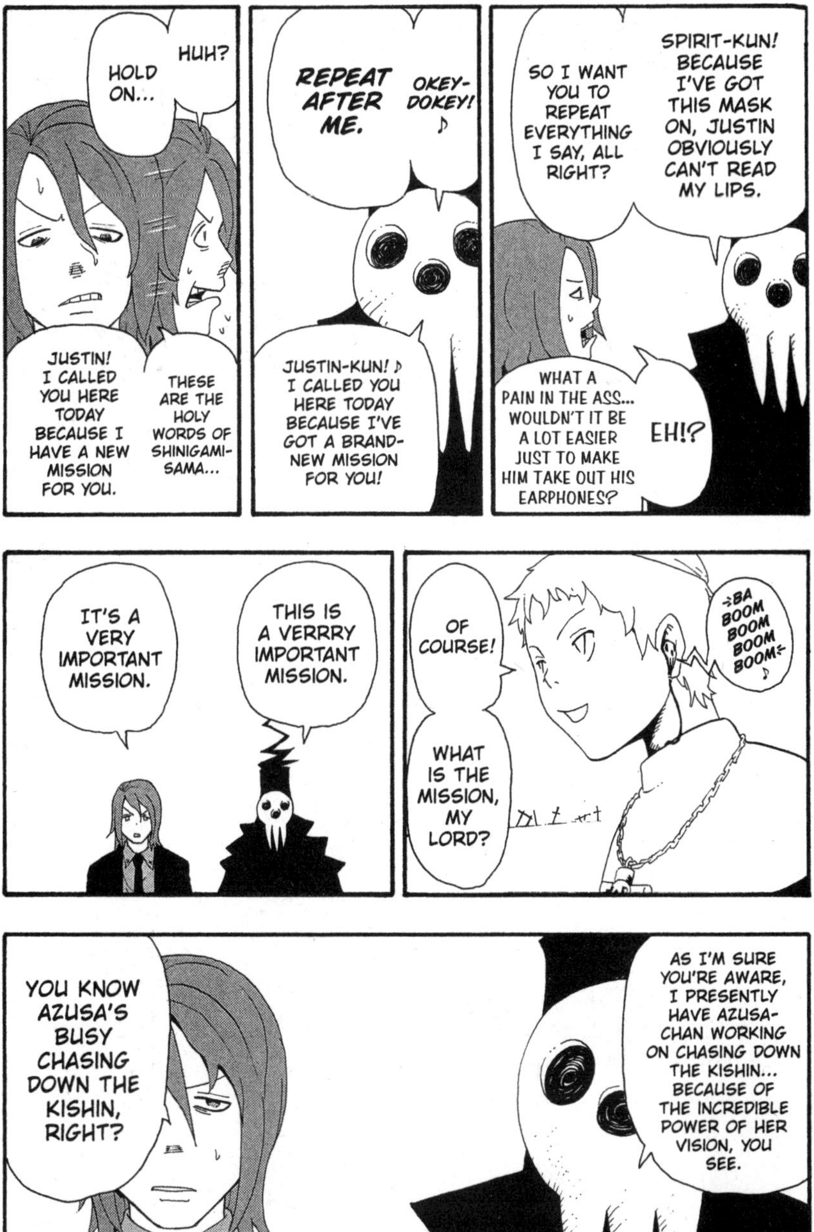
SPIRIT-KUN! BECAUSE I'VE GOT THIS MASK ON, JUSTIN OBVIOUSLY CAN'T READ MY LIPS.
SO I WANT YOU TO REPEAT EVERYTHING I SAY, ALL RIGHT?
EH!?
WHAT A PAIN IN THE ASS... WOULDN'T IT BE A LOT EASIER JUST TO MAKE HIM TAKE OUT HIS EARPHONES?
OKEY-DOKEY! ♪
REPEAT AFTER ME.
JUSTIN-KUN! ♪ I CALLED YOU HERE TODAY BECAUSE I'VE GOT A BRAND-NEW MISSION FOR YOU!
HUH?
HOLD ON...
THESE ARE THE HOLY WORDS OF SHINIGAMI-SAMA...
JUSTIN! I CALLED YOU HERE TODAY BECAUSE I HAVE A NEW MISSION FOR YOU.
⇒BA BOOM BOOM BOOM BOOM⇐ ♪
OF COURSE!
WHAT IS THE MISSION, MY LORD?
THIS IS A VERRRY IMPORTANT MISSION.
IT'S A VERY IMPORTANT MISSION.
AS I'M SURE YOU'RE AWARE, I PRESENTLY HAVE AZUSA-CHAN WORKING ON CHASING DOWN THE KISHIN... BECAUSE OF THE INCREDIBLE POWER OF HER VISION, YOU SEE.
YOU KNOW AZUSA'S BUSY CHASING DOWN THE KISHIN, RIGHT?

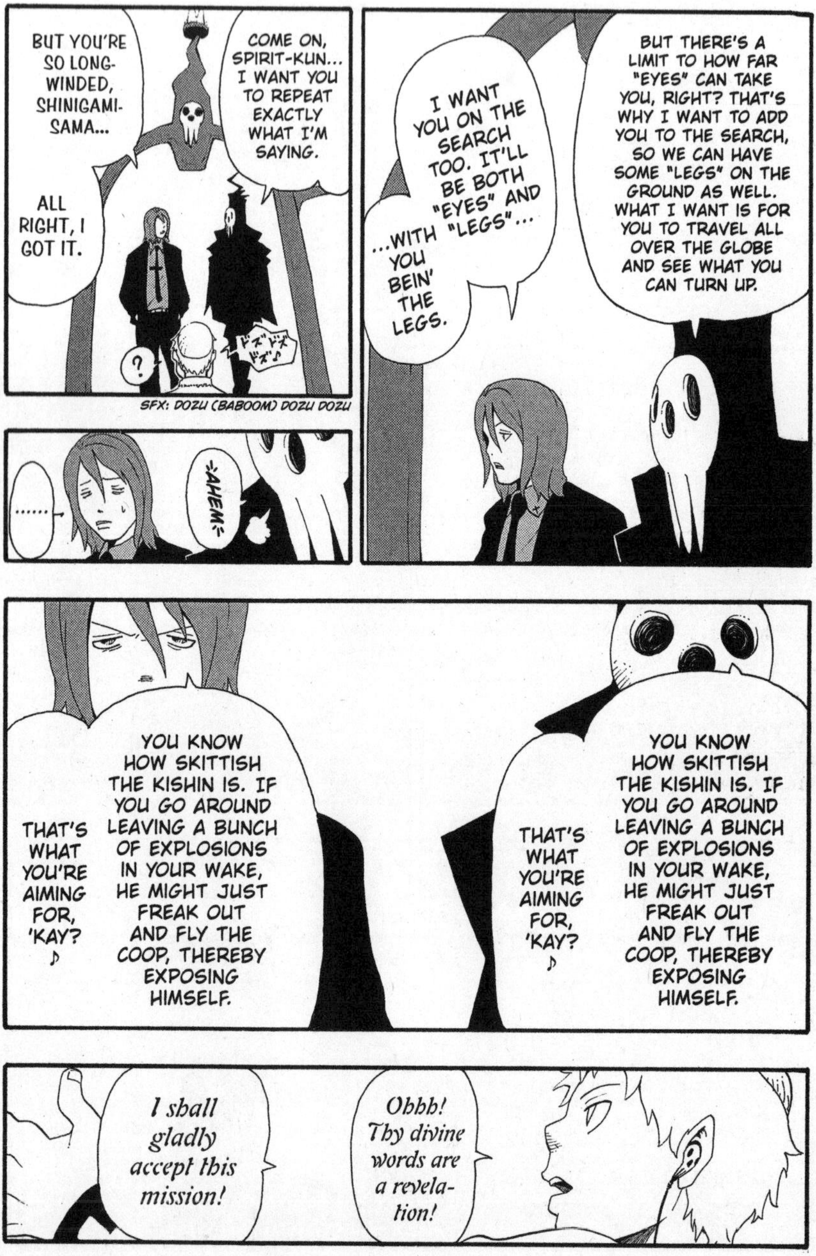
BUT THERE'S A LIMIT TO HOW FAR "EYES" CAN TAKE YOU, RIGHT? THAT'S WHY I WANT TO ADD YOU TO THE SEARCH, SO WE CAN HAVE SOME "LEGS" ON THE GROUND AS WELL. WHAT I WANT IS FOR YOU TO TRAVEL ALL OVER THE GLOBE AND SEE WHAT YOU CAN TURN UP.
I WANT YOU ON THE SEARCH TOO. IT'LL BE BOTH "EYES" AND
...WITH "LEGS"... YOU BEIN' THE LEGS.
COME ON, SPIRIT-KUN... I WANT YOU TO REPEAT EXACTLY WHAT I'M SAYING.
BUT YOU'RE SO LONG-WINDED, SHINIGAMI-SAMA...
ALL RIGHT, I GOT IT.
ドズドズドズ♪
?
AHEM
......
YOU KNOW HOW SKITTISH THE KISHIN IS. IF YOU GO AROUND LEAVING A BUNCH OF EXPLOSIONS IN YOUR WAKE, HE MIGHT JUST FREAK OUT AND FLY THE COOP, THEREBY EXPOSING HIMSELF.
THAT'S WHAT YOU'RE AIMING FOR, 'KAY? ♪
YOU KNOW HOW SKITTISH THE KISHIN IS. IF YOU GO AROUND LEAVING A BUNCH OF EXPLOSIONS IN YOUR WAKE, HE MIGHT JUST FREAK OUT AND FLY THE COOP, THEREBY EXPOSING HIMSELF.
THAT'S WHAT YOU'RE AIMING FOR, 'KAY? ♪
Ohhh! Thy divine words are a revelation!
I shall gladly accept this mission!

SFX: DOZU (BABOOM) DOZU DOZU

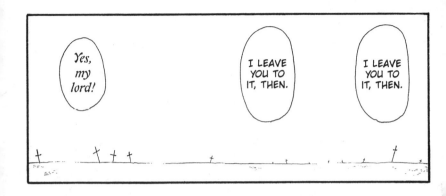

Yes, my lord!

I LEAVE YOU TO IT, THEN.

I LEAVE YOU TO IT, THEN.

...

LOOKS LIKE IT'S OFF-LIMITS BEYOND THIS POINT.

GOO-PI-PI! WE MIGHTA JUST FOUND THE SECRET VAULT UP AHEAD!

SUI
(SWIP)

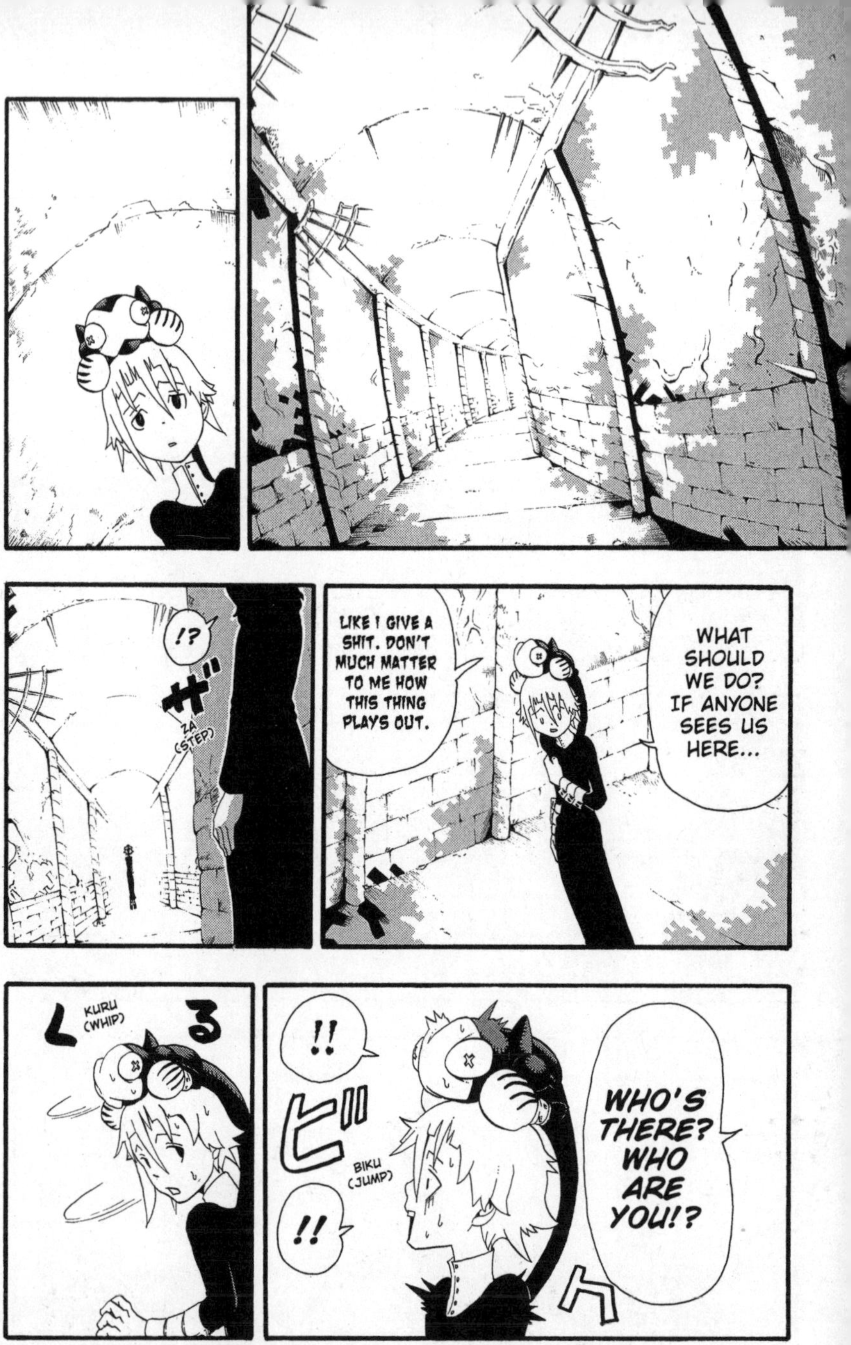
WHAT SHOULD WE DO? IF ANYONE SEES US HERE...
LIKE I GIVE A SHIT. DON'T MUCH MATTER TO ME HOW THIS THING PLAYS OUT.
!?
ザ
ZA (STEP)
WHO'S THERE? WHO ARE YOU!?
!!
BIKU (JUMP)
!!
くる
KURU (WHIP)

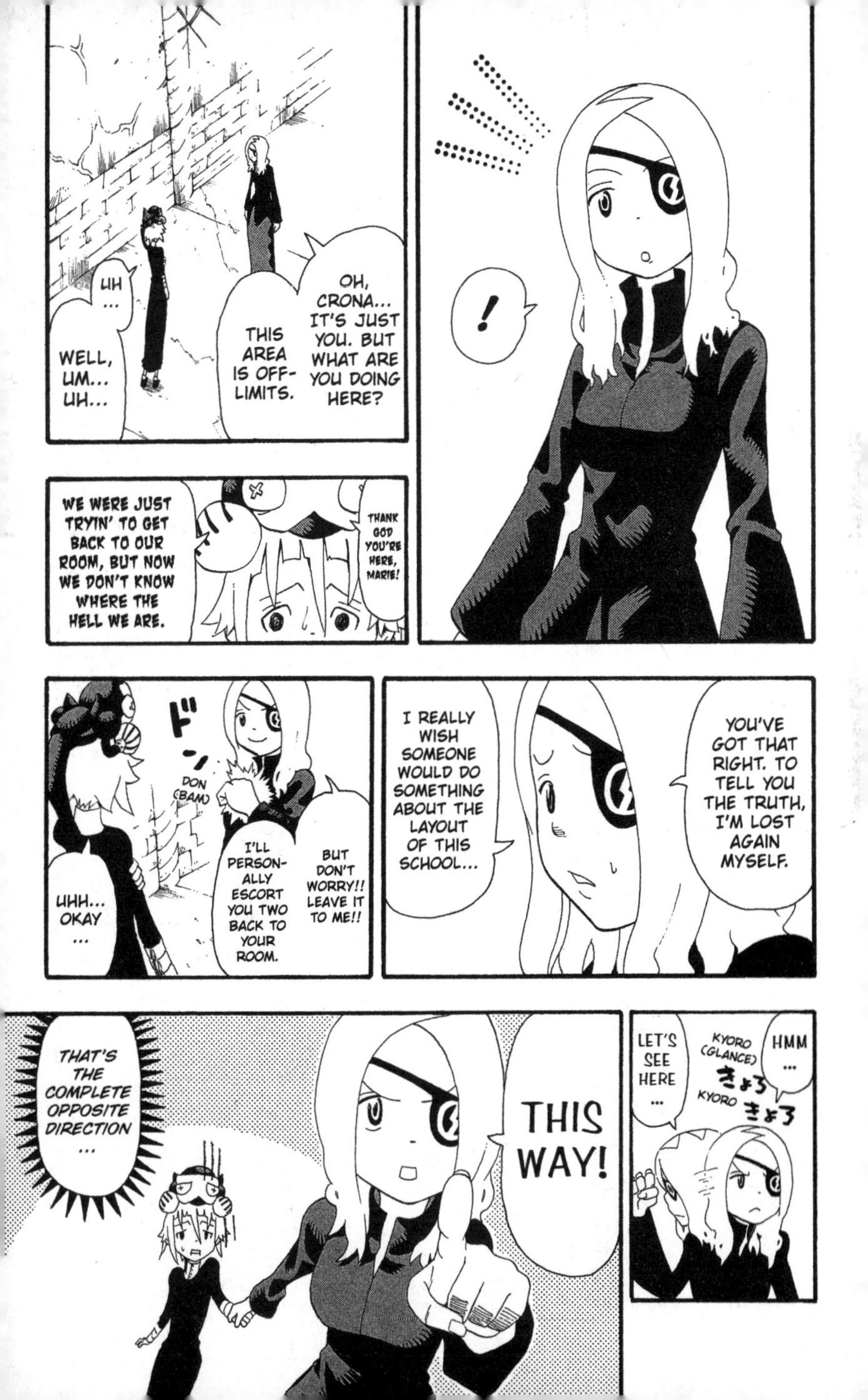

!
OH, CRONA... IT'S JUST YOU. BUT WHAT ARE YOU DOING HERE?
THIS AREA IS OFF-LIMITS.
UH ...
WELL, UM... UH...
THANK GOD YOU'RE HERE, MARIE!
WE WERE JUST TRYIN' TO GET BACK TO OUR ROOM, BUT NOW WE DON'T KNOW WHERE THE HELL WE ARE.
YOU'VE GOT THAT RIGHT. TO TELL YOU THE TRUTH, I'M LOST AGAIN MYSELF.
I REALLY WISH SOMEONE WOULD DO SOMETHING ABOUT THE LAYOUT OF THIS SCHOOL...
ドン
DON (BAM)
BUT DON'T WORRY!! LEAVE IT TO ME!!
I'LL PERSONALLY ESCORT YOU TWO BACK TO YOUR ROOM.
UHH... OKAY ...
HMM ...
KYORO (GLANCE)
きょろ
KYORO
きょろ
LET'S SEE HERE ...
THIS WAY!
THAT'S THE COMPLETE OPPOSITE DIRECTION ...

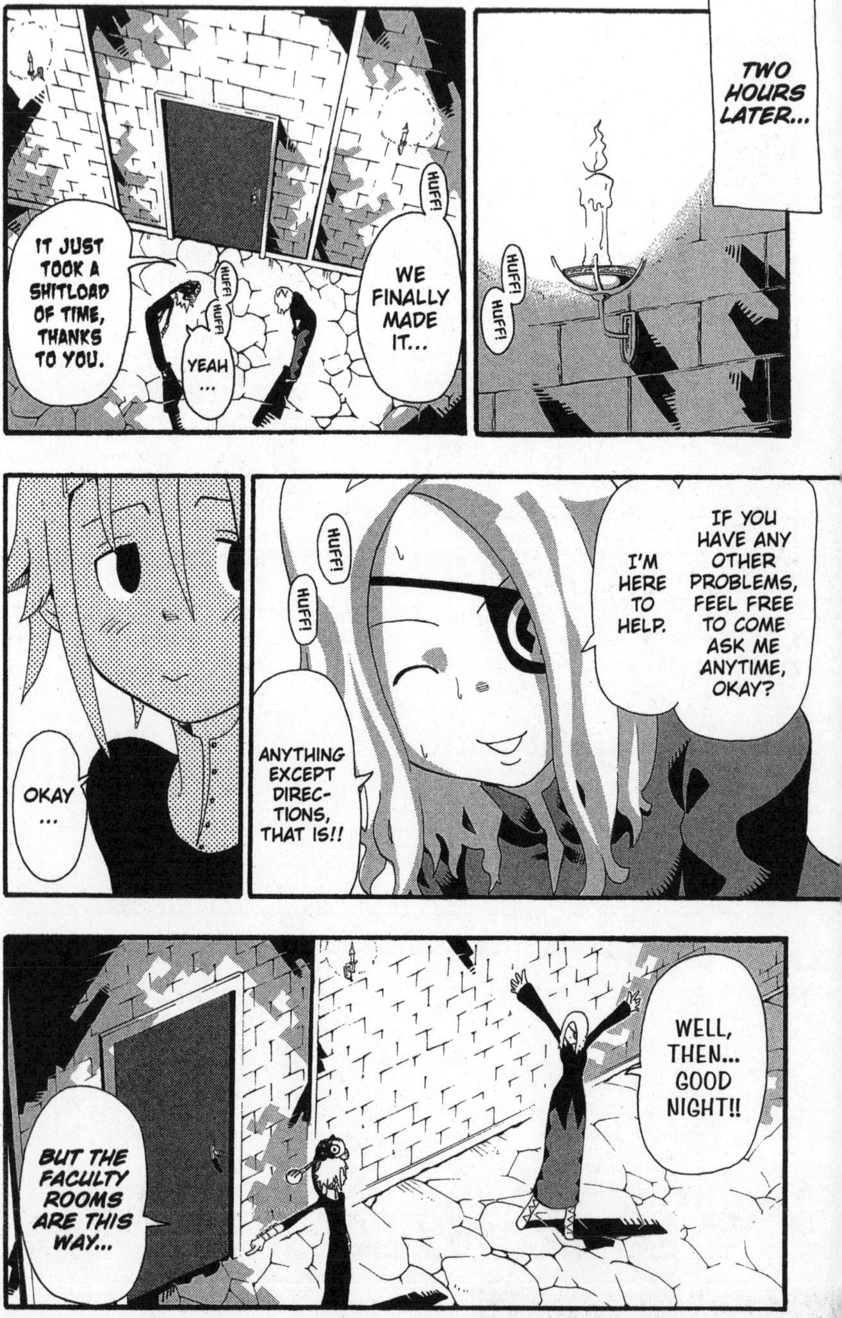
TWO HOURS LATER...
HUFF!
HUFF!
HUFF!
WE FINALLY MADE IT...
HUFF!
HUFF!
YEAH ...
IT JUST TOOK A SHITLOAD OF TIME, THANKS TO YOU.
IF YOU HAVE ANY OTHER PROBLEMS, FEEL FREE TO COME ASK ME ANYTIME, OKAY?
I'M HERE TO HELP.
HUFF!
HUFF!
ANYTHING EXCEPT DIREC-TIONS, THAT IS!!
OKAY ...
WELL, THEN... GOOD NIGHT!!
BUT THE FACULTY ROOMS ARE THIS WAY...

BATAN
(SLAM)

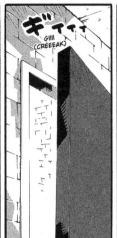
ギイイイ
GIII
(CREEEAK)

TEE-HEE-HEE!

⇒CROAK⇐

HIKO
(SHAKY)

PETA
(SPLAT)
ペタ

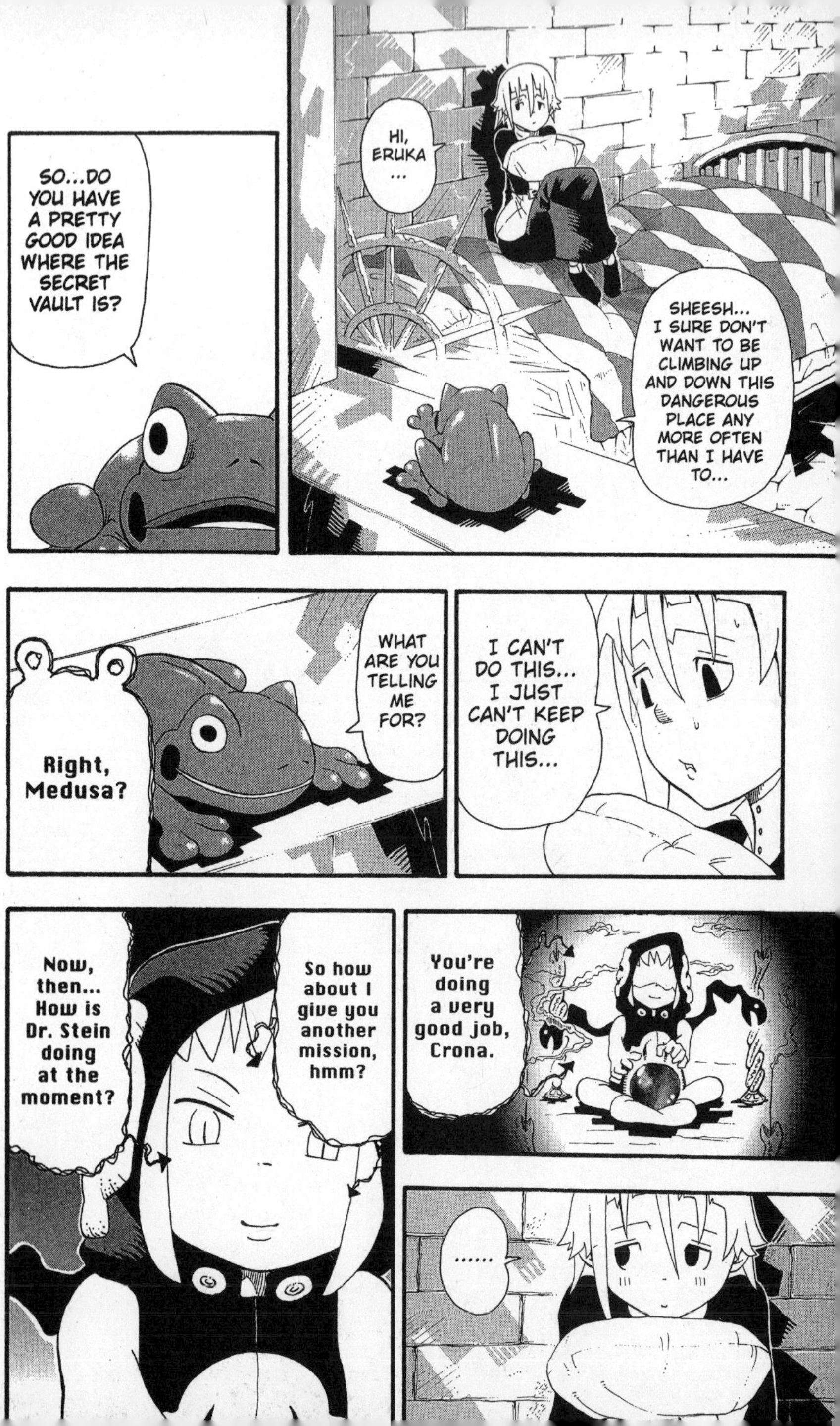
HI, ERUKA...
SHEESH... I SURE DON'T WANT TO BE CLIMBING UP AND DOWN THIS DANGEROUS PLACE ANY MORE OFTEN THAN I HAVE TO...
SO...DO YOU HAVE A PRETTY GOOD IDEA WHERE THE SECRET VAULT IS?
I CAN'T DO THIS... I JUST CAN'T KEEP DOING THIS...
WHAT ARE YOU TELLING ME FOR?
Right, Medusa?
You're doing a very good job, Crona.
......
So how about I give you another mission, hmm?
Now, then... How is Dr. Stein doing at the moment?

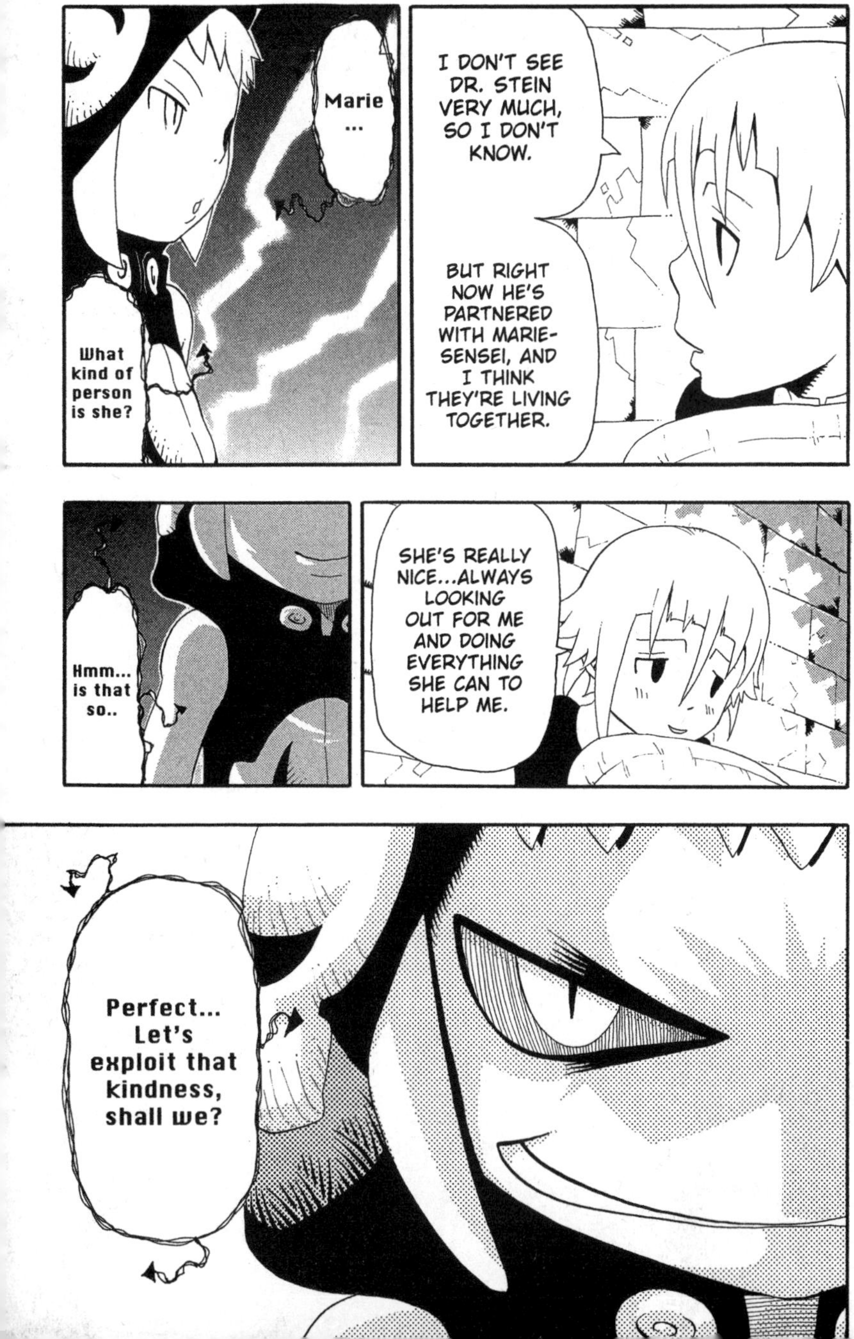
I DON'T SEE DR. STEIN VERY MUCH, SO I DON'T KNOW.
BUT RIGHT NOW HE'S PARTNERED WITH MARIE-SENSEI, AND I THINK THEY'RE LIVING TOGETHER.
Marie ...
What kind of person is she?
SHE'S REALLY NICE...ALWAYS LOOKING OUT FOR ME AND DOING EVERYTHING SHE CAN TO HELP ME.
Hmm... is that so..
Perfect... Let's exploit that kindness, shall we?

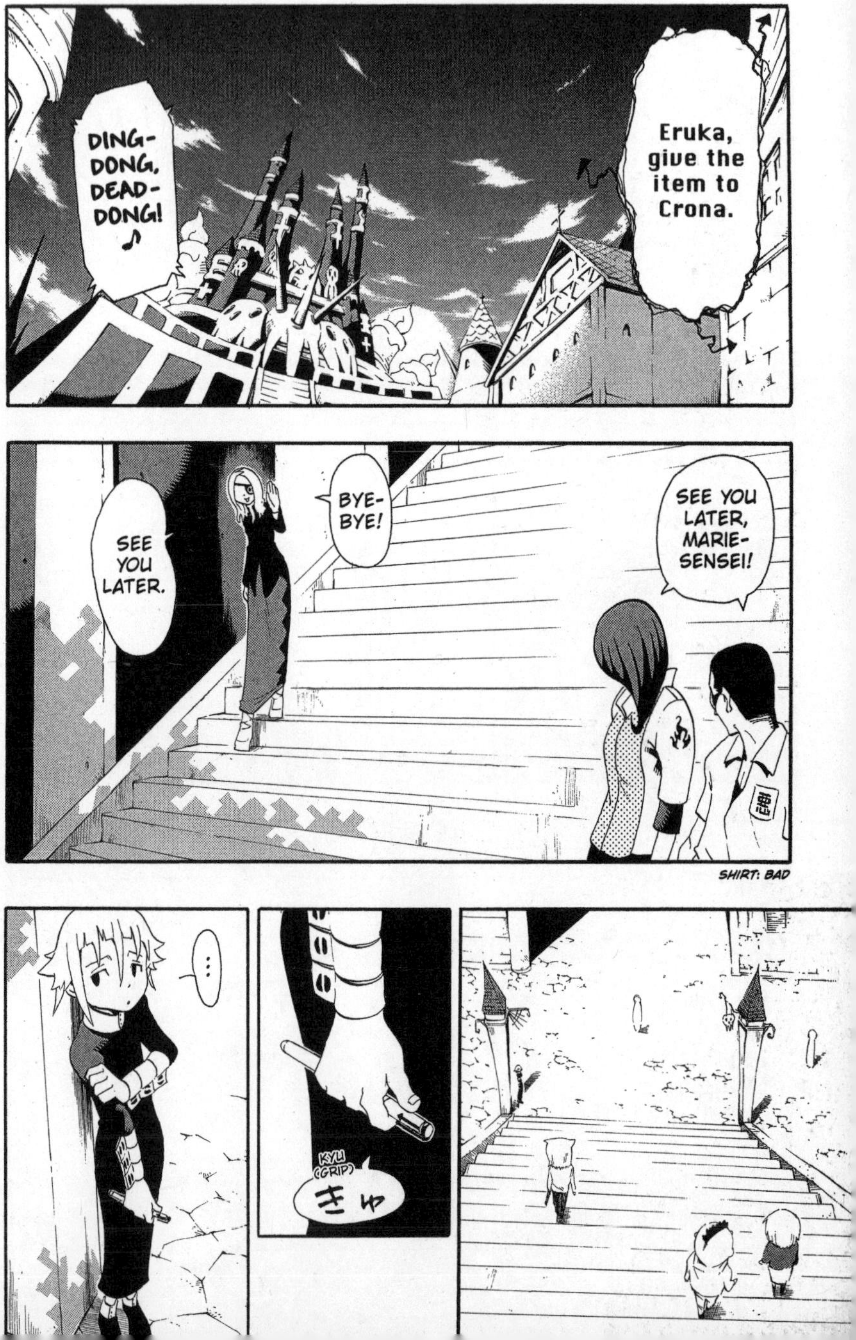
Eruka, give the item to Crona.
DING-DONG, DEAD-DONG! ♪
SEE YOU LATER, MARIE-SENSEI!
BYE-BYE!
SEE YOU LATER.
SHIRT: BAD
KYU (GRIP)
きゅ
...

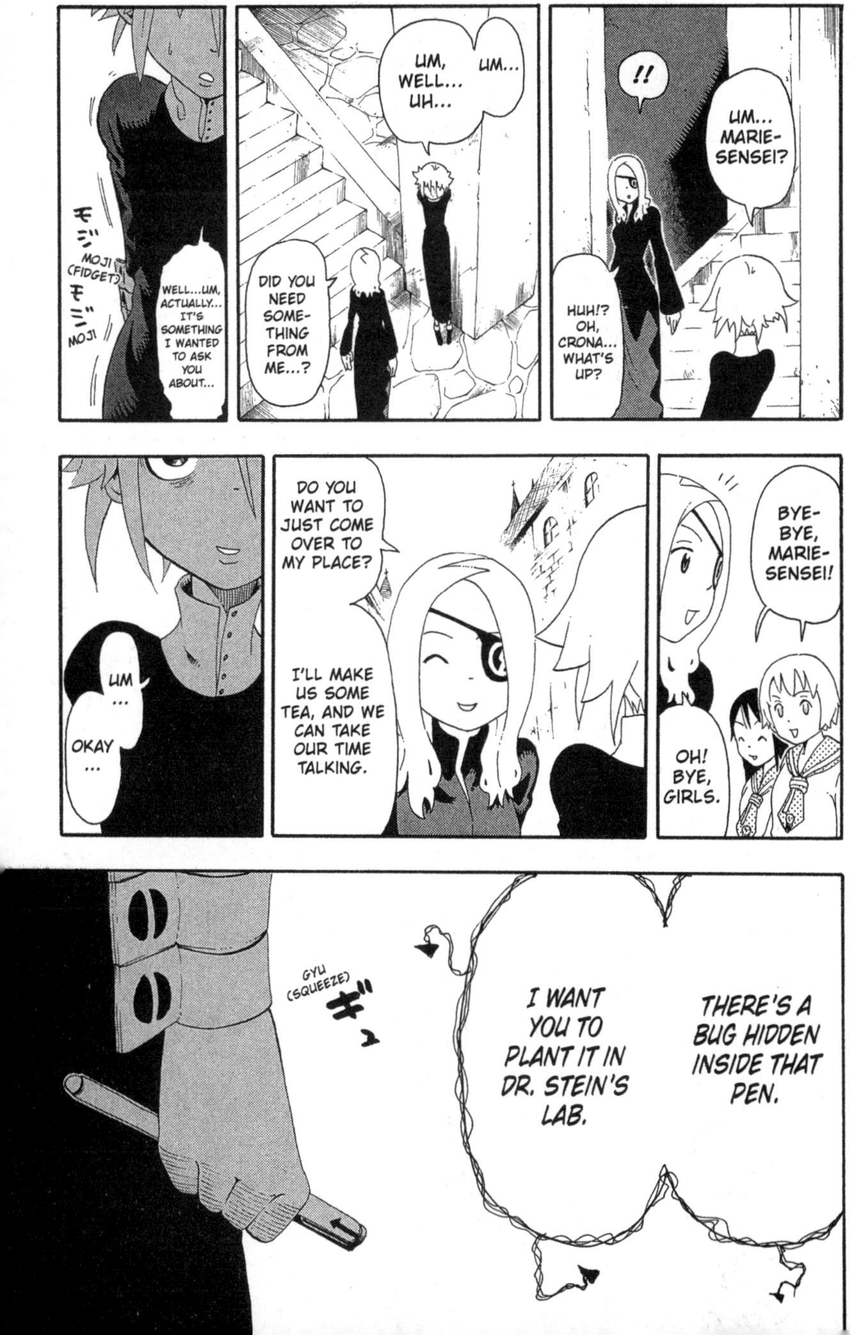
!!
UM... MARIE-SENSEI?
HUH!? OH, CRONA... WHAT'S UP?
UM...
UM, WELL... UH...
DID YOU NEED SOMETHING FROM ME...?
モジ MOJI (FIDGET) モジ MOJI
WELL...UM, ACTUALLY... IT'S SOMETHING I WANTED TO ASK YOU ABOUT...
BYE-BYE, MARIE-SENSEI!
OH! BYE, GIRLS.
DO YOU WANT TO JUST COME OVER TO MY PLACE?
I'LL MAKE US SOME TEA, AND WE CAN TAKE OUR TIME TALKING.
UM ...
OKAY ...
THERE'S A BUG HIDDEN INSIDE THAT PEN.
I WANT YOU TO PLANT IT IN DR. STEIN'S LAB.
GYU (SQUEEZE) ギュ

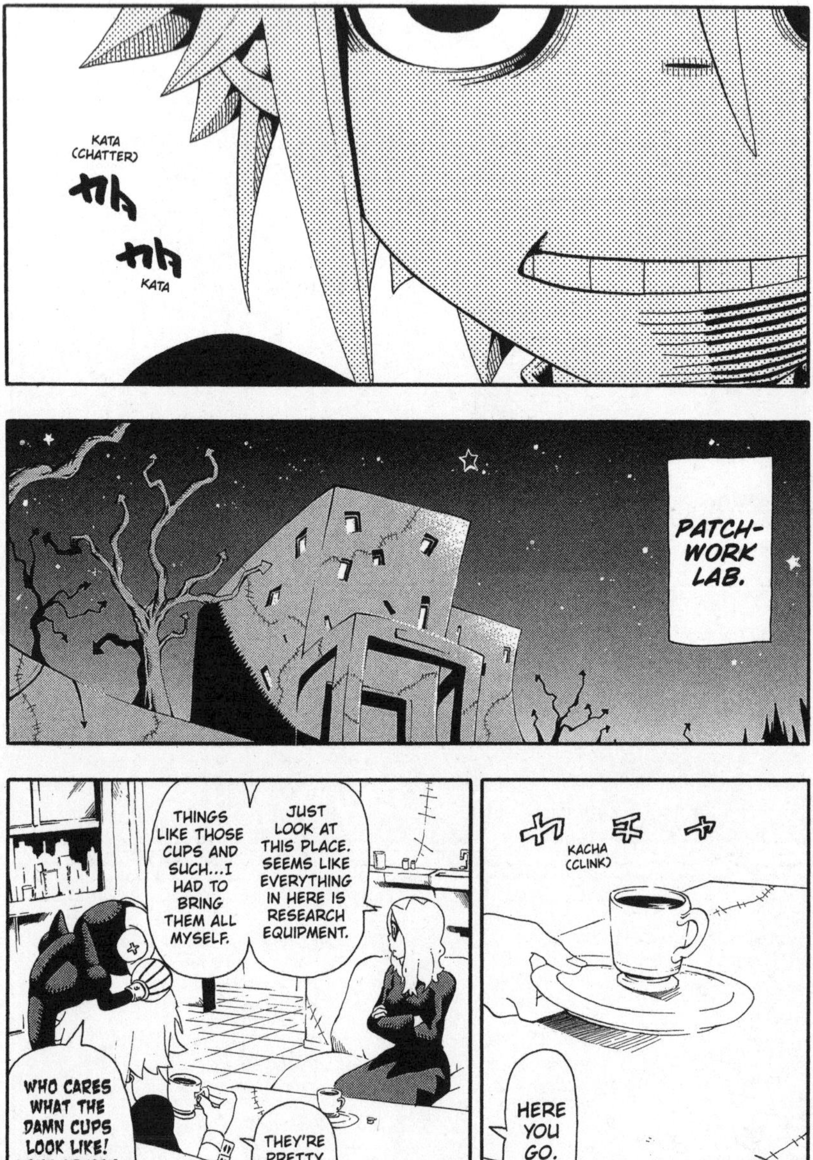
KATA (CHATTER)
KATA
PATCH-WORK LAB.
KACHA (CLINK)
HERE YOU GO.
JUST LOOK AT THIS PLACE. SEEMS LIKE EVERYTHING IN HERE IS RESEARCH EQUIPMENT.
THINGS LIKE THOSE CUPS AND SUCH...I HAD TO BRING THEM ALL MYSELF.
THEY'RE PRETTY CUPS.
WHO CARES WHAT THE DAMN CUPS LOOK LIKE! LONG AS YOU CAN DRINK OUTTA 'EM.

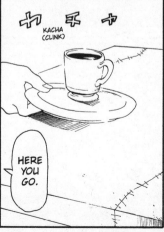

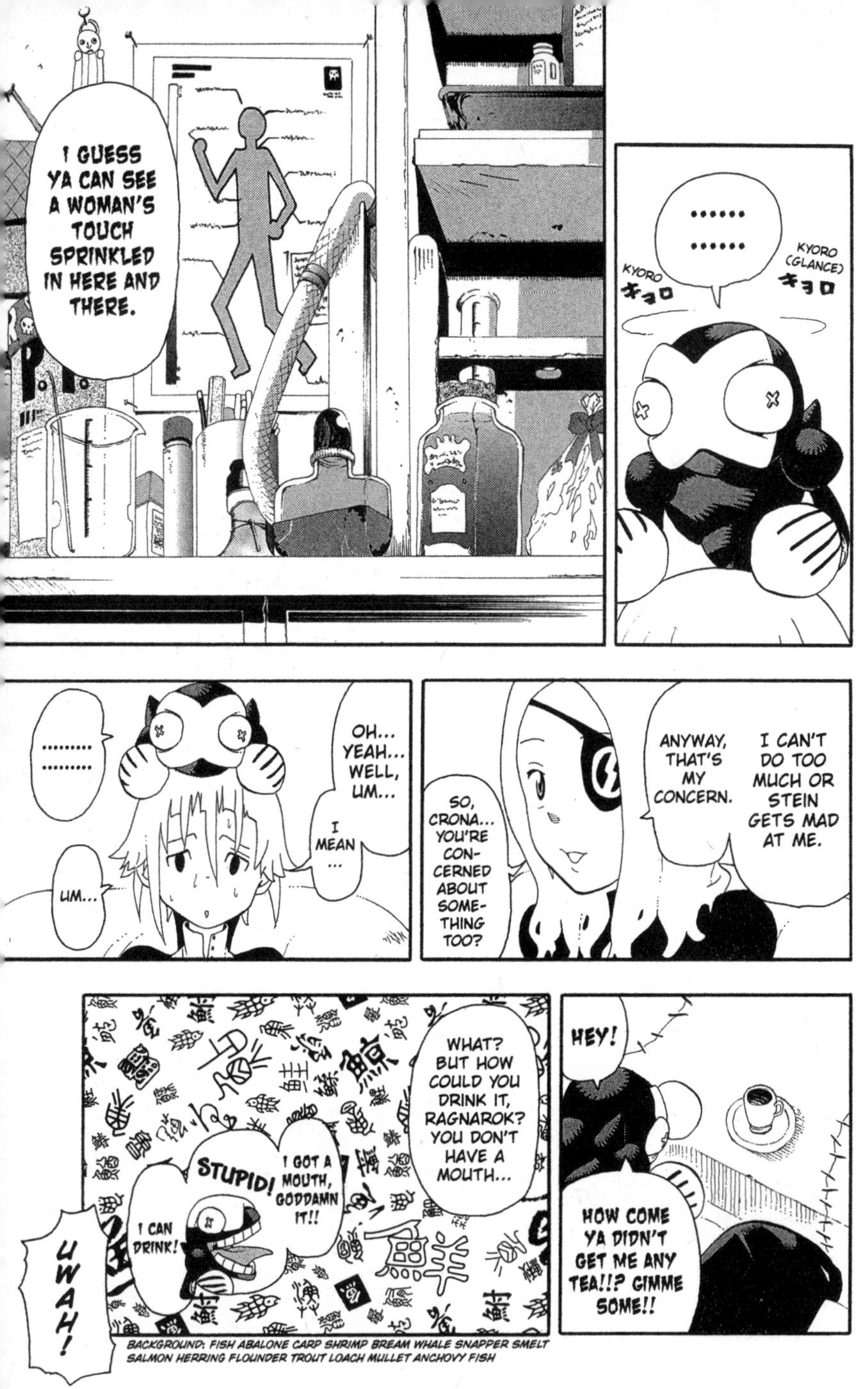

......
......
KYORO (GLANCE)
キョロ
KYORO
キョロ
I GUESS YA CAN SEE A WOMAN'S TOUCH SPRINKLED IN HERE AND THERE.
I CAN'T DO TOO MUCH OR STEIN GETS MAD AT ME.
ANYWAY, THAT'S MY CONCERN.
SO, CRONA... YOU'RE CONCERNED ABOUT SOMETHING TOO?
OH... YEAH... WELL, UM...
I MEAN...
....
....
UM...
HEY!
HOW COME YA DIDN'T GET ME ANY TEA!!? GIMME SOME!!
WHAT? BUT HOW COULD YOU DRINK IT, RAGNAROK? YOU DON'T HAVE A MOUTH...
STUPID!
I GOT A MOUTH, GODDAMN IT!!
I CAN DRINK!
UWAH!

BACKGROUND: FISH ABALONE CARP SHRIMP BREAM WHALE SNAPPER SMELT SALMON HERRING FLOUNDER TROUT LOACH MULLET ANCHOVY FISH

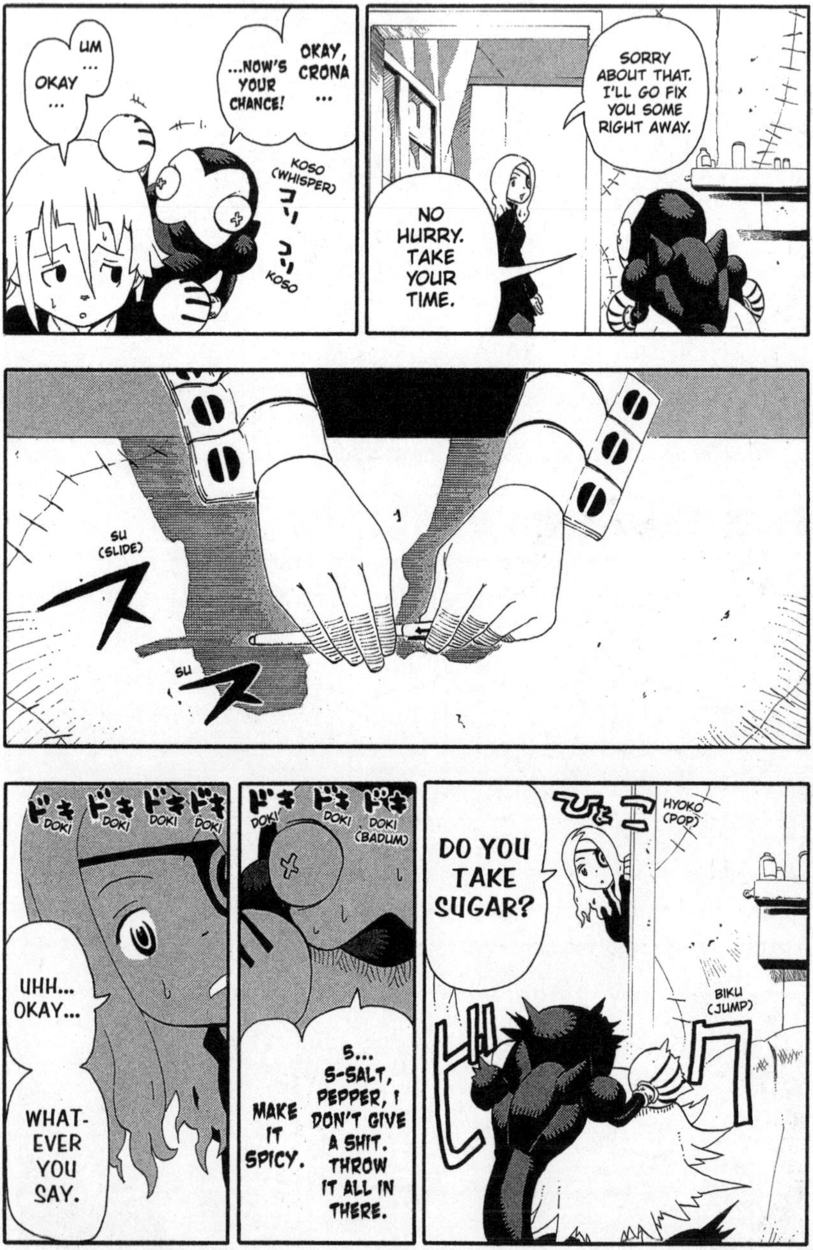
SORRY ABOUT THAT. I'LL GO FIX YOU SOME RIGHT AWAY.
NO HURRY. TAKE YOUR TIME.
OKAY, CRONA ...
...NOW'S YOUR CHANCE!
KOSO (WHISPER)
KOSO
UM ... OKAY ...
SU (SLIDE)
SU
HYOKO (POP)
DO YOU TAKE SUGAR?
BIKU (JUMP)
DOKI DOKI DOKI (BADUM)
S... S-SALT, PEPPER, I DON'T GIVE A SHIT. THROW IT ALL IN THERE.
MAKE IT SPICY.
DOKI DOKI DOKI DOKI
UHH... OKAY...
WHATEVER YOU SAY.

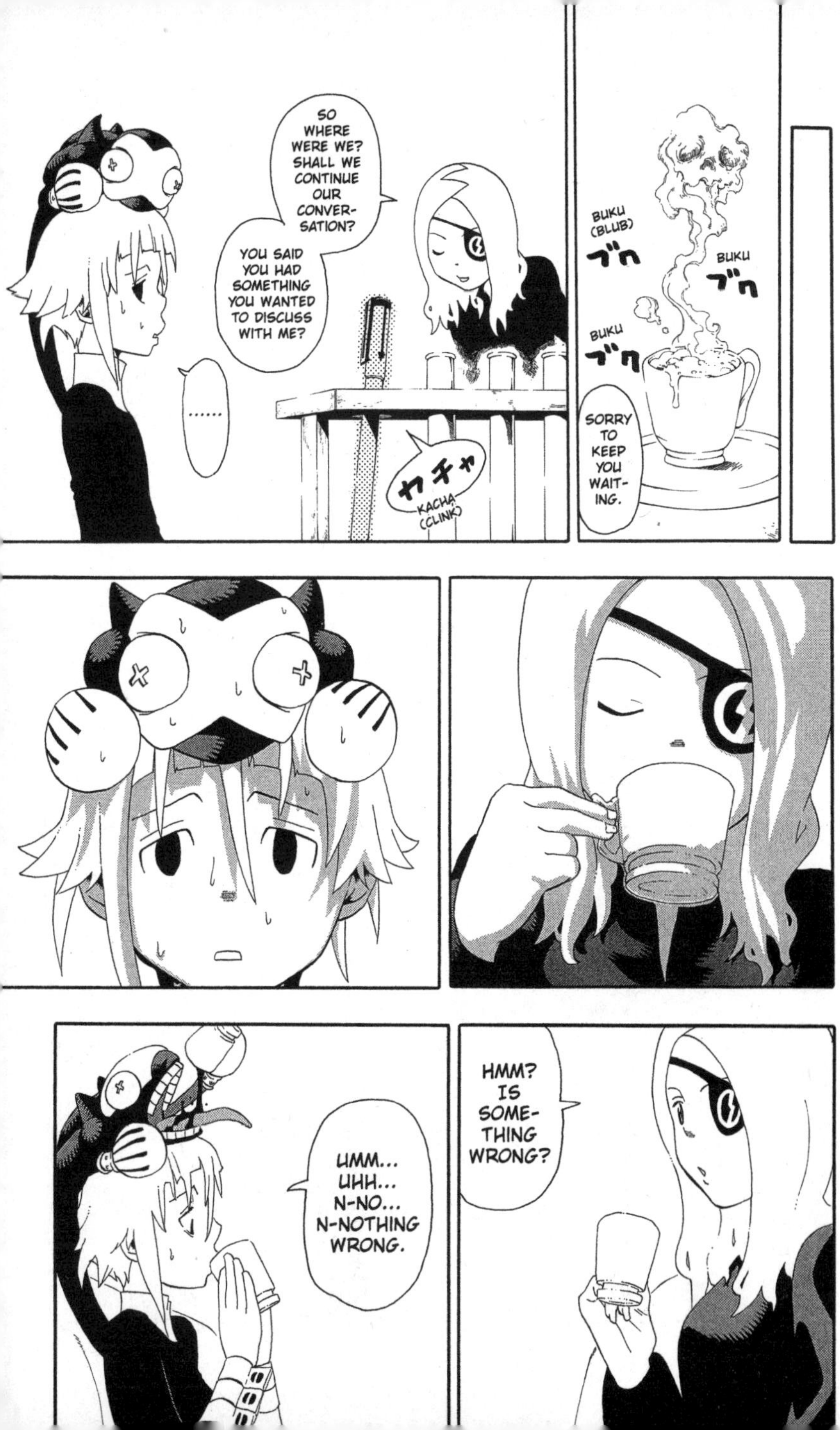
BUKU (BLUB)
ブク
BUKU
ブク
BUKU
ブク
SORRY TO KEEP YOU WAIT-ING.
SO WHERE WERE WE? SHALL WE CONTINUE OUR CONVER-SATION?
YOU SAID YOU HAD SOMETHING YOU WANTED TO DISCUSS WITH ME?
......
カチャ
KACHA (CLINK)
HMM? IS SOME-THING WRONG?
UMM... UHH... N-NO... N-NOTHING WRONG.

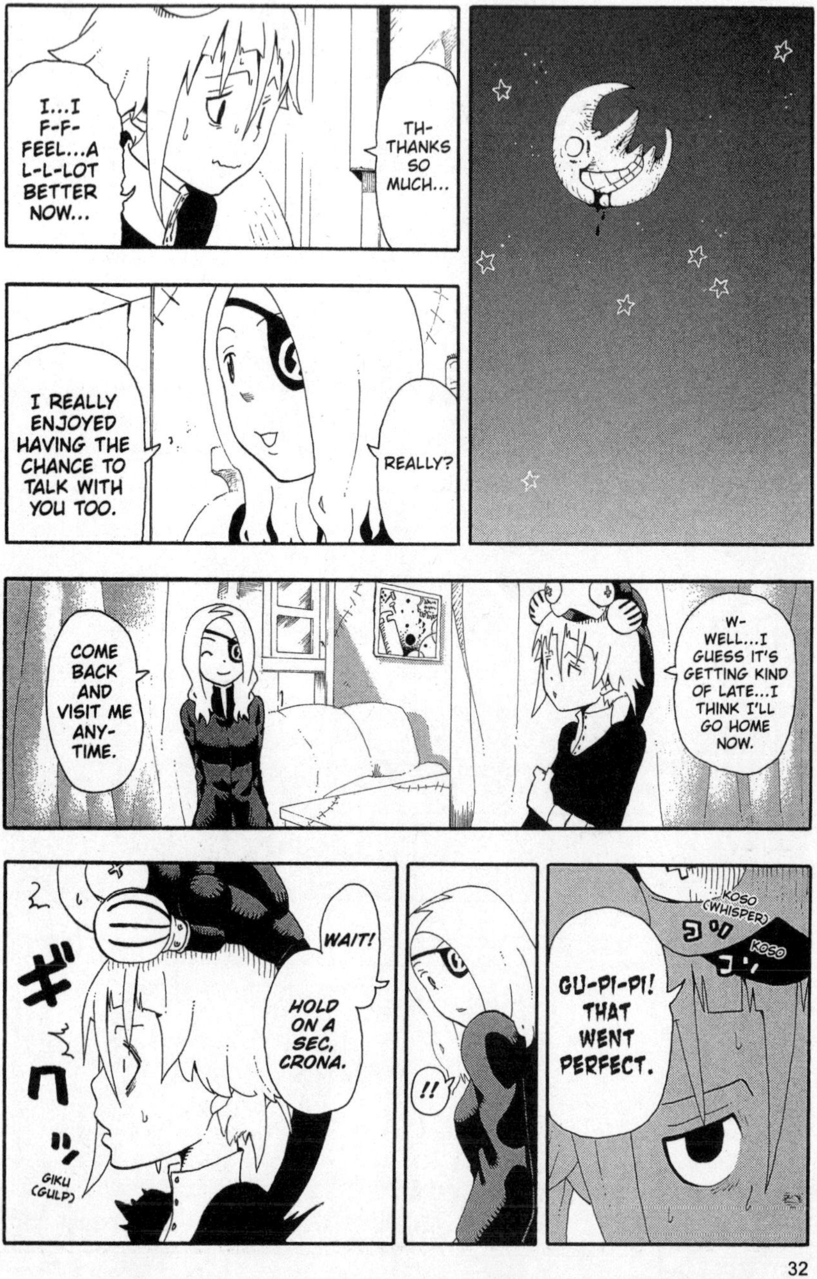
TH-THANKS SO MUCH...
I...I F-F-FEEL...A L-L-LOT BETTER NOW...
REALLY?
I REALLY ENJOYED HAVING THE CHANCE TO TALK WITH YOU TOO.
W-WELL...I GUESS IT'S GETTING KIND OF LATE...I THINK I'LL GO HOME NOW.
COME BACK AND VISIT ME ANY-TIME.
KOSO (WHISPER)
KOSO
GU-PI-PI! THAT WENT PERFECT.
!!
WAIT!
HOLD ON A SEC, CRONA.
GIKU (GULP)

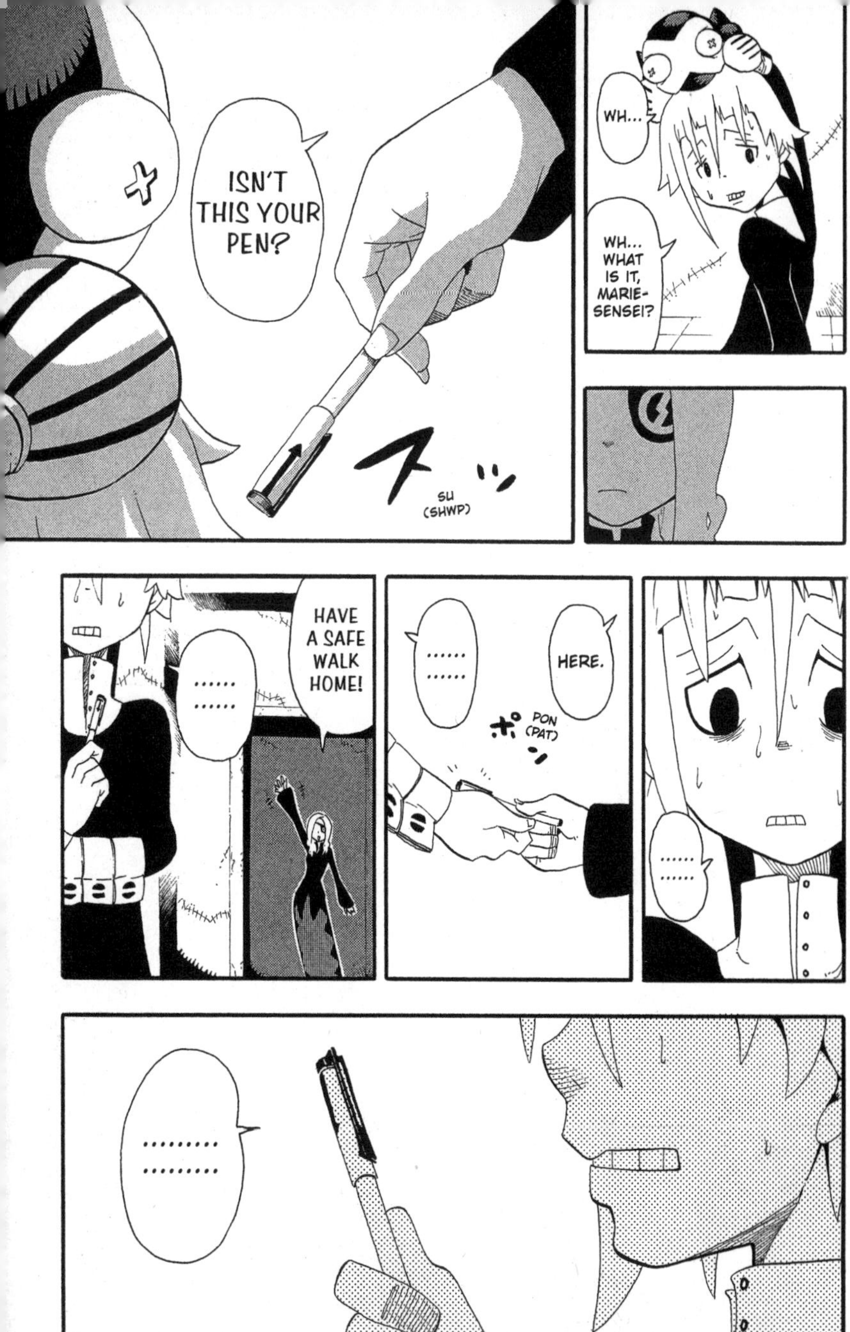
WH...
WH... WHAT IS IT, MARIE-SENSEI?
ISN'T THIS YOUR PEN?
ス ッ
SU (SHWP)
....
HERE.
....
ポ ン
PON (PAT)
HAVE A SAFE WALK HOME!
....
....

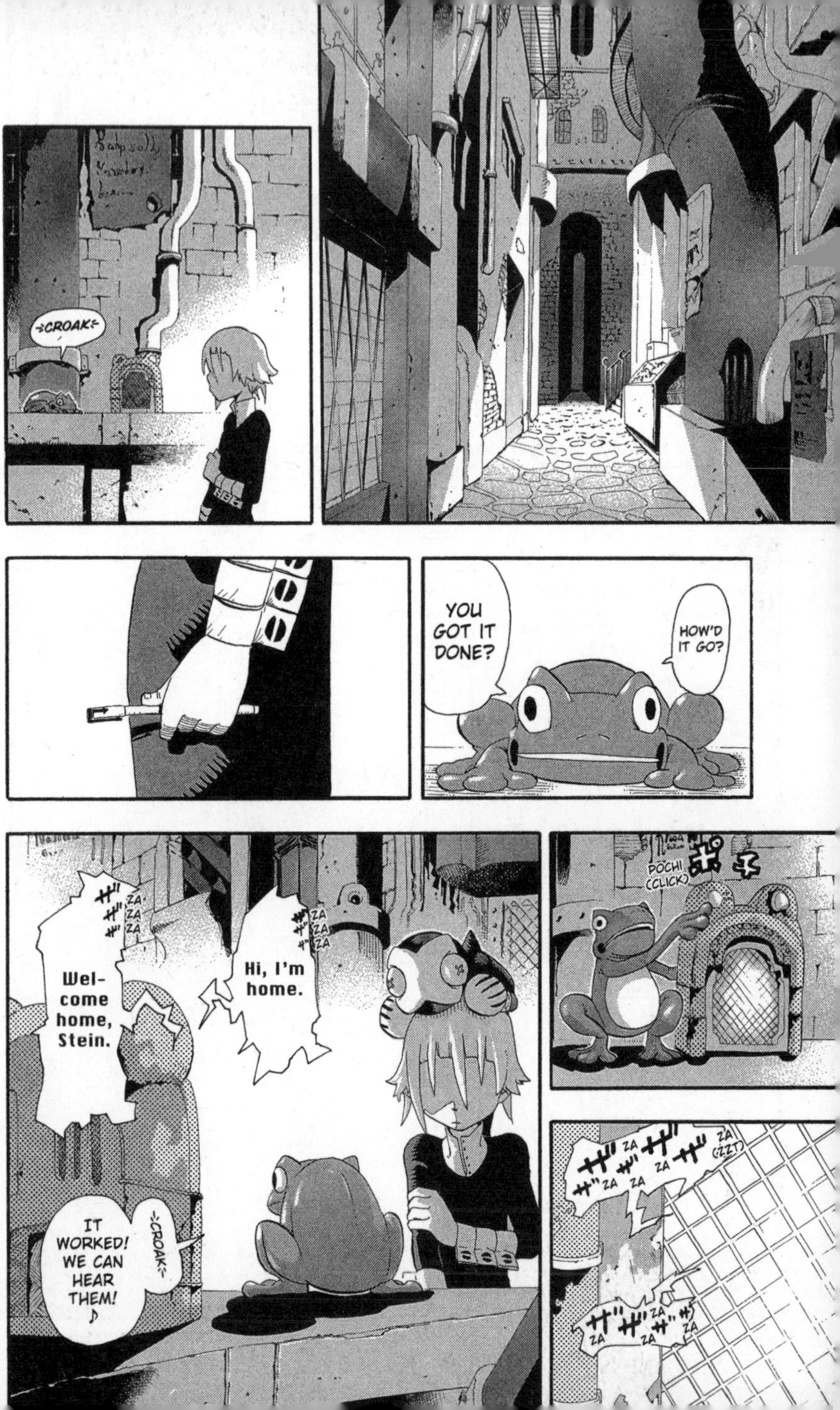

CROAK
HOW'D IT GO?
YOU GOT IT DONE?
POCHI (CLICK)
ZA ZA ZA ZA ZA ZA ZA (ZZT)
ZA ZA ZA ZA ZA
ZA ZA ZA
Hi, I'm home.
ZA ZA ZA
Wel-come home, Stein.
CROAK
IT WORKED! WE CAN HEAR THEM! ♪

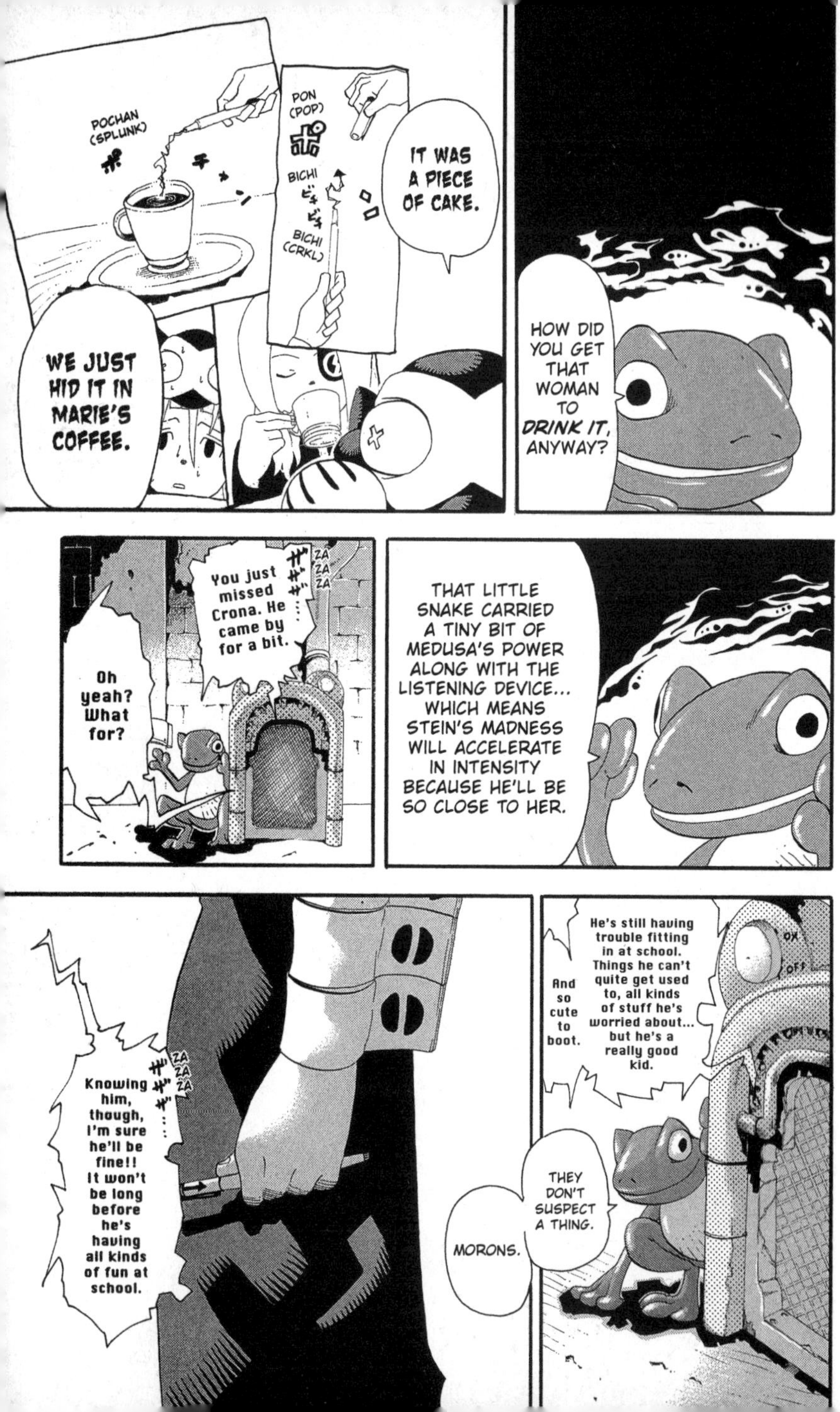
HOW DID YOU GET THAT WOMAN TO *DRINK IT*, ANYWAY?
IT WAS A PIECE OF CAKE.
PON (POP)
BICHI
BICHI (CRKL)
POCHAN (SPLUNK)
WE JUST HID IT IN MARIE'S COFFEE.
THAT LITTLE SNAKE CARRIED A TINY BIT OF MEDUSA'S POWER ALONG WITH THE LISTENING DEVICE... WHICH MEANS STEIN'S MADNESS WILL ACCELERATE IN INTENSITY BECAUSE HE'LL BE SO CLOSE TO HER.
ZA ZA ZA
You just missed Crona. He came by for a bit.
Oh yeah? What for?
He's still having trouble fitting in at school. Things he can't quite get used to, all kinds of stuff he's worried about... but he's a really good kid.
And so cute to boot.
THEY DON'T SUSPECT A THING.
MORONS.
ZA ZA ZA
Knowing him, though, I'm sure he'll be fine!! It won't be long before he's having all kinds of fun at school.

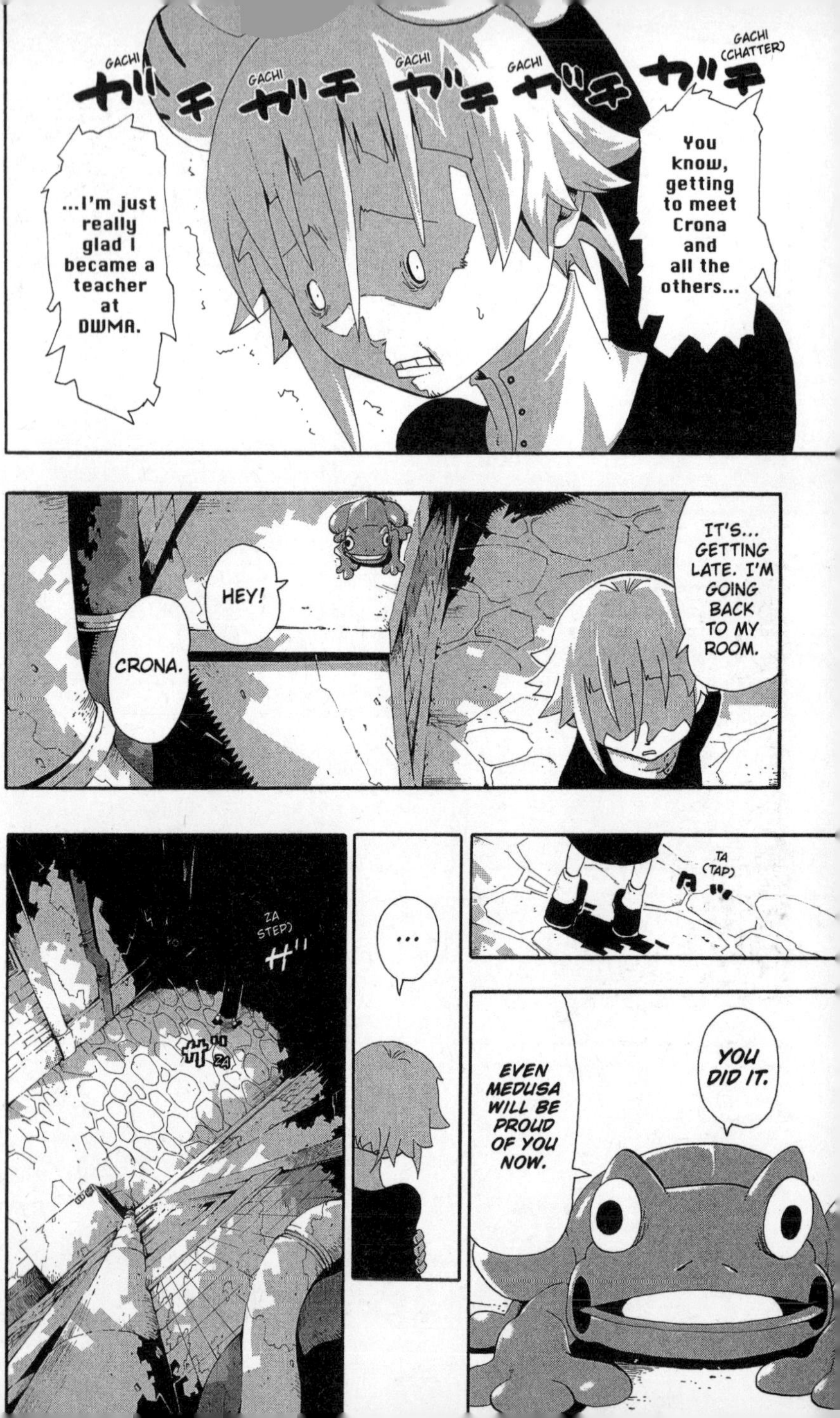
GACHI (CHATTER)
GACHI
GACHI
GACHI
You know, getting to meet Crona and all the others...
...I'm just really glad I became a teacher at DWMA.
IT'S... GETTING LATE. I'M GOING BACK TO MY ROOM.
HEY!
CRONA.
TA (TAP)
YOU DID IT.
EVEN MEDUSA WILL BE PROUD OF YOU NOW.
...
ZA STEP)
ZA

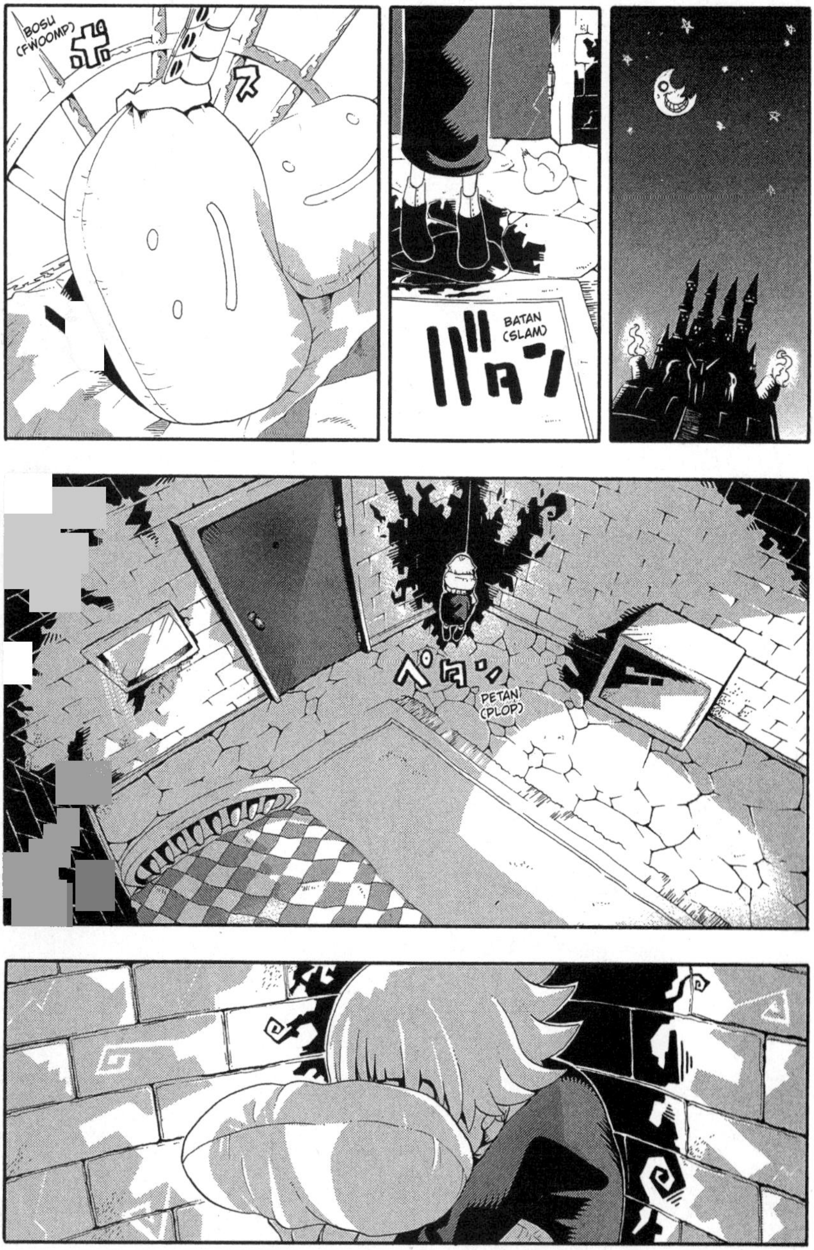
BATAN (SLAM)
バタン
BOSU (FWOOMP)
ボス
ペタン
PETAN (PLOP)

ギュゥゥゥ…
GYUUUUU
(SQUEEEEEZE)

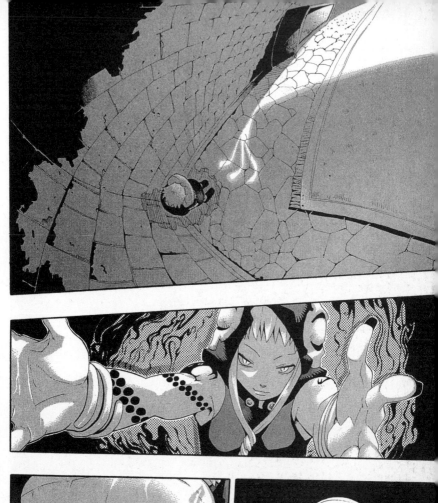

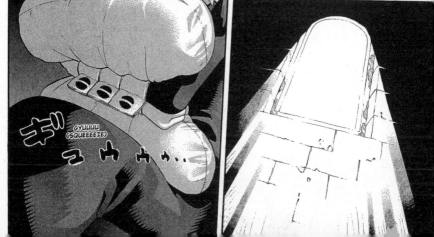

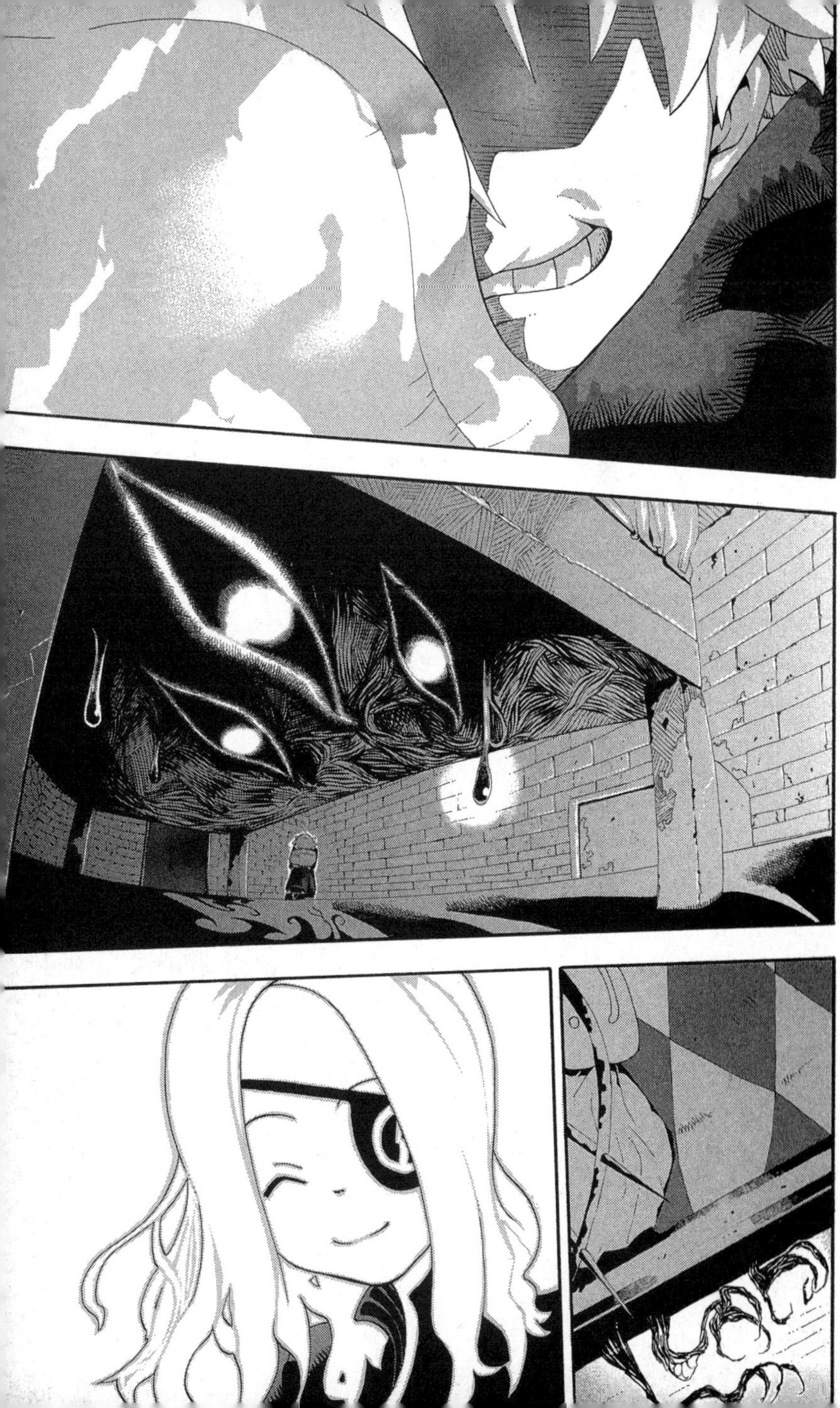

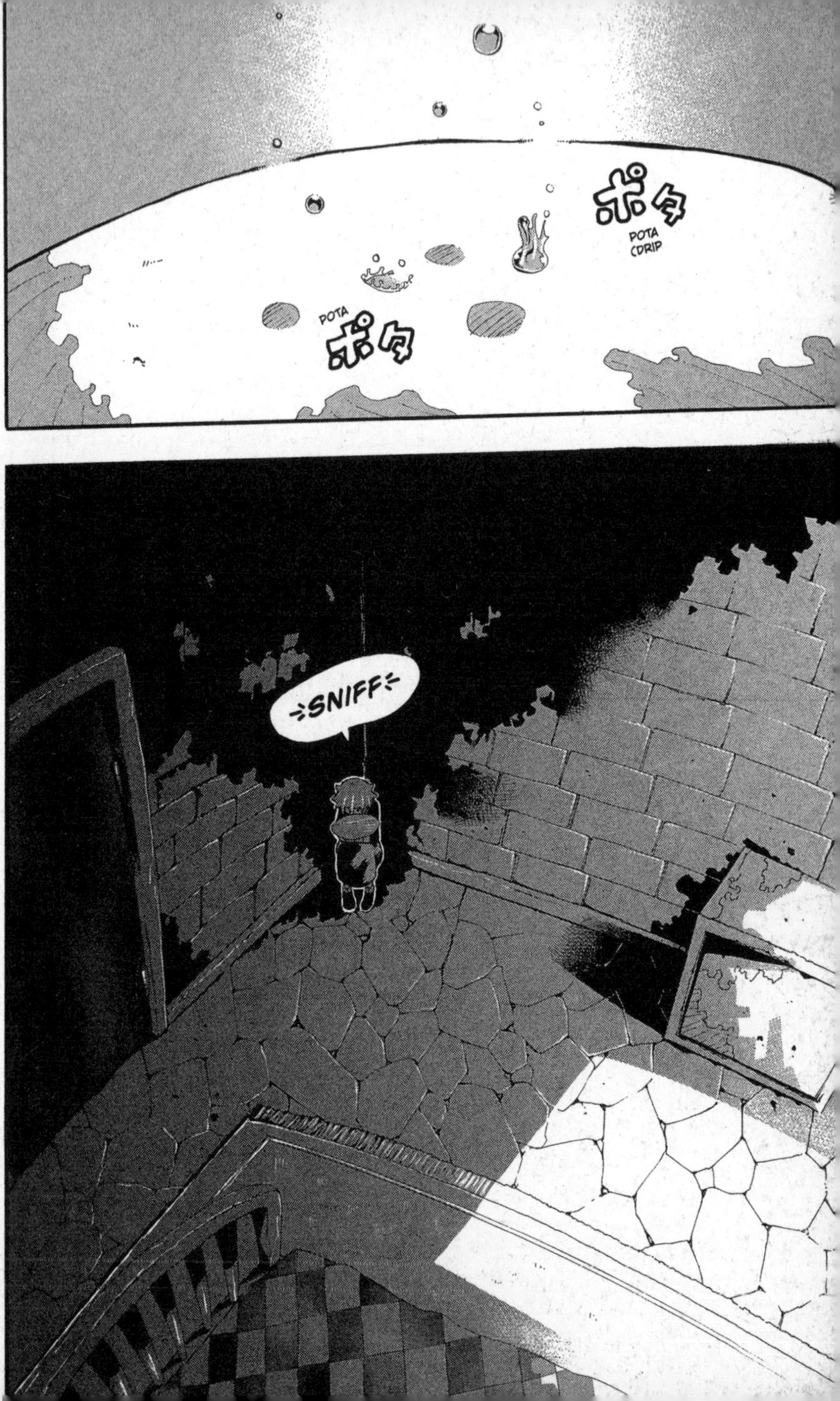
ポタ
POTA
(DRIP)
POTA
ポタ
SNIFF

SOUL EATER

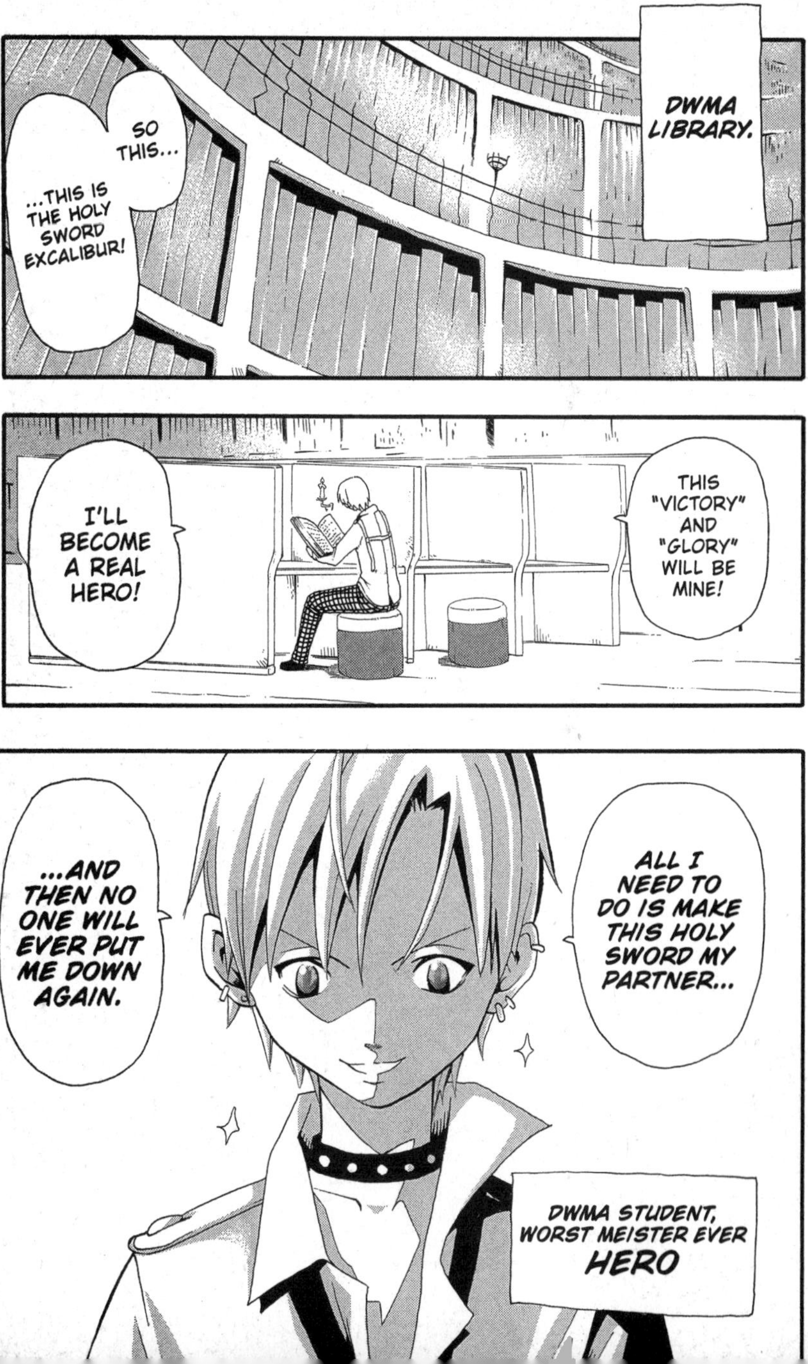
DWMA LIBRARY.
SO THIS...
...THIS IS THE HOLY SWORD EXCALIBUR!
THIS "VICTORY" AND "GLORY" WILL BE MINE!
I'LL BECOME A REAL HERO!
ALL I NEED TO DO IS MAKE THIS HOLY SWORD MY PARTNER...
...AND THEN NO ONE WILL EVER PUT ME DOWN AGAIN.
DWMA STUDENT, WORST MEISTER EVER
HERO

BONUS CHAPTER: LEGEND OF THE HOLY SWORD

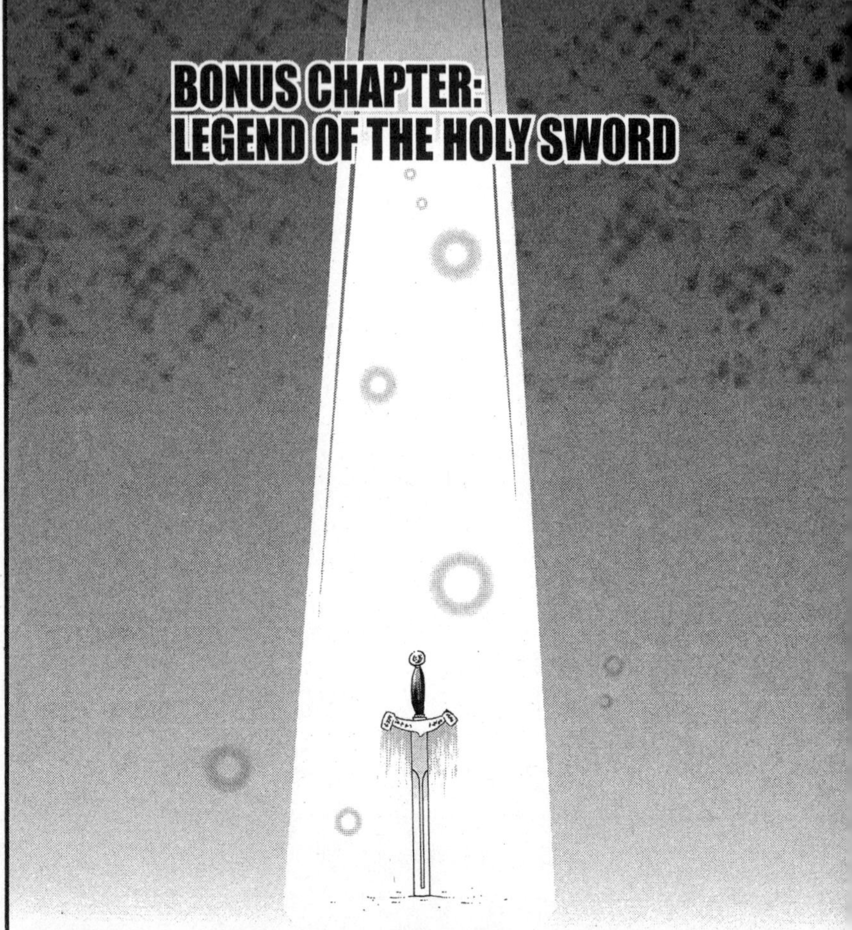

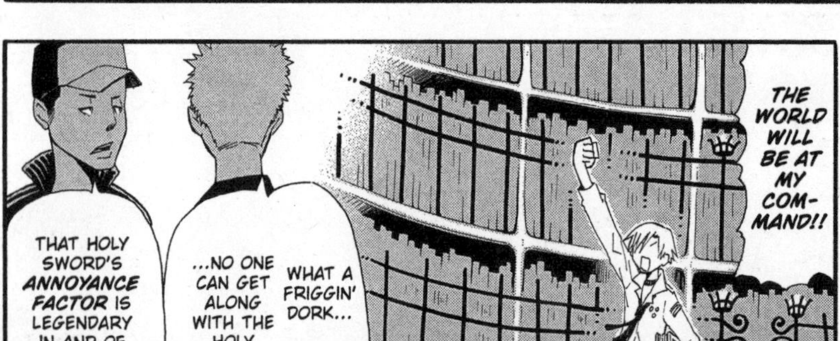
THE WORLD WILL BE AT MY COM-MAND!!
WHAT A FRIGGIN' DORK...
...NO ONE CAN GET ALONG WITH THE HOLY SWORD.
THAT HOLY SWORD'S *ANNOYANCE FACTOR* IS LEGENDARY IN AND OF ITSELF.

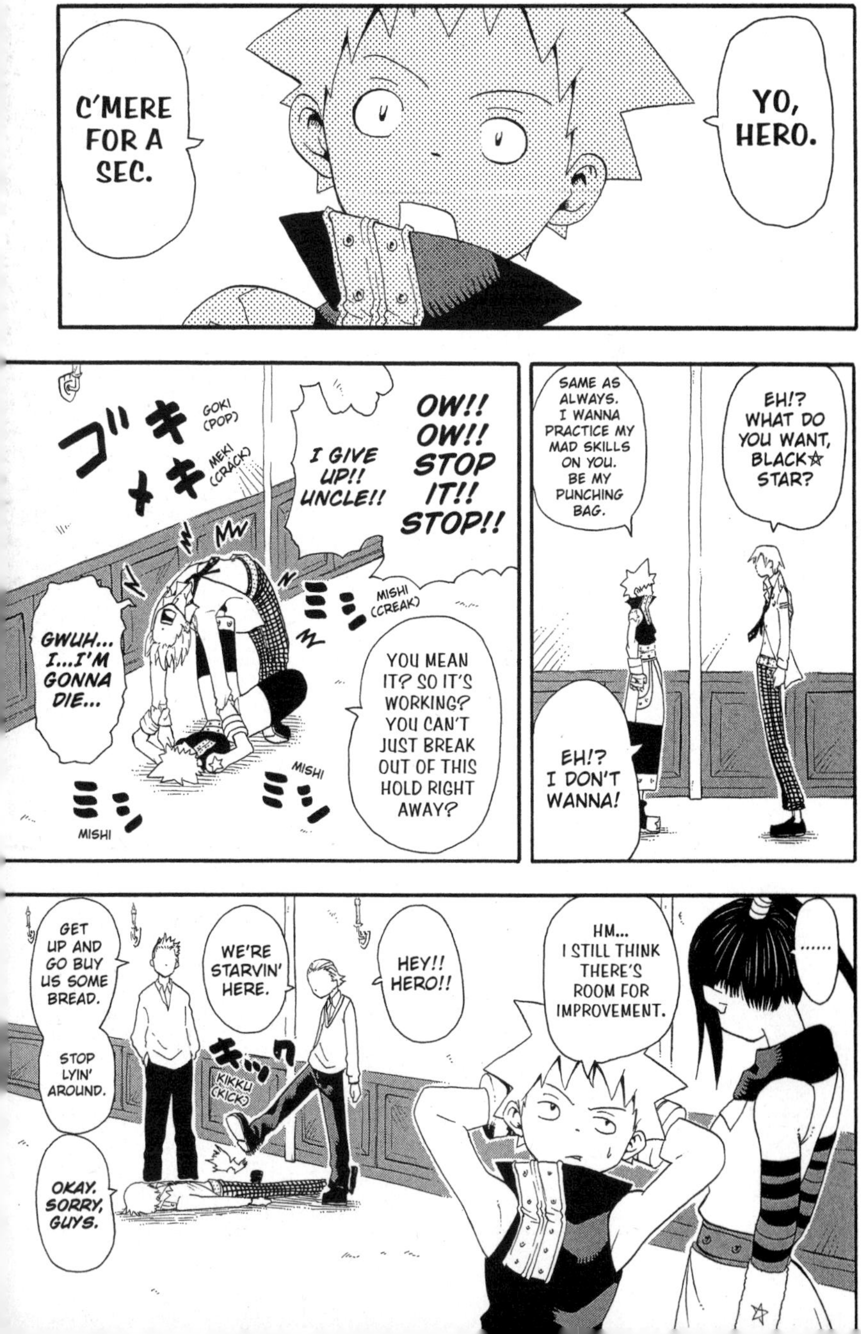
YO, HERO.
C'MERE FOR A SEC.
EH!? WHAT DO YOU WANT, BLACK☆STAR?
SAME AS ALWAYS. I WANNA PRACTICE MY MAD SKILLS ON YOU. BE MY PUNCHING BAG.
EH!? I DON'T WANNA!
OW!! OW!! STOP IT!! STOP!!
I GIVE UP!! UNCLE!!
ゴキ
GOKI (POP)
メキ
MEKI (CRACK)
ミシ
MISHI (CREAK)
YOU MEAN IT? SO IT'S WORKING? YOU CAN'T JUST BREAK OUT OF THIS HOLD RIGHT AWAY?
GWUH... I...I'M GONNA DIE...
ミシ
MISHI
ミシ
MISHI
......
HM... I STILL THINK THERE'S ROOM FOR IMPROVEMENT.
HEY!! HERO!!
WE'RE STARVIN' HERE.
GET UP AND GO BUY US SOME BREAD.
キック
KIKKU (KICK)
STOP LYIN' AROUND.
OKAY. SORRY, GUYS.

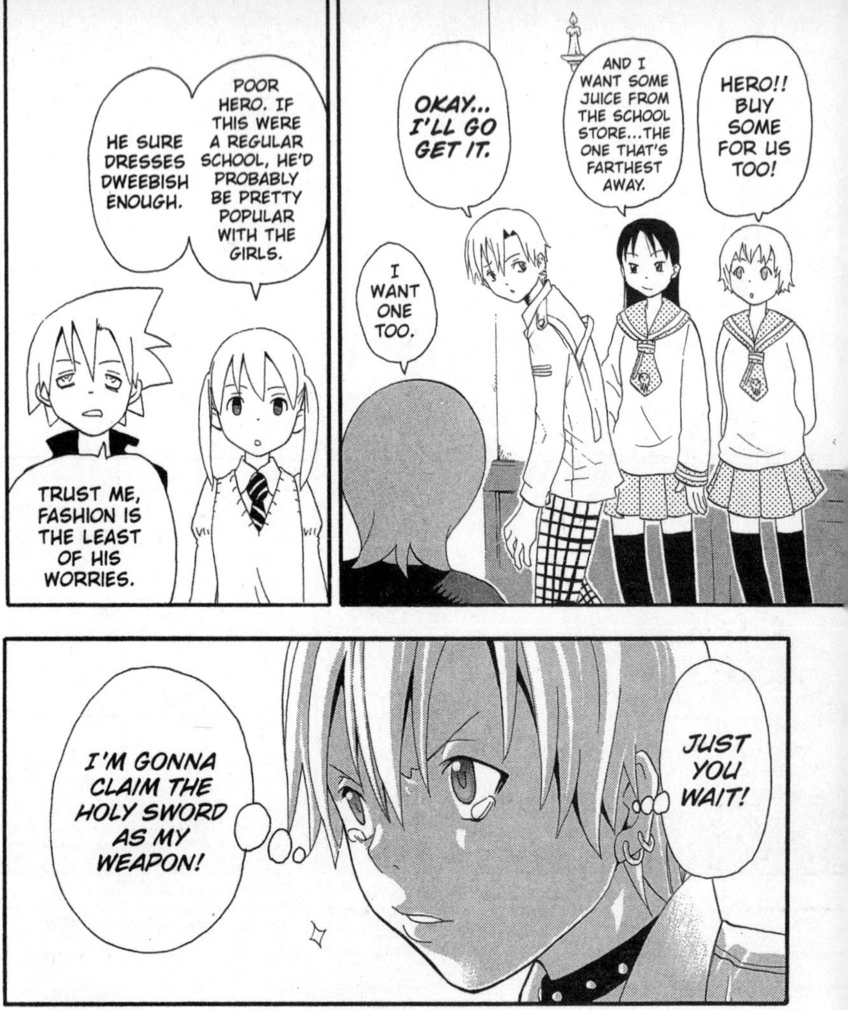
HERO!! BUY SOME FOR US TOO!
AND I WANT SOME JUICE FROM THE SCHOOL STORE...THE ONE THAT'S FARTHEST AWAY.
OKAY... I'LL GO GET IT.
I WANT ONE TOO.
POOR HERO. IF THIS WERE A REGULAR SCHOOL, HE'D PROBABLY BE PRETTY POPULAR WITH THE GIRLS.
HE SURE DRESSES DWEEBISH ENOUGH.
TRUST ME, FASHION IS THE LEAST OF HIS WORRIES.
JUST YOU WAIT!
I'M GONNA CLAIM THE HOLY SWORD AS MY WEAPON!

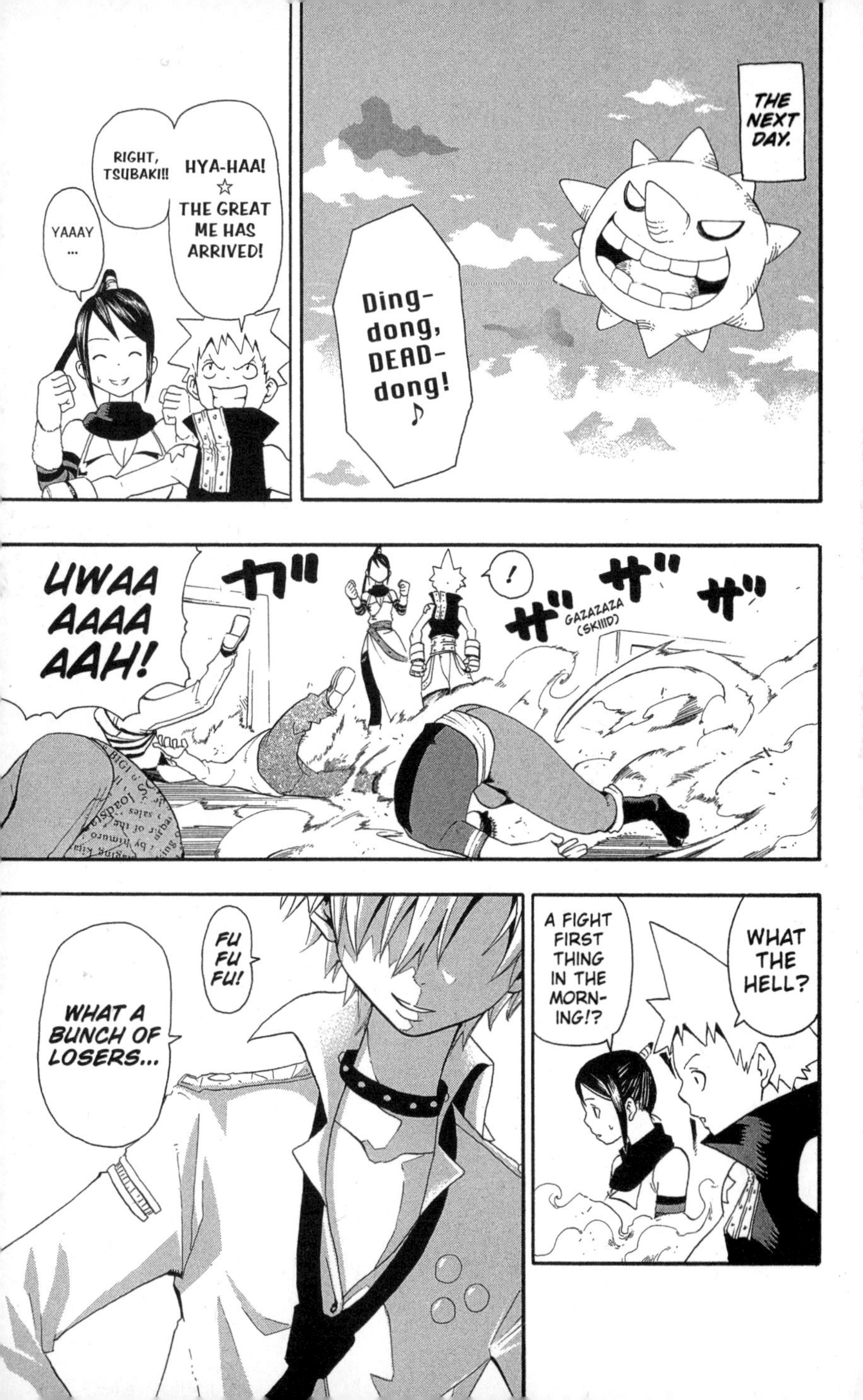
THE NEXT DAY.
Ding-dong, DEAD-dong! ♪
HYA-HAA! ☆ THE GREAT ME HAS ARRIVED!
RIGHT, TSUBAKI!!
YAAAY ...
ザ ザ ザ
GAZAZAZA (SKIIID)
!
ガ
UWAA AAAA AAH!
WHAT THE HELL?
A FIGHT FIRST THING IN THE MORNING!?
FU FU FU!
WHAT A BUNCH OF LOSERS...

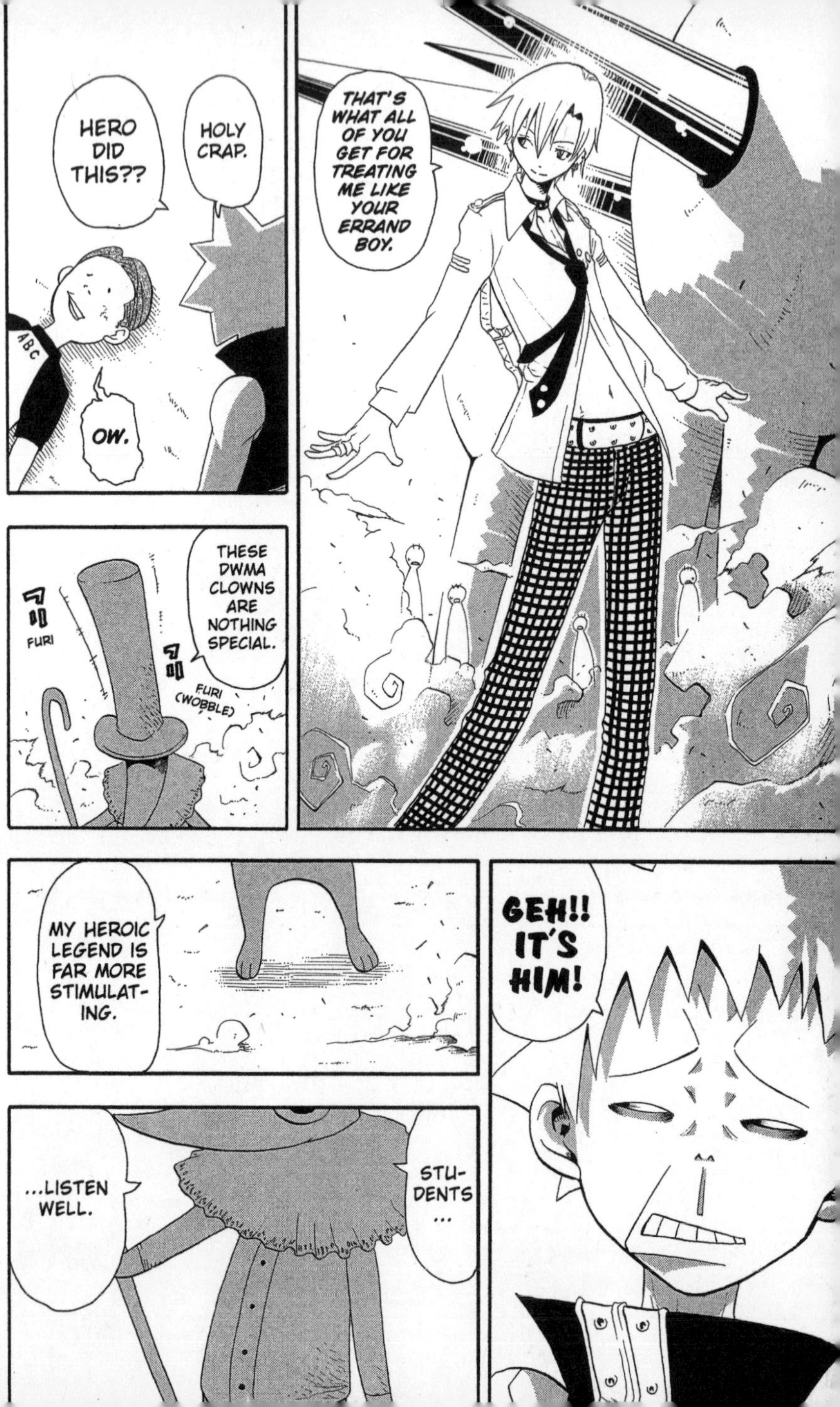

THAT'S WHAT ALL OF YOU GET FOR TREATING ME LIKE YOUR ERRAND BOY.
HOLY CRAP.
HERO DID THIS??
OW.
THESE DWMA CLOWNS ARE NOTHING SPECIAL.
FURI (WOBBLE)
FURI
GEH!! IT'S HIM!
MY HEROIC LEGEND IS FAR MORE STIMULAT-ING.
STU-DENTS...
...LISTEN WELL.

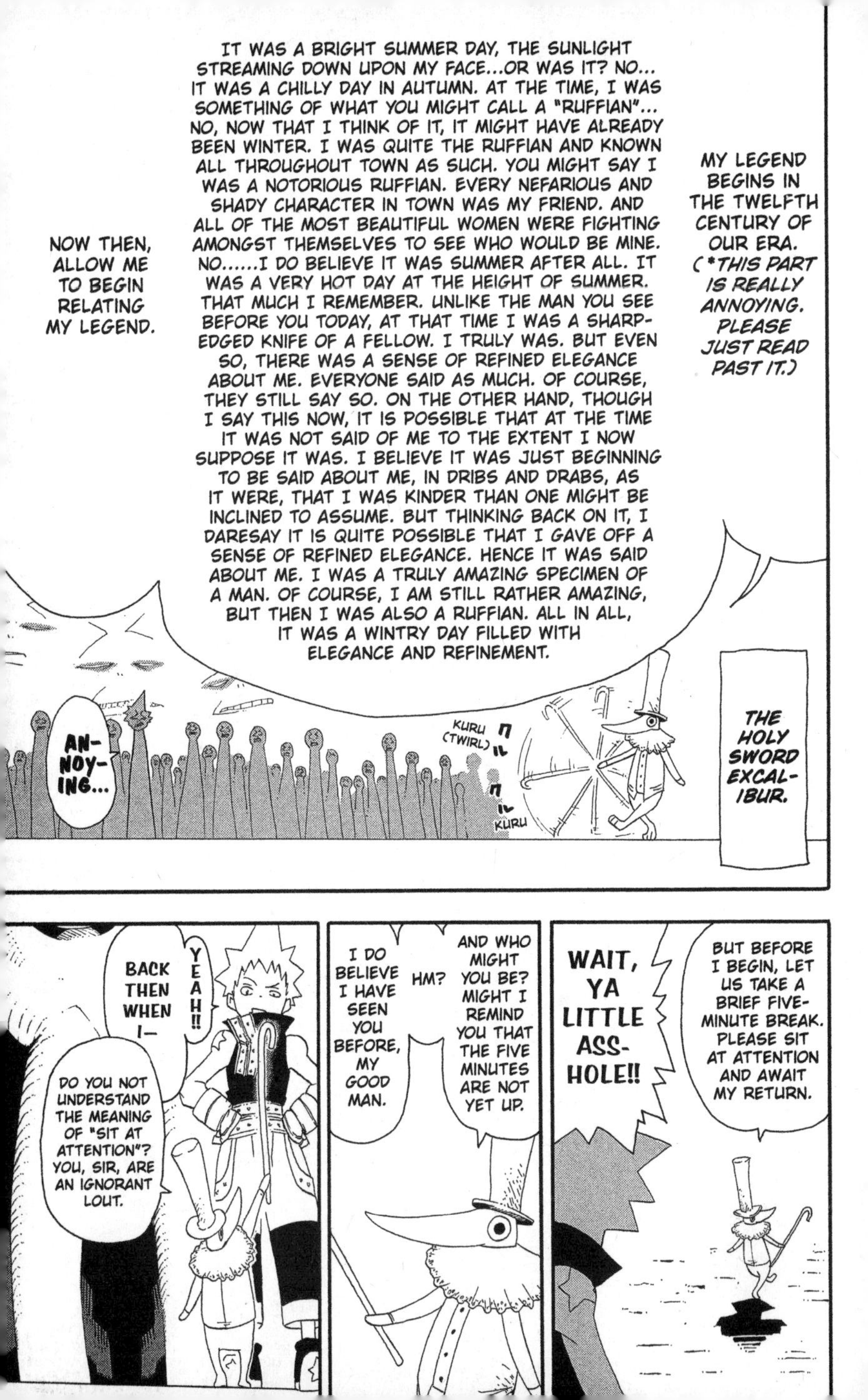
THE HOLY SWORD EXCALIBUR.
MY LEGEND BEGINS IN THE TWELFTH CENTURY OF OUR ERA. (*THIS PART IS REALLY ANNOYING. PLEASE JUST READ PAST IT.)
IT WAS A BRIGHT SUMMER DAY, THE SUNLIGHT STREAMING DOWN UPON MY FACE...OR WAS IT? NO... IT WAS A CHILLY DAY IN AUTUMN. AT THE TIME, I WAS SOMETHING OF WHAT YOU MIGHT CALL A "RUFFIAN"... NO, NOW THAT I THINK OF IT, IT MIGHT HAVE ALREADY BEEN WINTER. I WAS QUITE THE RUFFIAN AND KNOWN ALL THROUGHOUT TOWN AS SUCH. YOU MIGHT SAY I WAS A NOTORIOUS RUFFIAN. EVERY NEFARIOUS AND SHADY CHARACTER IN TOWN WAS MY FRIEND. AND ALL OF THE MOST BEAUTIFUL WOMEN WERE FIGHTING AMONGST THEMSELVES TO SEE WHO WOULD BE MINE. NO......I DO BELIEVE IT WAS SUMMER AFTER ALL. IT WAS A VERY HOT DAY AT THE HEIGHT OF SUMMER. THAT MUCH I REMEMBER. UNLIKE THE MAN YOU SEE BEFORE YOU TODAY, AT THAT TIME I WAS A SHARP-EDGED KNIFE OF A FELLOW. I TRULY WAS. BUT EVEN SO, THERE WAS A SENSE OF REFINED ELEGANCE ABOUT ME. EVERYONE SAID AS MUCH. OF COURSE, THEY STILL SAY SO. ON THE OTHER HAND, THOUGH I SAY THIS NOW, IT IS POSSIBLE THAT AT THE TIME IT WAS NOT SAID OF ME TO THE EXTENT I NOW SUPPOSE IT WAS. I BELIEVE IT WAS JUST BEGINNING TO BE SAID ABOUT ME, IN DRIBS AND DRABS, AS IT WERE, THAT I WAS KINDER THAN ONE MIGHT BE INCLINED TO ASSUME. BUT THINKING BACK ON IT, I DARESAY IT IS QUITE POSSIBLE THAT I GAVE OFF A SENSE OF REFINED ELEGANCE. HENCE IT WAS SAID ABOUT ME. I WAS A TRULY AMAZING SPECIMEN OF A MAN. OF COURSE, I AM STILL RATHER AMAZING, BUT THEN I WAS ALSO A RUFFIAN. ALL IN ALL, IT WAS A WINTRY DAY FILLED WITH ELEGANCE AND REFINEMENT.
NOW THEN, ALLOW ME TO BEGIN RELATING MY LEGEND.
KURU (TWIRL)
KURU
AN-NOY-ING...
BUT BEFORE I BEGIN, LET US TAKE A BRIEF FIVE-MINUTE BREAK. PLEASE SIT AT ATTENTION AND AWAIT MY RETURN.
WAIT, YA LITTLE ASS-HOLE!!
AND WHO MIGHT YOU BE? MIGHT I REMIND YOU THAT THE FIVE MINUTES ARE NOT YET UP.
HM?
I DO BELIEVE I HAVE SEEN YOU BEFORE, MY GOOD MAN.
YEAH!!
BACK THEN WHEN I—
DO YOU NOT UNDERSTAND THE MEANING OF "SIT AT ATTENTION"? YOU, SIR, ARE AN IGNORANT LOUT.

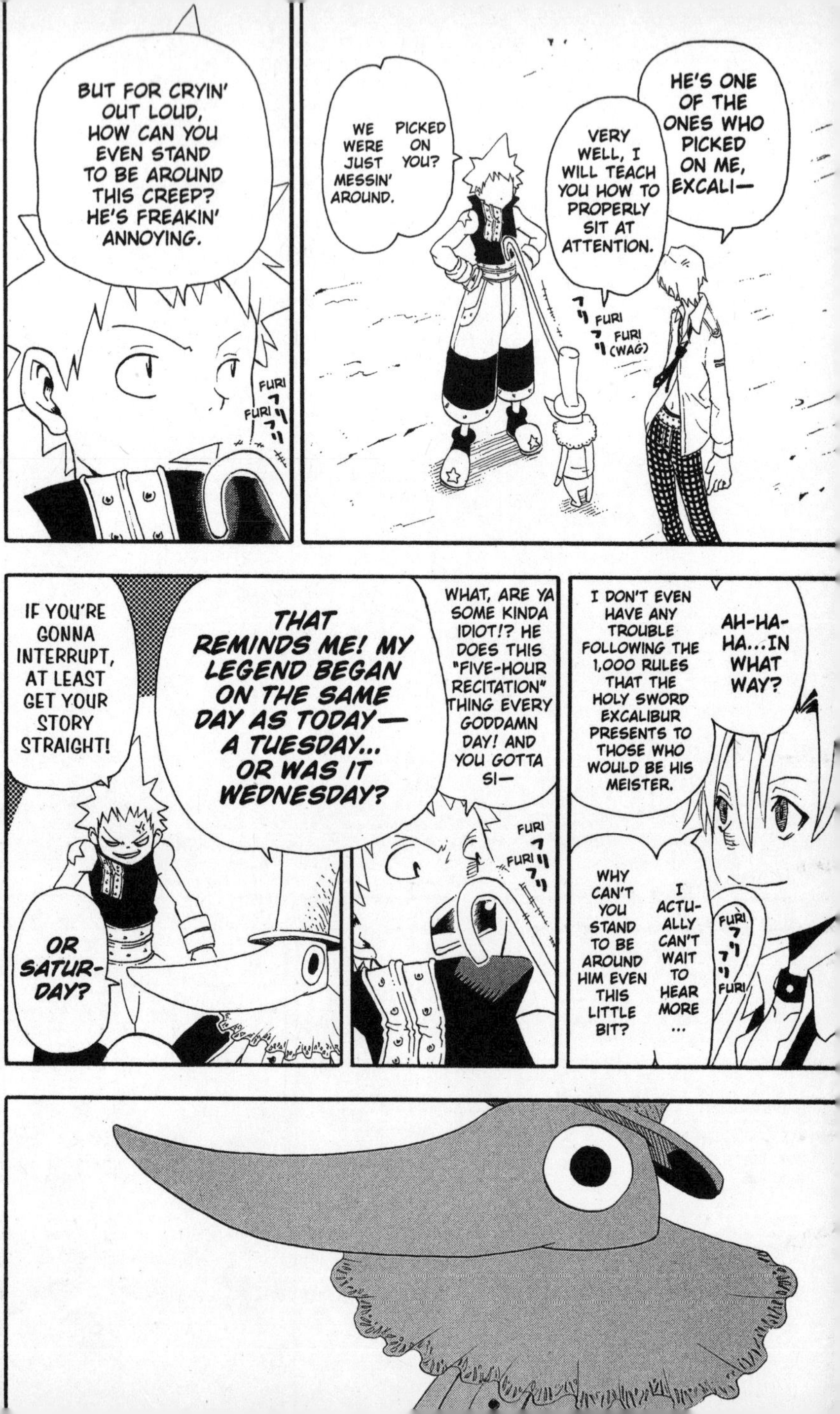
HE'S ONE OF THE ONES WHO PICKED ON ME, EXCALI—
VERY WELL, I WILL TEACH YOU HOW TO PROPERLY SIT AT ATTENTION.
FURI FURI (WAG)
PICKED ON YOU? WE WERE JUST MESSIN' AROUND.
BUT FOR CRYIN' OUT LOUD, HOW CAN YOU EVEN STAND TO BE AROUND THIS CREEP? HE'S FREAKIN' ANNOYING.
FURI FURI
AH-HA-HA...IN WHAT WAY?
I DON'T EVEN HAVE ANY TROUBLE FOLLOWING THE 1,000 RULES THAT THE HOLY SWORD EXCALIBUR PRESENTS TO THOSE WHO WOULD BE HIS MEISTER.
FURI FURI
I ACTUALLY CAN'T WAIT TO HEAR MORE...
WHY CAN'T YOU STAND TO BE AROUND HIM EVEN THIS LITTLE BIT?
WHAT, ARE YA SOME KINDA IDIOT!? HE DOES THIS "FIVE-HOUR RECITATION" THING EVERY GODDAMN DAY! AND YOU GOTTA SI—
FURI FURI
THAT REMINDS ME! MY LEGEND BEGAN ON THE SAME DAY AS TODAY—A TUESDAY... OR WAS IT WEDNESDAY?
IF YOU'RE GONNA INTERRUPT, AT LEAST GET YOUR STORY STRAIGHT!
OR SATURDAY?

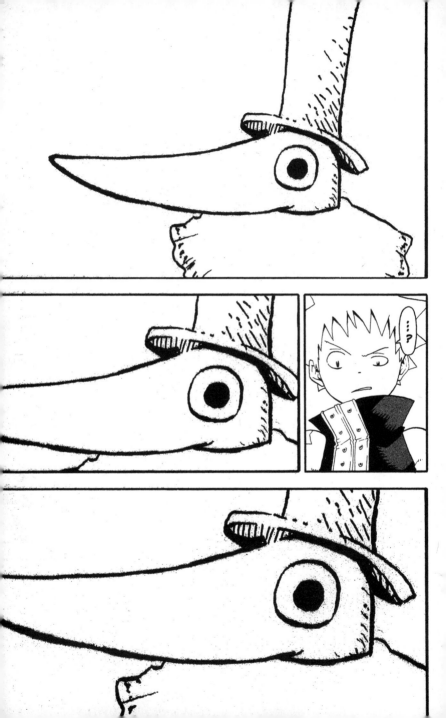

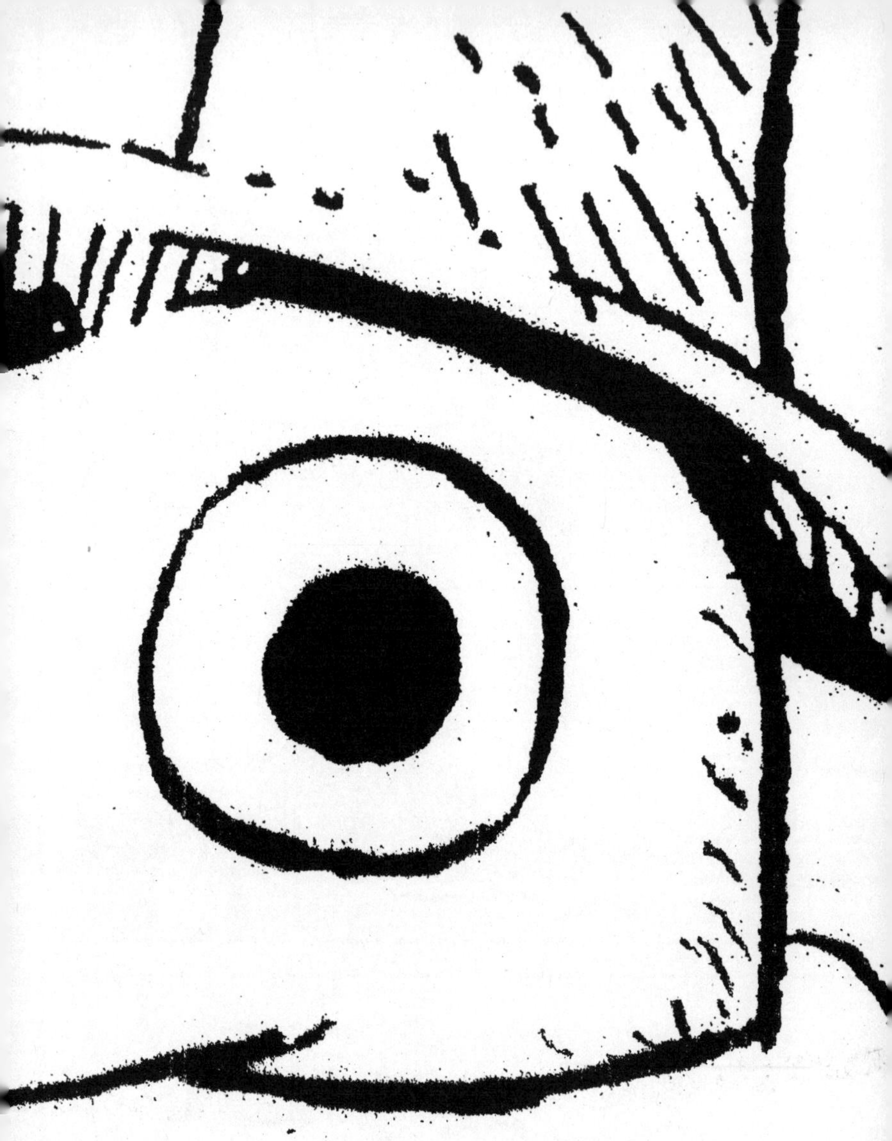

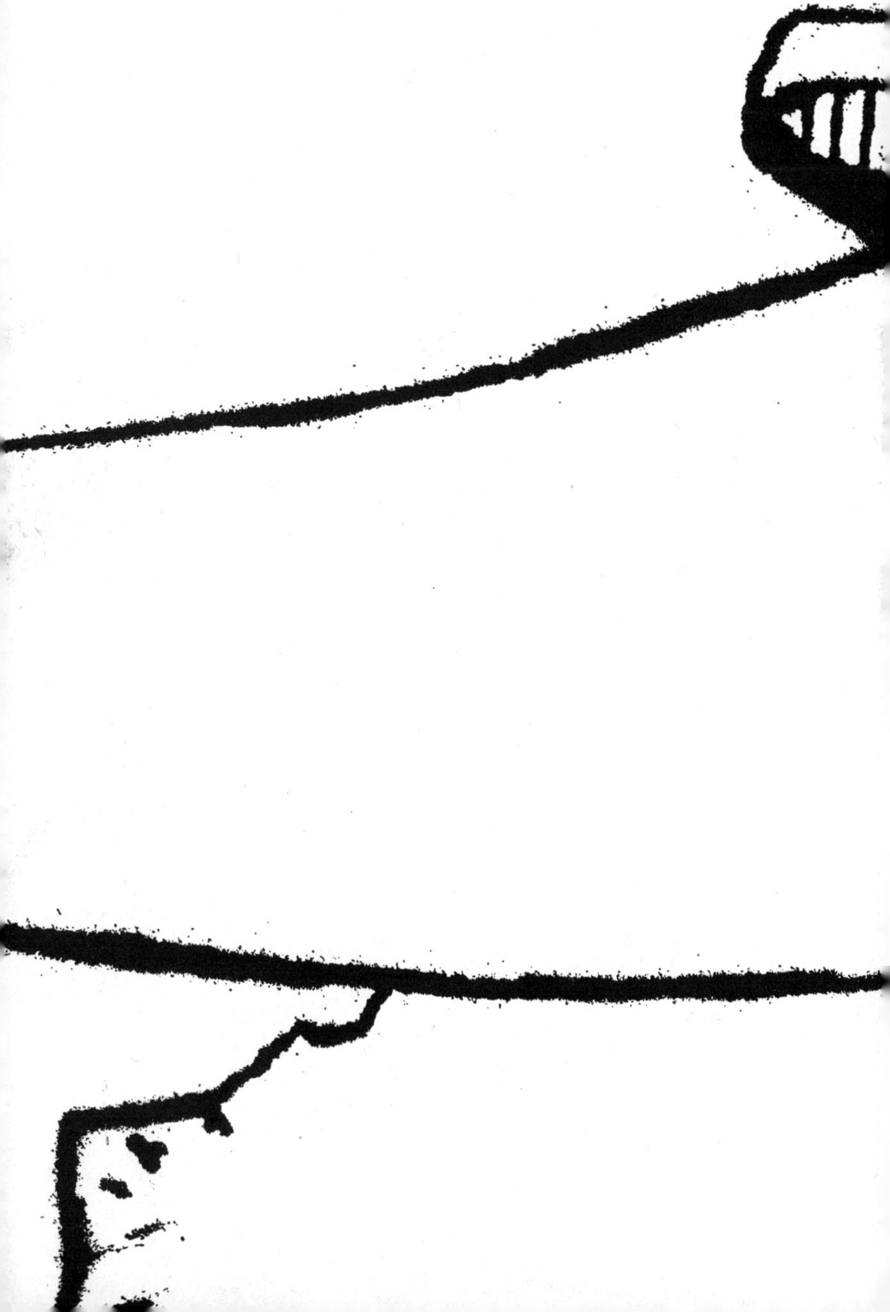

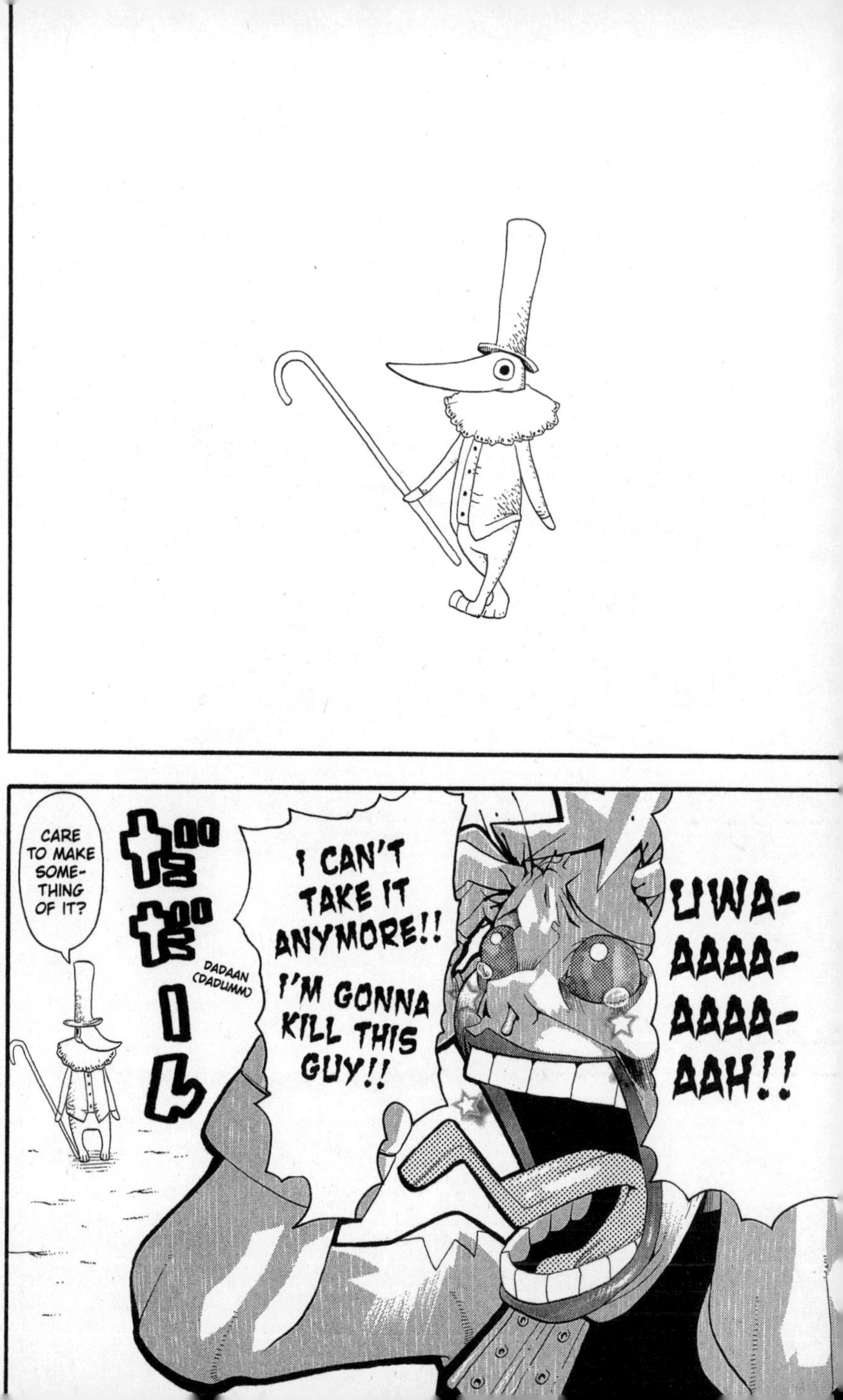
UWA-AAAA-AAAA-AAH!!
I CAN'T TAKE IT ANYMORE!! I'M GONNA KILL THIS GUY!!
DADAAN (DADUMM)
CARE TO MAKE SOME-THING OF IT?

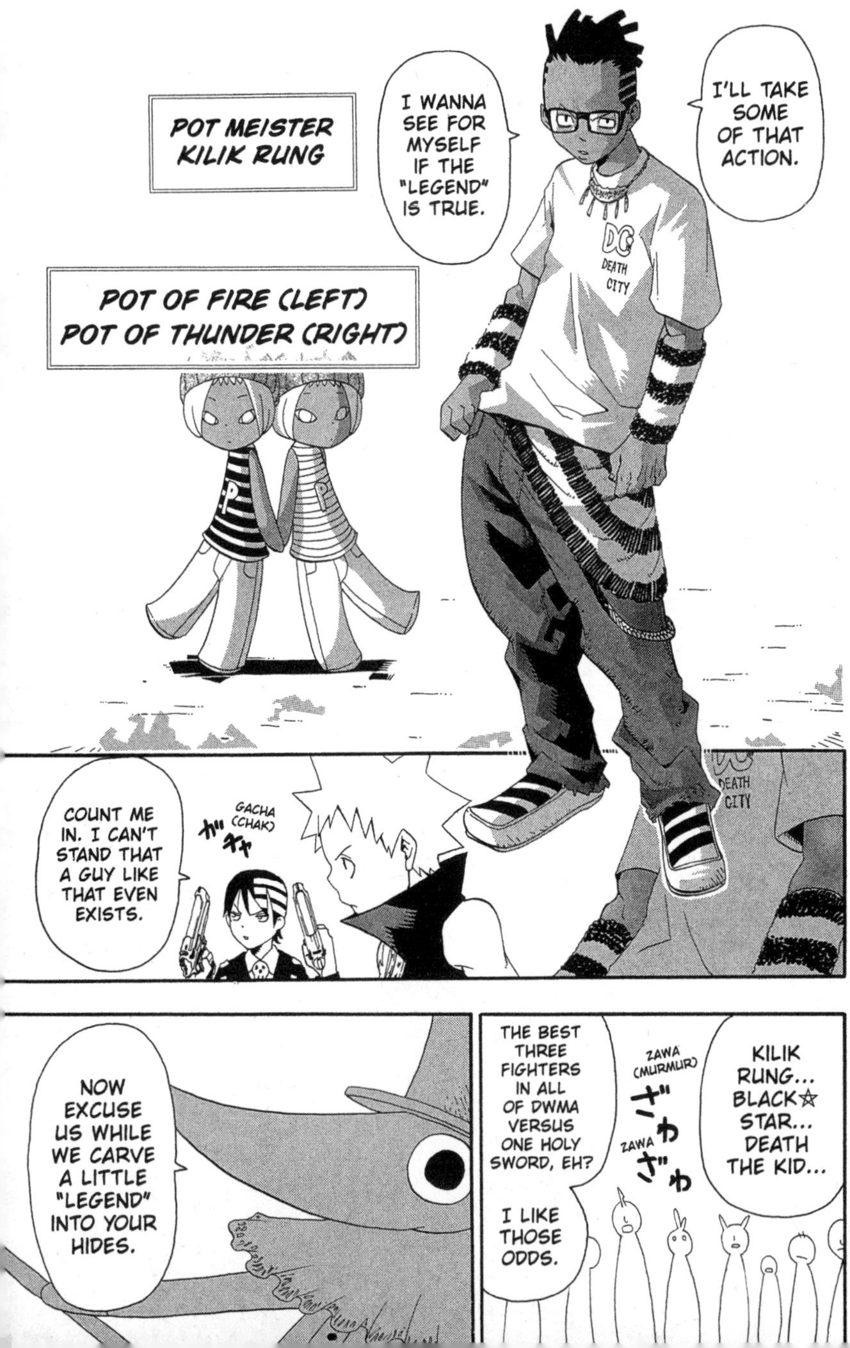
I'LL TAKE SOME OF THAT ACTION.
I WANNA SEE FOR MYSELF IF THE "LEGEND" IS TRUE.
POT MEISTER KILIK RUNG
POT OF FIRE (LEFT) POT OF THUNDER (RIGHT)
DEATH CITY
GACHA (CHAK)
COUNT ME IN. I CAN'T STAND THAT A GUY LIKE THAT EVEN EXISTS.
KILIK RUNG... BLACK☆STAR... DEATH THE KID...
ZAWA (MURMUR)
ZAWA
THE BEST THREE FIGHTERS IN ALL OF DWMA VERSUS ONE HOLY SWORD, EH?
I LIKE THOSE ODDS.
NOW EXCUSE US WHILE WE CARVE A LITTLE "LEGEND" INTO YOUR HIDES.

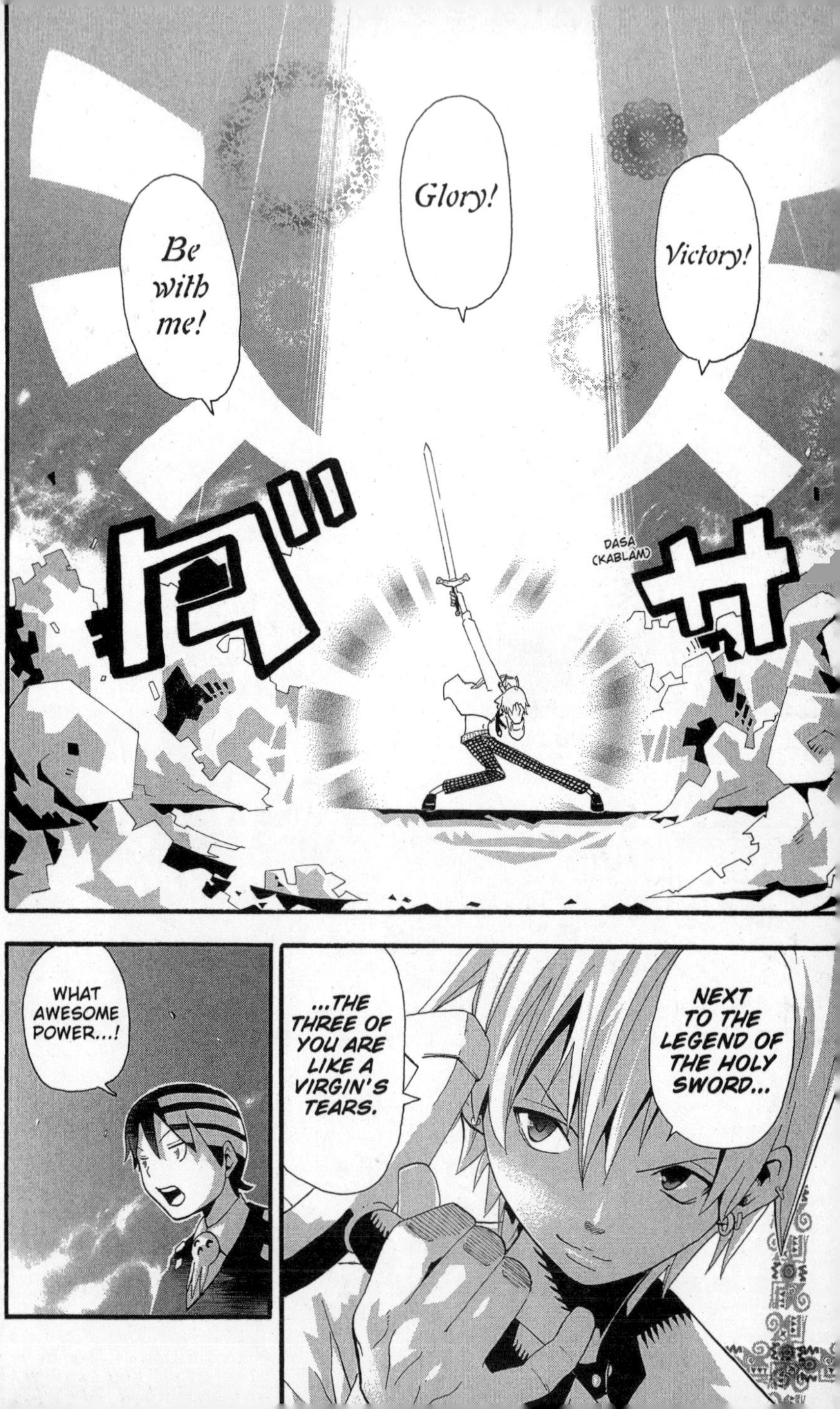
Victory!
Glory!
Be with me!
DASA (KABLAM)
NEXT TO THE LEGEND OF THE HOLY SWORD...
...THE THREE OF YOU ARE LIKE A VIRGIN'S TEARS.
WHAT AWESOME POWER...!

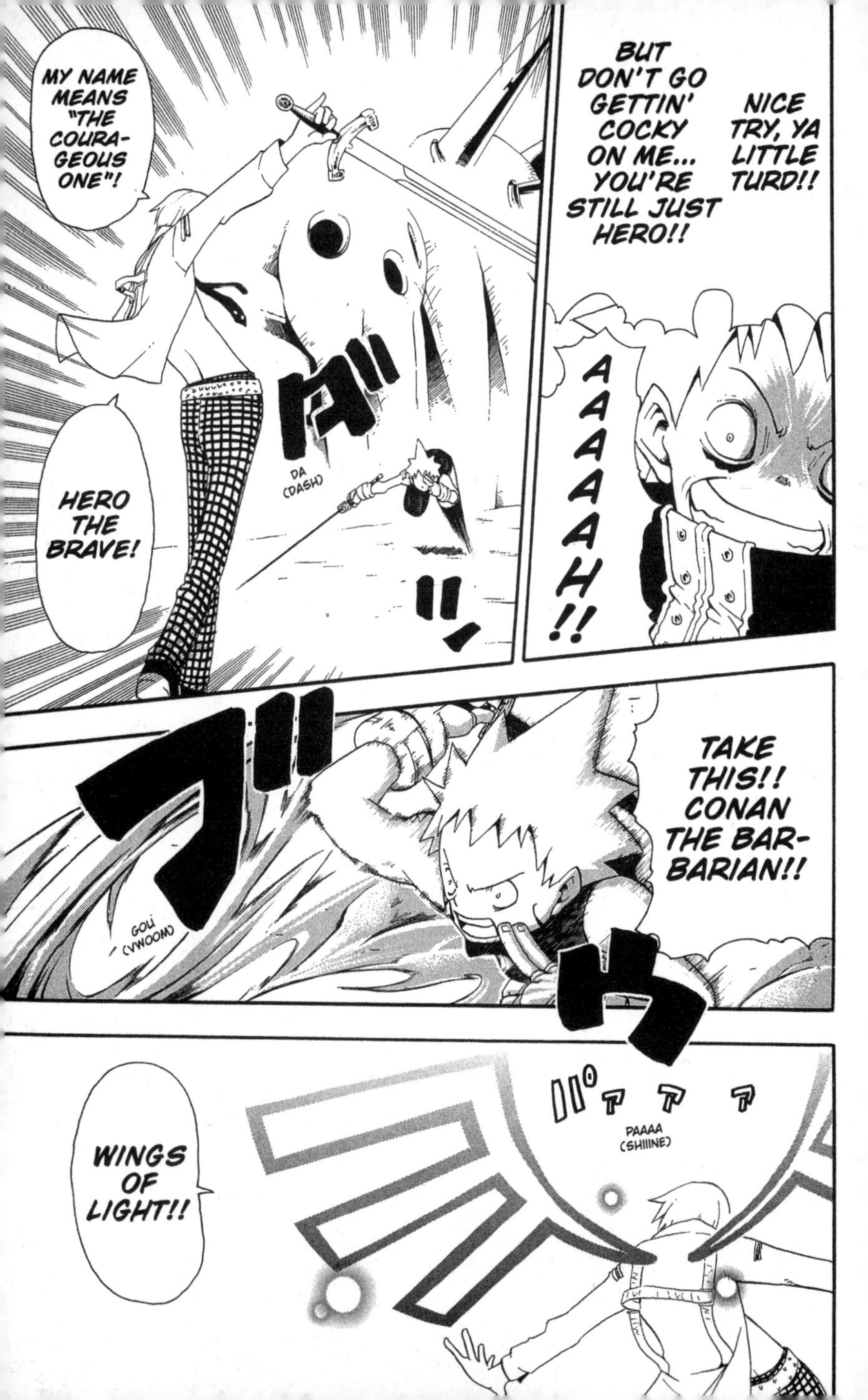
NICE TRY, YA LITTLE TURD!!
BUT DON'T GO GETTIN' COCKY ON ME... YOU'RE STILL JUST HERO!!
AAAAAAAH!!
MY NAME MEANS "THE COURAGEOUS ONE"!
DA (DASH)
HERO THE BRAVE!
TAKE THIS!! CONAN THE BARBARIAN!!
GOU (VWOOM)
PAAAA (SHIIINE)
WINGS OF LIGHT!!

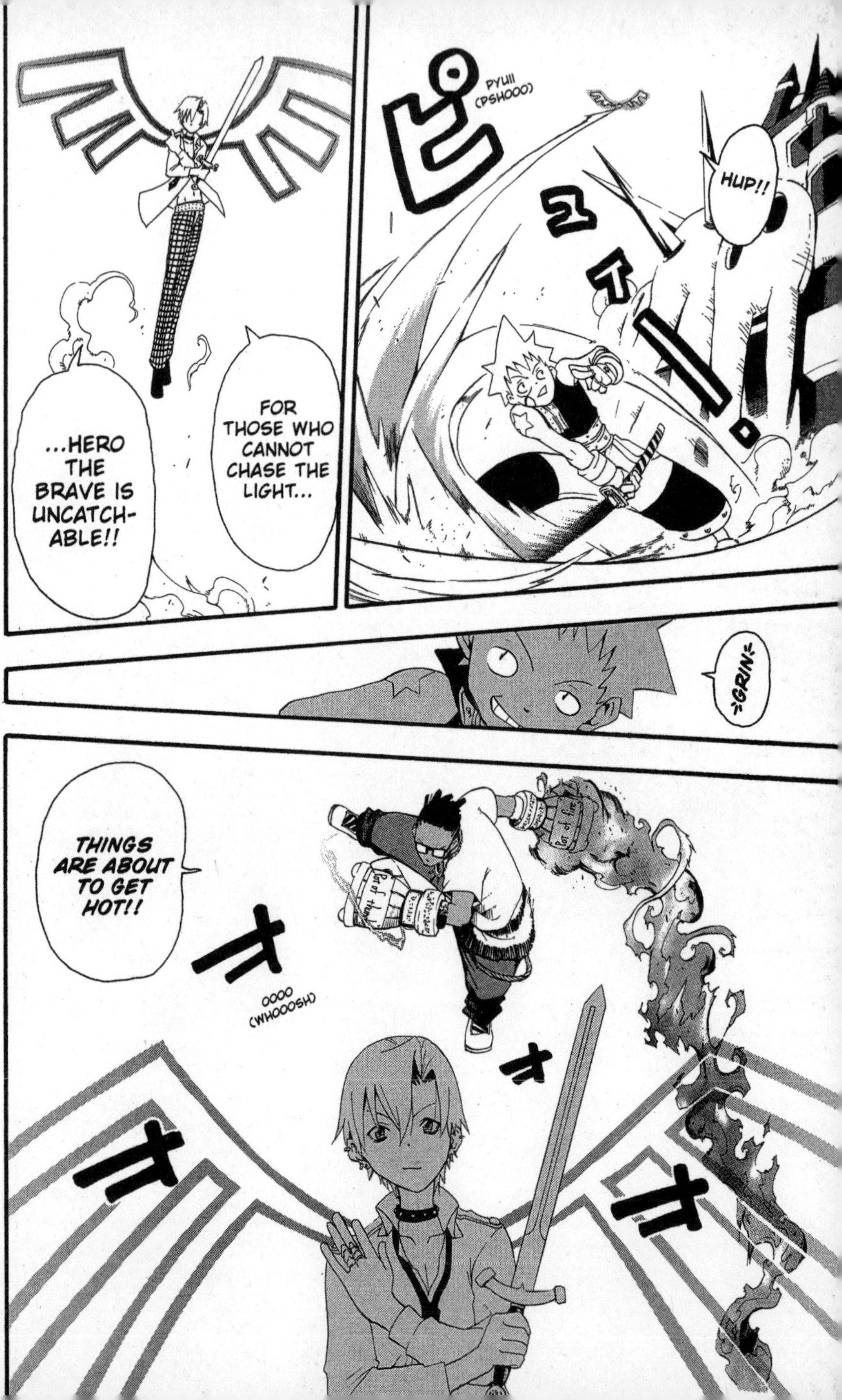
HUP!!
PYUII (PSHOOO)
FOR THOSE WHO CANNOT CHASE THE LIGHT...
...HERO THE BRAVE IS UNCATCH-ABLE!!
GRIN
THINGS ARE ABOUT TO GET HOT!!
OOOO (WHOOOSH)

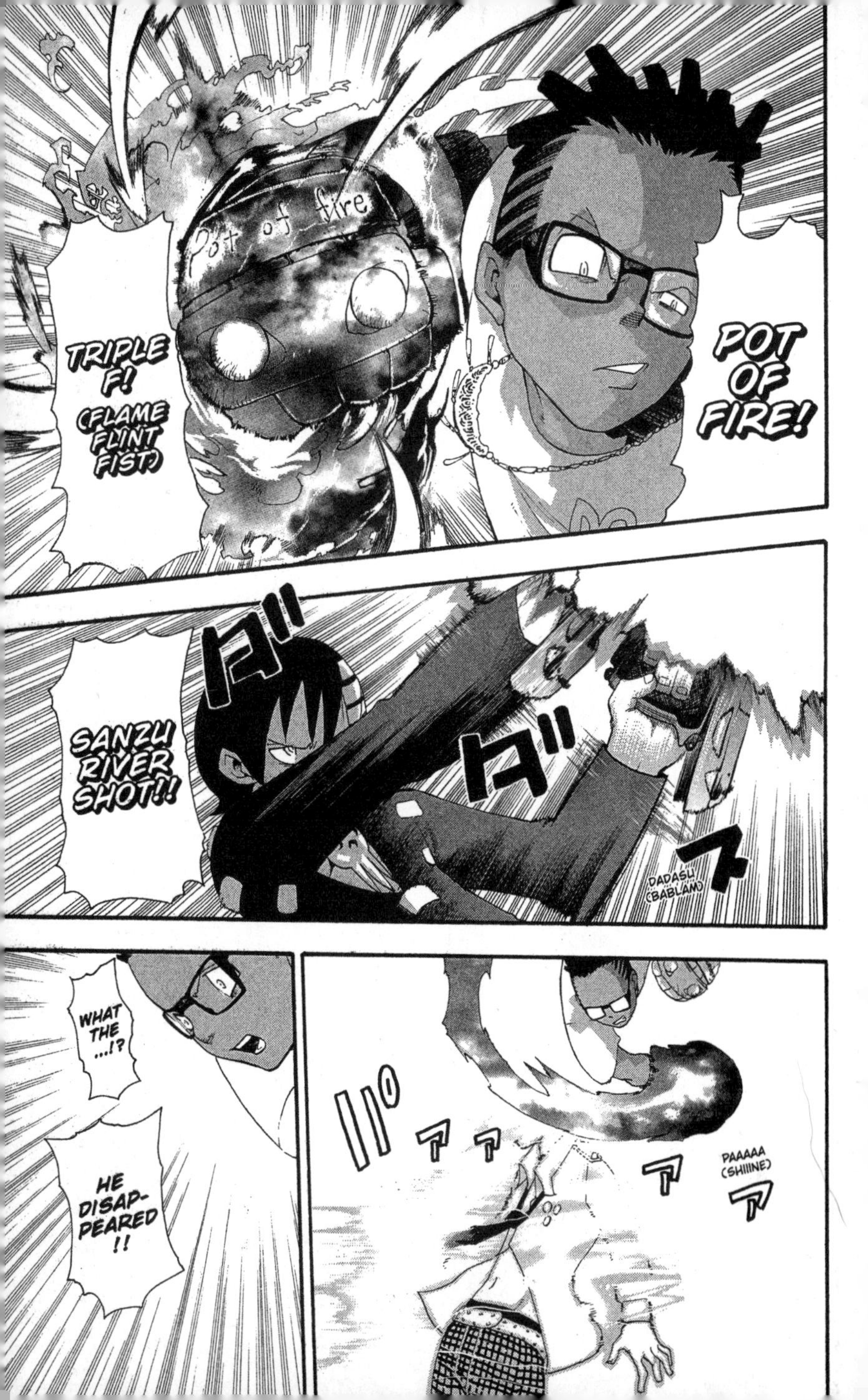

POT OF FIRE!
Pot of fire
TRIPLE F! (FLAME FLINT FIST)
SANZU RIVER SHOT!!
DADASU (BABLAM)
PAAAAA (SHIINE)
WHAT THE ...!?
HE DISAP-PEARED!!

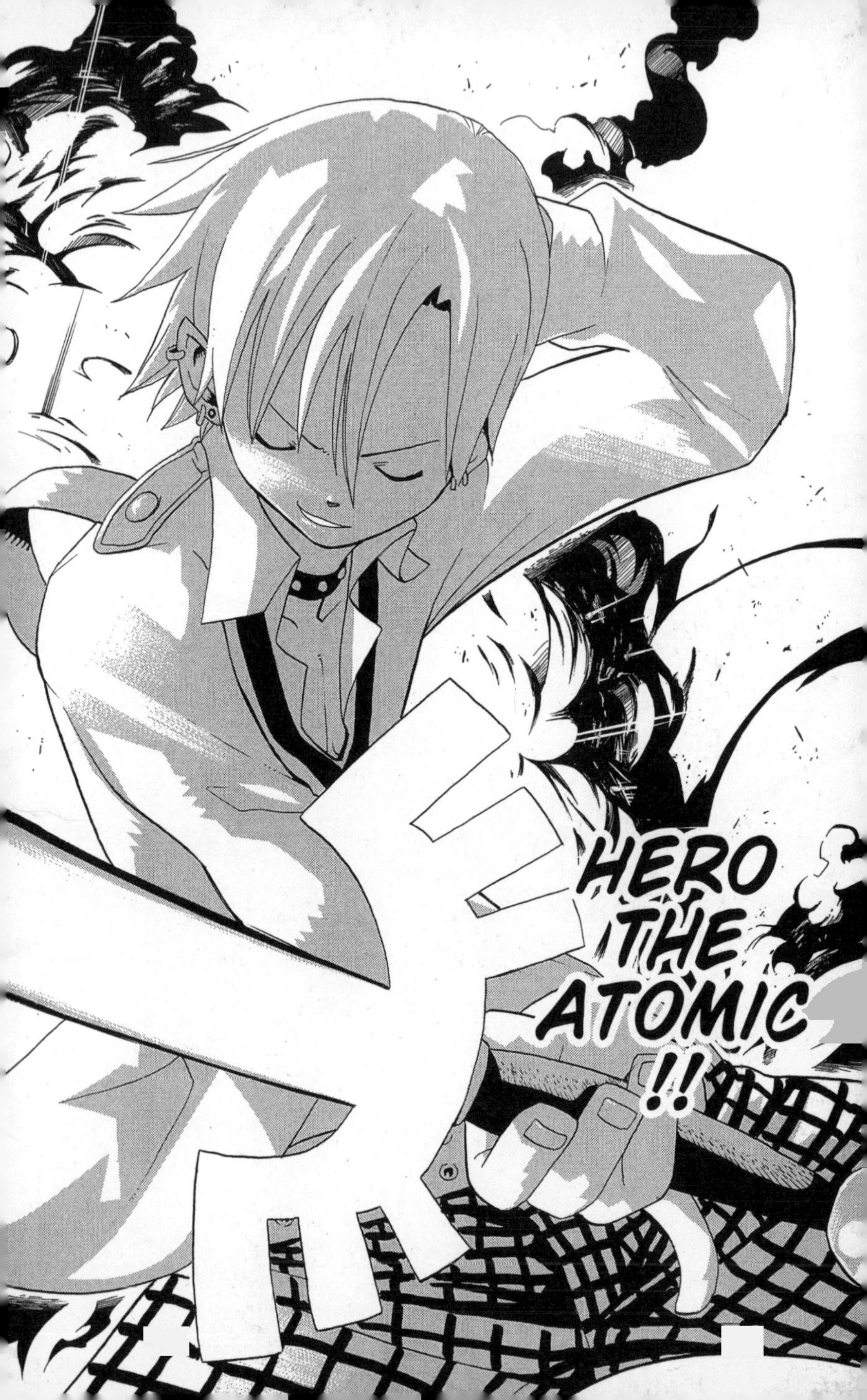
HERO THE ATOMIC !!

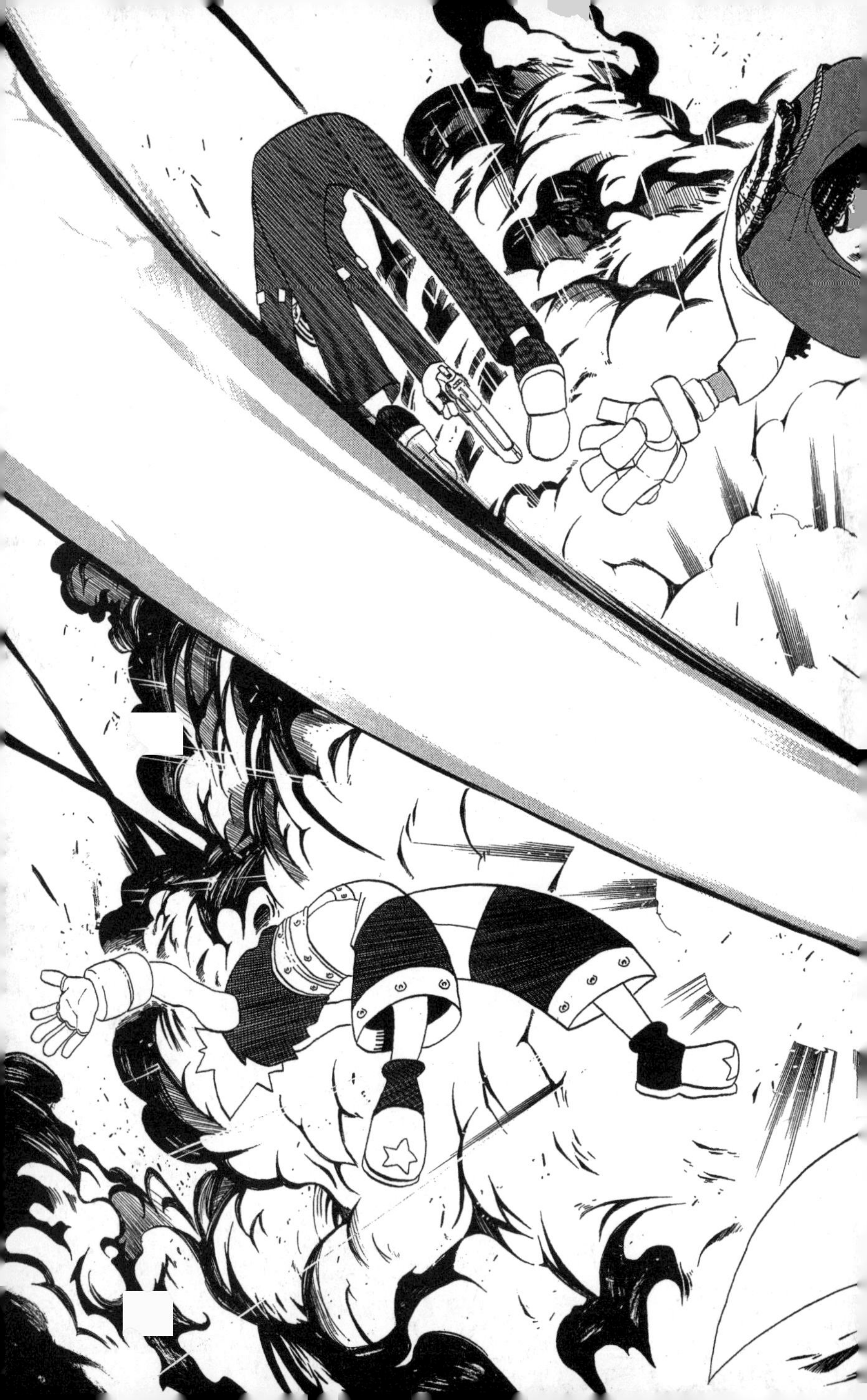

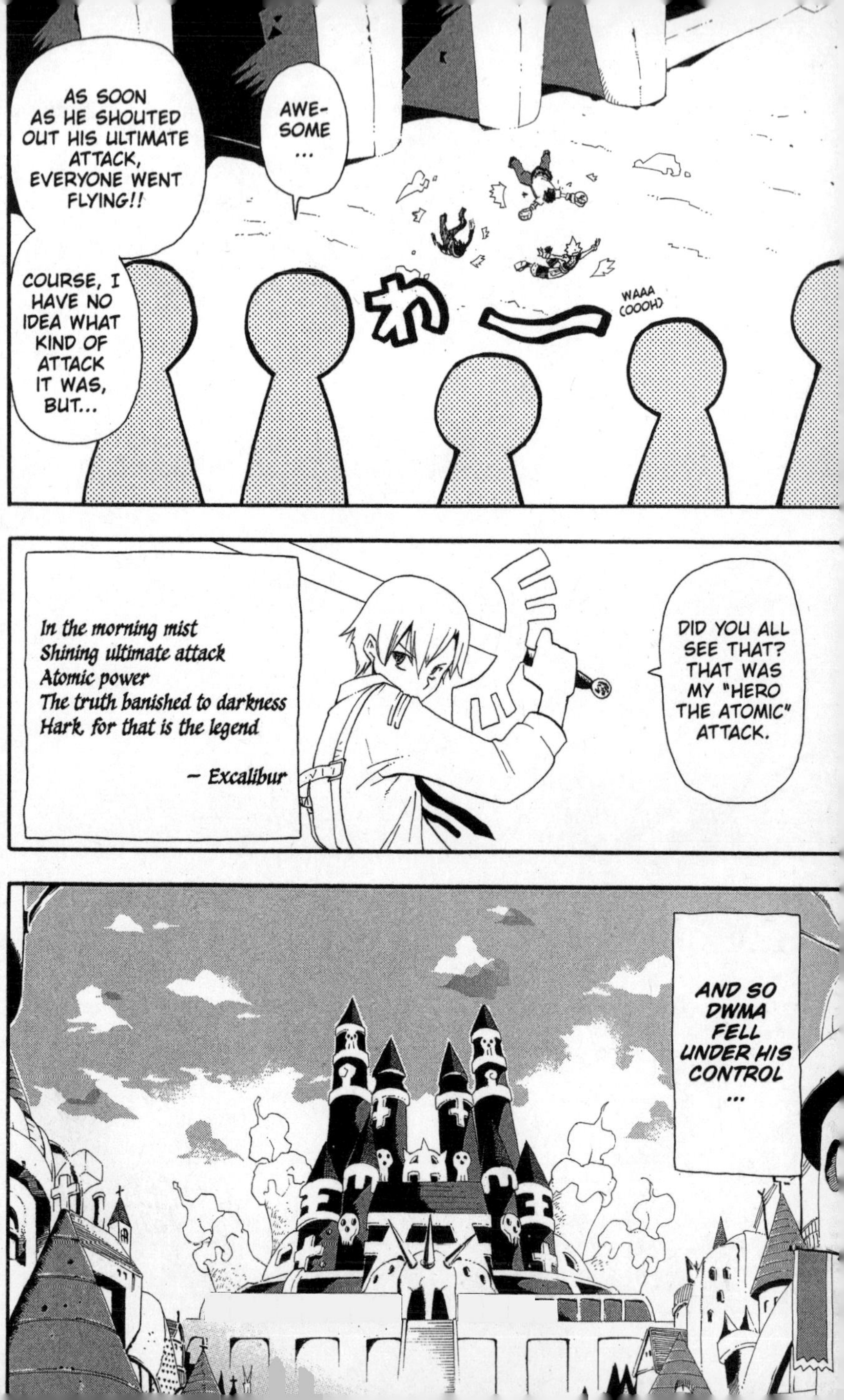
AWE-SOME...
AS SOON AS HE SHOUTED OUT HIS ULTIMATE ATTACK, EVERYONE WENT FLYING!!
わー
WAAA (OOOH)
COURSE, I HAVE NO IDEA WHAT KIND OF ATTACK IT WAS, BUT...
DID YOU ALL SEE THAT? THAT WAS MY "HERO THE ATOMIC" ATTACK.
In the morning mist
Shining ultimate attack
Atomic power
The truth banished to darkness
Hark, for that is the legend
– Excalibur
AND SO DWMA FELL UNDER HIS CONTROL...

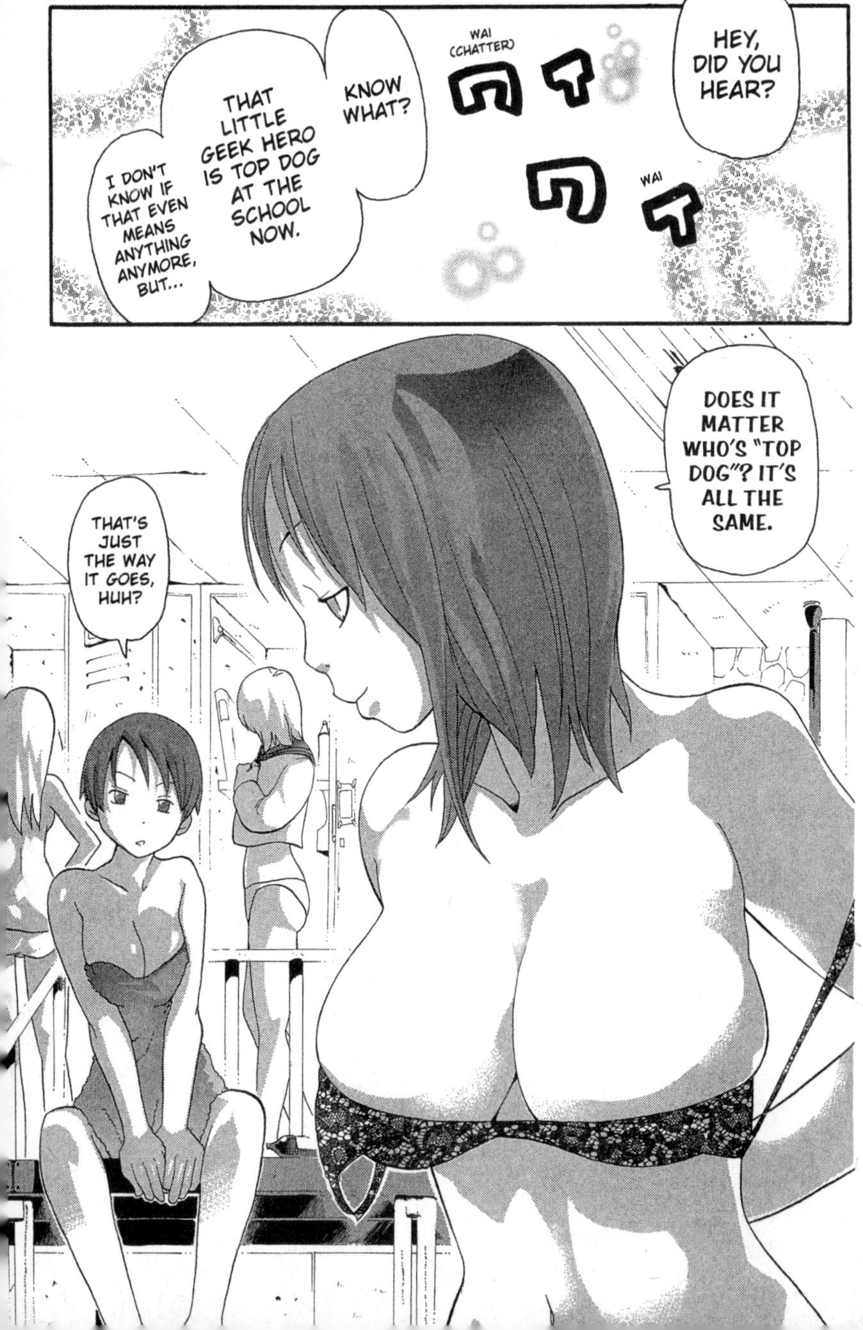
HEY, DID YOU HEAR?
WAI (CHATTER)
WAI
KNOW WHAT?
THAT LITTLE GEEK HERO IS TOP DOG AT THE SCHOOL NOW.
I DON'T KNOW IF THAT EVEN MEANS ANYTHING ANYMORE, BUT...
DOES IT MATTER WHO'S "TOP DOG"? IT'S ALL THE SAME.
THAT'S JUST THE WAY IT GOES, HUH?

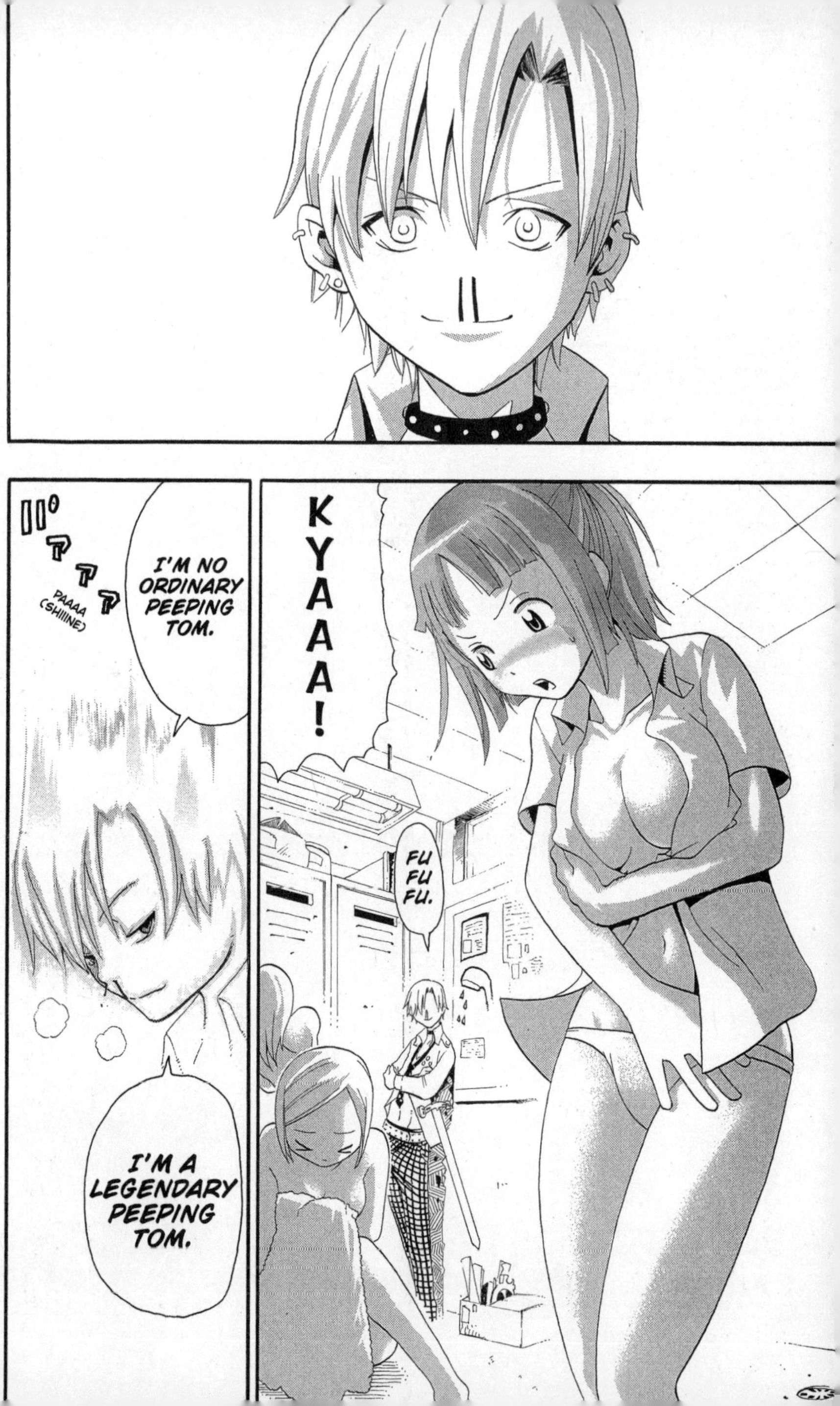
KYAAAA!
FU FU FU.
PAAAA (SHIIINE)
I'M NO ORDINARY PEEPING TOM.
I'M A LEGENDARY PEEPING TOM.

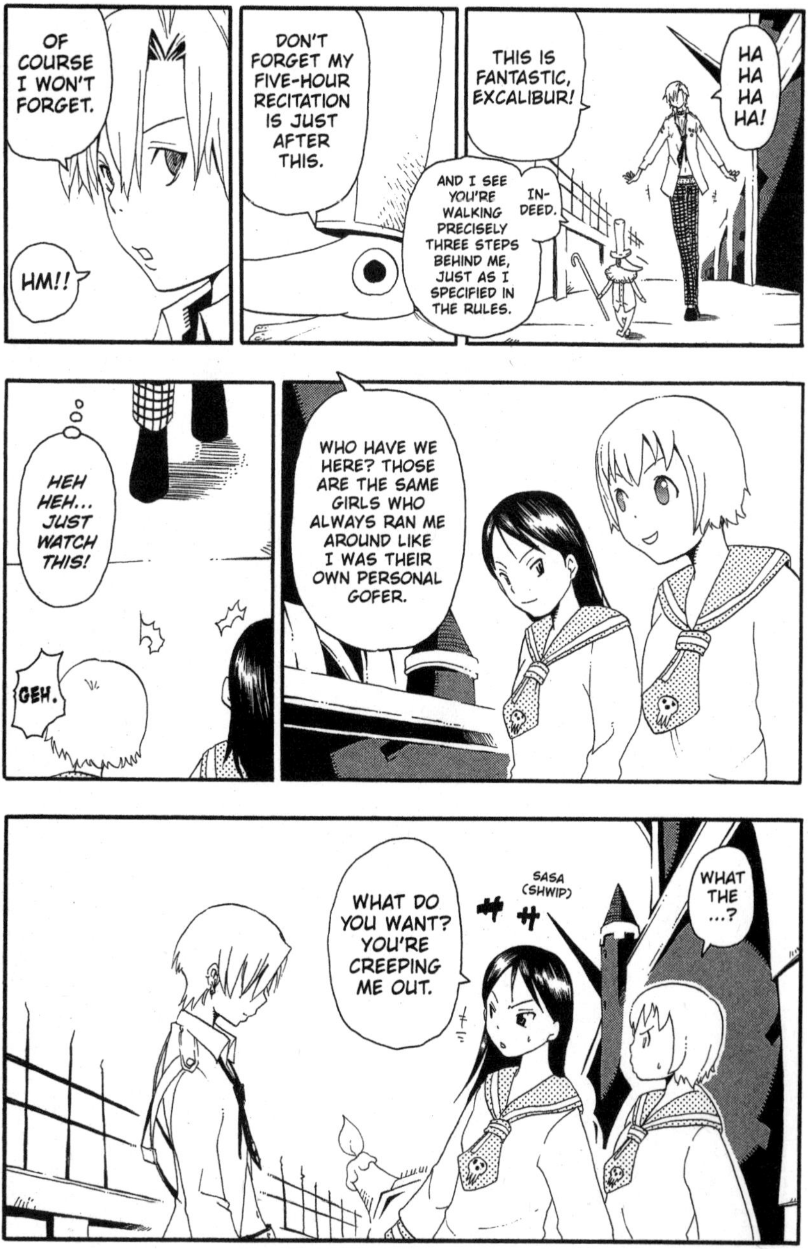
HA HA HA HA!
THIS IS FANTASTIC, EXCALIBUR!
AND I SEE YOU'RE WALKING PRECISELY THREE STEPS BEHIND ME, JUST AS I SPECIFIED IN THE RULES.
IN-DEED.
DON'T FORGET MY FIVE-HOUR RECITATION IS JUST AFTER THIS.
OF COURSE I WON'T FORGET.
HM!!
WHO HAVE WE HERE? THOSE ARE THE SAME GIRLS WHO ALWAYS RAN ME AROUND LIKE I WAS THEIR OWN PERSONAL GOFER.
HEH HEH... JUST WATCH THIS!
GEH.
WHAT THE ...?
SASA (SHWIP)
WHAT DO YOU WANT? YOU'RE CREEPING ME OUT.

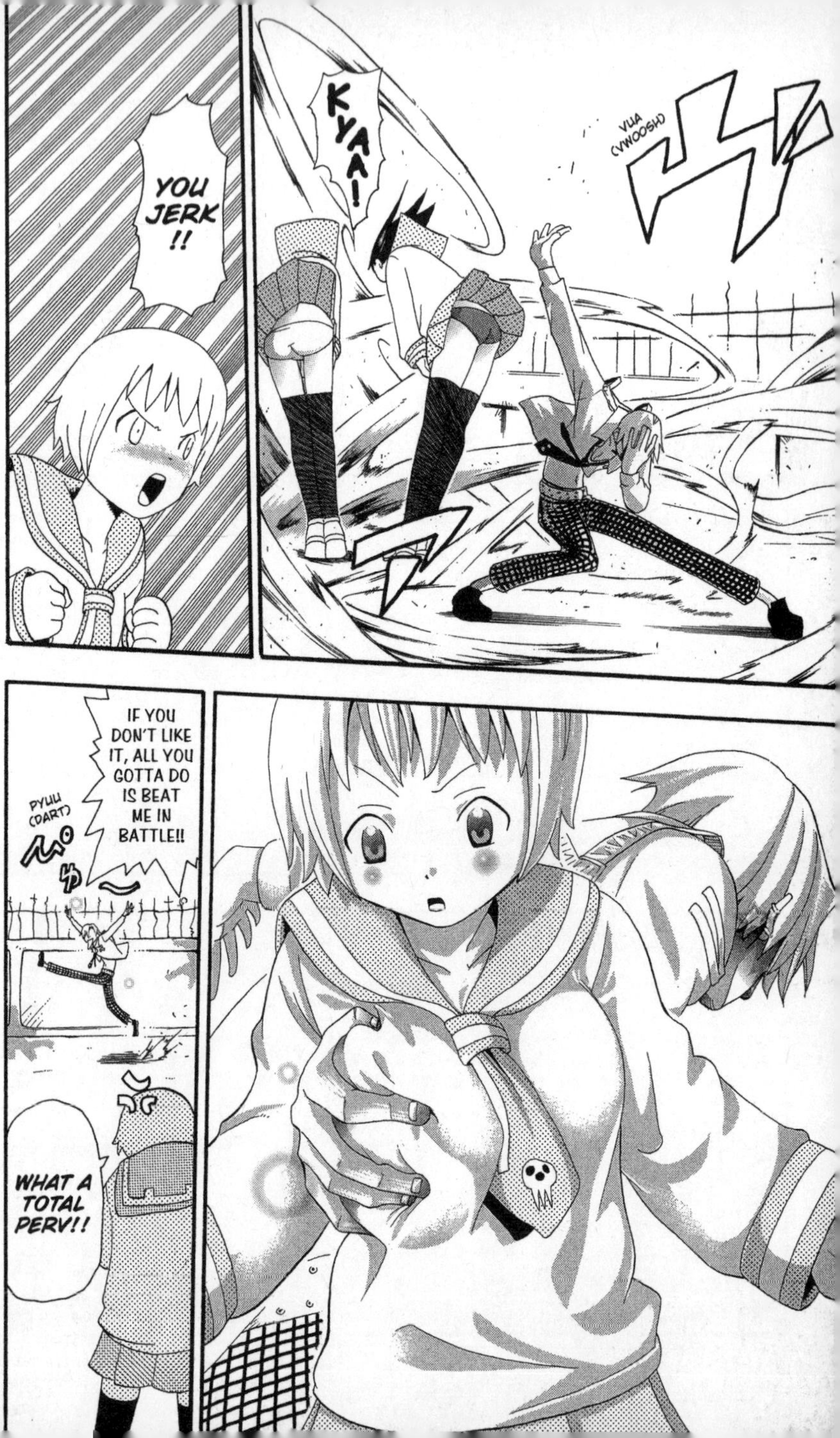
VUA (VWOOSH)
KYAAA!
YOU JERK!!
IF YOU DON'T LIKE IT, ALL YOU GOTTA DO IS BEAT ME IN BATTLE!!
PYUU (DART)
WHAT A TOTAL PERV!!

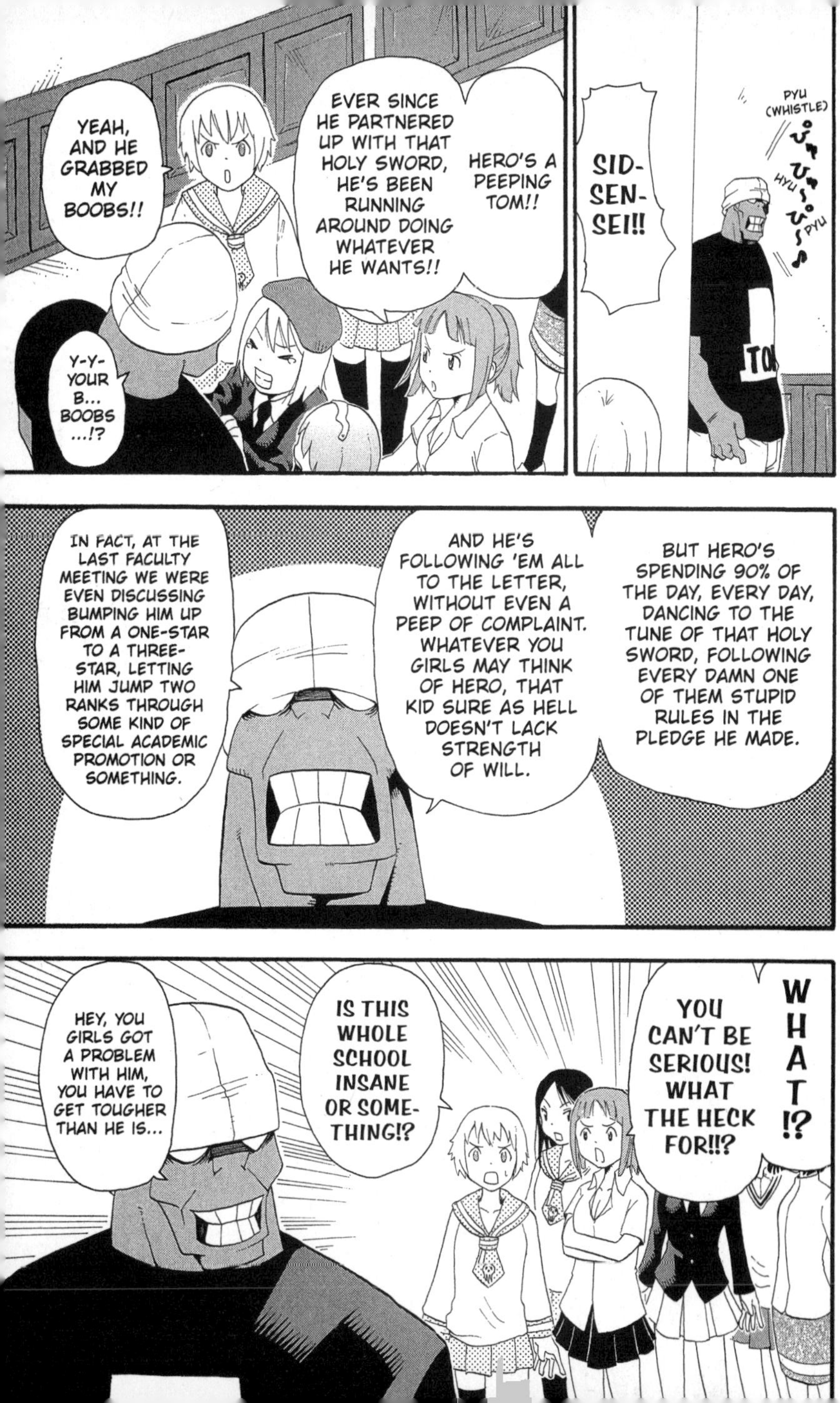
PYU (WHISTLE)
HYU
PYU
SID-SENSEI!!
TO
HERO'S A PEEPING TOM!!
EVER SINCE HE PARTNERED UP WITH THAT HOLY SWORD, HE'S BEEN RUNNING AROUND DOING WHATEVER HE WANTS!!
YEAH, AND HE GRABBED MY BOOBS!!
Y-Y-YOUR B... BOOBS ...!?
BUT HERO'S SPENDING 90% OF THE DAY, EVERY DAY, DANCING TO THE TUNE OF THAT HOLY SWORD, FOLLOWING EVERY DAMN ONE OF THEM STUPID RULES IN THE PLEDGE HE MADE.
AND HE'S FOLLOWING 'EM ALL TO THE LETTER, WITHOUT EVEN A PEEP OF COMPLAINT. WHATEVER YOU GIRLS MAY THINK OF HERO, THAT KID SURE AS HELL DOESN'T LACK STRENGTH OF WILL.
IN FACT, AT THE LAST FACULTY MEETING WE WERE EVEN DISCUSSING BUMPING HIM UP FROM A ONE-STAR TO A THREE-STAR, LETTING HIM JUMP TWO RANKS THROUGH SOME KIND OF SPECIAL ACADEMIC PROMOTION OR SOMETHING.
WHAT!?
YOU CAN'T BE SERIOUS! WHAT THE HECK FOR!!?
IS THIS WHOLE SCHOOL INSANE OR SOME-THING!?
HEY, YOU GIRLS GOT A PROBLEM WITH HIM, YOU HAVE TO GET TOUGHER THAN HE IS...

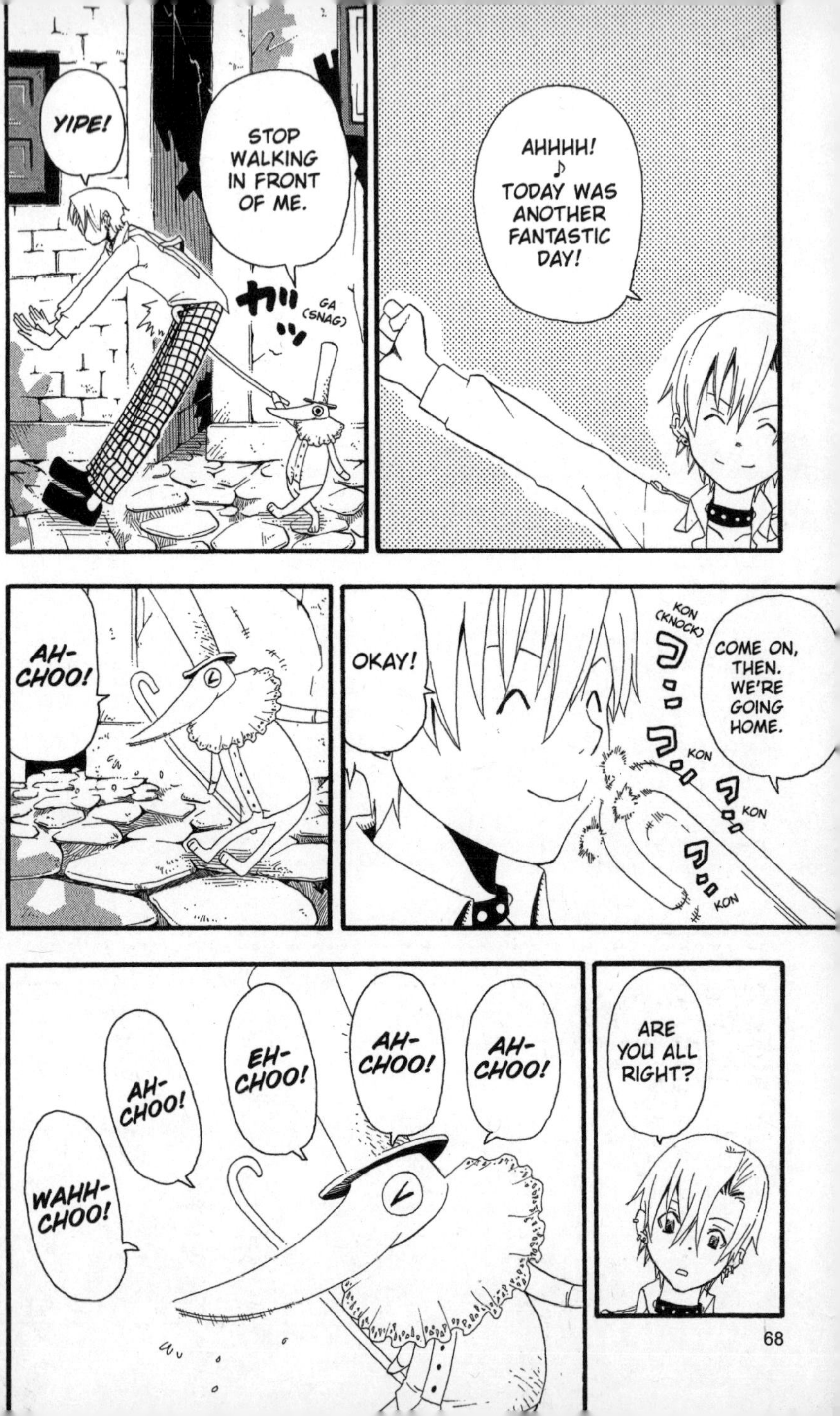
AHHHH! ♪ TODAY WAS ANOTHER FANTASTIC DAY!
STOP WALKING IN FRONT OF ME.
YIPE!
GA (SNAG)
KON (KNOCK)
COME ON, THEN. WE'RE GOING HOME.
KON
KON
KON
OKAY!
AH-CHOO!
ARE YOU ALL RIGHT?
AH-CHOO!
AH-CHOO!
EH-CHOO!
AH-CHOO!
WAHH-CHOO!

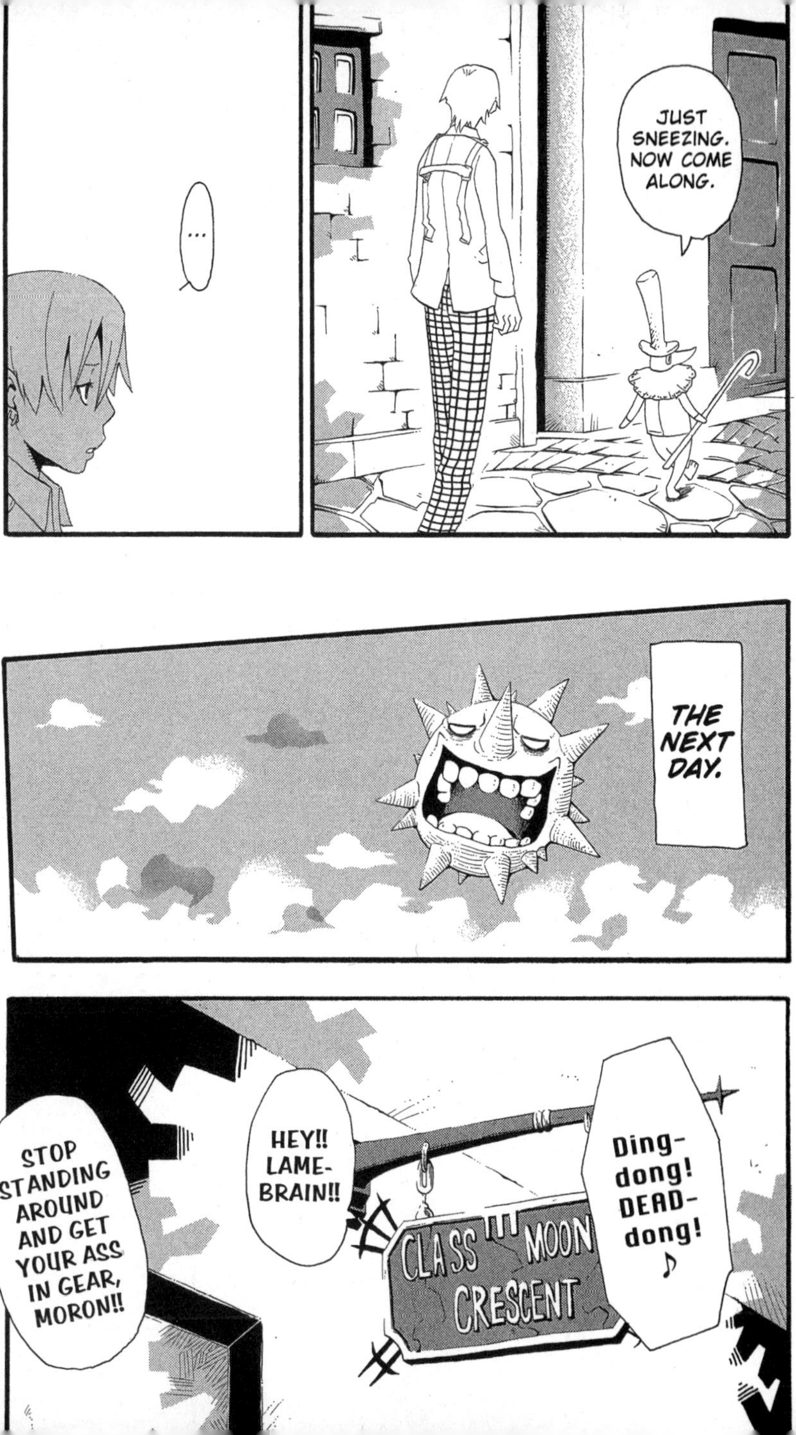
JUST SNEEZING. NOW COME ALONG.
...
THE NEXT DAY.
Ding-dong! DEAD-dong! ♪
CLASS MOON
CRESCENT
HEY!! LAME-BRAIN!!
STOP STANDING AROUND AND GET YOUR ASS IN GEAR, MORON!!

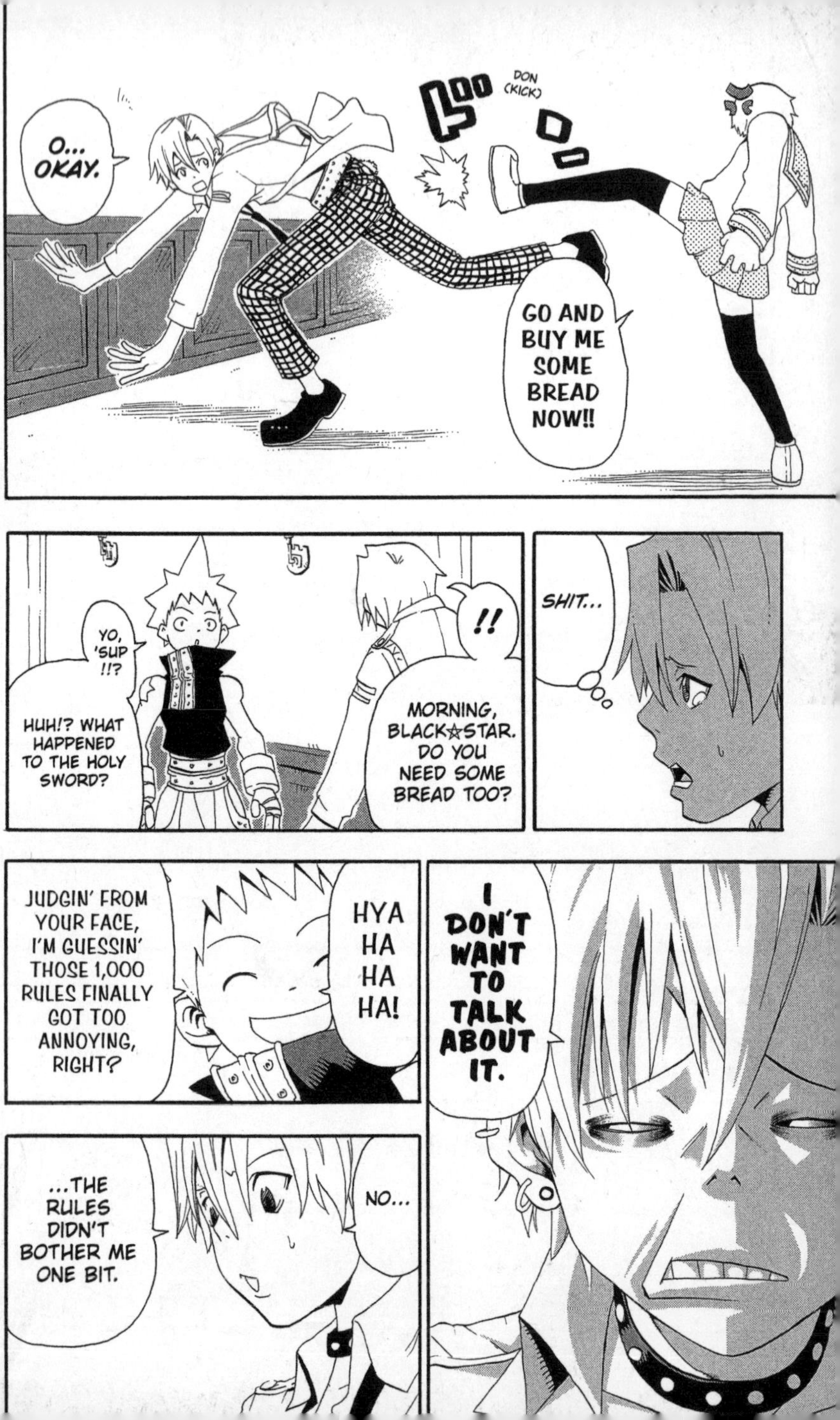
DON (KICK)
GO AND BUY ME SOME BREAD NOW!!
O... OKAY.
SHIT...
!!
MORNING, BLACK☆STAR. DO YOU NEED SOME BREAD TOO?
YO, 'SUP !!?
HUH!? WHAT HAPPENED TO THE HOLY SWORD?
I DON'T WANT TO TALK ABOUT IT.
HYA HA HA HA!
JUDGIN' FROM YOUR FACE, I'M GUESSIN' THOSE 1,000 RULES FINALLY GOT TOO ANNOYING, RIGHT?
NO...
...THE RULES DIDN'T BOTHER ME ONE BIT.

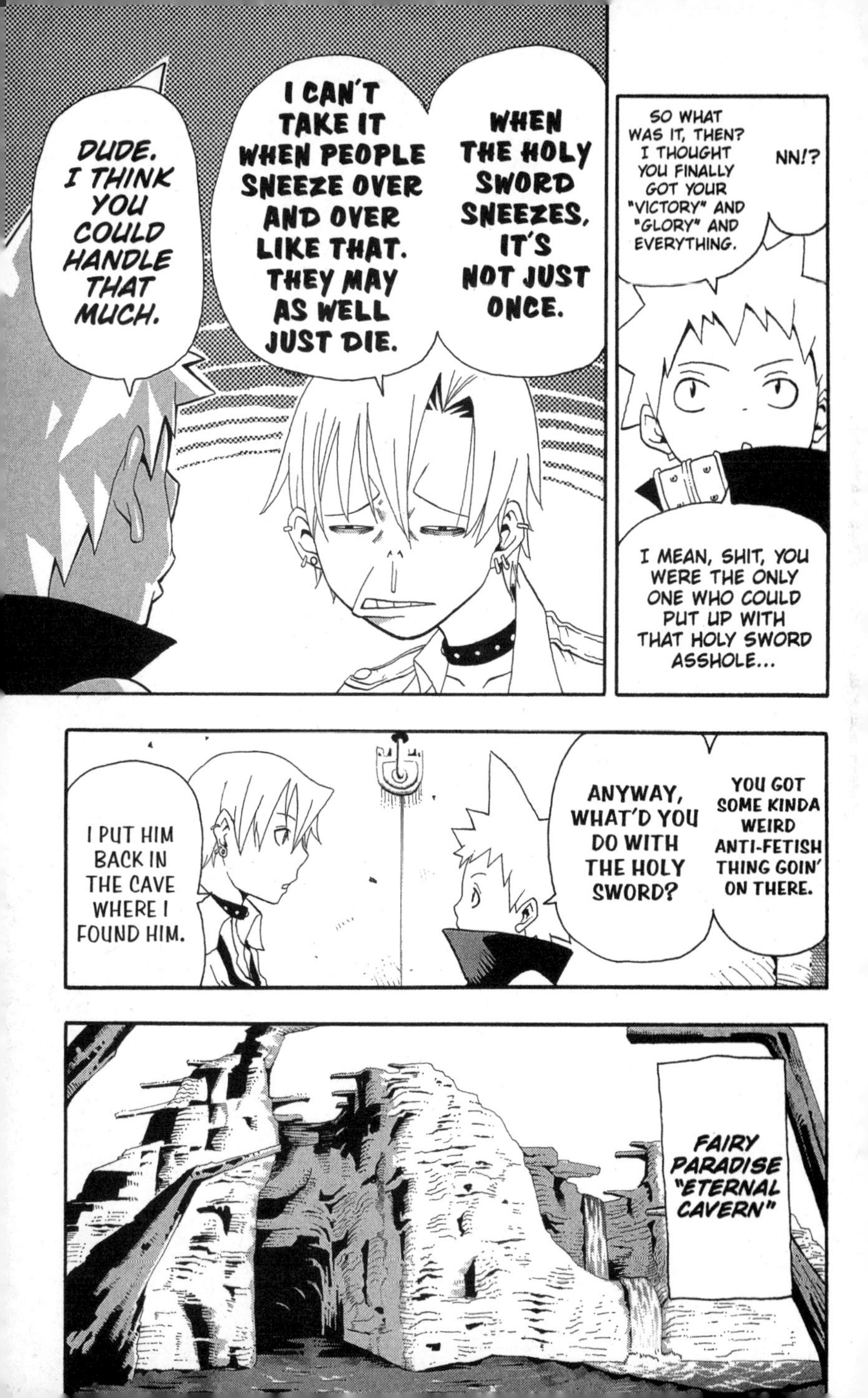
SO WHAT WAS IT, THEN? I THOUGHT YOU FINALLY GOT YOUR "VICTORY" AND "GLORY" AND EVERYTHING.
NN!?
I MEAN, SHIT, YOU WERE THE ONLY ONE WHO COULD PUT UP WITH THAT HOLY SWORD ASSHOLE...
WHEN THE HOLY SWORD SNEEZES, IT'S NOT JUST ONCE.
I CAN'T TAKE IT WHEN PEOPLE SNEEZE OVER AND OVER LIKE THAT. THEY MAY AS WELL JUST DIE.
DUDE. I THINK YOU COULD HANDLE THAT MUCH.
YOU GOT SOME KINDA WEIRD ANTI-FETISH THING GOIN' ON THERE.
ANYWAY, WHAT'D YOU DO WITH THE HOLY SWORD?
I PUT HIM BACK IN THE CAVE WHERE I FOUND HIM.
FAIRY PARADISE "ETERNAL CAVERN"

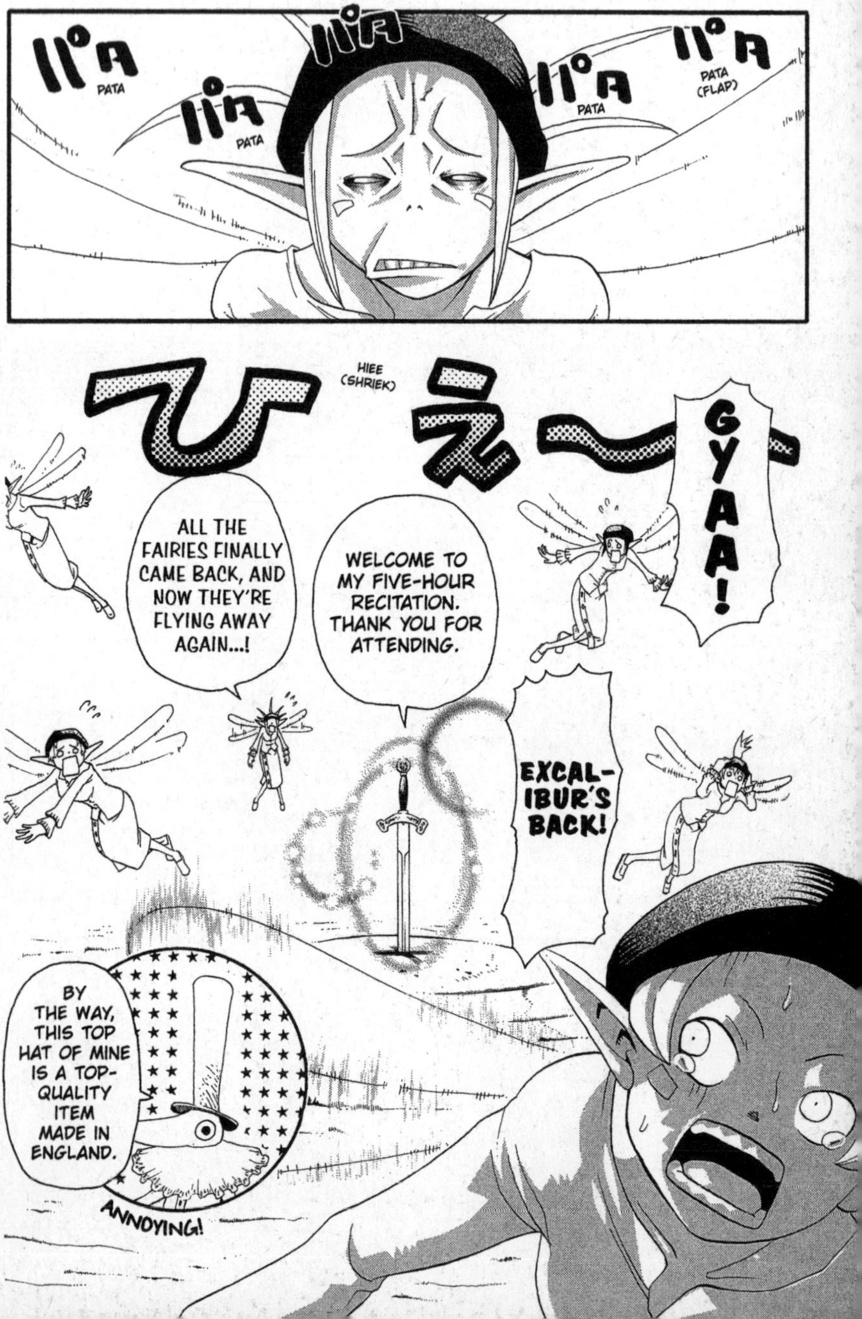
パタ
PATA (FLAP)
パタ
PATA
パタ
パタ
PATA
パタ
PATA
ひえ〜
HIEE (SHRIEK)
GYAA!
WELCOME TO MY FIVE-HOUR RECITATION. THANK YOU FOR ATTENDING.
ALL THE FAIRIES FINALLY CAME BACK, AND NOW THEY'RE FLYING AWAY AGAIN...!
EXCAL-IBUR'S BACK!
BY THE WAY, THIS TOP HAT OF MINE IS A TOP-QUALITY ITEM MADE IN ENGLAND.
ANNOYING!

SOUL EATER

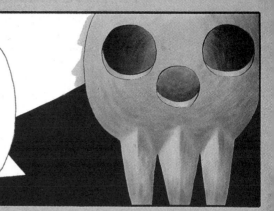

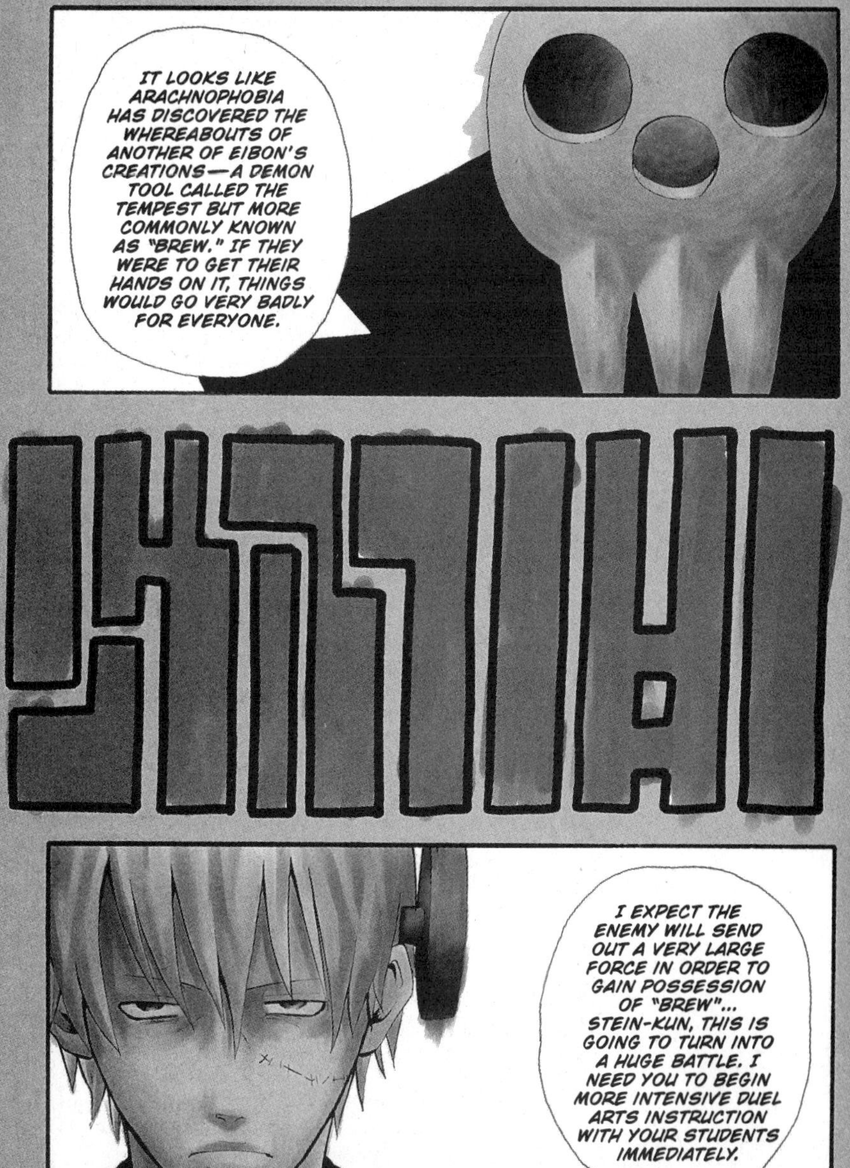

IT LOOKS LIKE ARACHNOPHOBIA HAS DISCOVERED THE WHEREABOUTS OF ANOTHER OF EIBON'S CREATIONS—A DEMON TOOL CALLED THE TEMPEST BUT MORE COMMONLY KNOWN AS "BREW." IF THEY WERE TO GET THEIR HANDS ON IT, THINGS WOULD GO VERY BADLY FOR EVERYONE.

I EXPECT THE ENEMY WILL SEND OUT A VERY LARGE FORCE IN ORDER TO GAIN POSSESSION OF "BREW"... STEIN-KUN, THIS IS GOING TO TURN INTO A HUGE BATTLE. I NEED YOU TO BEGIN MORE INTENSIVE DUEL ARTS INSTRUCTION WITH YOUR STUDENTS IMMEDIATELY.

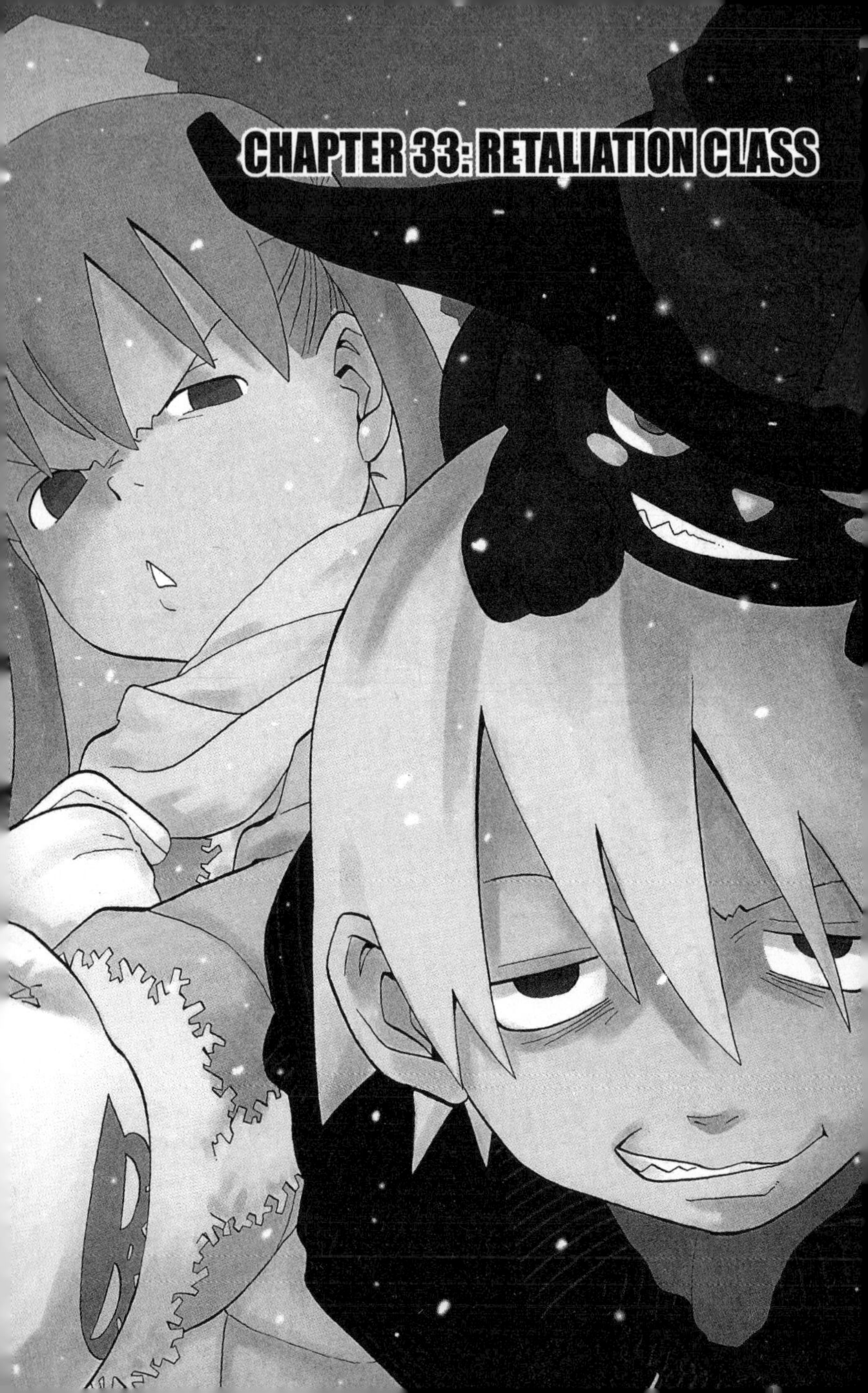
CHAPTER 33: RETALIATION CLASS

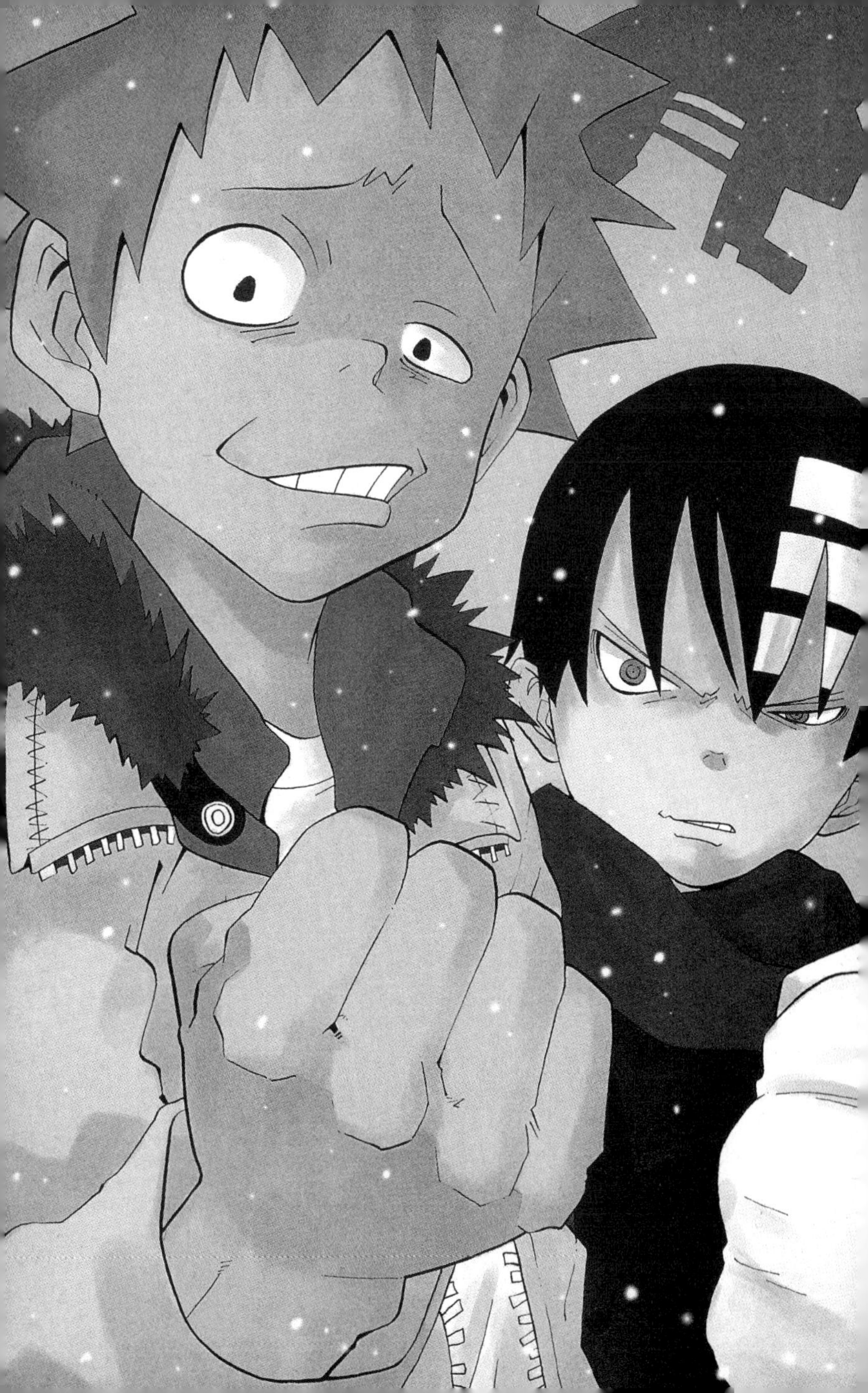

SOUL EATER

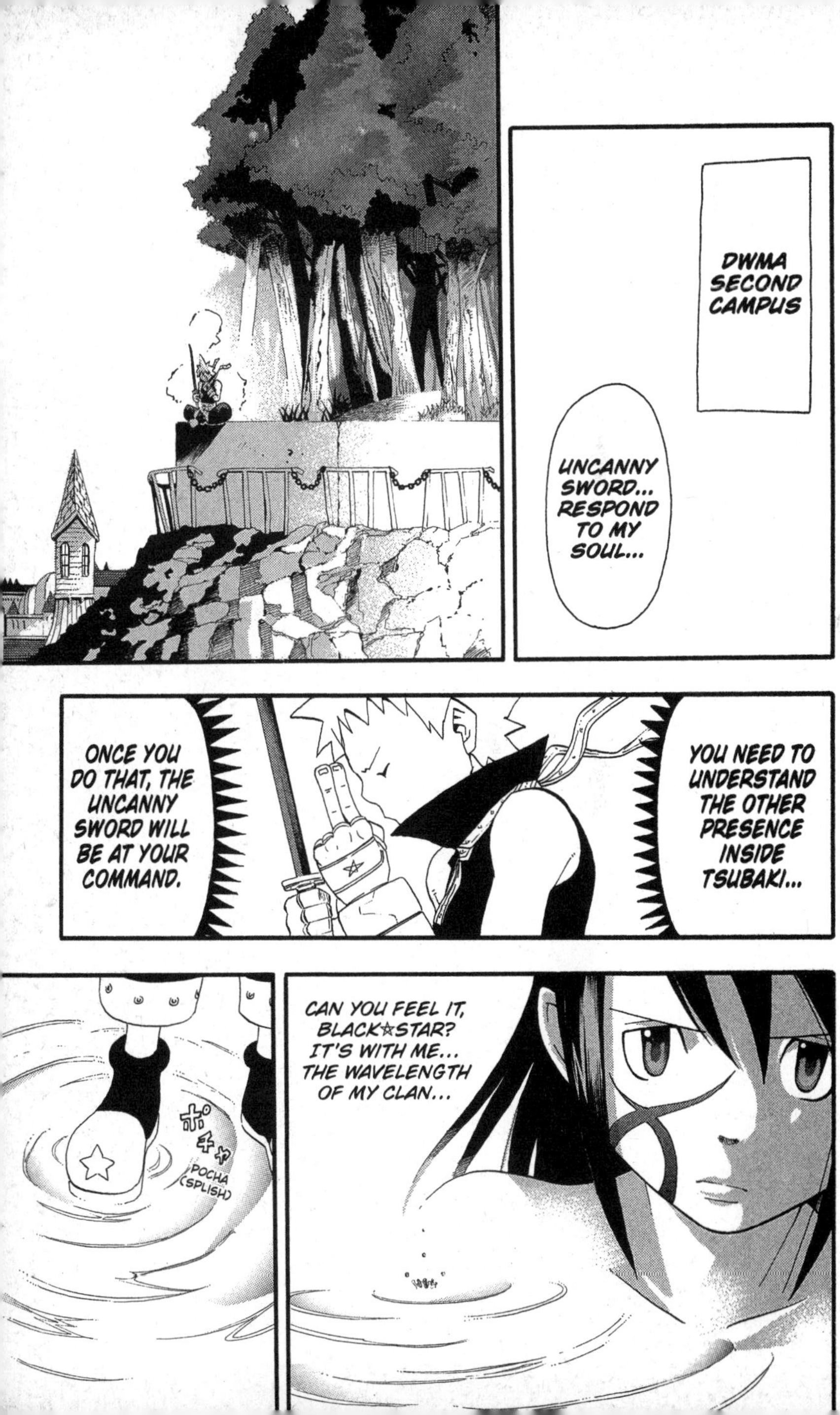
DWMA SECOND CAMPUS
UNCANNY SWORD... RESPOND TO MY SOUL...
YOU NEED TO UNDERSTAND THE OTHER PRESENCE INSIDE TSUBAKI...
ONCE YOU DO THAT, THE UNCANNY SWORD WILL BE AT YOUR COMMAND.
CAN YOU FEEL IT, BLACK☆STAR? IT'S WITH ME... THE WAVELENGTH OF MY CLAN...
ポチャ
POCHA (SPLISH)

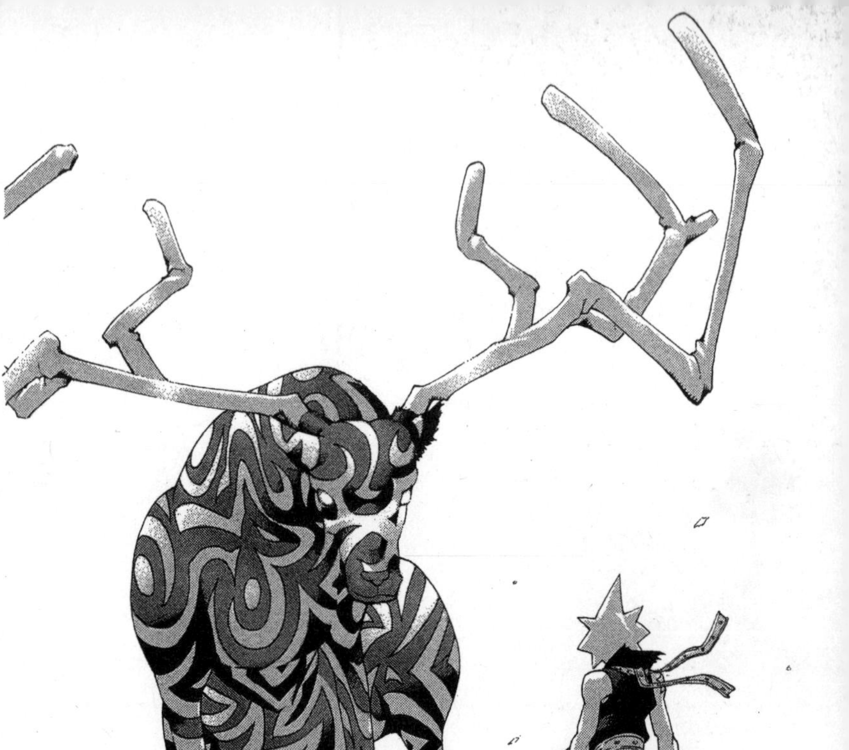
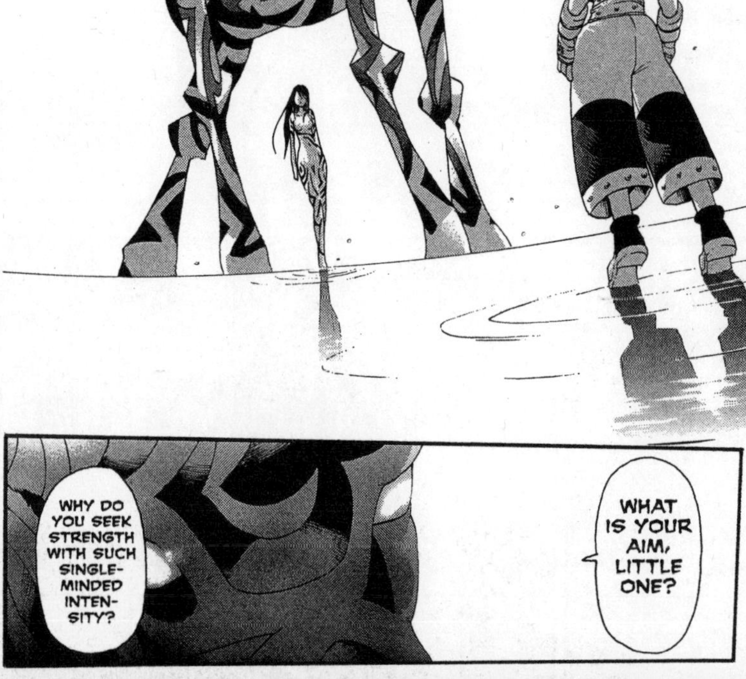
WHAT IS YOUR AIM, LITTLE ONE?
WHY DO YOU SEEK STRENGTH WITH SUCH SINGLE-MINDED INTEN-SITY?

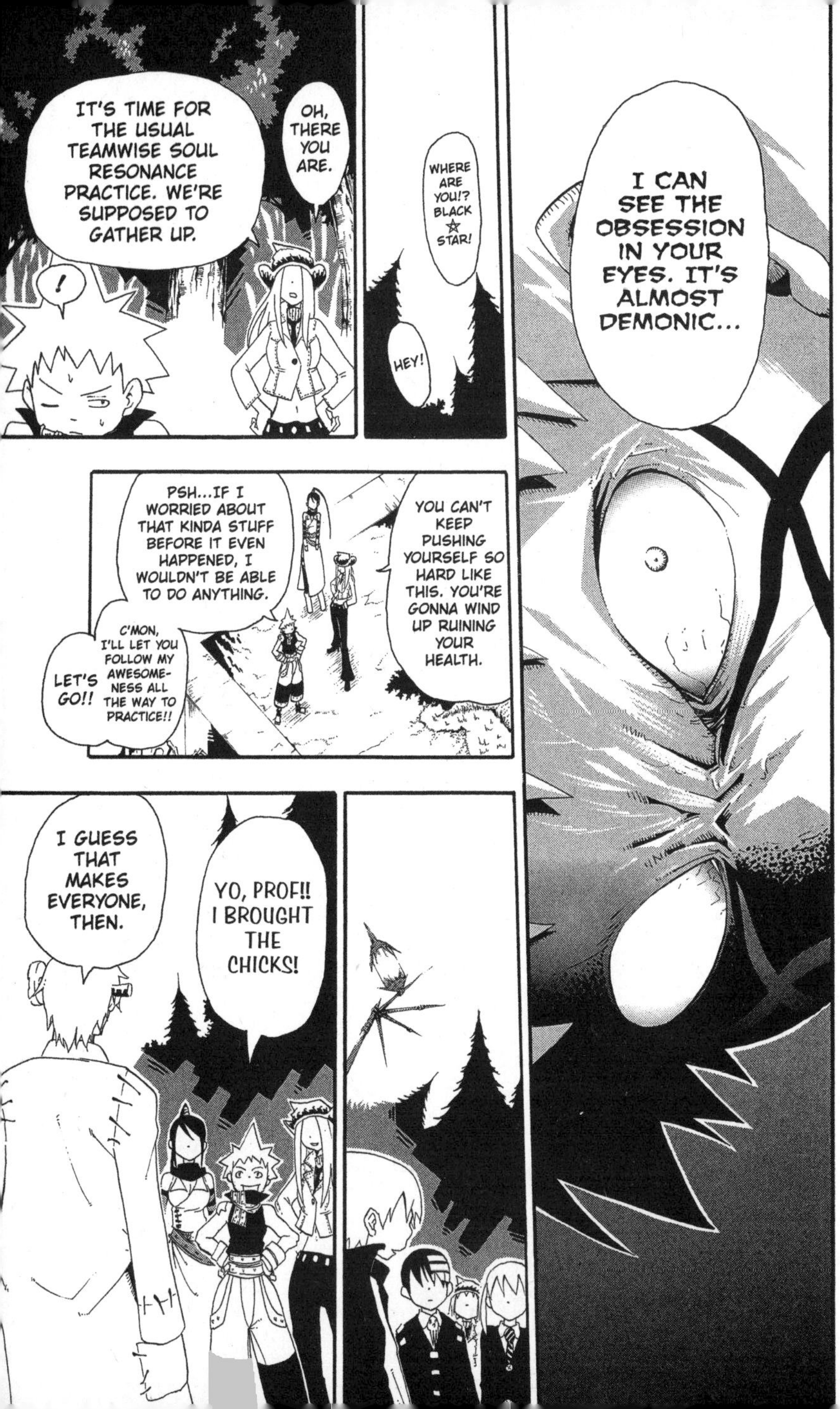
I CAN SEE THE OBSESSION IN YOUR EYES. IT'S ALMOST DEMONIC...
WHERE ARE YOU!? BLACK☆STAR!
HEY!
OH, THERE YOU ARE.
IT'S TIME FOR THE USUAL TEAMWISE SOUL RESONANCE PRACTICE. WE'RE SUPPOSED TO GATHER UP.
!
YOU CAN'T KEEP PUSHING YOURSELF SO HARD LIKE THIS. YOU'RE GONNA WIND UP RUINING YOUR HEALTH.
PSH...IF I WORRIED ABOUT THAT KINDA STUFF BEFORE IT EVEN HAPPENED, I WOULDN'T BE ABLE TO DO ANYTHING.
C'MON, I'LL LET YOU FOLLOW MY AWESOME-NESS ALL THE WAY TO PRACTICE!!
LET'S GO!!
YO, PROF!! I BROUGHT THE CHICKS!
I GUESS THAT MAKES EVERYONE, THEN.

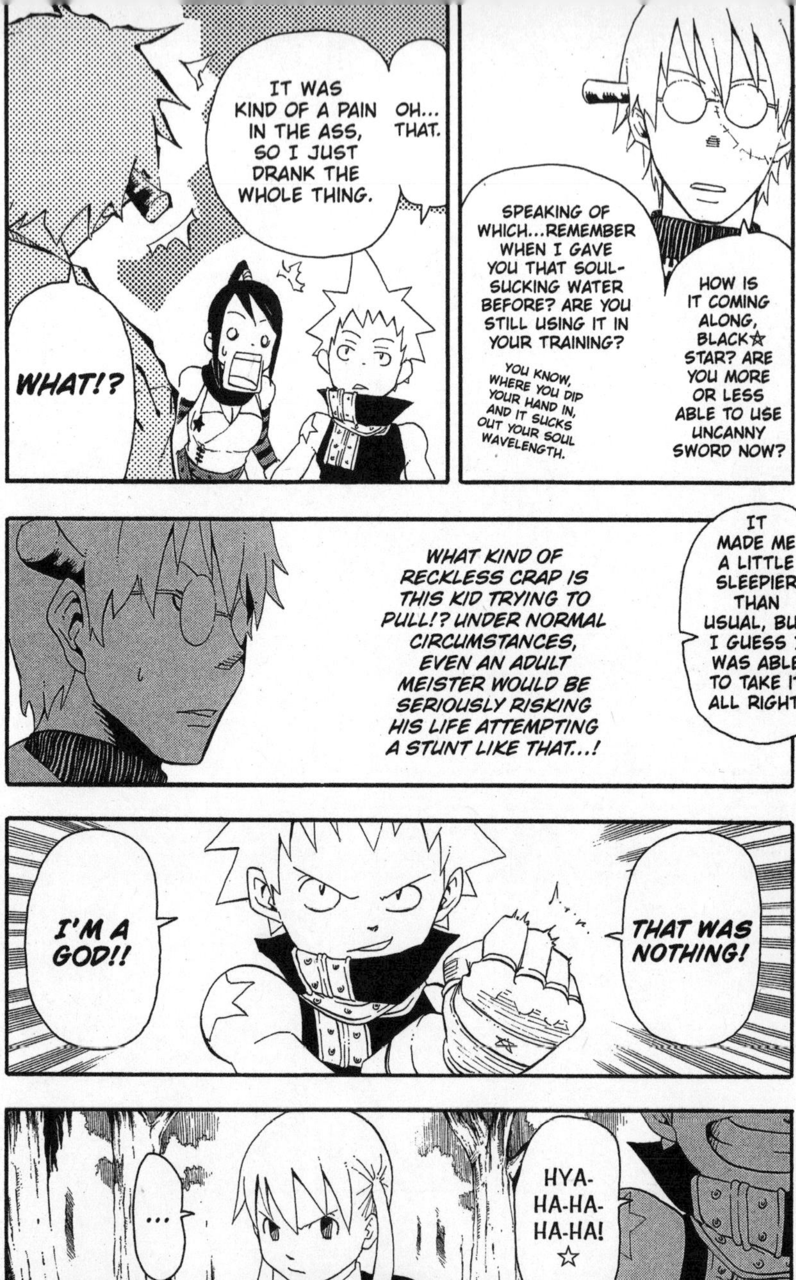
SPEAKING OF WHICH...REMEMBER WHEN I GAVE YOU THAT SOUL-SUCKING WATER BEFORE? ARE YOU STILL USING IT IN YOUR TRAINING?
YOU KNOW, WHERE YOU DIP YOUR HAND IN, AND IT SUCKS OUT YOUR SOUL WAVELENGTH.
HOW IS IT COMING ALONG, BLACK☆STAR? ARE YOU MORE OR LESS ABLE TO USE UNCANNY SWORD NOW?
OH... THAT.
IT WAS KIND OF A PAIN IN THE ASS, SO I JUST DRANK THE WHOLE THING.
WHAT!?
IT MADE ME A LITTLE SLEEPIER THAN USUAL, BUT I GUESS I WAS ABLE TO TAKE IT ALL RIGHT.
WHAT KIND OF RECKLESS CRAP IS THIS KID TRYING TO PULL!? UNDER NORMAL CIRCUMSTANCES, EVEN AN ADULT MEISTER WOULD BE SERIOUSLY RISKING HIS LIFE ATTEMPTING A STUNT LIKE THAT...!
THAT WAS NOTHING!
I'M A GOD!!
HYA-HA-HA-HA-HA! ☆
...

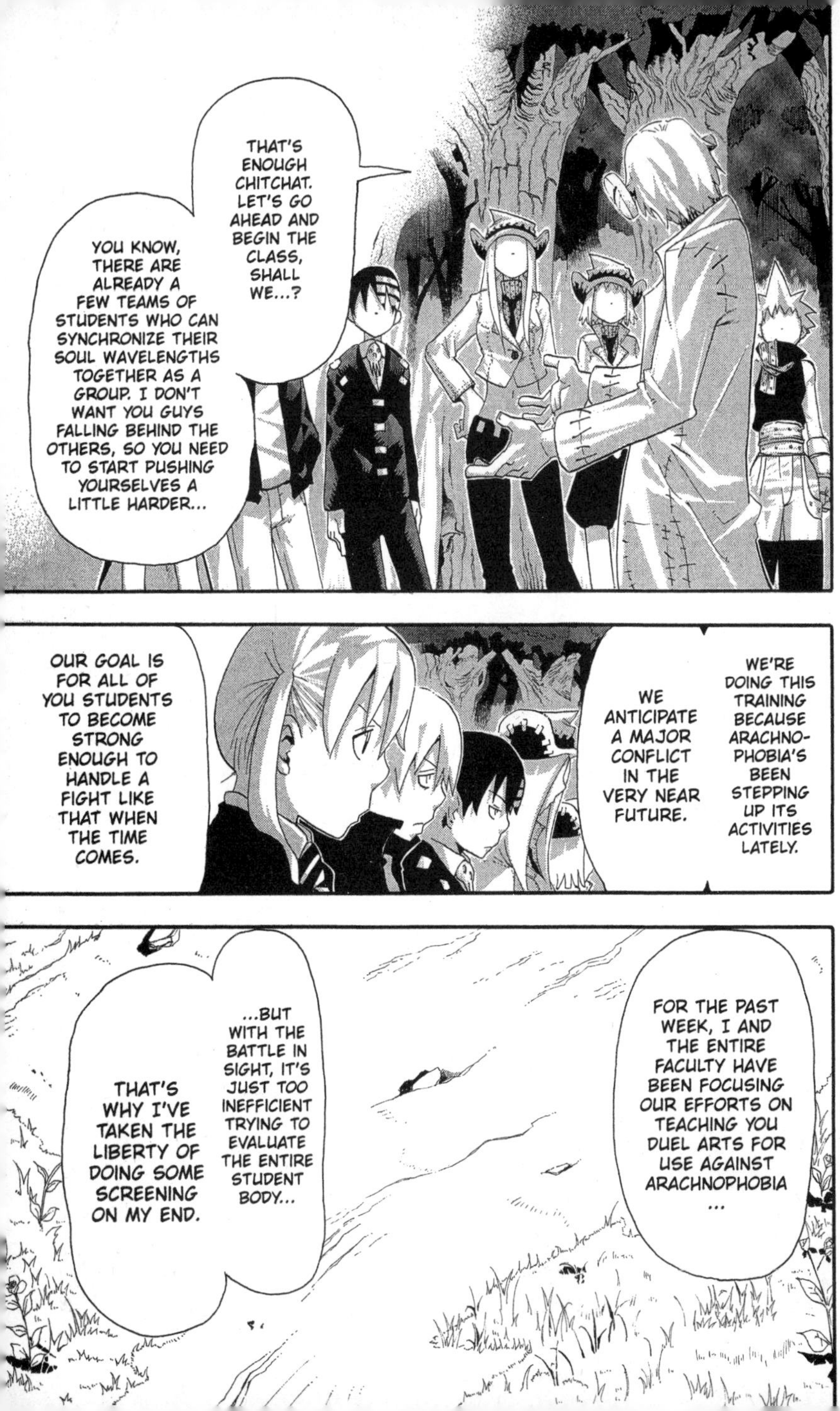
THAT'S ENOUGH CHITCHAT. LET'S GO AHEAD AND BEGIN THE CLASS, SHALL WE...?
YOU KNOW, THERE ARE ALREADY A FEW TEAMS OF STUDENTS WHO CAN SYNCHRONIZE THEIR SOUL WAVELENGTHS TOGETHER AS A GROUP. I DON'T WANT YOU GUYS FALLING BEHIND THE OTHERS, SO YOU NEED TO START PUSHING YOURSELVES A LITTLE HARDER...
WE'RE DOING THIS TRAINING BECAUSE ARACHNO-PHOBIA'S BEEN STEPPING UP ITS ACTIVITIES LATELY.
WE ANTICIPATE A MAJOR CONFLICT IN THE VERY NEAR FUTURE.
OUR GOAL IS FOR ALL OF YOU STUDENTS TO BECOME STRONG ENOUGH TO HANDLE A FIGHT LIKE THAT WHEN THE TIME COMES.
FOR THE PAST WEEK, I AND THE ENTIRE FACULTY HAVE BEEN FOCUSING OUR EFFORTS ON TEACHING YOU DUEL ARTS FOR USE AGAINST ARACHNOPHOBIA...
...BUT WITH THE BATTLE IN SIGHT, IT'S JUST TOO INEFFICIENT TRYING TO EVALUATE THE ENTIRE STUDENT BODY...
THAT'S WHY I'VE TAKEN THE LIBERTY OF DOING SOME SCREENING ON MY END.

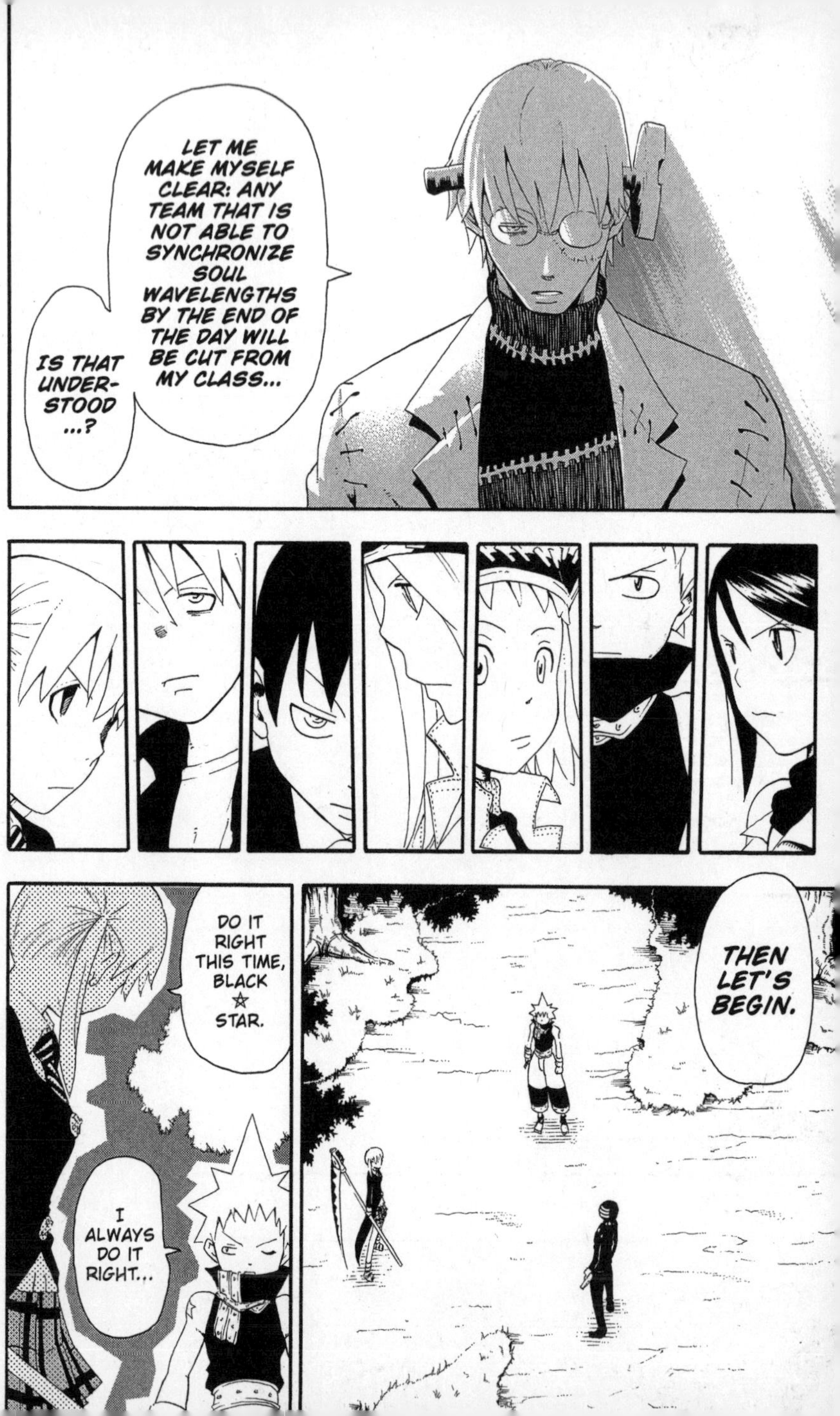
LET ME MAKE MYSELF CLEAR: ANY TEAM THAT IS NOT ABLE TO SYNCHRONIZE SOUL WAVELENGTHS BY THE END OF THE DAY WILL BE CUT FROM MY CLASS...
IS THAT UNDER-STOOD ...?
THEN LET'S BEGIN.
DO IT RIGHT THIS TIME, BLACK☆STAR.
I ALWAYS DO IT RIGHT...

YEAH.

LET'S DO IT.

MAKA...

KID...

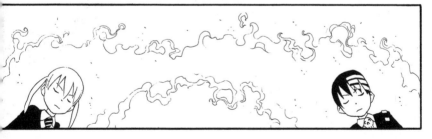

BLACK☆STAR
...

WE'RE
CONNECTED...

SO FAR SO
GOOD...

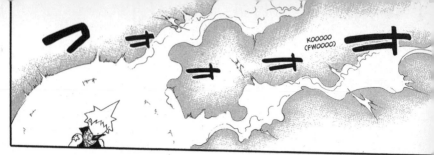

KOOOOO
(FWOOOO)

PAN
(POP)

PAN

NO
GOOD,
HUH
...

......

ONE
MORE
TIME.

OKAY!

SHIT
...

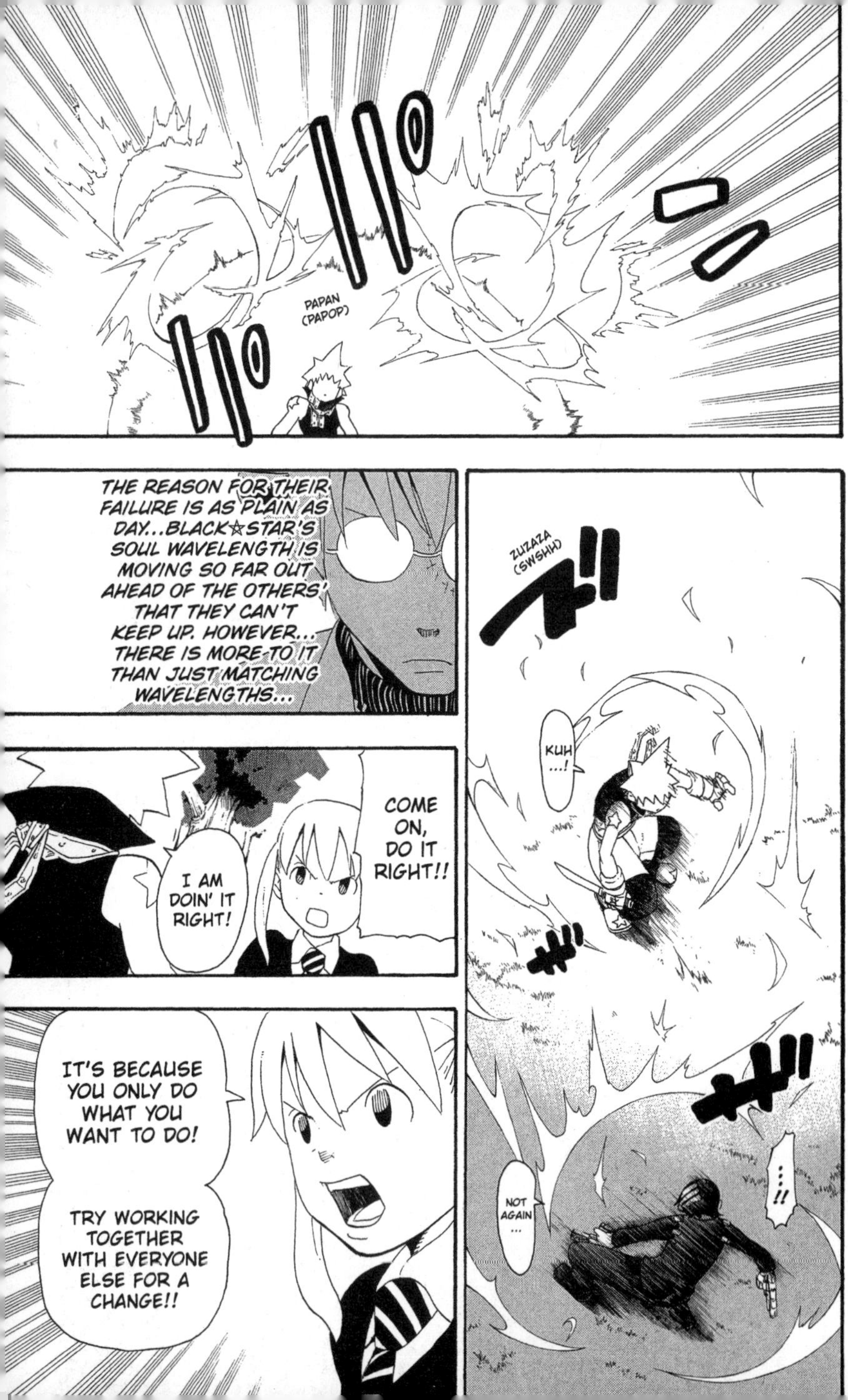
PAPAN (PAPOP)
ZUZAZA (SWSHH)
KUH ...!
NOT AGAIN ...
...!!
THE REASON FOR THEIR FAILURE IS AS PLAIN AS DAY...BLACK☆STAR'S SOUL WAVELENGTH IS MOVING SO FAR OUT AHEAD OF THE OTHERS' THAT THEY CAN'T KEEP UP. HOWEVER... THERE IS MORE TO IT THAN JUST MATCHING WAVELENGTHS...
COME ON, DO IT RIGHT!!
I AM DOIN' IT RIGHT!
IT'S BECAUSE YOU ONLY DO WHAT YOU WANT TO DO!
TRY WORKING TOGETHER WITH EVERYONE ELSE FOR A CHANGE!!

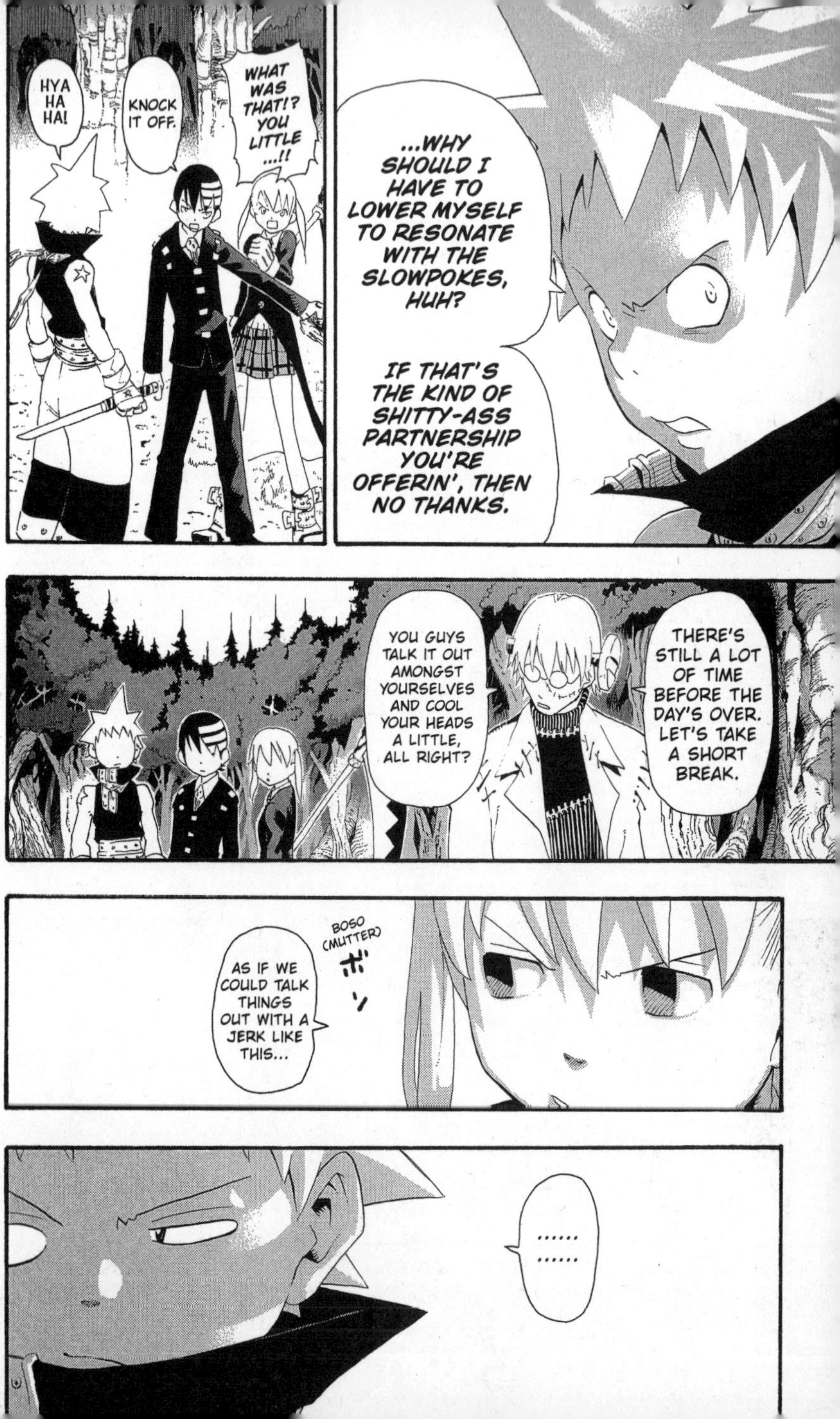
...WHY SHOULD I HAVE TO LOWER MYSELF TO RESONATE WITH THE SLOWPOKES, HUH?
IF THAT'S THE KIND OF SHITTY-ASS PARTNERSHIP YOU'RE OFFERIN', THEN NO THANKS.
WHAT WAS THAT!? YOU LITTLE ...!!
KNOCK IT OFF.
HYA HA HA!
THERE'S STILL A LOT OF TIME BEFORE THE DAY'S OVER. LET'S TAKE A SHORT BREAK.
YOU GUYS TALK IT OUT AMONGST YOURSELVES AND COOL YOUR HEADS A LITTLE, ALL RIGHT?
ボソ
BOSO (MUTTER)
AS IF WE COULD TALK THINGS OUT WITH A JERK LIKE THIS...
....

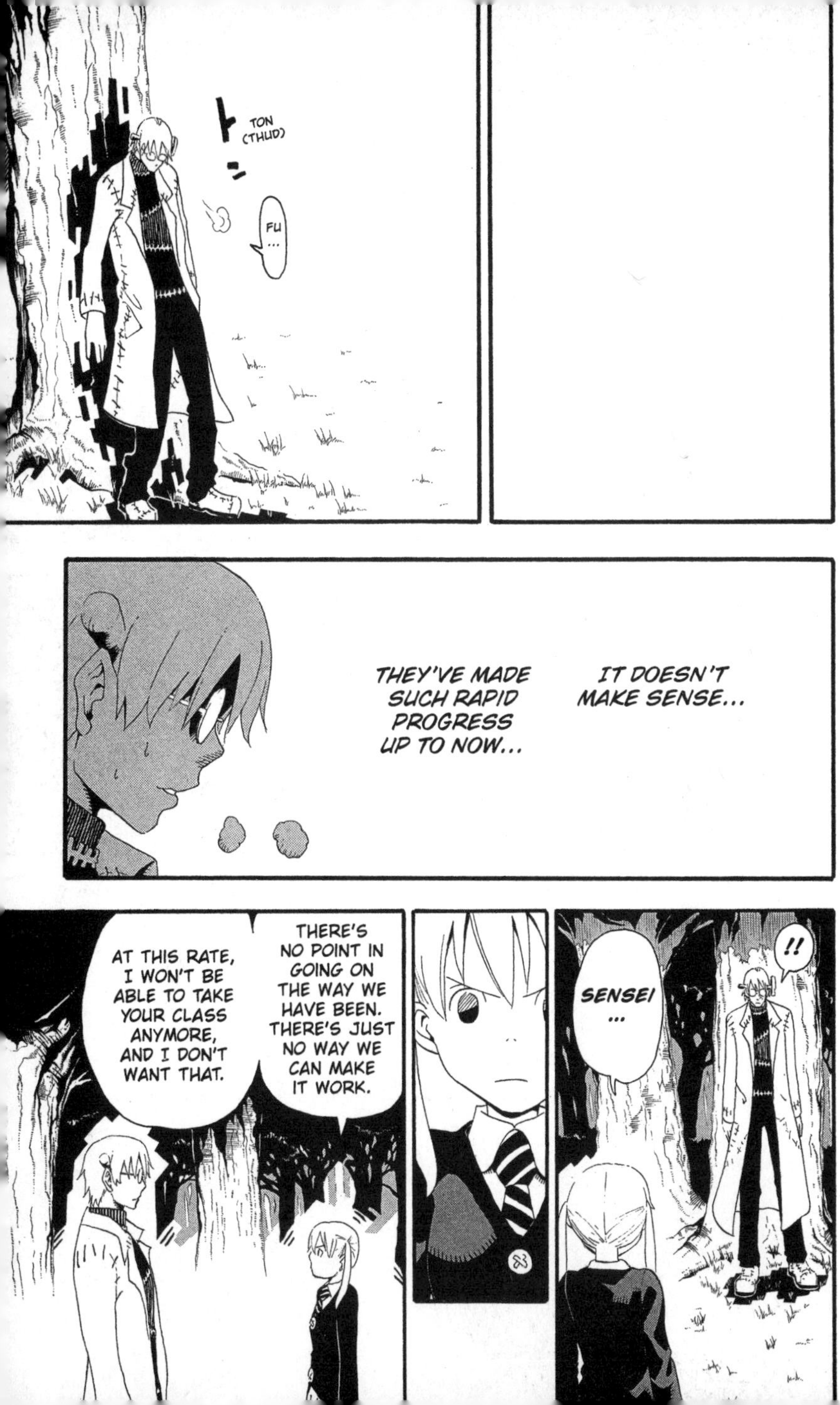
TON (THUD)
FU ...
IT DOESN'T MAKE SENSE...
THEY'VE MADE SUCH RAPID PROGRESS UP TO NOW...
!!
SENSEI ...
THERE'S NO POINT IN GOING ON THE WAY WE HAVE BEEN. THERE'S JUST NO WAY WE CAN MAKE IT WORK.
AT THIS RATE, I WON'T BE ABLE TO TAKE YOUR CLASS ANYMORE, AND I DON'T WANT THAT.

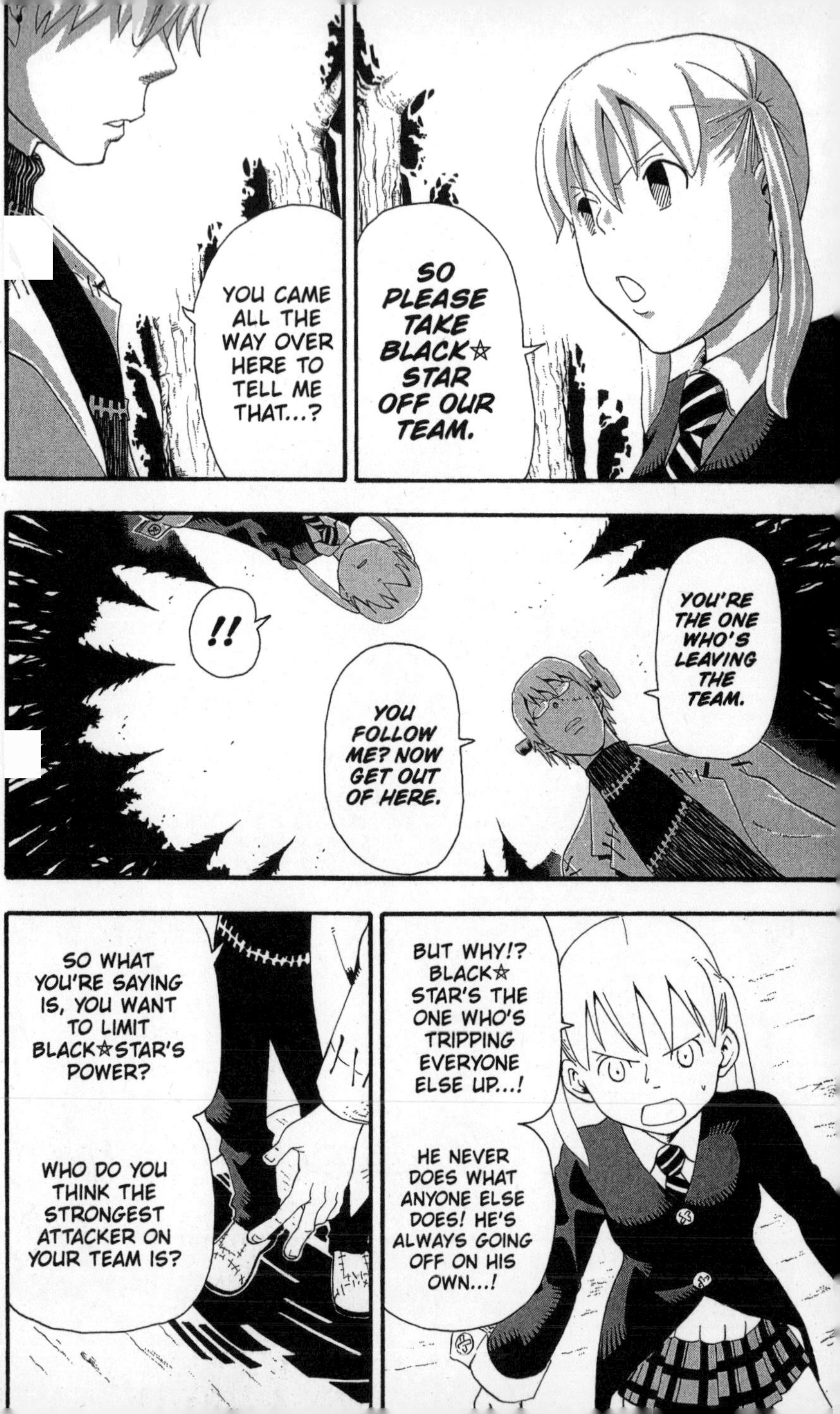
SO PLEASE TAKE BLACK☆STAR OFF OUR TEAM.
YOU CAME ALL THE WAY OVER HERE TO TELL ME THAT...?
YOU'RE THE ONE WHO'S LEAVING THE TEAM.
!!
YOU FOLLOW ME? NOW GET OUT OF HERE.
BUT WHY!? BLACK☆STAR'S THE ONE WHO'S TRIPPING EVERYONE ELSE UP...!
HE NEVER DOES WHAT ANYONE ELSE DOES! HE'S ALWAYS GOING OFF ON HIS OWN...!
SO WHAT YOU'RE SAYING IS, YOU WANT TO LIMIT BLACK☆STAR'S POWER?
WHO DO YOU THINK THE STRONGEST ATTACKER ON YOUR TEAM IS?

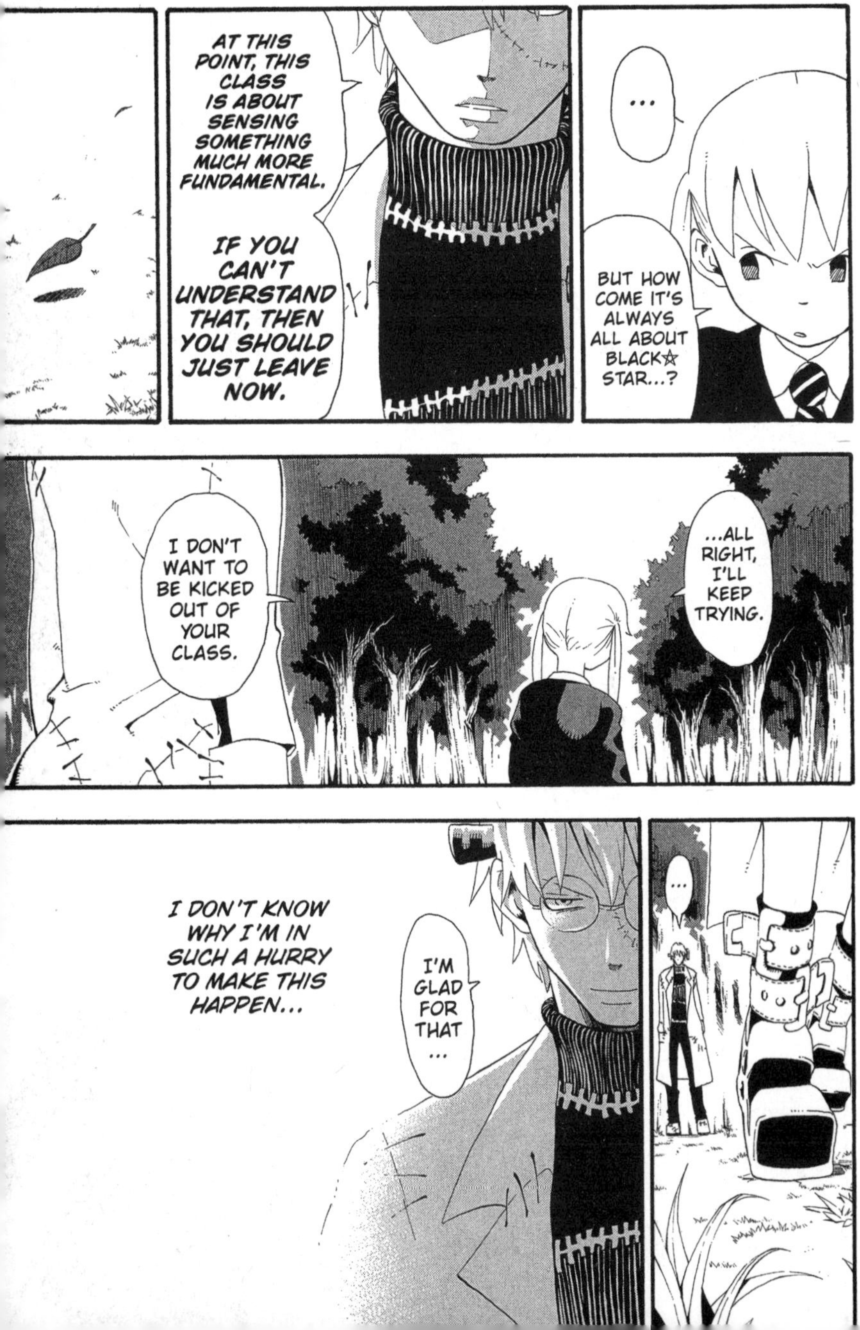
...
BUT HOW COME IT'S ALWAYS ALL ABOUT BLACK☆STAR...?
AT THIS POINT, THIS CLASS IS ABOUT SENSING SOMETHING MUCH MORE FUNDAMENTAL.
IF YOU CAN'T UNDERSTAND THAT, THEN YOU SHOULD JUST LEAVE NOW.
...ALL RIGHT, I'LL KEEP TRYING.
I DON'T WANT TO BE KICKED OUT OF YOUR CLASS.
...
I'M GLAD FOR THAT...
I DON'T KNOW WHY I'M IN SUCH A HURRY TO MAKE THIS HAPPEN...

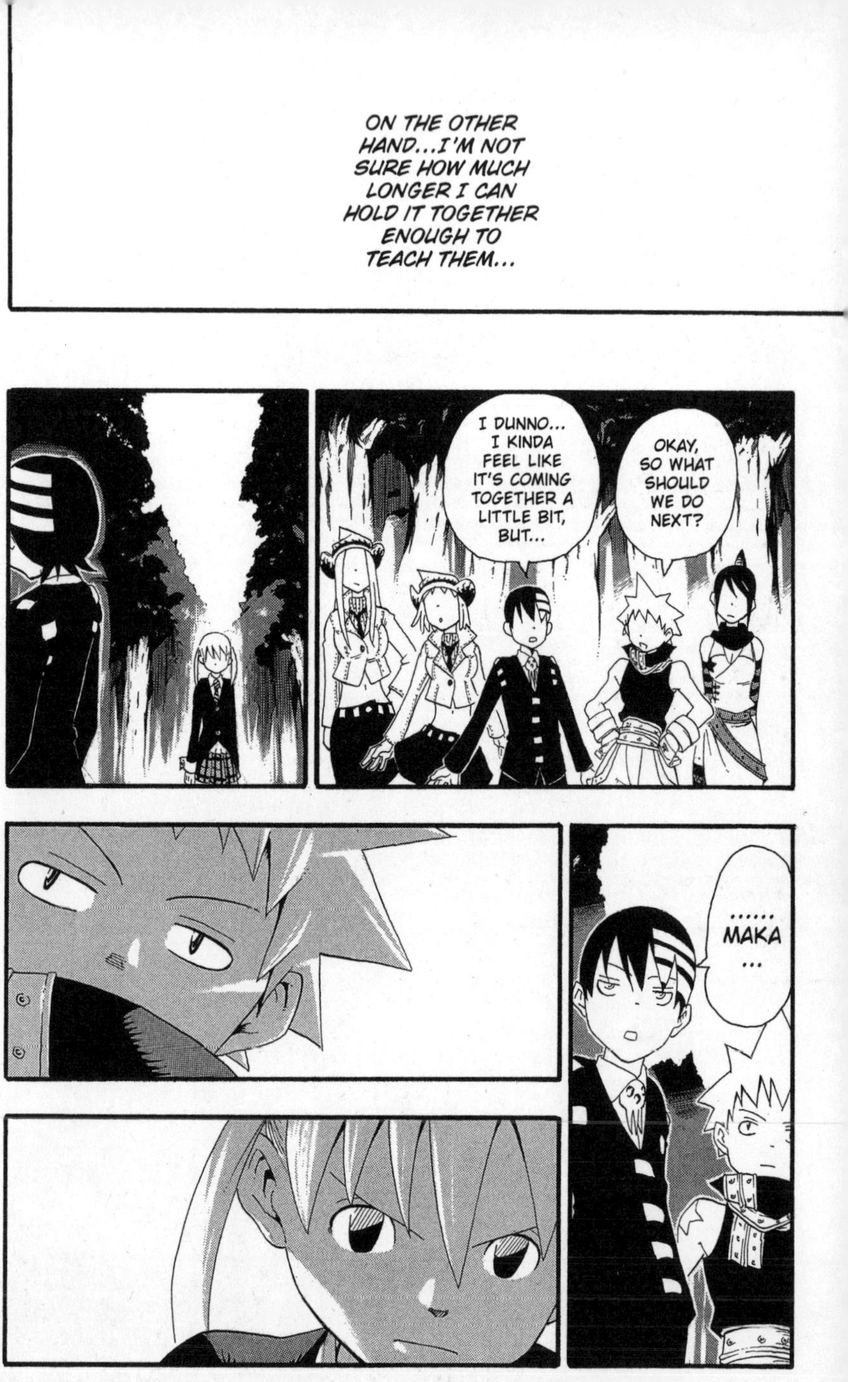
ON THE OTHER HAND...I'M NOT SURE HOW MUCH LONGER I CAN HOLD IT TOGETHER ENOUGH TO TEACH THEM...
OKAY, SO WHAT SHOULD WE DO NEXT?
I DUNNO... I KINDA FEEL LIKE IT'S COMING TOGETHER A LITTLE BIT, BUT...
...... MAKA ...

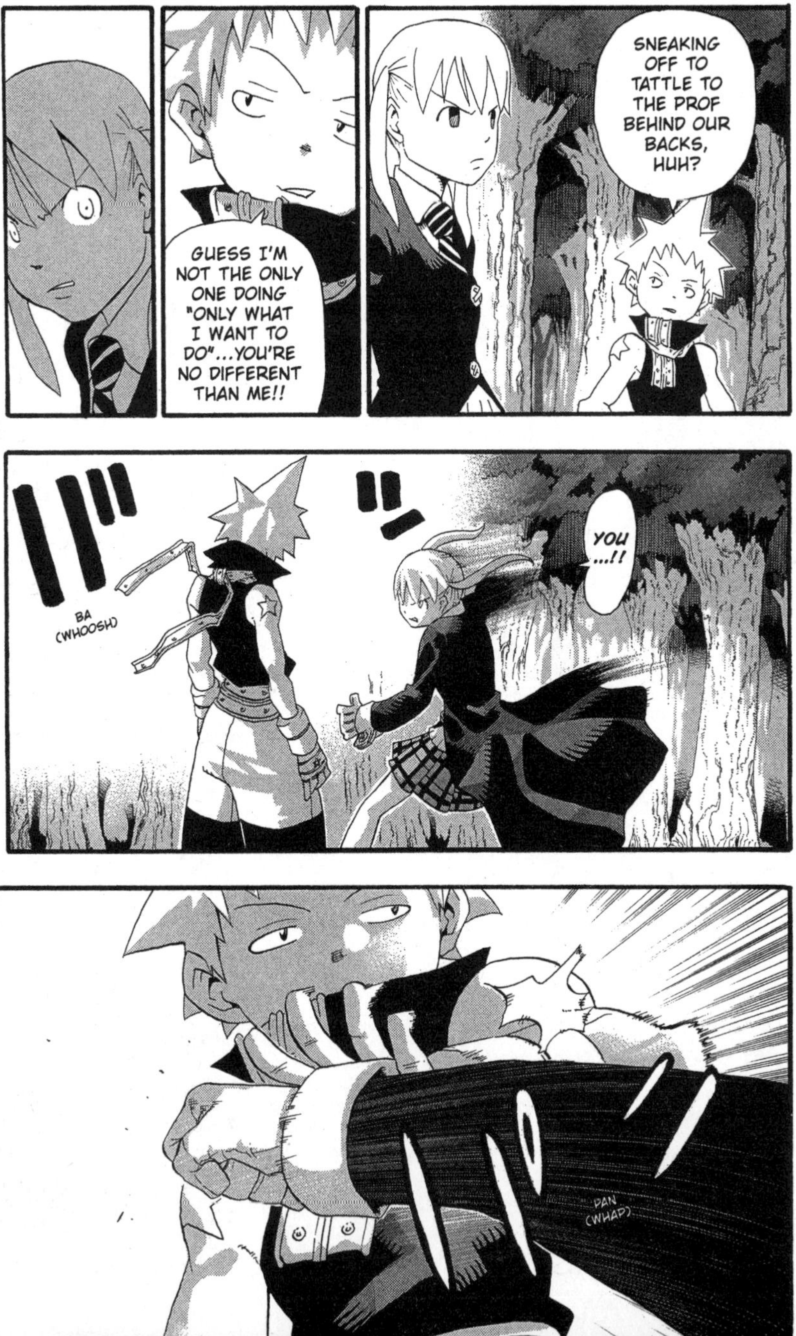
SNEAKING OFF TO TATTLE TO THE PROF BEHIND OUR BACKS, HUH?
GUESS I'M NOT THE ONLY ONE DOING "ONLY WHAT I WANT TO DO"...YOU'RE NO DIFFERENT THAN ME!!
YOU ...!!
BA (WHOOSH)
PAN (WHAP)

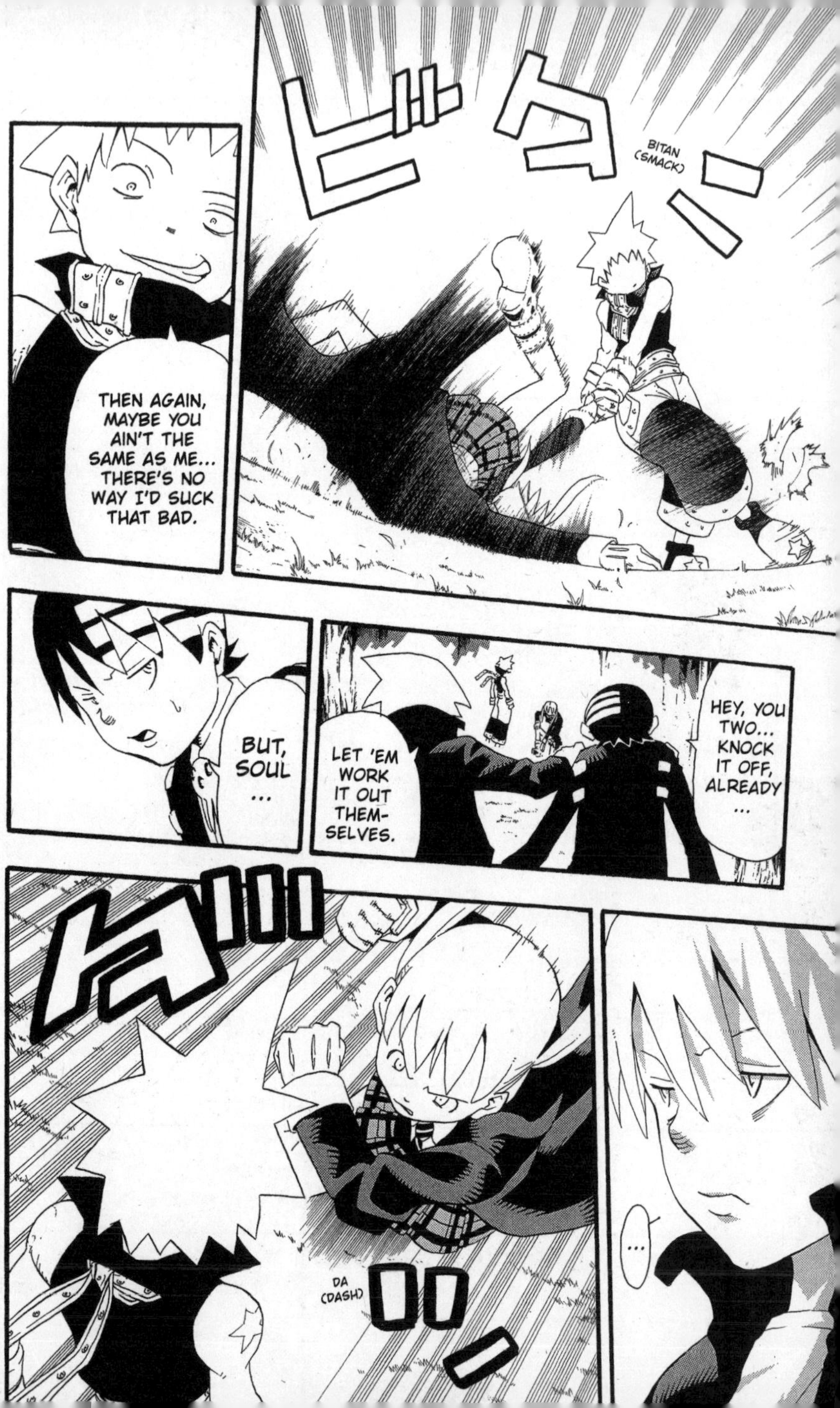
BITAN (SMACK)
THEN AGAIN, MAYBE YOU AIN'T THE SAME AS ME... THERE'S NO WAY I'D SUCK THAT BAD.
HEY, YOU TWO... KNOCK IT OFF, ALREADY...
LET 'EM WORK IT OUT THEM-SELVES.
BUT, SOUL...
...
DA (DASH)

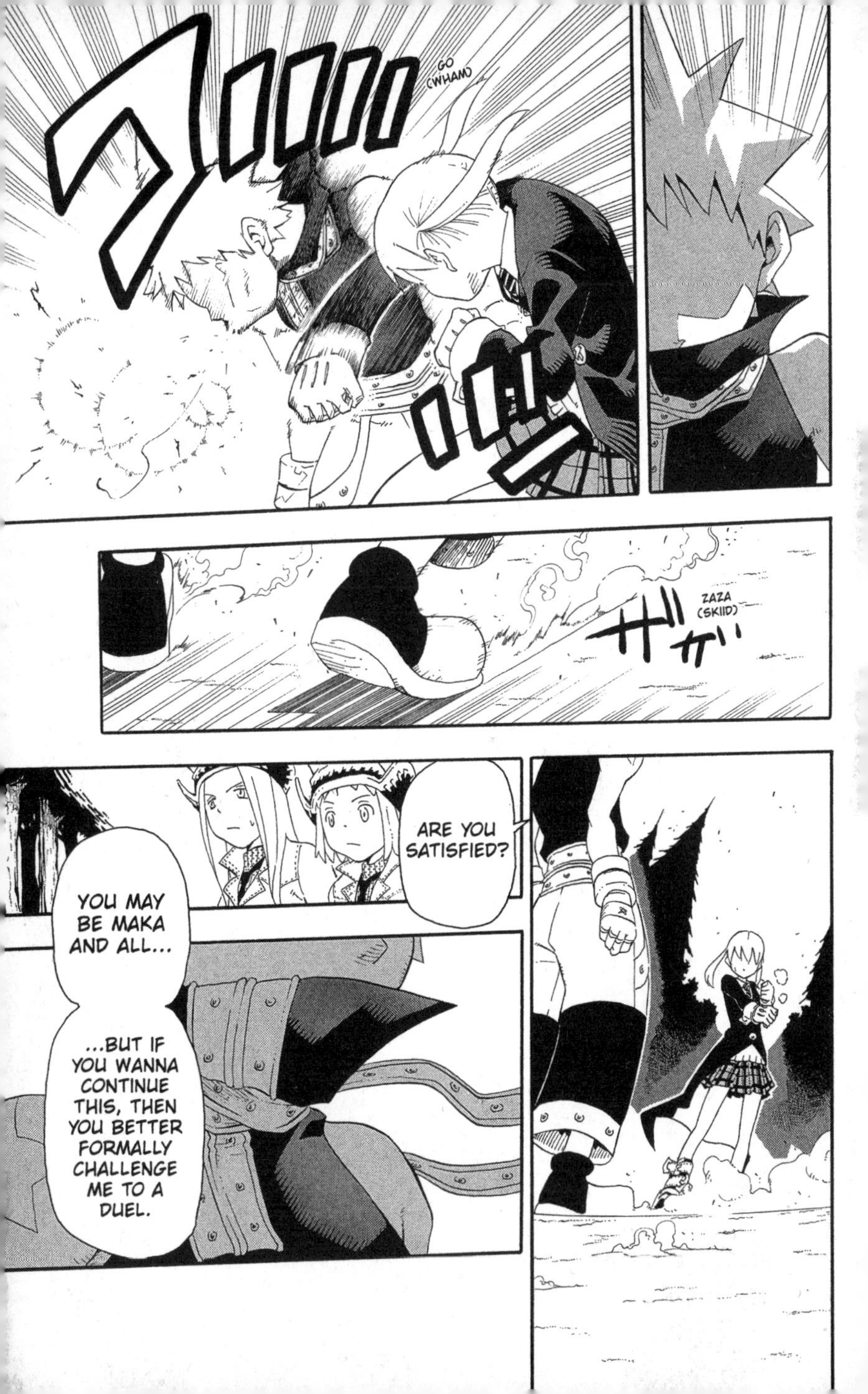
GO
(WHAM)
ZAZA
(SKIID)
ARE YOU SATISFIED?
YOU MAY BE MAKA AND ALL...
...BUT IF YOU WANNA CONTINUE THIS, THEN YOU BETTER FORMALLY CHALLENGE ME TO A DUEL.

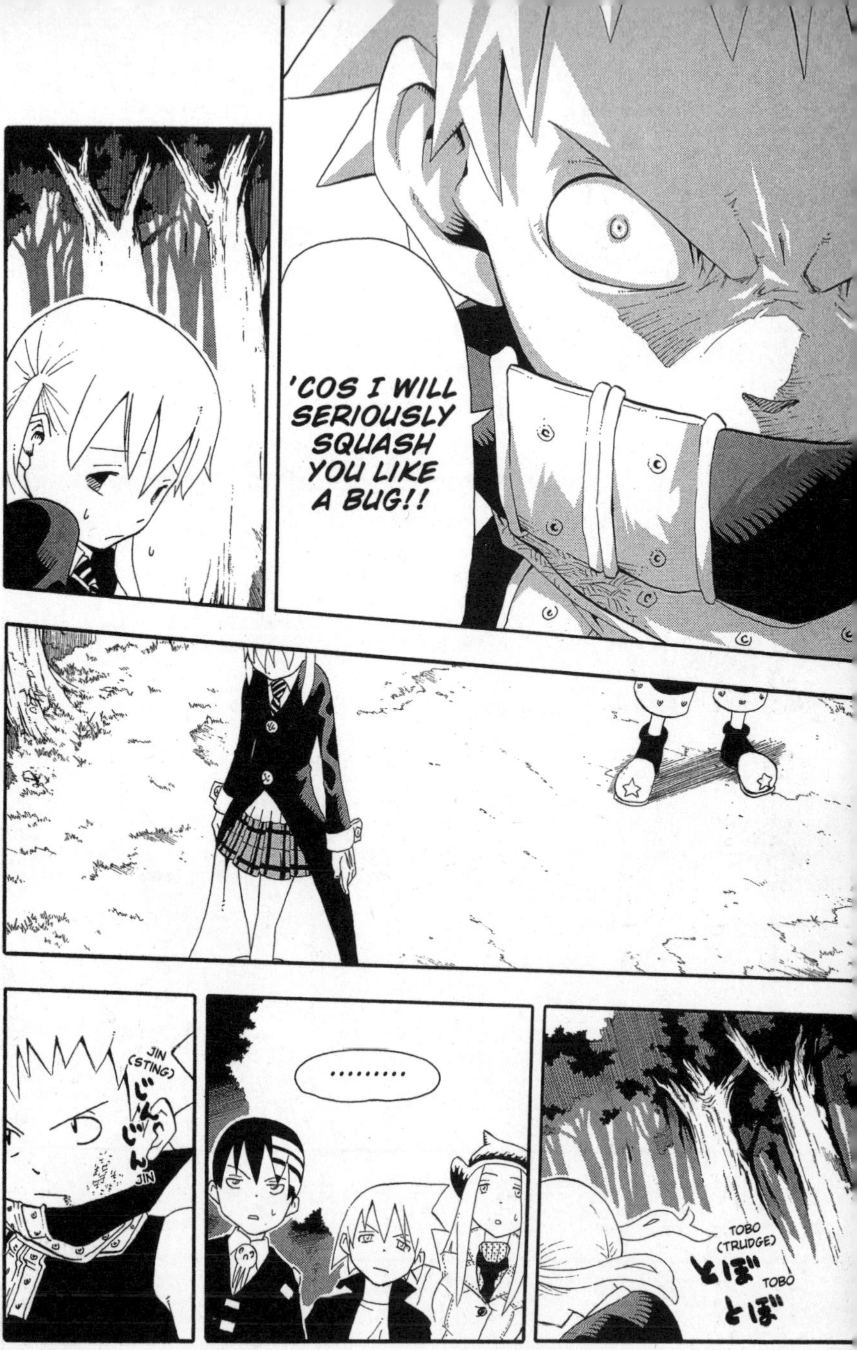
'COS I WILL SERIOUSLY SQUASH YOU LIKE A BUG!!
TOBO (TRUDGE)
とぼ
TOBO
とぼ
....
JIN (STING)
じん
じん
JIN

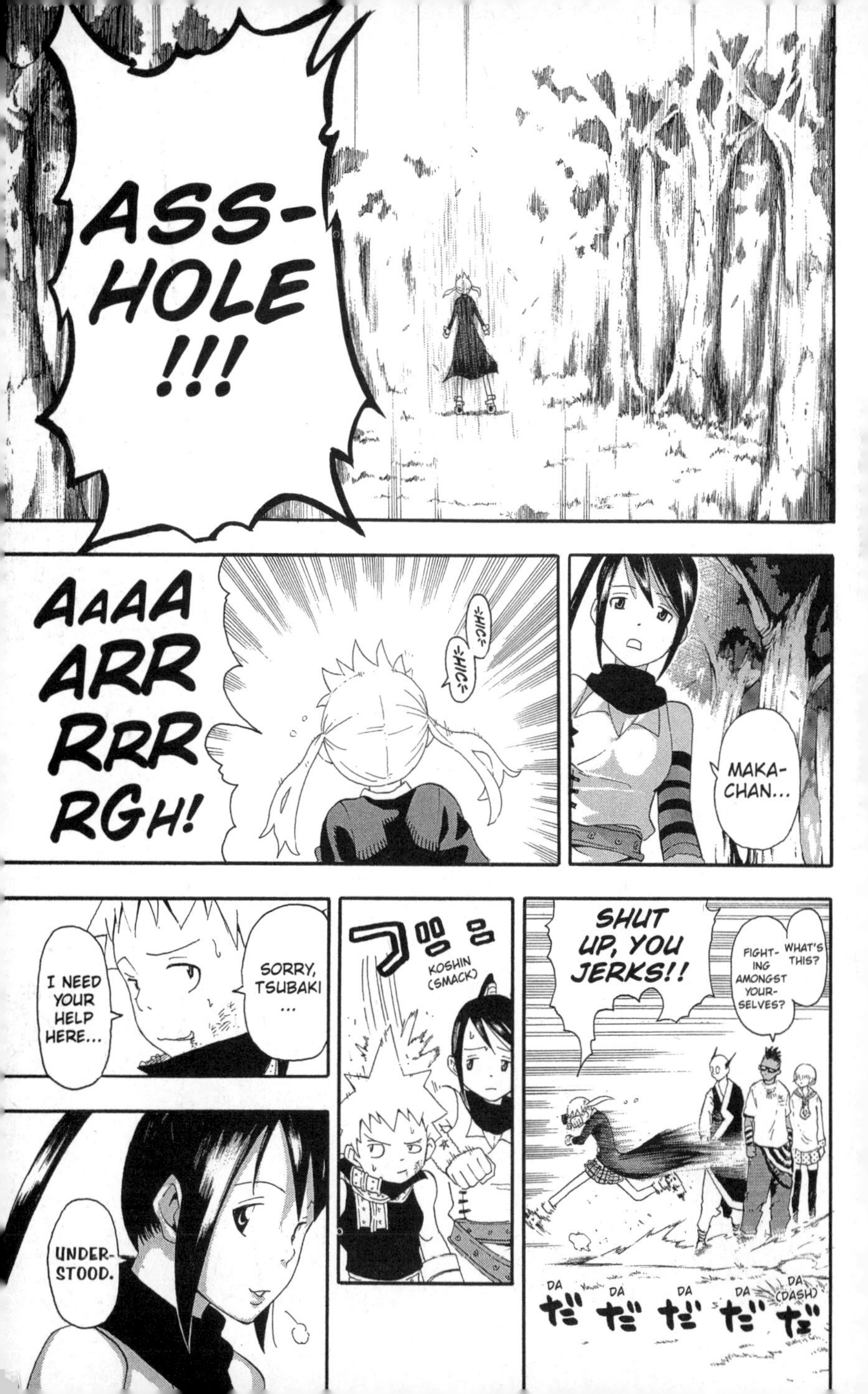
ASS-HOLE!!!
MAKA-CHAN...
HIC
HIC
AAAAARRRRRRRGH!
WHAT'S THIS?
FIGHTING AMONGST YOURSELVES?
SHUT UP, YOU JERKS!!
DA DA DA DA DA (DASH)
KOSHIN (SMACK)
SORRY, TSUBAKI...
I NEED YOUR HELP HERE...
UNDERSTOOD.

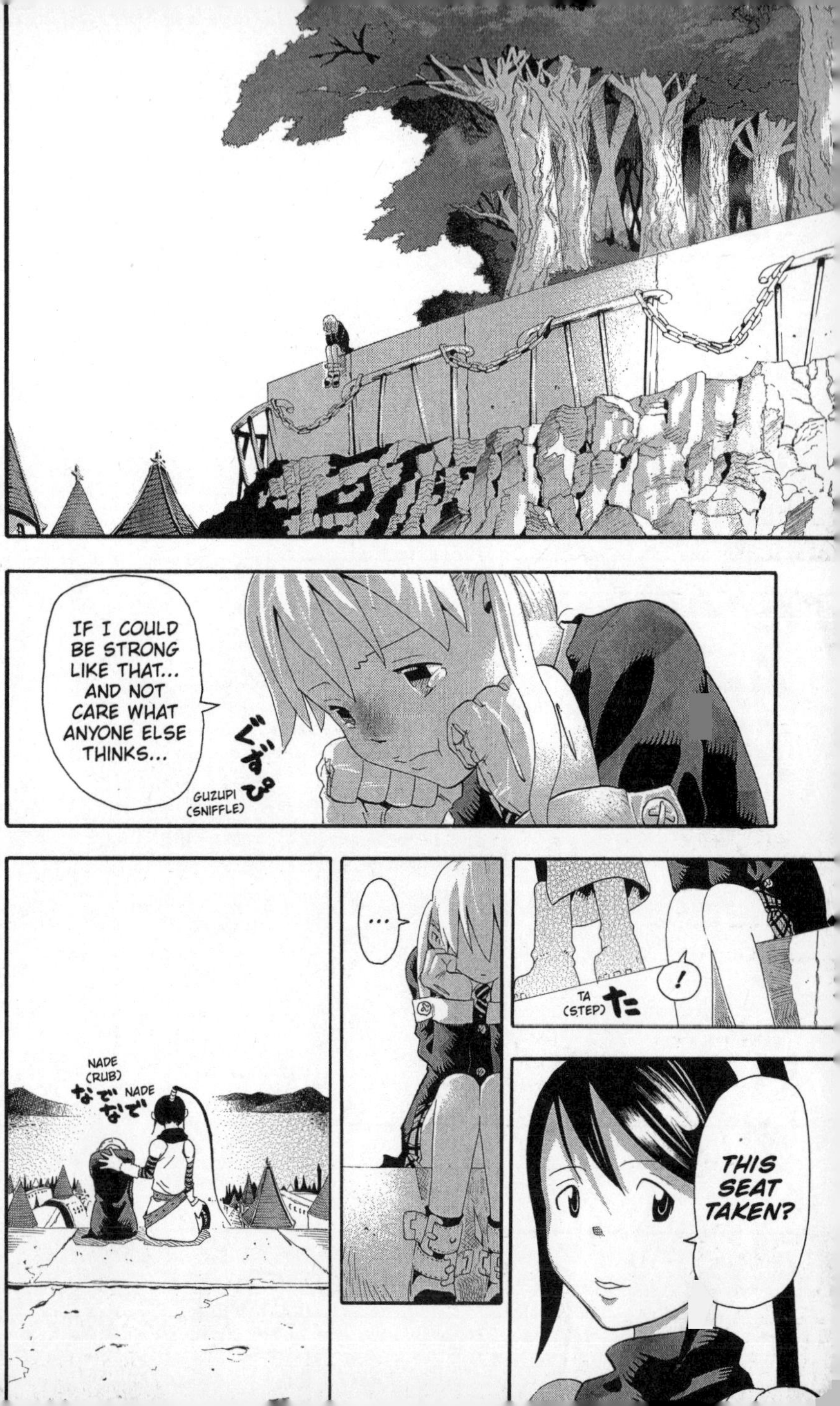
IF I COULD BE STRONG LIKE THAT... AND NOT CARE WHAT ANYONE ELSE THINKS...
ぐずぴ
GUZUPI (SNIFFLE)
!
たっ
TA (STEP)
THIS SEAT TAKEN?
...
なでなで
NADE (RUB) NADE

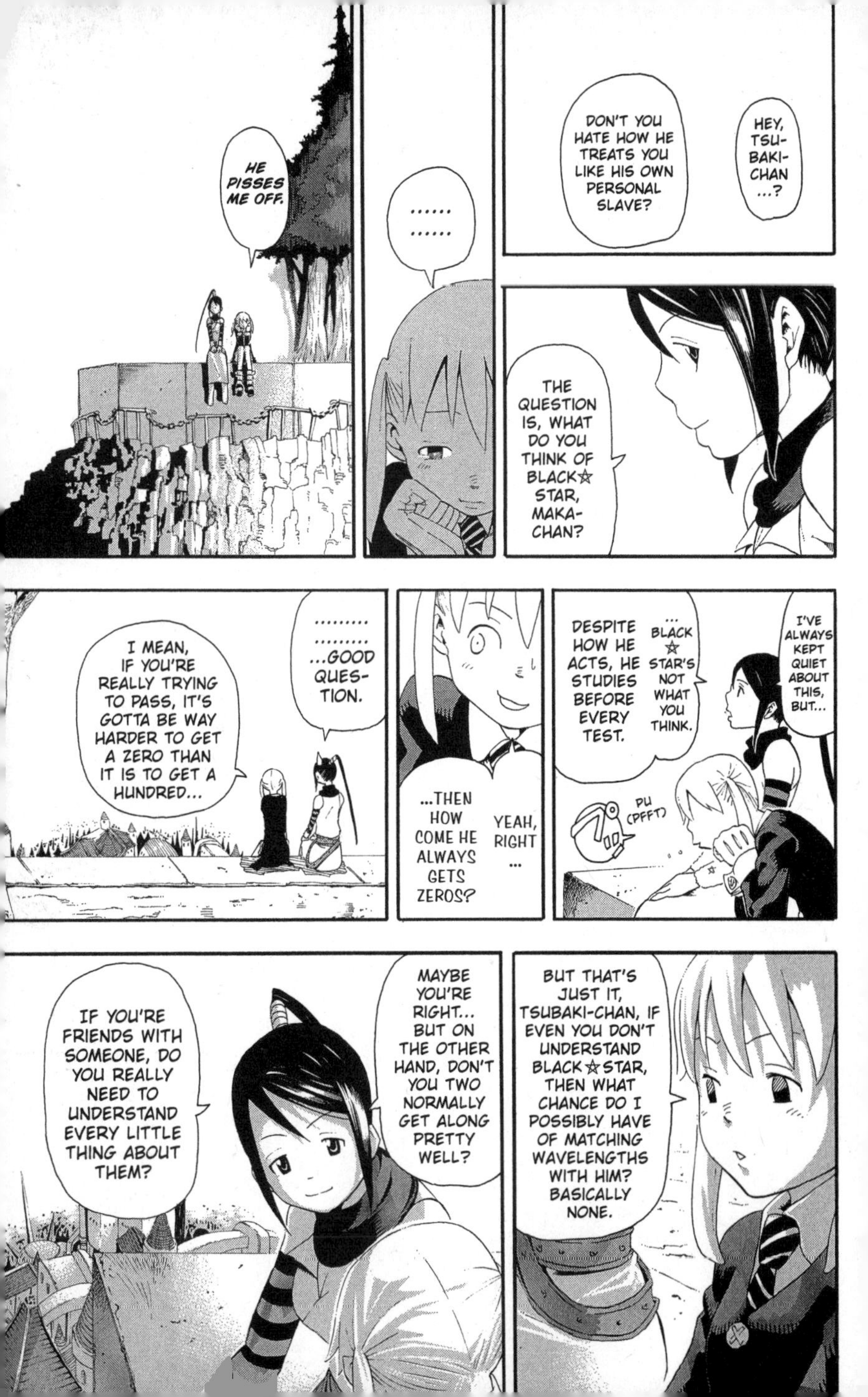
HEY, TSUBAKI-CHAN...?
DON'T YOU HATE HOW HE TREATS YOU LIKE HIS OWN PERSONAL SLAVE?
THE QUESTION IS, WHAT DO YOU THINK OF BLACK☆STAR, MAKA-CHAN?
....
HE PISSES ME OFF.
I'VE ALWAYS KEPT QUIET ABOUT THIS, BUT...
...BLACK☆STAR'S NOT WHAT YOU THINK.
DESPITE HOW HE ACTS, HE STUDIES BEFORE EVERY TEST.
PU (PFFT)
YEAH, RIGHT...
...THEN HOW COME HE ALWAYS GETS ZEROS?
....GOOD QUESTION.
I MEAN, IF YOU'RE REALLY TRYING TO PASS, IT'S GOTTA BE WAY HARDER TO GET A ZERO THAN IT IS TO GET A HUNDRED...
BUT THAT'S JUST IT, TSUBAKI-CHAN, IF EVEN YOU DON'T UNDERSTAND BLACK☆STAR, THEN WHAT CHANCE DO I POSSIBLY HAVE OF MATCHING WAVELENGTHS WITH HIM? BASICALLY NONE.
MAYBE YOU'RE RIGHT... BUT ON THE OTHER HAND, DON'T YOU TWO NORMALLY GET ALONG PRETTY WELL?
IF YOU'RE FRIENDS WITH SOMEONE, DO YOU REALLY NEED TO UNDERSTAND EVERY LITTLE THING ABOUT THEM?

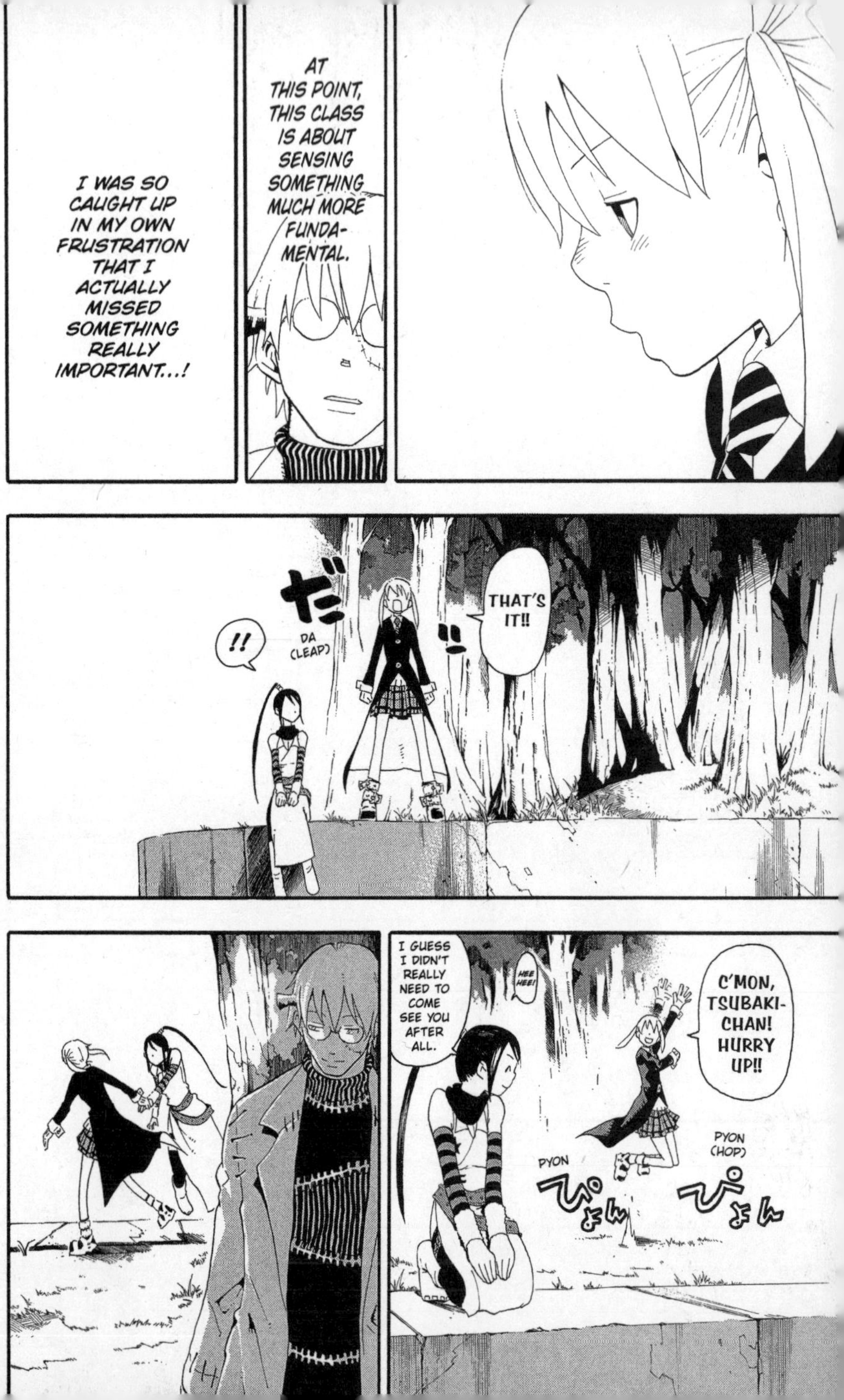
AT THIS POINT, THIS CLASS IS ABOUT SENSING SOMETHING MUCH MORE FUNDA-MENTAL.
I WAS SO CAUGHT UP IN MY OWN FRUSTRATION THAT I ACTUALLY MISSED SOMETHING REALLY IMPORTANT...!
THAT'S IT!!
DA (LEAP)
!!
C'MON, TSUBAKI-CHAN! HURRY UP!!
PYON (HOP)
PYON
HEE HEE!
I GUESS I DIDN'T REALLY NEED TO COME SEE YOU AFTER ALL.

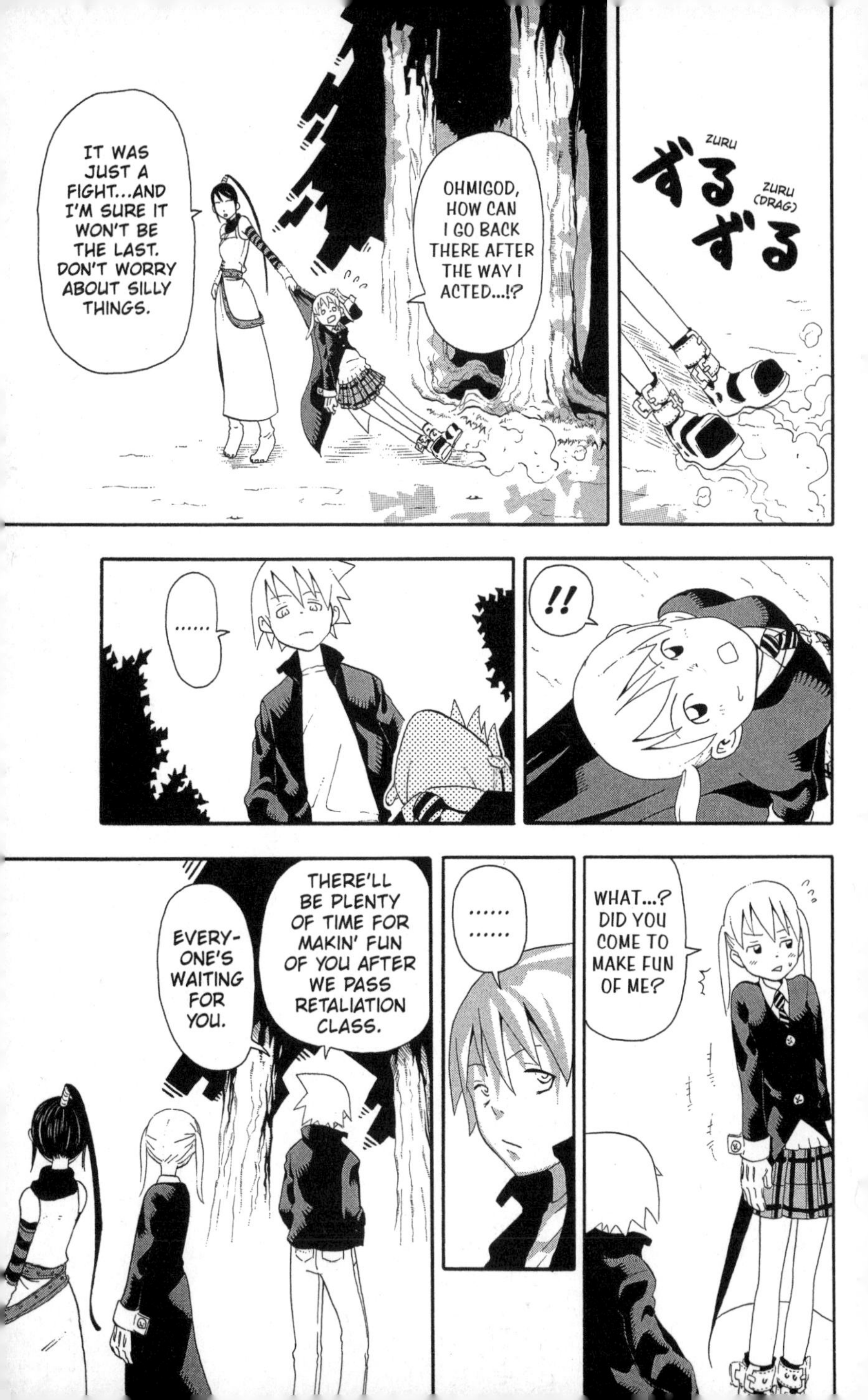
ZURU
ずるずる
ZURU (DRAG)
OHMIGOD, HOW CAN I GO BACK THERE AFTER THE WAY I ACTED...!?
IT WAS JUST A FIGHT...AND I'M SURE IT WON'T BE THE LAST. DON'T WORRY ABOUT SILLY THINGS.
!!
......
WHAT...? DID YOU COME TO MAKE FUN OF ME?
....
THERE'LL BE PLENTY OF TIME FOR MAKIN' FUN OF YOU AFTER WE PASS RETALIATION CLASS.
EVERY-ONE'S WAITING FOR YOU.

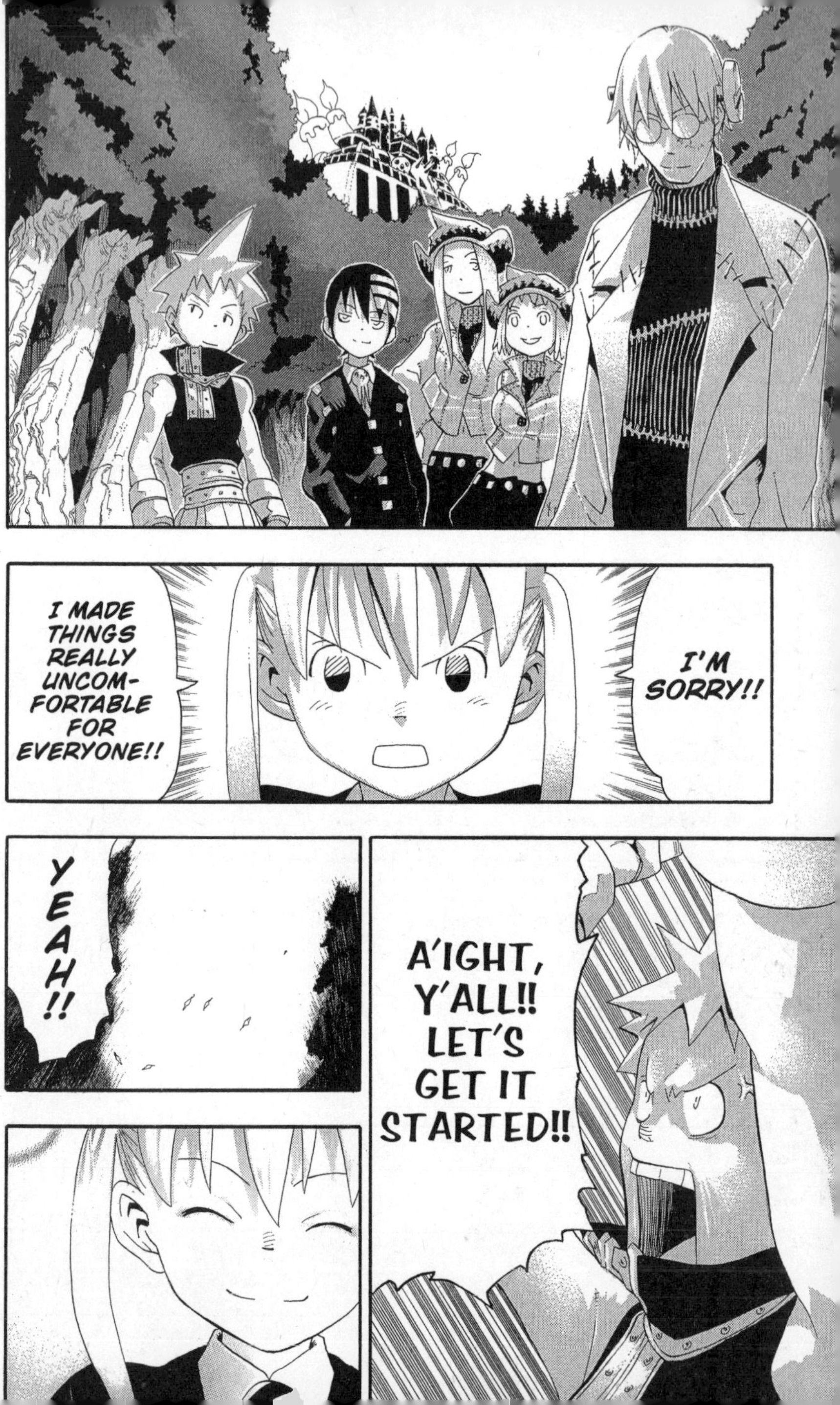
I'M SORRY!!
I MADE THINGS REALLY UNCOMFORTABLE FOR EVERYONE!!
A'IGHT, Y'ALL!! LET'S GET IT STARTED!!
YEAH!!

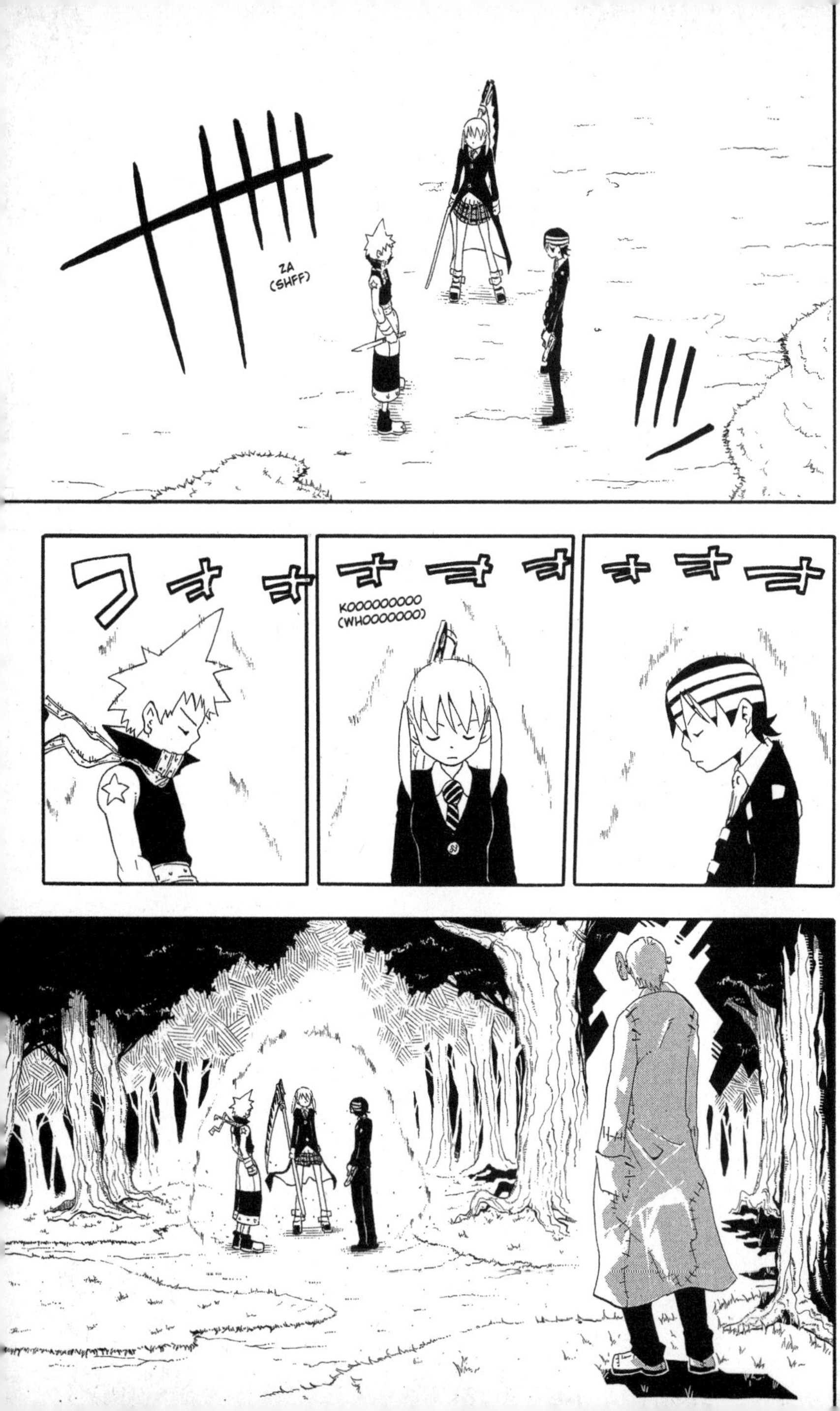
ZA
(SHFF)
フォォォォォォォォ
KOOOOOOOOO
(WHOOOOOOO)

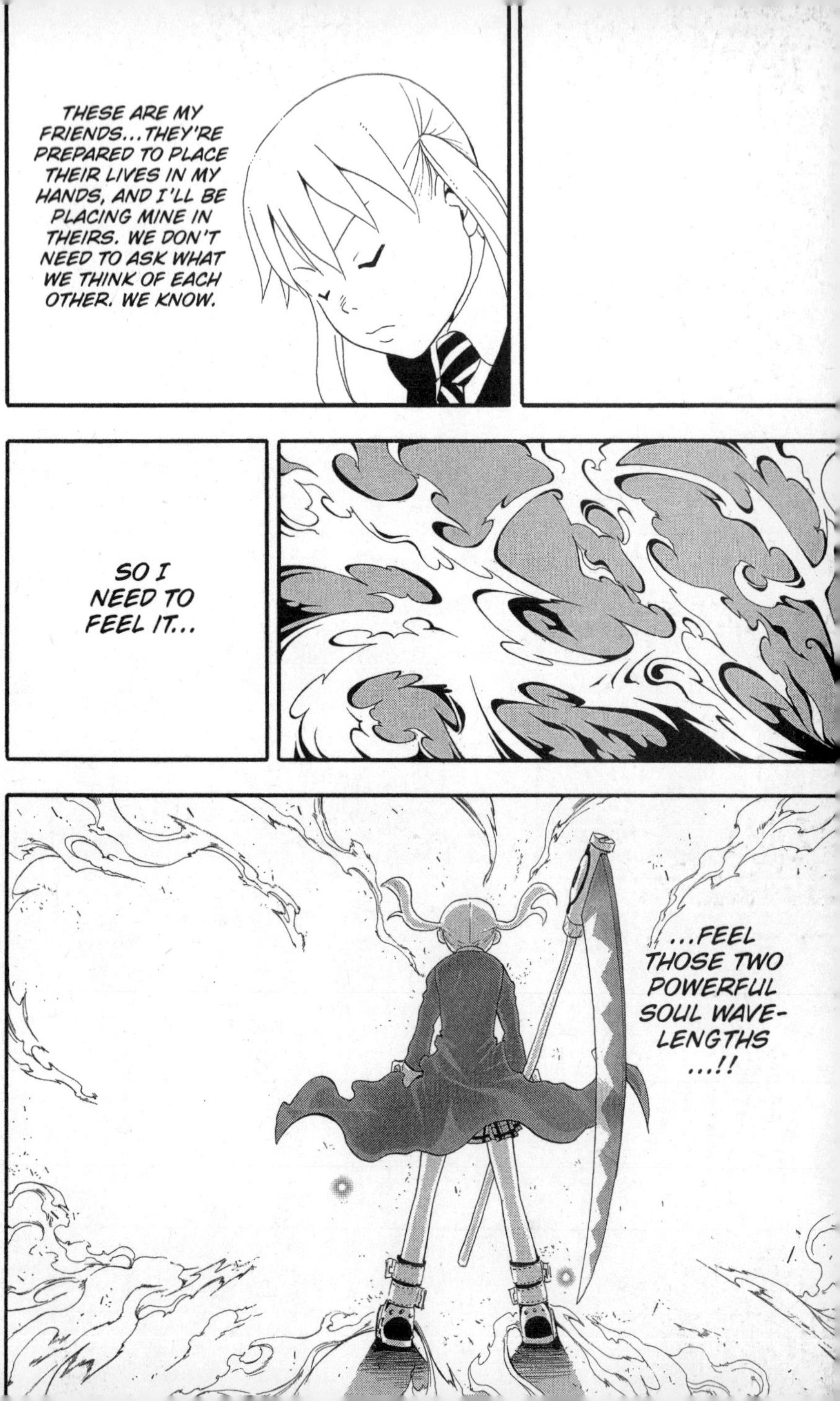
THESE ARE MY FRIENDS...THEY'RE PREPARED TO PLACE THEIR LIVES IN MY HANDS, AND I'LL BE PLACING MINE IN THEIRS. WE DON'T NEED TO ASK WHAT WE THINK OF EACH OTHER. WE KNOW.
SO I NEED TO FEEL IT...
...FEEL THOSE TWO POWERFUL SOUL WAVE-LENGTHS ...!!

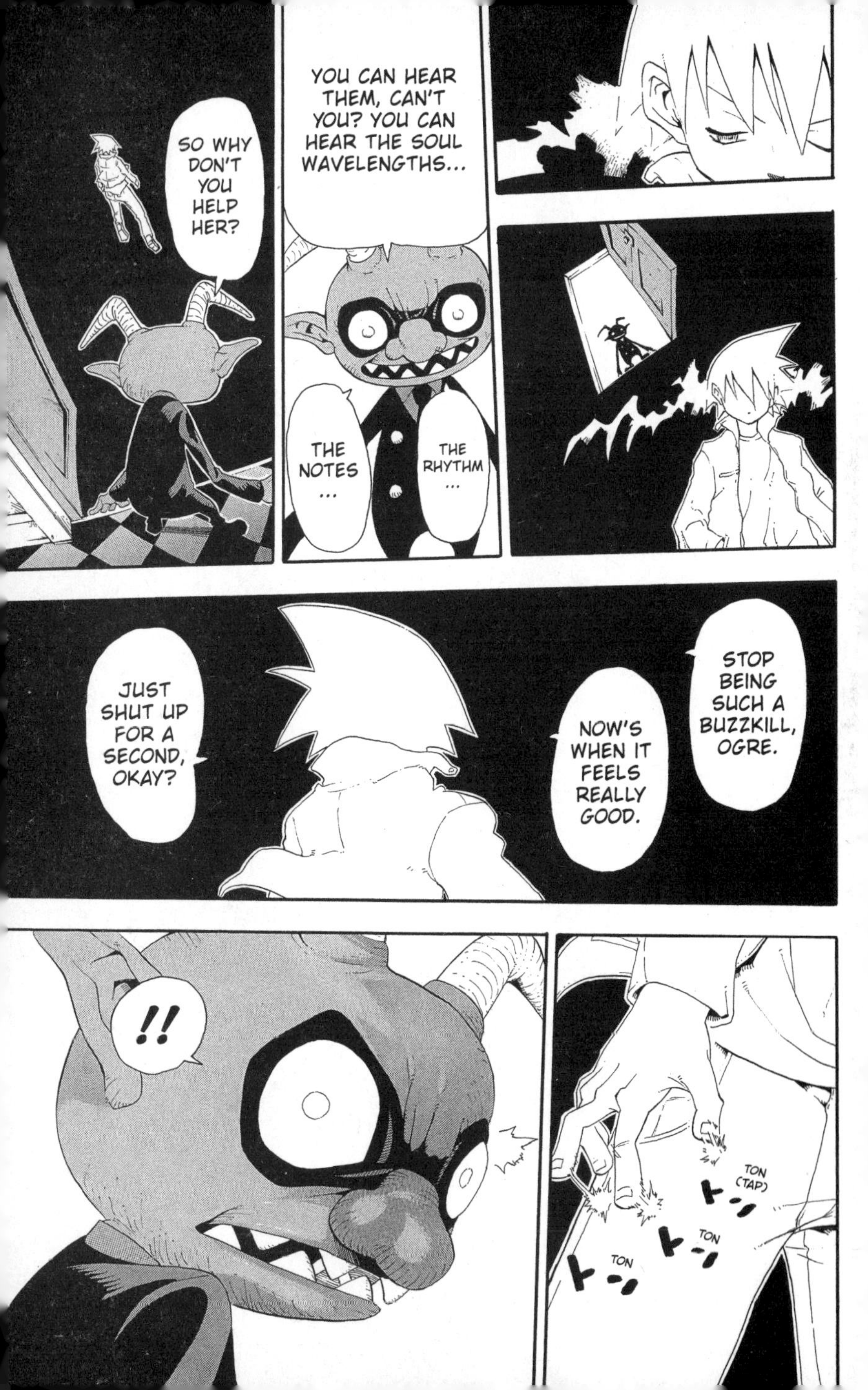
YOU CAN HEAR THEM, CAN'T YOU? YOU CAN HEAR THE SOUL WAVELENGTHS...
THE RHYTHM ...
THE NOTES ...
SO WHY DON'T YOU HELP HER?
STOP BEING SUCH A BUZZKILL, OGRE.
NOW'S WHEN IT FEELS REALLY GOOD.
JUST SHUT UP FOR A SECOND, OKAY?
TON (TAP)
TON
TON
!!

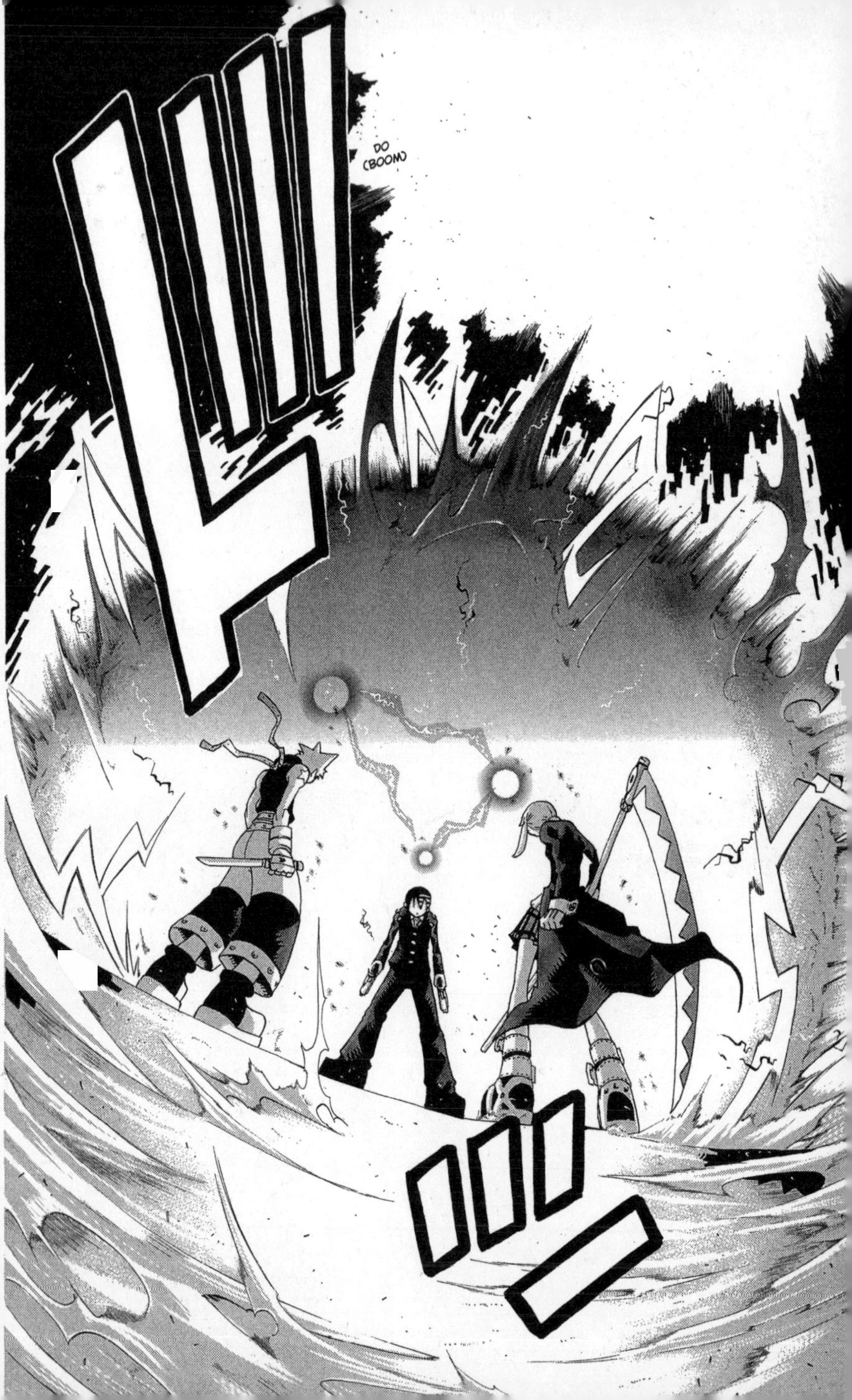
DO
(BOOM)

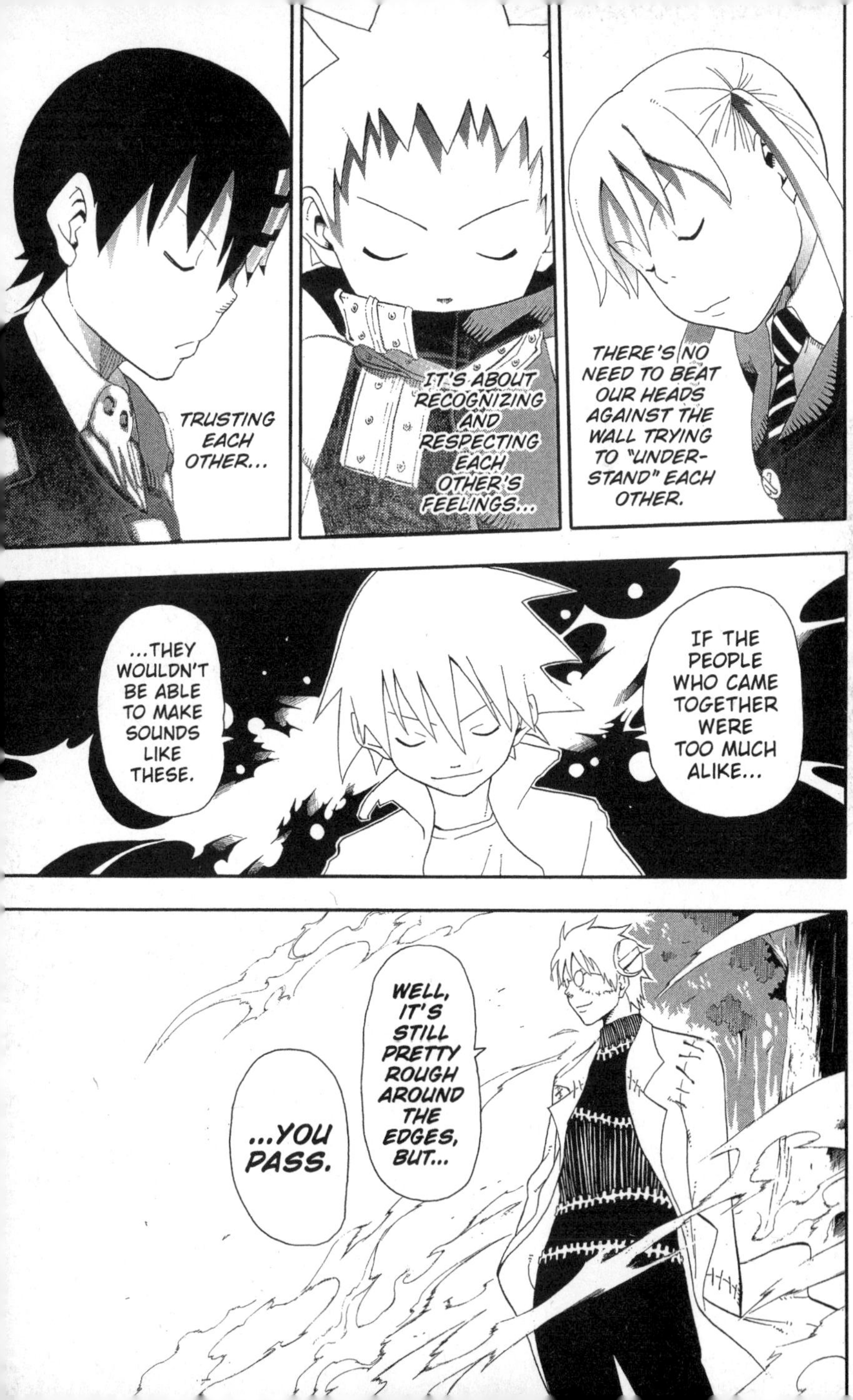
THERE'S NO NEED TO BEAT OUR HEADS AGAINST THE WALL TRYING TO "UNDER-STAND" EACH OTHER.
IT'S ABOUT RECOGNIZING AND RESPECTING EACH OTHER'S FEELINGS...
TRUSTING EACH OTHER...
IF THE PEOPLE WHO CAME TOGETHER WERE TOO MUCH ALIKE...
...THEY WOULDN'T BE ABLE TO MAKE SOUNDS LIKE THESE.
WELL, IT'S STILL PRETTY ROUGH AROUND THE EDGES, BUT...
...YOU PASS.

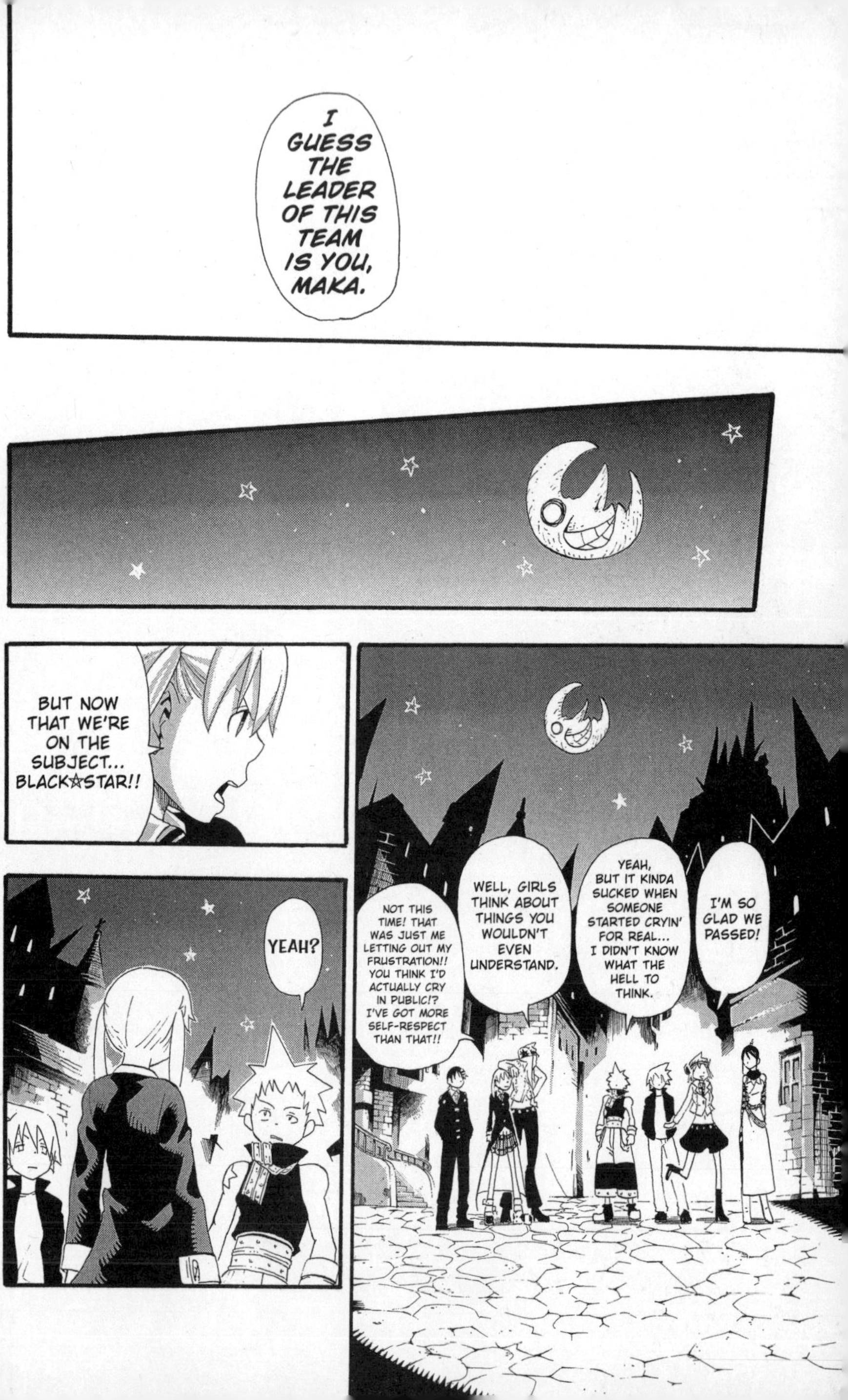
I GUESS THE LEADER OF THIS TEAM IS YOU, MAKA.
I'M SO GLAD WE PASSED!
YEAH, BUT IT KINDA SUCKED WHEN SOMEONE STARTED CRYIN' FOR REAL... I DIDN'T KNOW WHAT THE HELL TO THINK.
WELL, GIRLS THINK ABOUT THINGS YOU WOULDN'T EVEN UNDERSTAND.
NOT THIS TIME! THAT WAS JUST ME LETTING OUT MY FRUSTRATION!! YOU THINK I'D ACTUALLY CRY IN PUBLIC!? I'VE GOT MORE SELF-RESPECT THAN THAT!!
BUT NOW THAT WE'RE ON THE SUBJECT... BLACK☆STAR!!
YEAH?

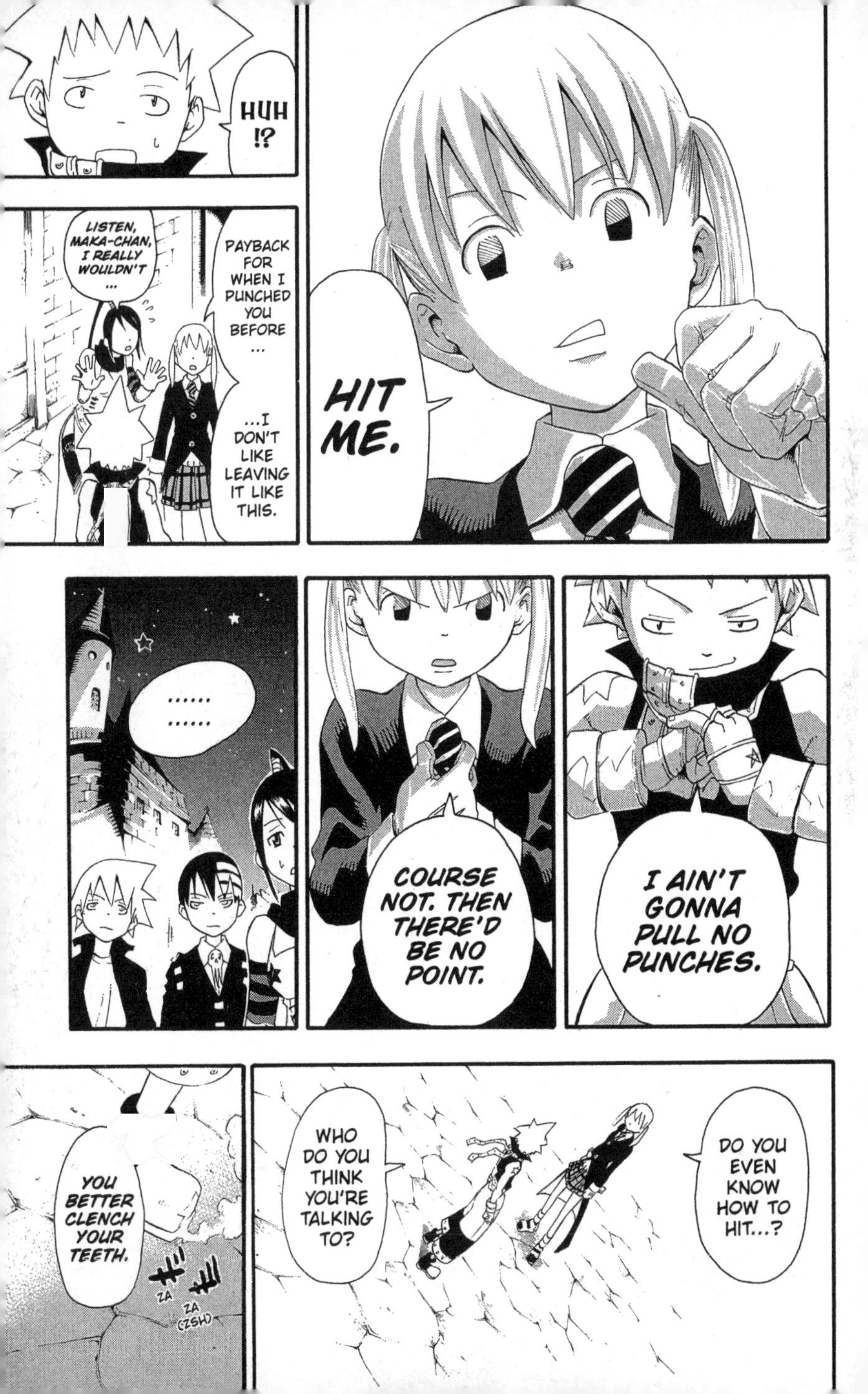
HIT ME.
HUH !?
PAYBACK FOR WHEN I PUNCHED YOU BEFORE ...
...I DON'T LIKE LEAVING IT LIKE THIS.
LISTEN, MAKA-CHAN, I REALLY WOULDN'T ...
I AIN'T GONNA PULL NO PUNCHES.
COURSE NOT. THEN THERE'D BE NO POINT.
....
DO YOU EVEN KNOW HOW TO HIT...?
WHO DO YOU THINK YOU'RE TALKING TO?
YOU BETTER CLENCH YOUR TEETH.
ZA
ZA
(ZSH)

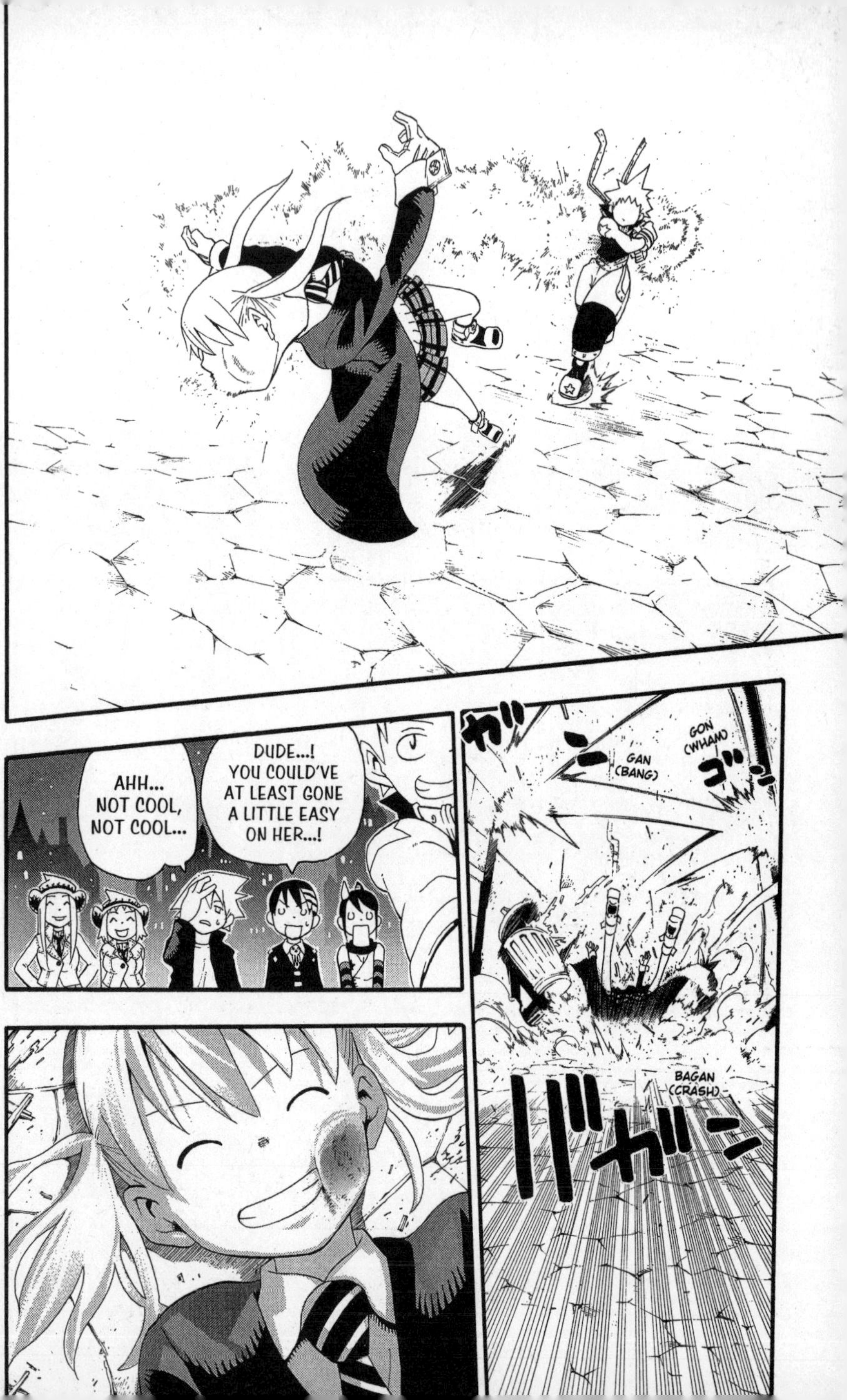

GON (WHAM)
GAN (BANG)
BAGAN (CRASH)
DUDE...! YOU COULD'VE AT LEAST GONE A LITTLE EASY ON HER...!
AHH... NOT COOL, NOT COOL...

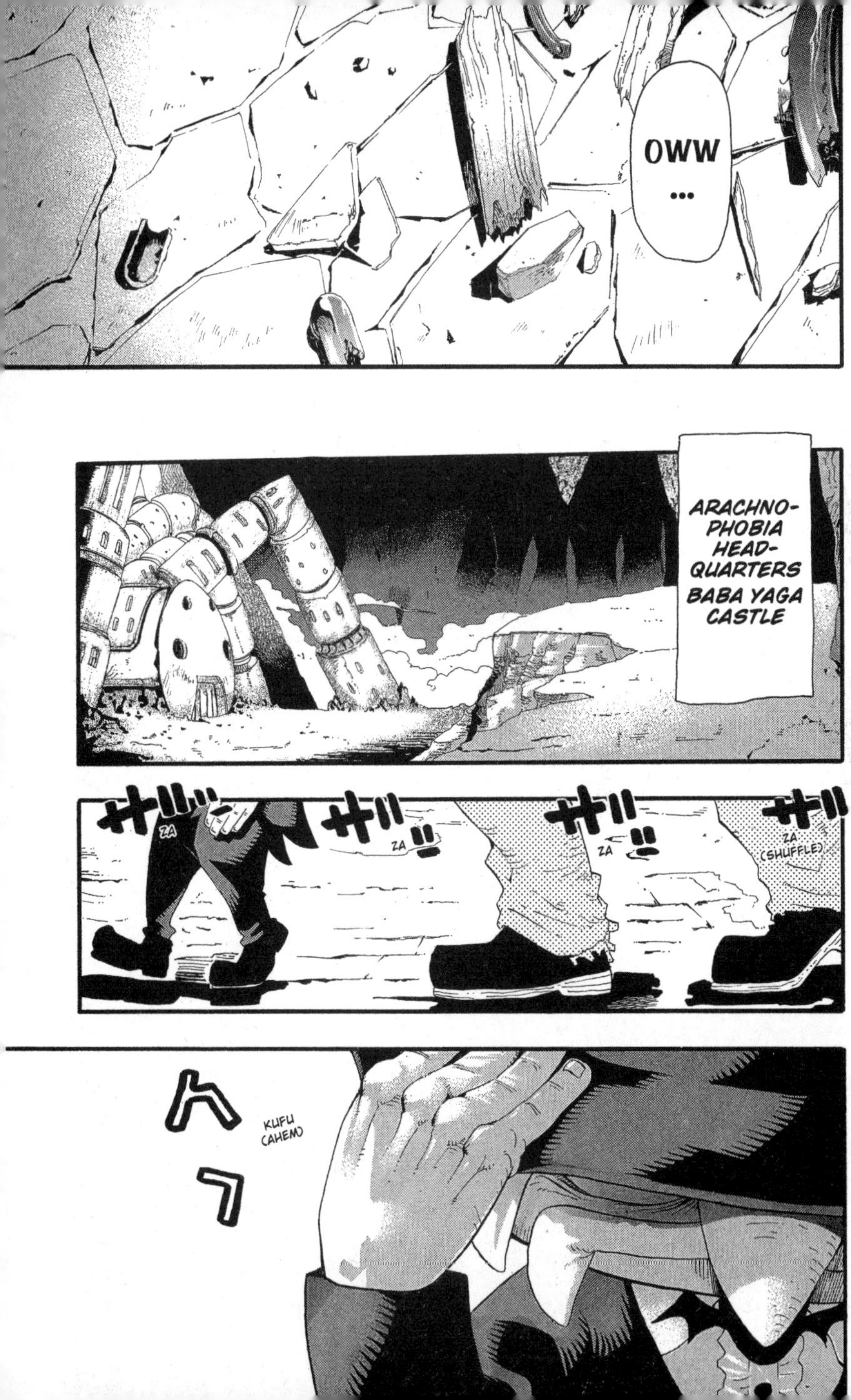
OWW...
ARACHNOPHOBIA HEADQUARTERS BABA YAGA CASTLE
ZA (SHUFFLE)
ZA
ZA
ZA
KUFU (AHEM)

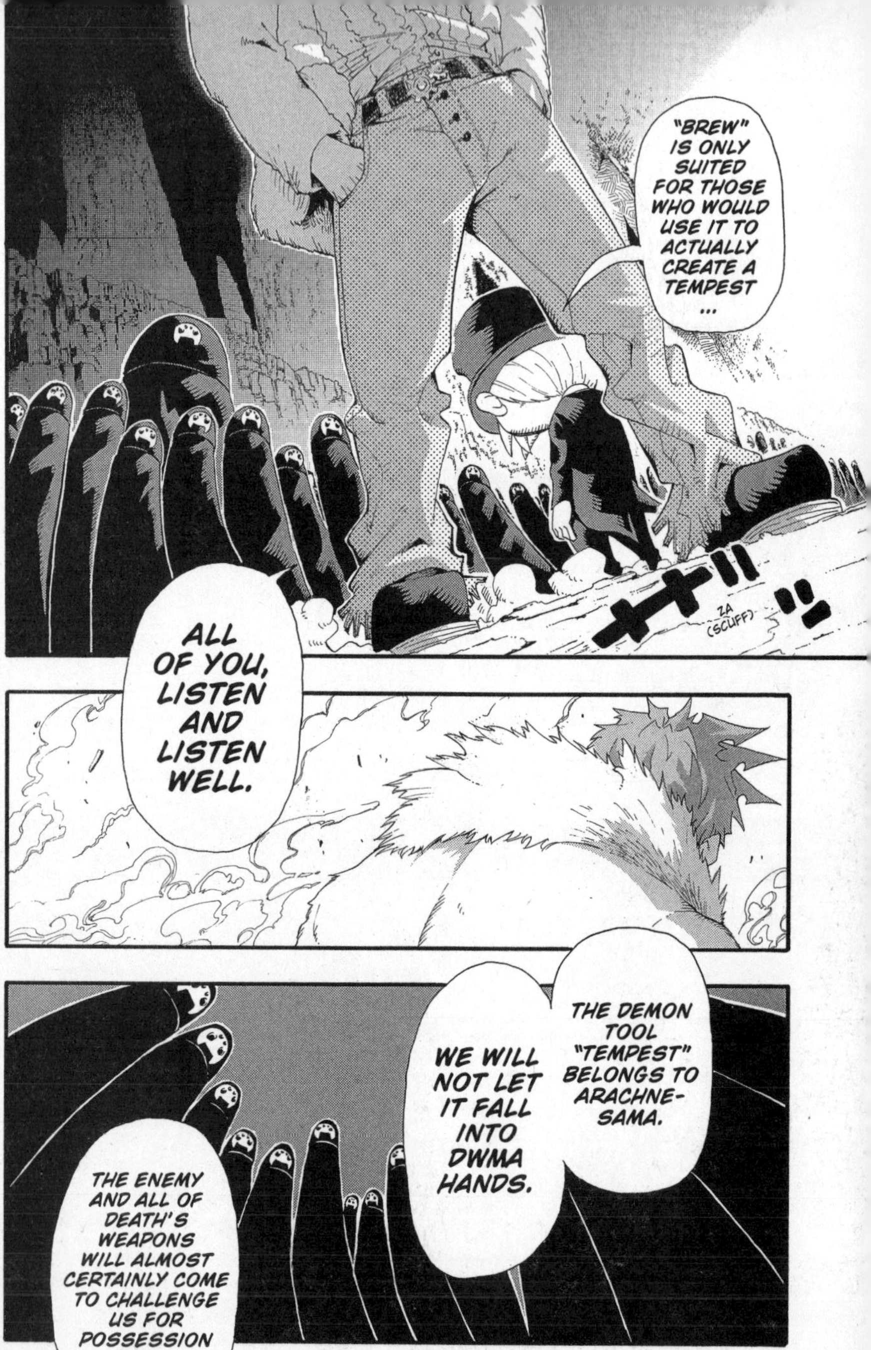
"BREW" IS ONLY SUITED FOR THOSE WHO WOULD USE IT TO ACTUALLY CREATE A TEMPEST ...
ZA (SCUFF)
ALL OF YOU, LISTEN AND LISTEN WELL.
THE DEMON TOOL "TEMPEST" BELONGS TO ARACHNE-SAMA.
WE WILL NOT LET IT FALL INTO DWMA HANDS.
THE ENEMY AND ALL OF DEATH'S WEAPONS WILL ALMOST CERTAINLY COME TO CHALLENGE US FOR POSSESSION OF IT.

SOUL EATER

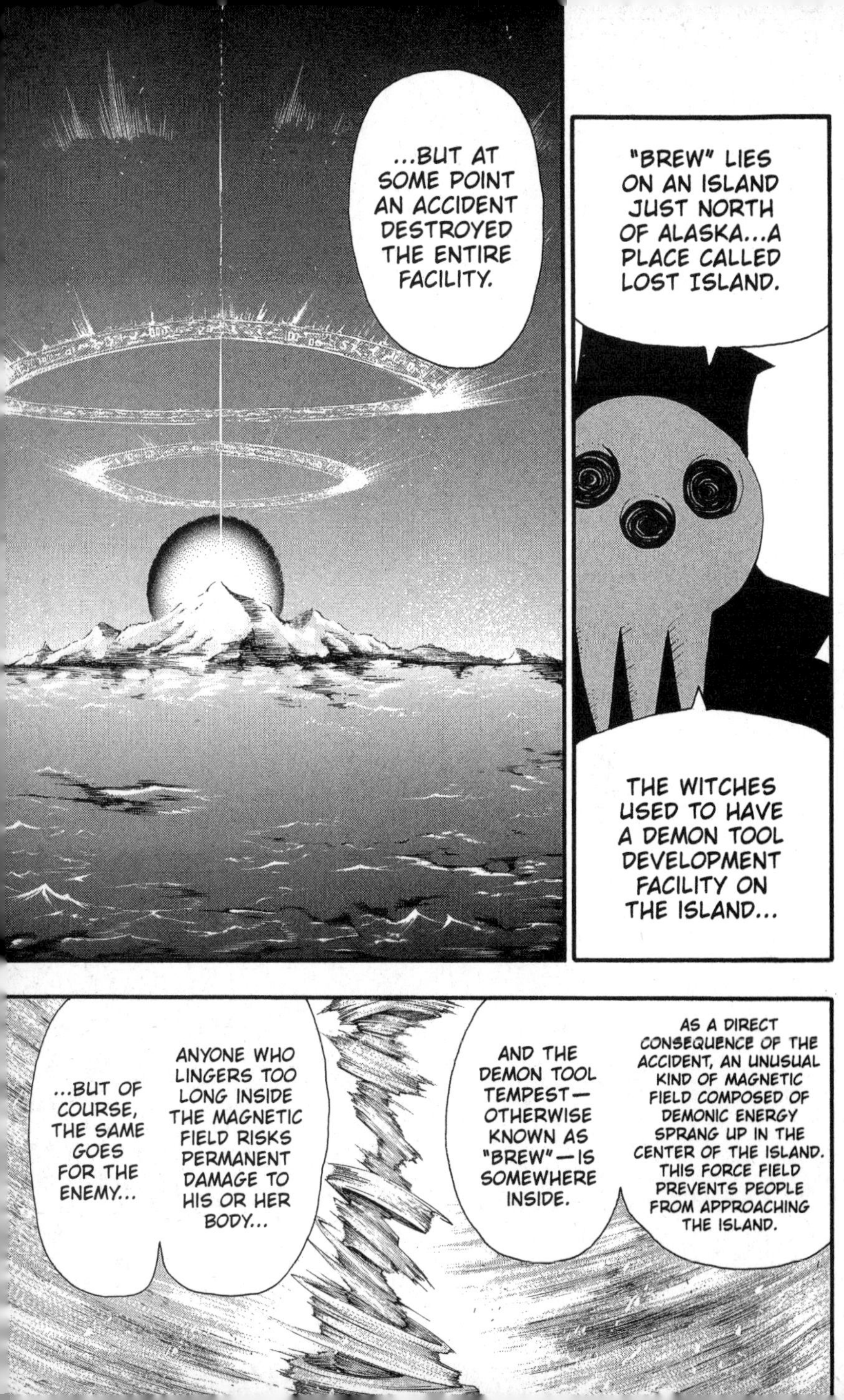
"BREW" LIES ON AN ISLAND JUST NORTH OF ALASKA...A PLACE CALLED LOST ISLAND.
THE WITCHES USED TO HAVE A DEMON TOOL DEVELOPMENT FACILITY ON THE ISLAND...
...BUT AT SOME POINT AN ACCIDENT DESTROYED THE ENTIRE FACILITY.
AS A DIRECT CONSEQUENCE OF THE ACCIDENT, AN UNUSUAL KIND OF MAGNETIC FIELD COMPOSED OF DEMONIC ENERGY SPRANG UP IN THE CENTER OF THE ISLAND. THIS FORCE FIELD PREVENTS PEOPLE FROM APPROACHING THE ISLAND.
AND THE DEMON TOOL TEMPEST—OTHERWISE KNOWN AS "BREW"—IS SOMEWHERE INSIDE.
ANYONE WHO LINGERS TOO LONG INSIDE THE MAGNETIC FIELD RISKS PERMANENT DAMAGE TO HIS OR HER BODY...
...BUT OF COURSE, THE SAME GOES FOR THE ENEMY...

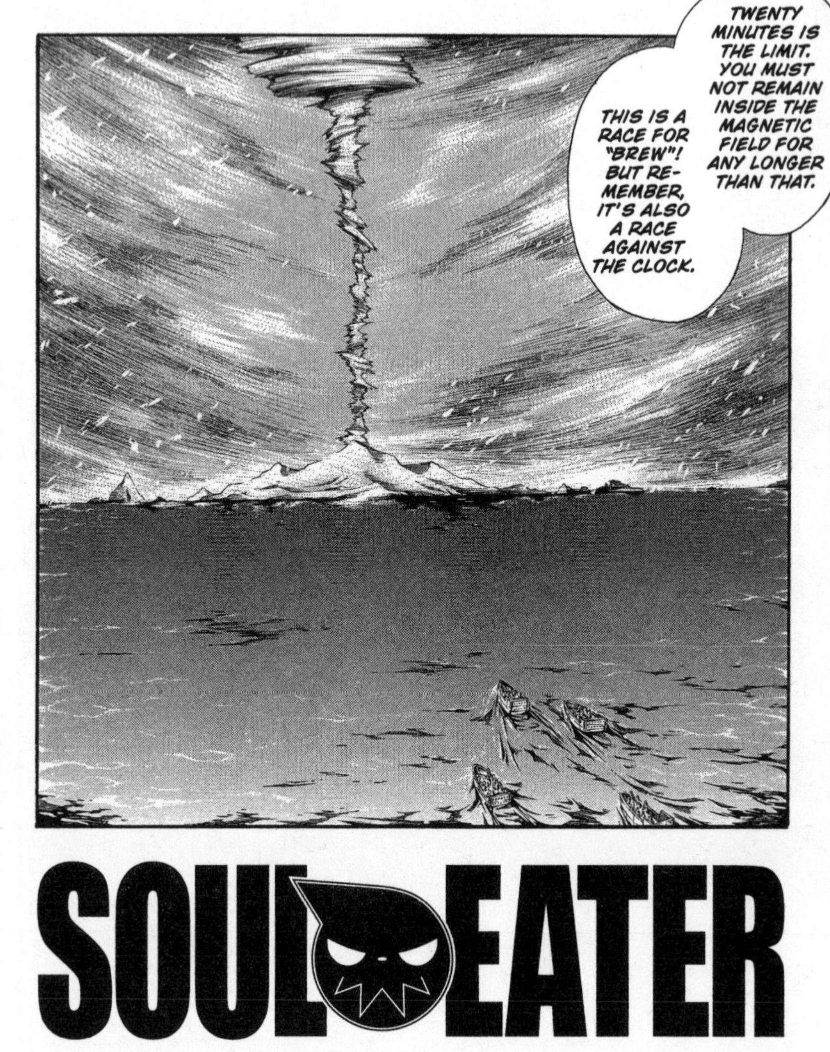
THIS IS A RACE FOR "BREW"! BUT RE-MEMBER, IT'S ALSO A RACE AGAINST THE CLOCK.
TWENTY MINUTES IS THE LIMIT. YOU MUST NOT REMAIN INSIDE THE MAGNETIC FIELD FOR ANY LONGER THAN THAT.

SOUL EATER

CHAPTER 34: "BREW"—THE TEMPEST (PART 1)

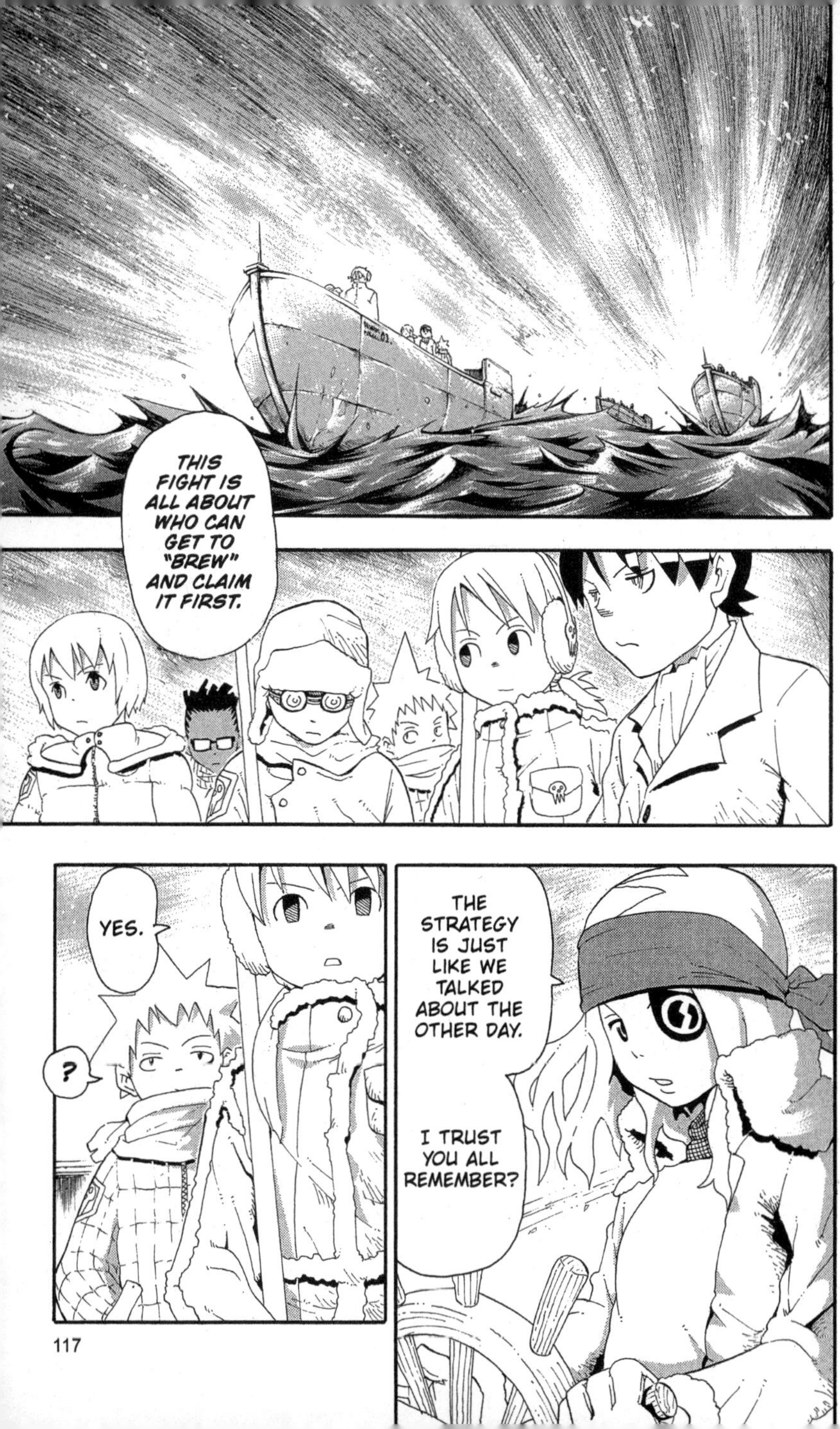
THIS FIGHT IS ALL ABOUT WHO CAN GET TO "BREW" AND CLAIM IT FIRST.
THE STRATEGY IS JUST LIKE WE TALKED ABOUT THE OTHER DAY.
I TRUST YOU ALL REMEMBER?
YES.
?

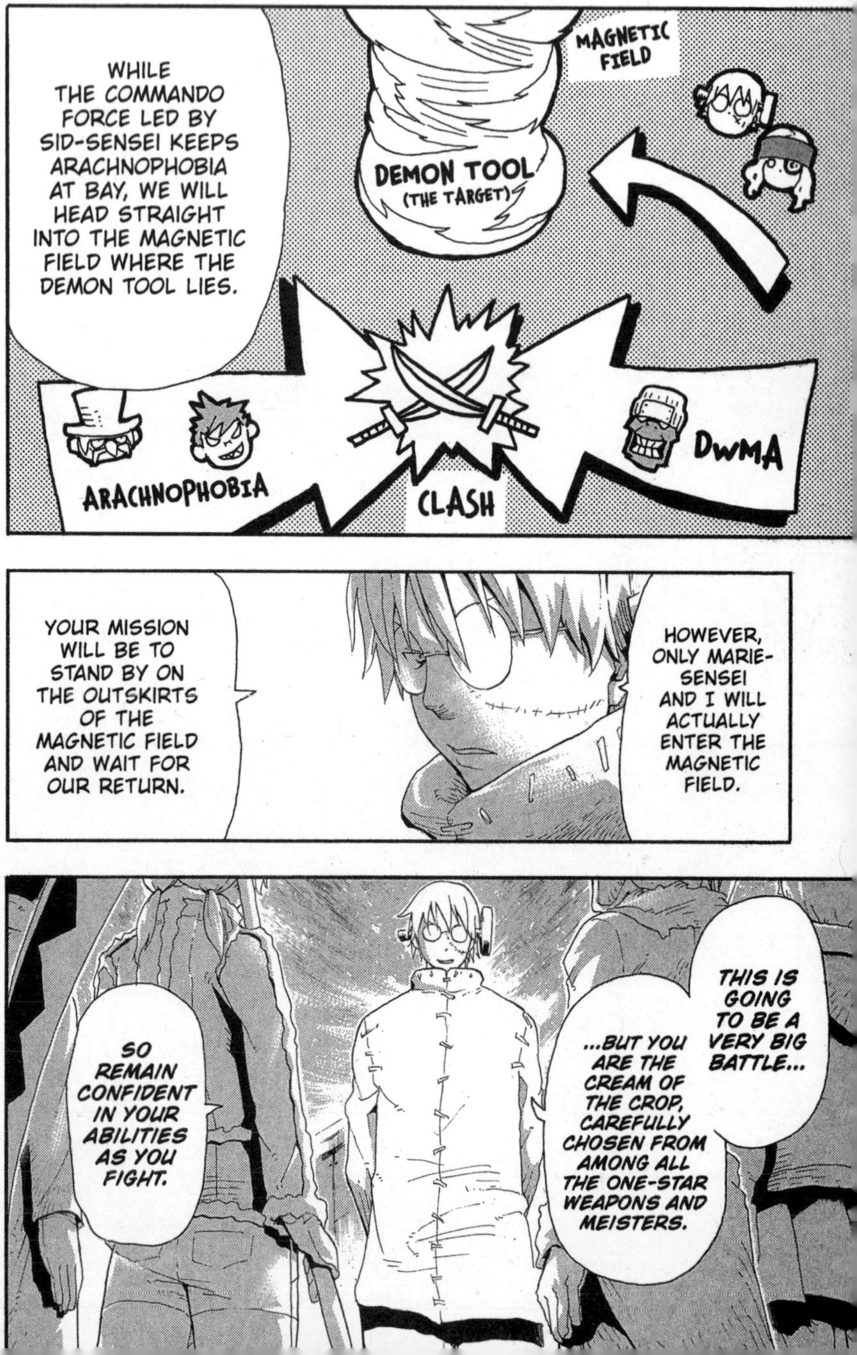
MAGNETIC FIELD
DEMON TOOL (THE TARGET)
WHILE THE COMMANDO FORCE LED BY SID-SENSEI KEEPS ARACHNOPHOBIA AT BAY, WE WILL HEAD STRAIGHT INTO THE MAGNETIC FIELD WHERE THE DEMON TOOL LIES.
DWMA
CLASH
ARACHNOPHOBIA
HOWEVER, ONLY MARIE-SENSEI AND I WILL ACTUALLY ENTER THE MAGNETIC FIELD.
YOUR MISSION WILL BE TO STAND BY ON THE OUTSKIRTS OF THE MAGNETIC FIELD AND WAIT FOR OUR RETURN.
THIS IS GOING TO BE A VERY BIG BATTLE...
...BUT YOU ARE THE CREAM OF THE CROP, CAREFULLY CHOSEN FROM AMONG ALL THE ONE-STAR WEAPONS AND MEISTERS.
SO REMAIN CONFIDENT IN YOUR ABILITIES AS YOU FIGHT.

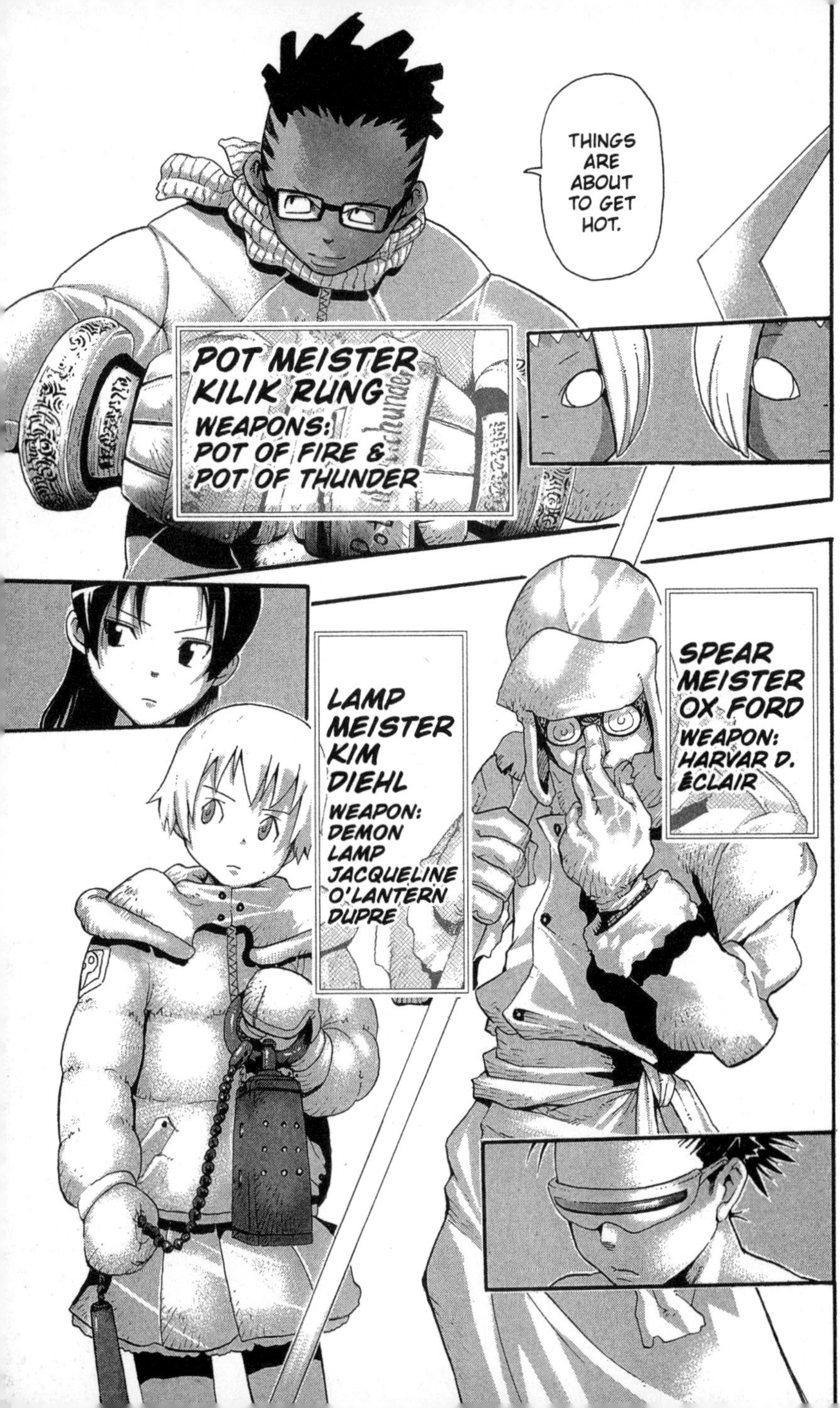
THINGS ARE ABOUT TO GET HOT.
POT MEISTER KILIK RUNG
WEAPONS: POT OF FIRE & POT OF THUNDER
SPEAR MEISTER OX FORD
WEAPON: HARVAR D. ÉCLAIR
LAMP MEISTER KIM DIEHL
WEAPON: DEMON LAMP JACQUELINE O'LANTERN DUPRE

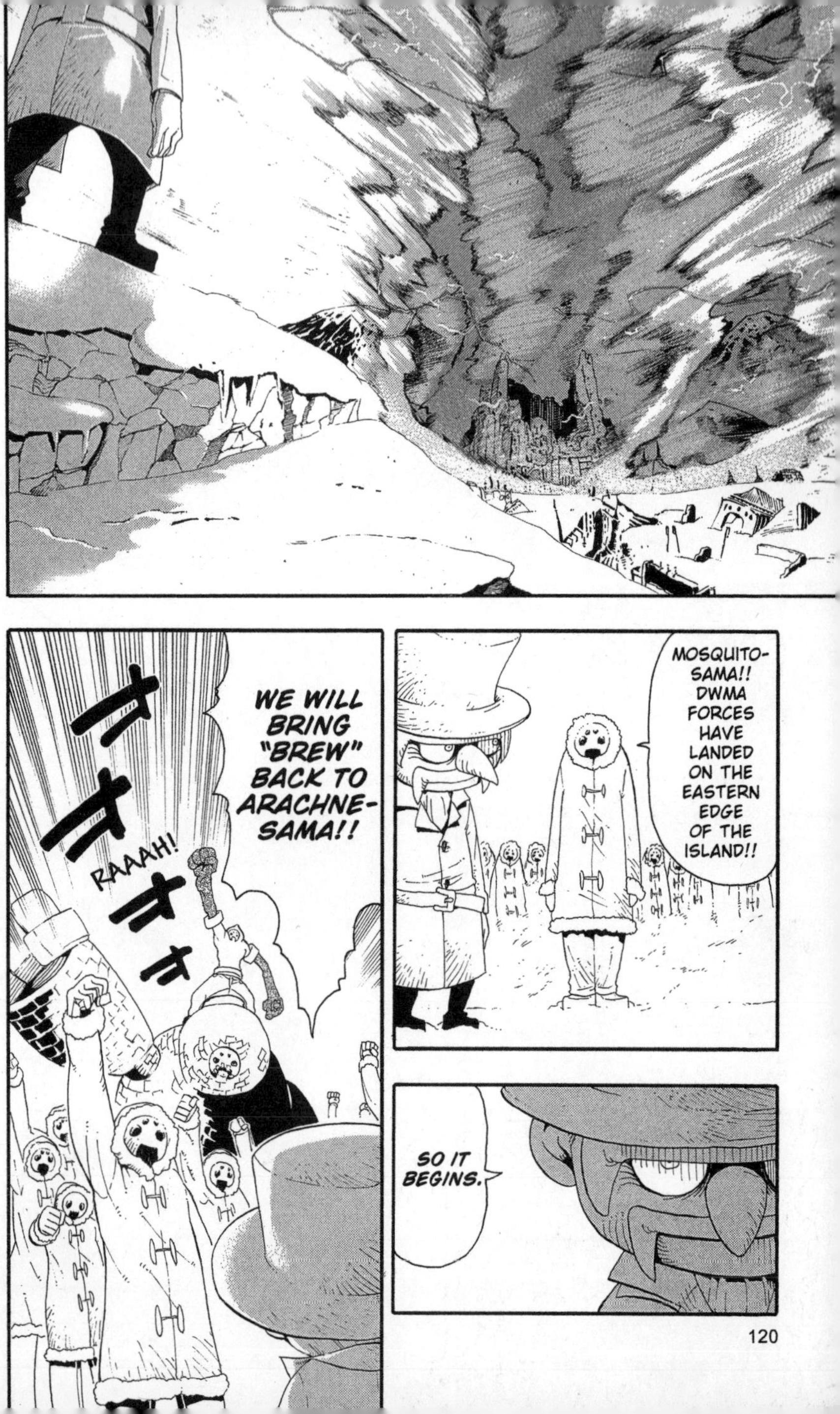
MOSQUITO-SAMA!! DWMA FORCES HAVE LANDED ON THE EASTERN EDGE OF THE ISLAND!!
SO IT BEGINS.
WE WILL BRING "BREW" BACK TO ARACHNE-SAMA!!
オオオォ
RAAAH!

AH...

CAPTAIN BARRETT, SIR... WHAT IS THIS PLACE?

THESE ARE THE REMAINS OF THE OLD DEMON TOOL DEVELOPMENT FACILITY.

MUST'VE BEEN ONE HELL OF AN ACCIDENT.

THIS WHOLE AREA'S IN RUINS.

ZA

ZA (CRUNCH)

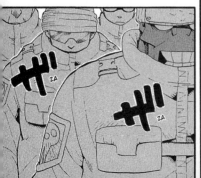

ZA

ZA

ROGER!

OOOO (WHOOO)

KEEP YOUR EYES PEELED, BOYS! SOUL-SENSING ABILITIES ARE BASICALLY USELESS HERE, AND OUR RADIOS ARE ON THE FRITZ TOO, ALL ON ACCOUNT OF THIS DAMN MAGNETIC FIELD.

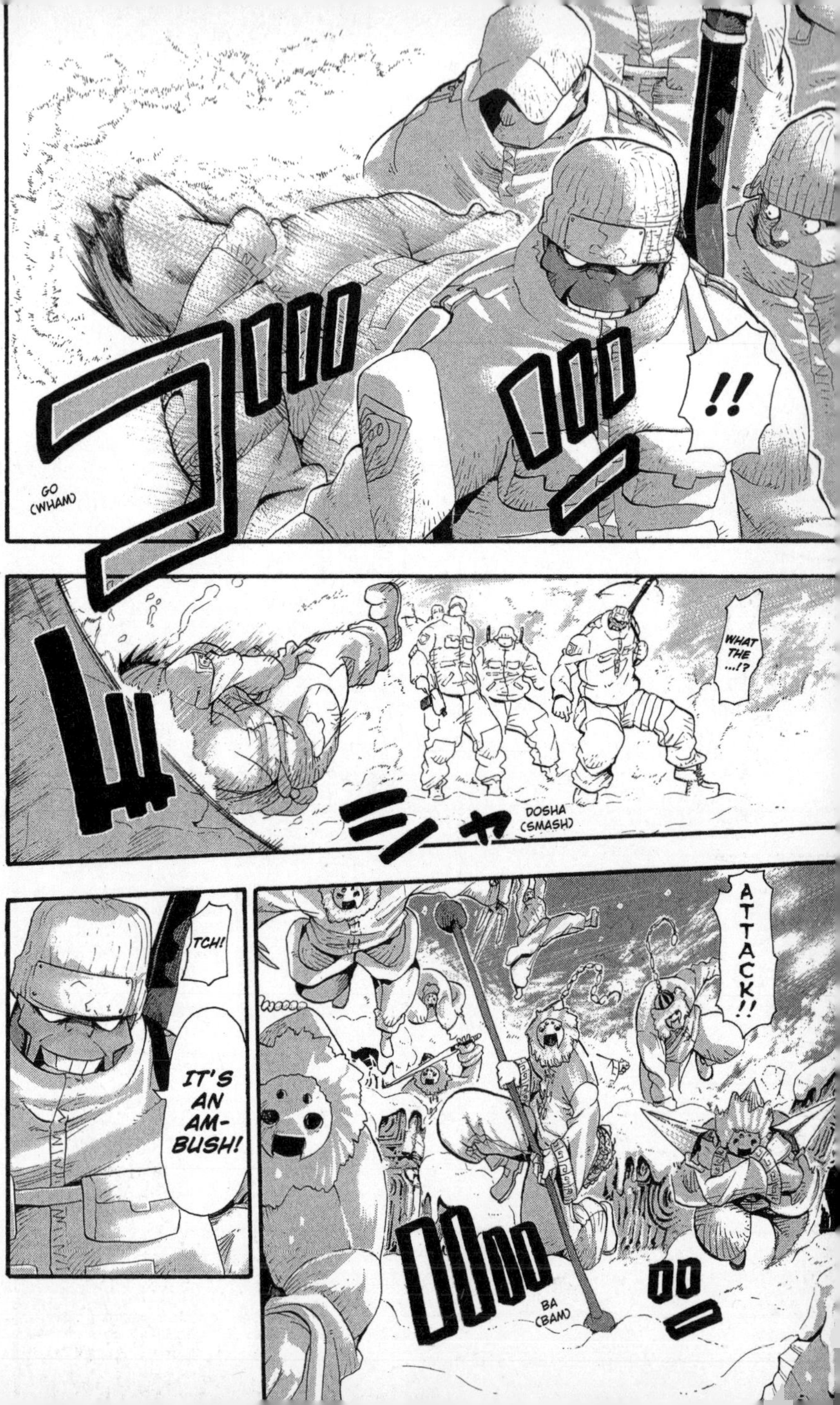
!!
GO (WHAM)
WHAT THE ...!?
DOSHA (SMASH)
ATTACK!!
BA (BAM)
TCH!
IT'S AN AM-BUSH!

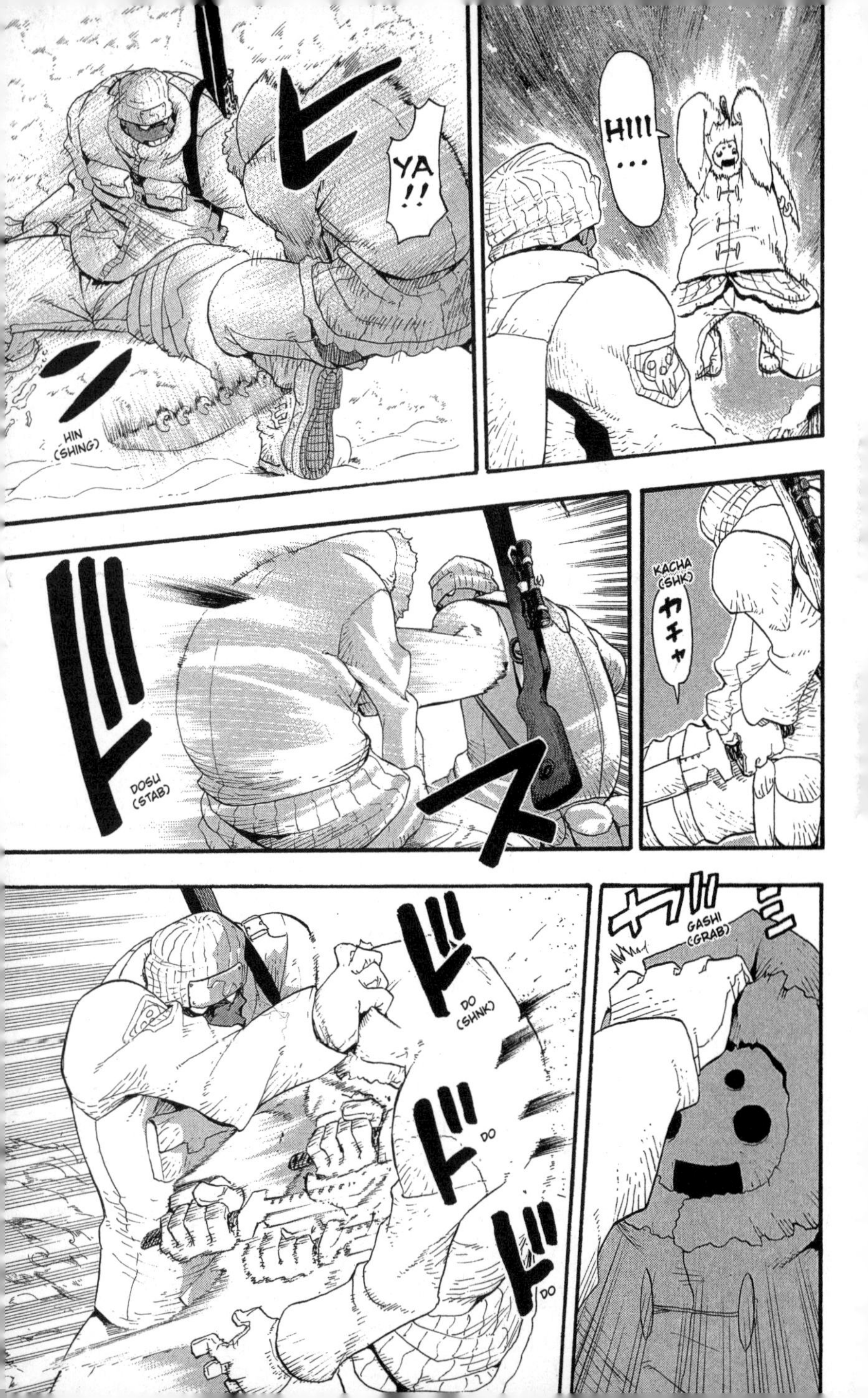
HI!!! ...
YA !!
HIN (SHING)
KACHA (SHK)
カチャ
DOSU (STAB)
GASHI (GRAB)
DO (SHNK)
DO
DO

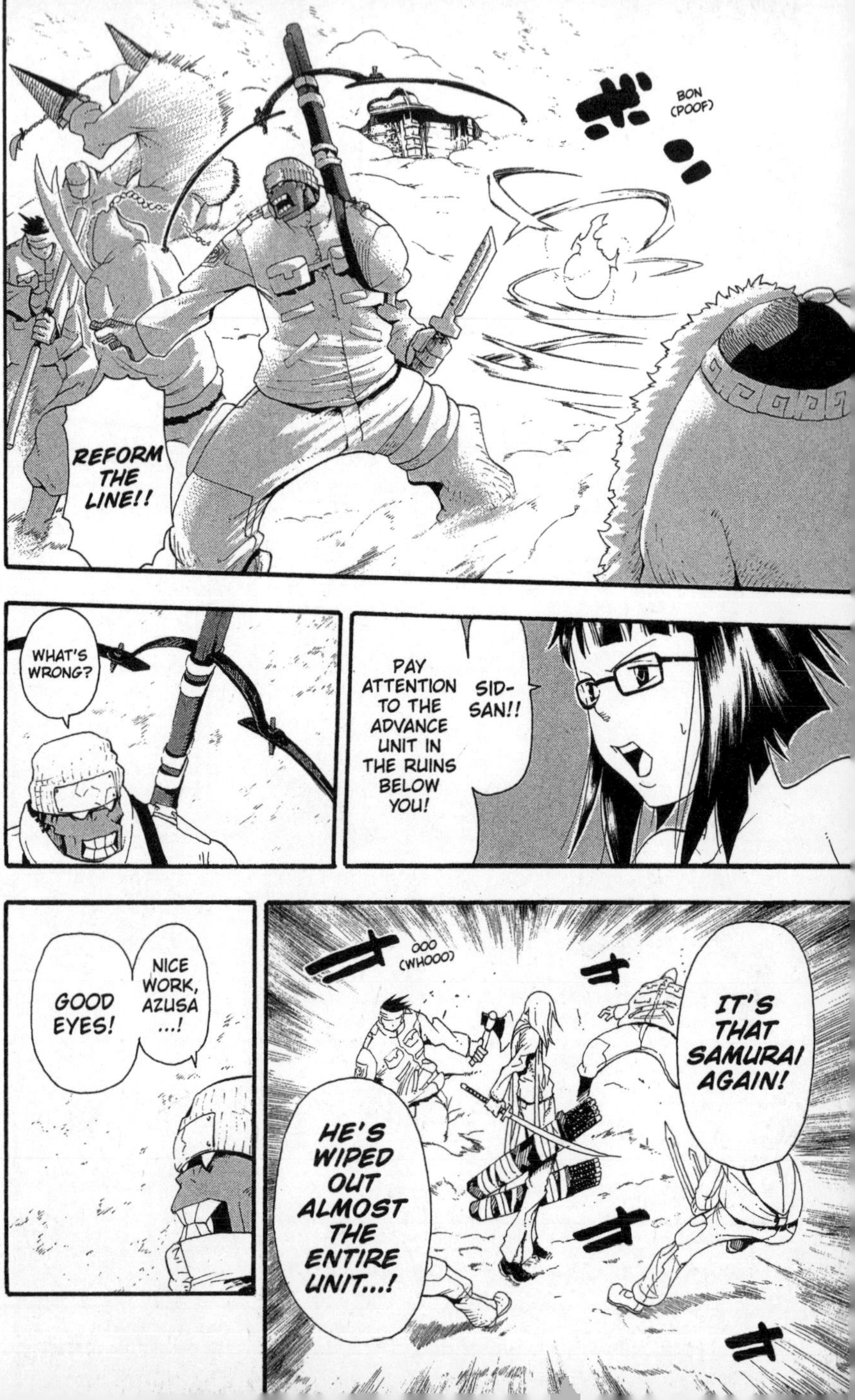
BON (POOF)
REFORM THE LINE!!
SID-SAN!!
PAY ATTENTION TO THE ADVANCE UNIT IN THE RUINS BELOW YOU!
WHAT'S WRONG?
OOO (WHOOO)
IT'S THAT SAMURAI AGAIN!
HE'S WIPED OUT ALMOST THE ENTIRE UNIT...!
NICE WORK, AZUSA...!
GOOD EYES!

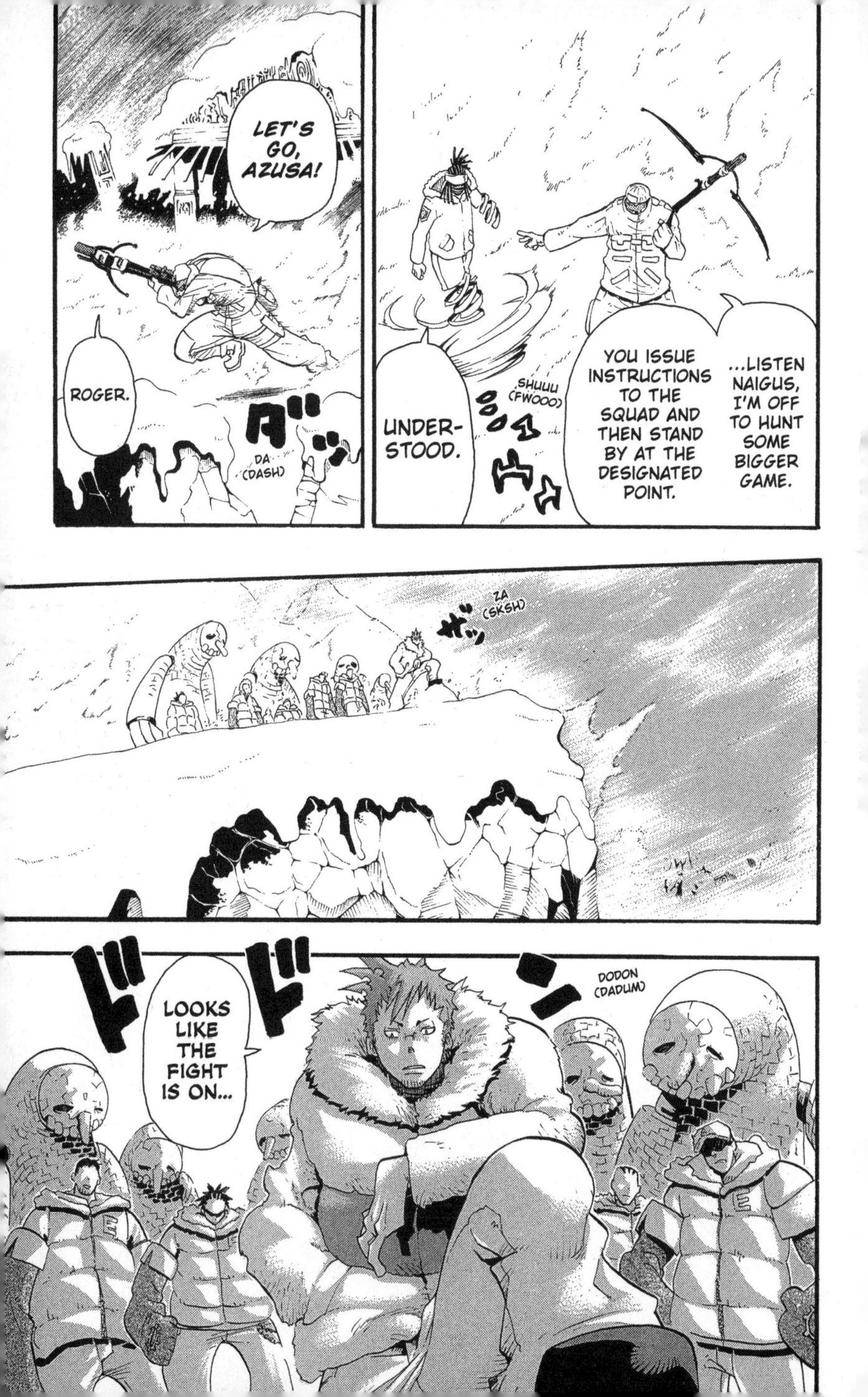
...LISTEN NAIGUS, I'M OFF TO HUNT SOME BIGGER GAME.
YOU ISSUE INSTRUCTIONS TO THE SQUAD AND THEN STAND BY AT THE DESIGNATED POINT.
UNDER-STOOD.
SHUUU (FWOOO)
LET'S GO, AZUSA!
ROGER.
DA (DASH)
ZA (SKSH)
DODON (DADUM)
LOOKS LIKE THE FIGHT IS ON...

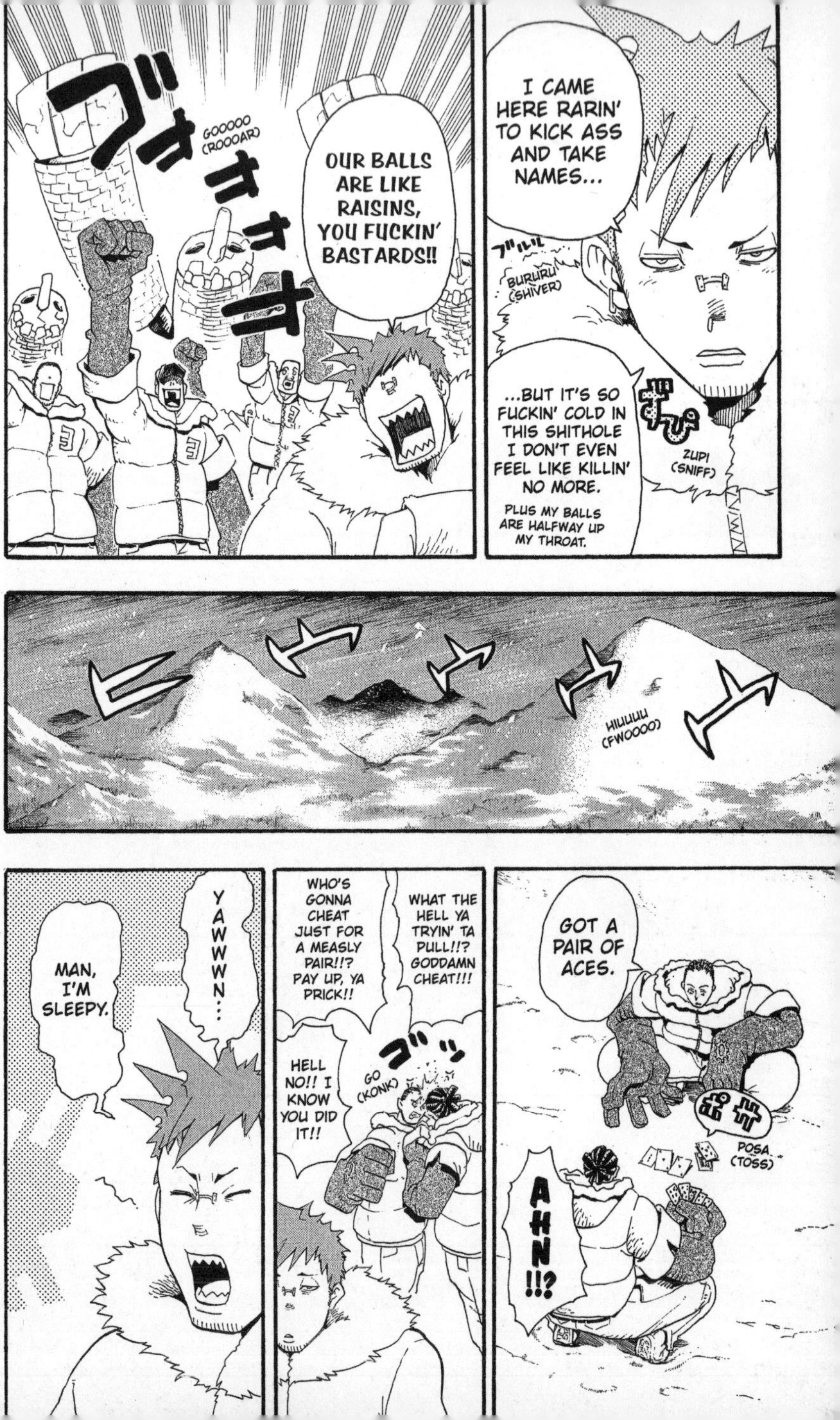
I CAME HERE RARIN' TO KICK ASS AND TAKE NAMES...
BURURU (SHIVER)
...BUT IT'S SO FUCKIN' COLD IN THIS SHITHOLE I DON'T EVEN FEEL LIKE KILLIN' NO MORE.
PLUS MY BALLS ARE HALFWAY UP MY THROAT.
ZUPI (SNIFF)
GOOOOO (ROOOAR)
OUR BALLS ARE LIKE RAISINS, YOU FUCKIN' BASTARDS!!
HIUUUU (FWOOOO)
GOT A PAIR OF ACES.
POSA (TOSS)
AHN!!?
WHAT THE HELL YA TRYIN' TA PULL!!? GODDAMN CHEAT!!!
WHO'S GONNA CHEAT JUST FOR A MEASLY PAIR!!? PAY UP, YA PRICK!!
GO (KONK)
HELL NO!! I KNOW YOU DID IT!!
YAWWWN...
MAN, I'M SLEEPY.

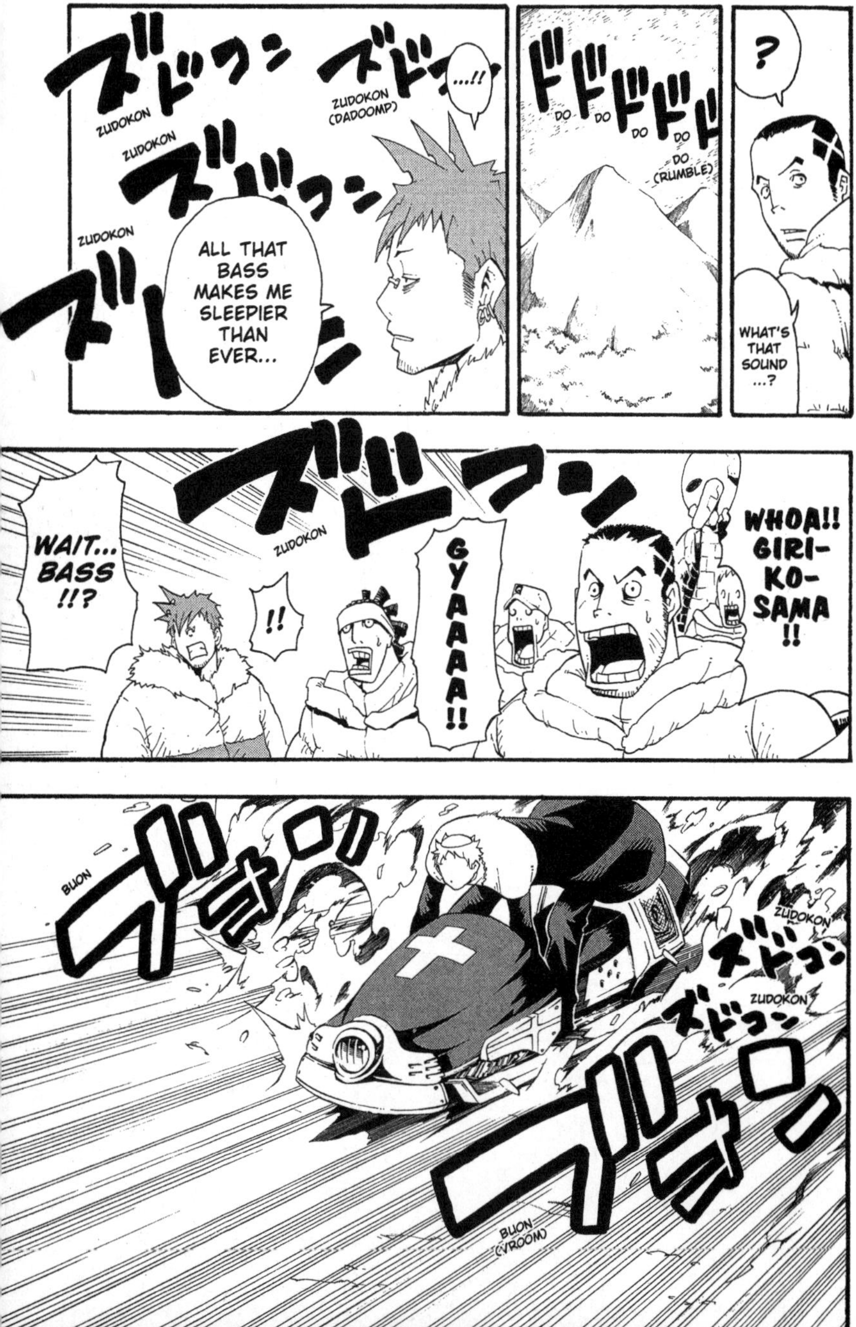
?
WHAT'S THAT SOUND ...?
DO
DO
DO
DO
DO (RUMBLE)
...!!
ZUDOKON (DADOOMP)
ZUDOKON
ZUDOKON
ALL THAT BASS MAKES ME SLEEPIER THAN EVER...
ZUDOKON
WHOA!! GIRI-KO-SAMA!!
GYAAAAA!!
ZUDOKON
!!
WAIT... BASS!!?
ZUDOKON
ZUDOKON
BUON (VROOM)
BUON

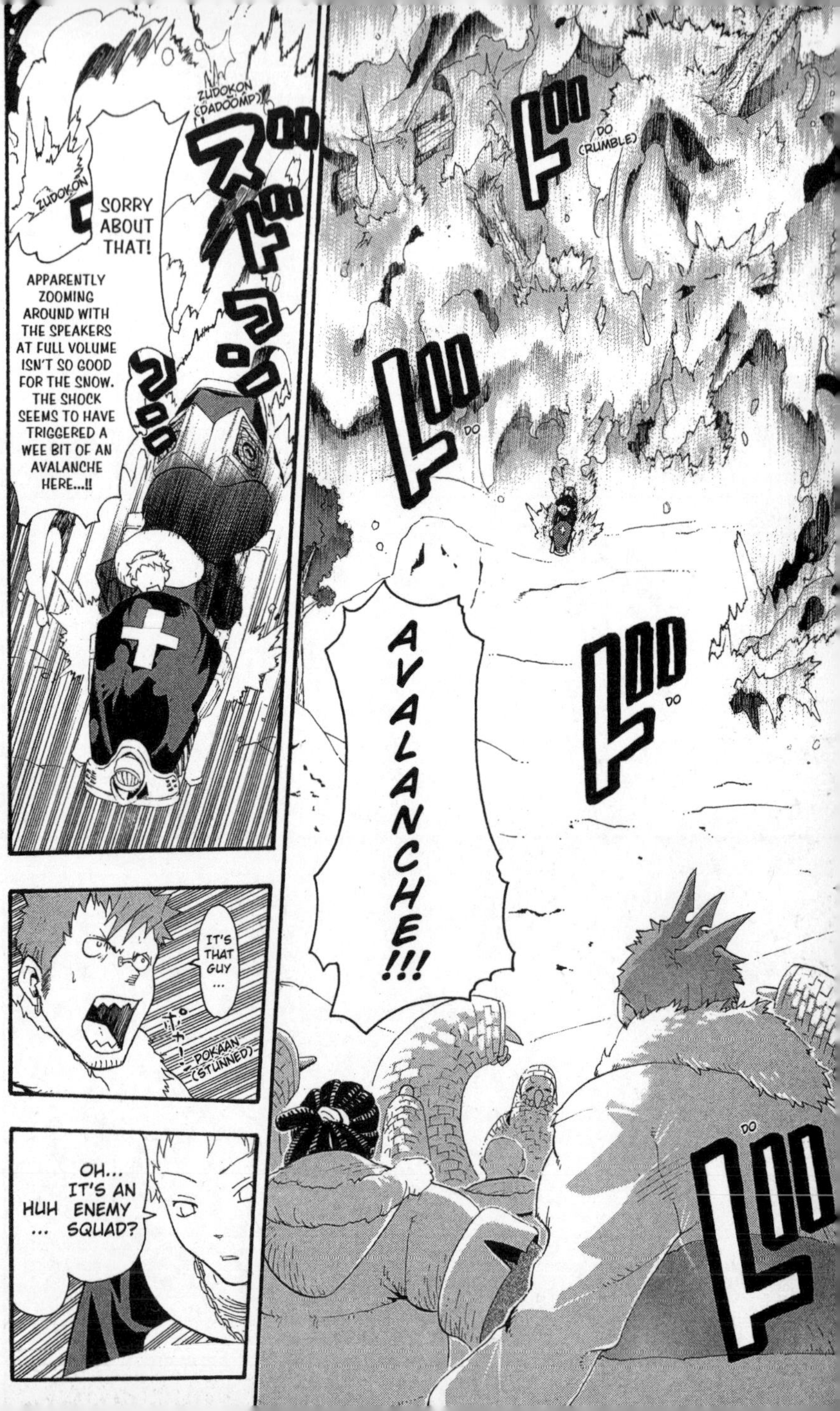
DO (RUMBLE)
DO
AVALANCHE!!!
DO
DO
ZUDOKON (DADOOMP)
ZUDOKON
SORRY ABOUT THAT!
APPARENTLY ZOOMING AROUND WITH THE SPEAKERS AT FULL VOLUME ISN'T SO GOOD FOR THE SNOW. THE SHOCK SEEMS TO HAVE TRIGGERED A WEE BIT OF AN AVALANCHE HERE...!!
IT'S THAT GUY...
POKAAN (STUNNED)
OH... IT'S AN ENEMY SQUAD?
HUH...

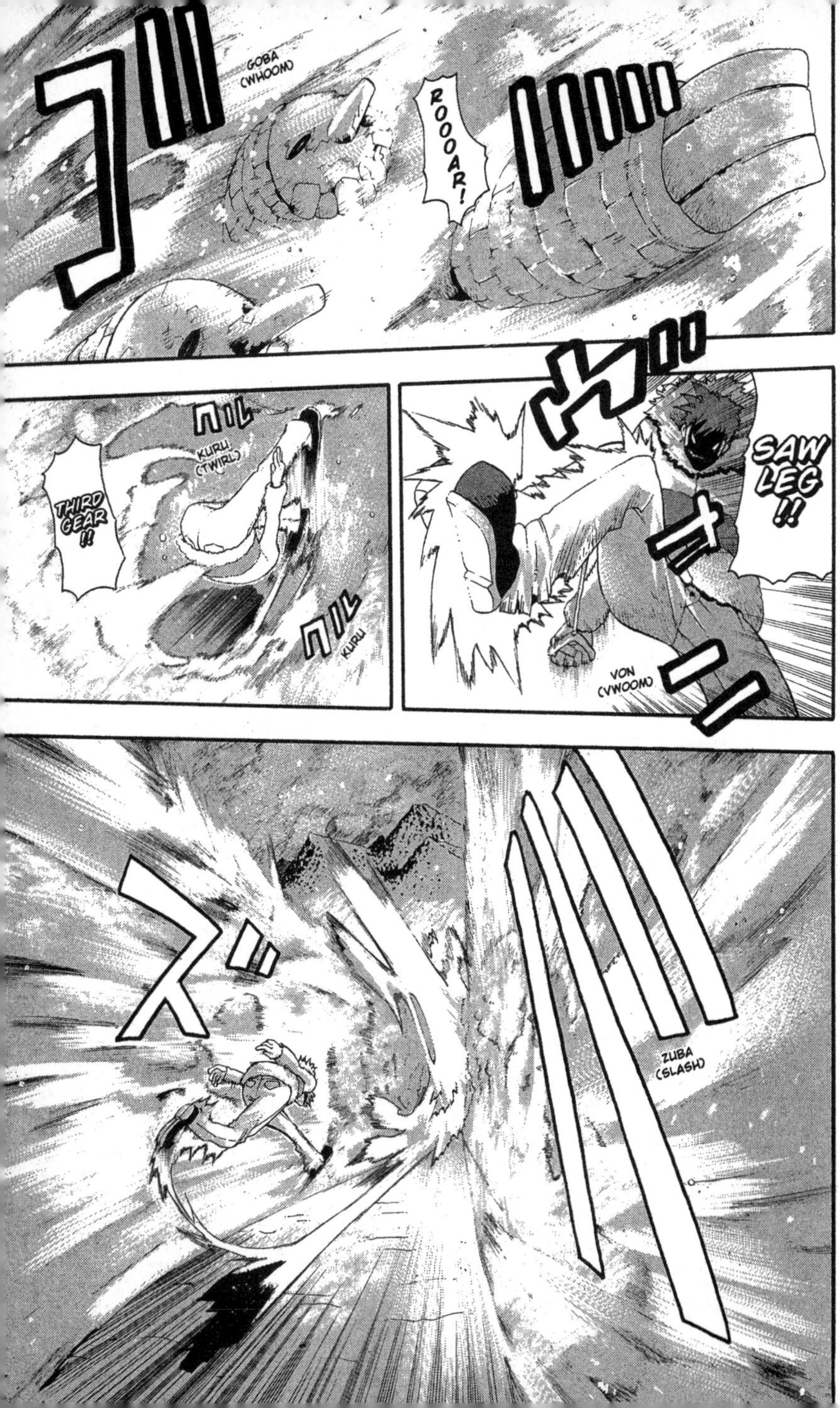
ROOOOAR!
GOBA (WHOOM)
SAW LEG!!
VON (VWOOM)
THIRD GEAR!!
KURU (TWIRL)
KURU
ZUBA (SLASH)

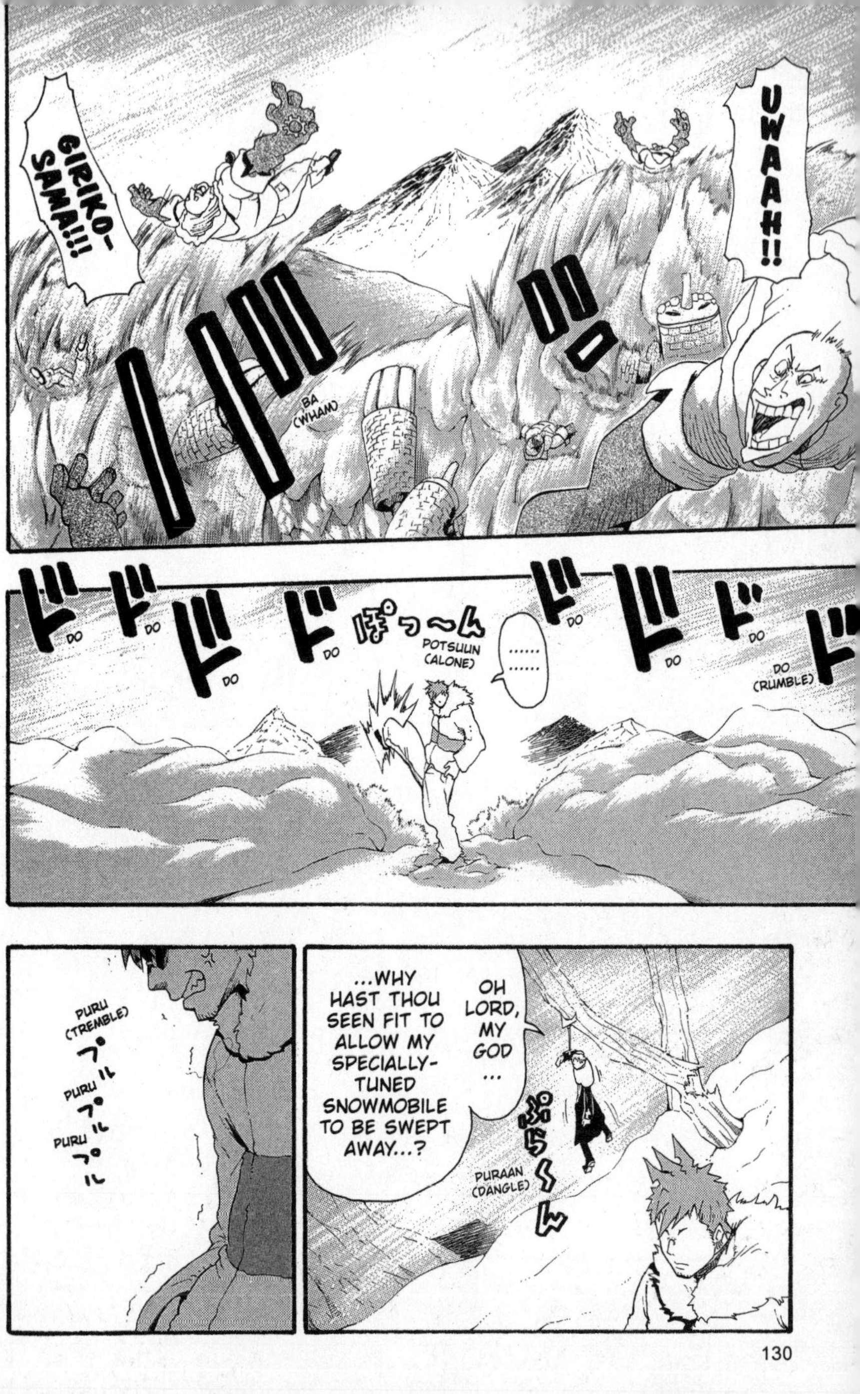
UWAAH!!
GIRIKO-SAMA!!!
BA (WHAM)
DO (RUMBLE)
DO
DO
DO
......
......
ぽっ～ん
POTSUUN (ALONE)
DO
DO
DO
DO
OH LORD, MY GOD ...
...WHY HAST THOU SEEN FIT TO ALLOW MY SPECIALLY-TUNED SNOWMOBILE TO BE SWEPT AWAY...?
PURAAN (DANGLE)
PURU (TREMBLE)
PURU
PURU

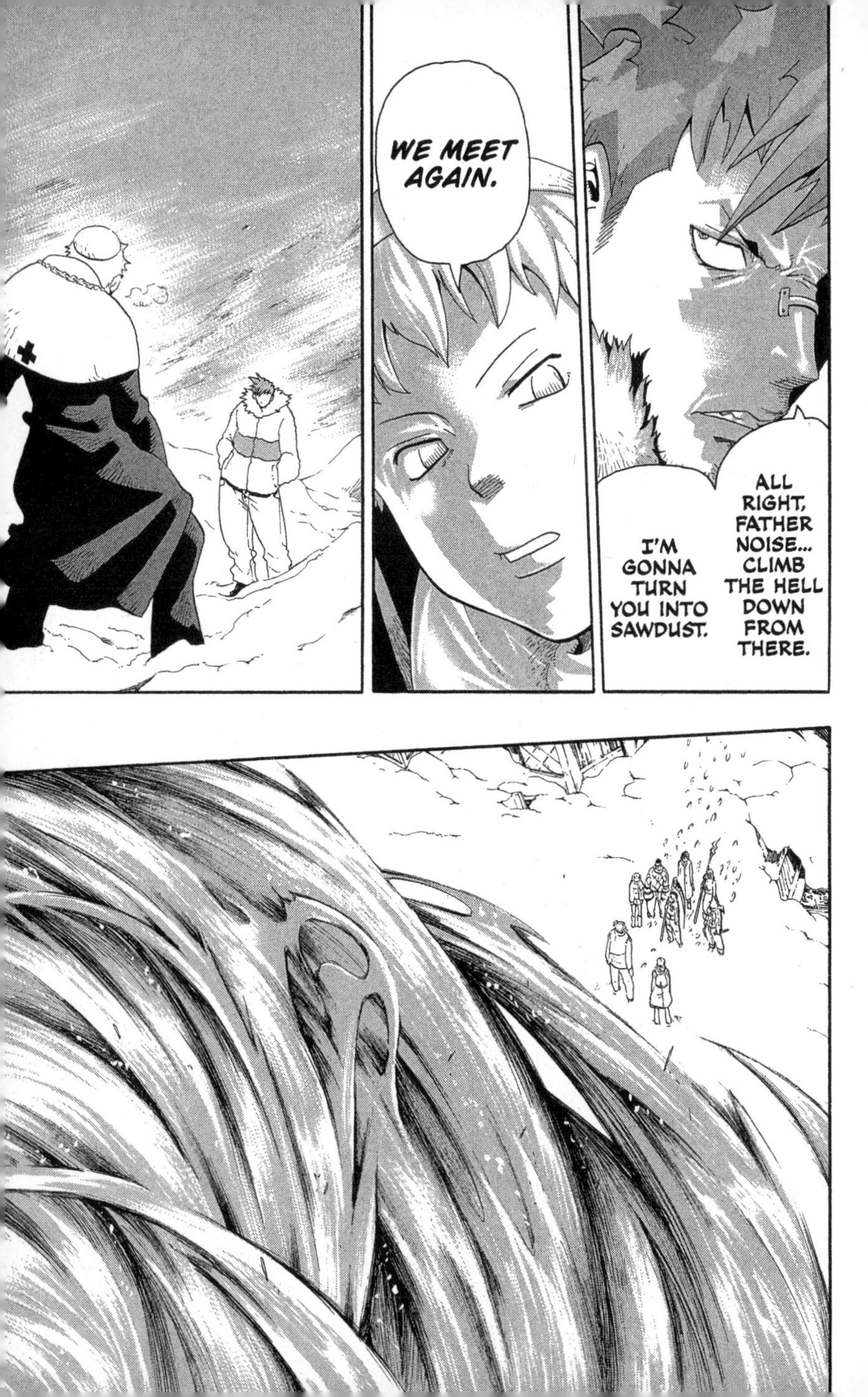
ALL RIGHT, FATHER NOISE... CLIMB THE HELL DOWN FROM THERE.
I'M GONNA TURN YOU INTO SAWDUST.
WE MEET AGAIN.

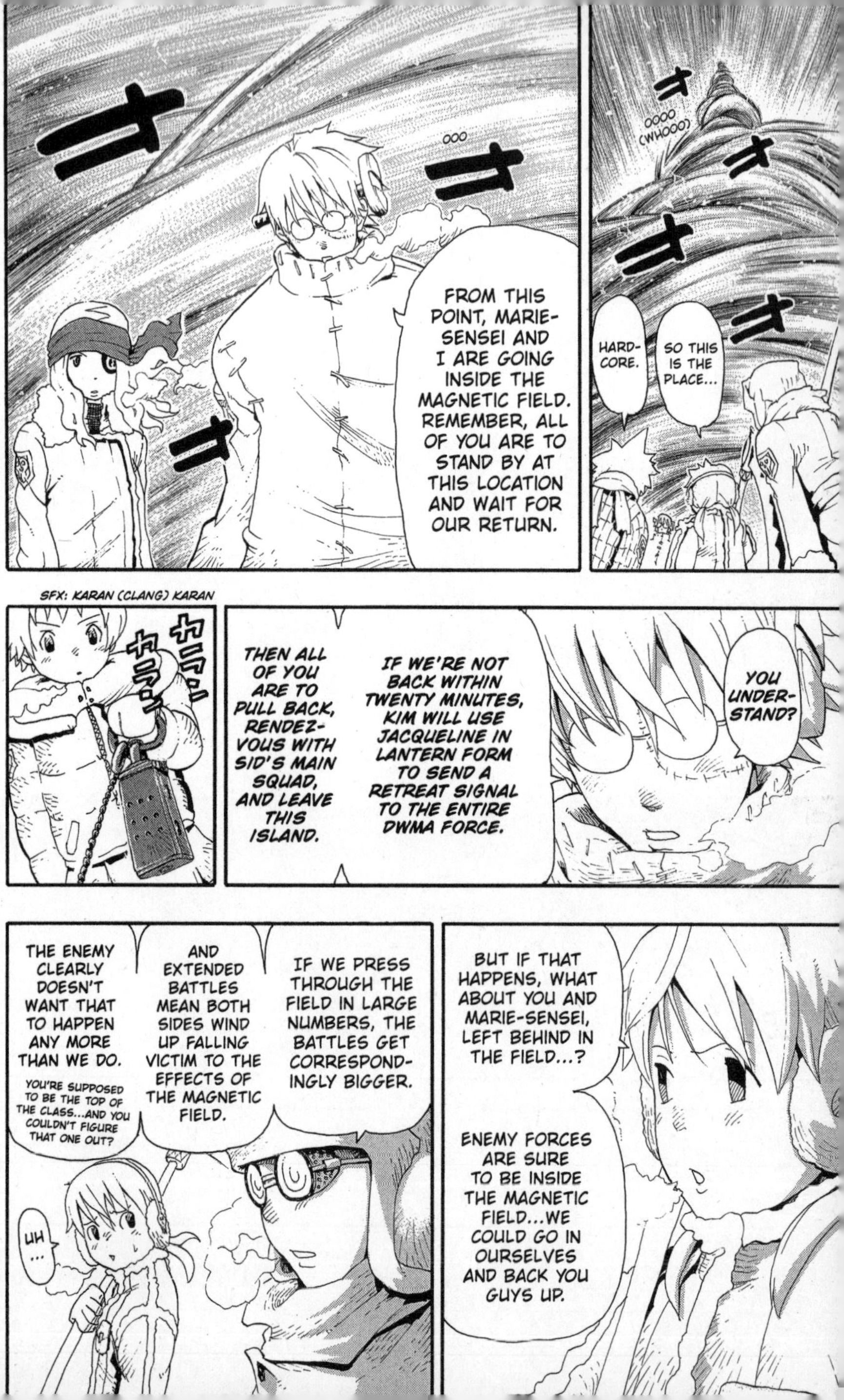
OOOO (WHOOO)
SO THIS IS THE PLACE...
HARD-CORE.
OOO
FROM THIS POINT, MARIE-SENSEI AND I ARE GOING INSIDE THE MAGNETIC FIELD. REMEMBER, ALL OF YOU ARE TO STAND BY AT THIS LOCATION AND WAIT FOR OUR RETURN.
YOU UNDERSTAND?
IF WE'RE NOT BACK WITHIN TWENTY MINUTES, KIM WILL USE JACQUELINE IN LANTERN FORM TO SEND A RETREAT SIGNAL TO THE ENTIRE DWMA FORCE.
THEN ALL OF YOU ARE TO PULL BACK, RENDEZVOUS WITH SID'S MAIN SQUAD, AND LEAVE THIS ISLAND.
SFX: KARAN (CLANG) KARAN
BUT IF THAT HAPPENS, WHAT ABOUT YOU AND MARIE-SENSEI, LEFT BEHIND IN THE FIELD...?
ENEMY FORCES ARE SURE TO BE INSIDE THE MAGNETIC FIELD...WE COULD GO IN OURSELVES AND BACK YOU GUYS UP.
IF WE PRESS THROUGH THE FIELD IN LARGE NUMBERS, THE BATTLES GET CORRESPONDINGLY BIGGER.
AND EXTENDED BATTLES MEAN BOTH SIDES WIND UP FALLING VICTIM TO THE EFFECTS OF THE MAGNETIC FIELD.
THE ENEMY CLEARLY DOESN'T WANT THAT TO HAPPEN ANY MORE THAN WE DO.
YOU'RE SUPPOSED TO BE THE TOP OF THE CLASS...AND YOU COULDN'T FIGURE THAT ONE OUT?
UH...

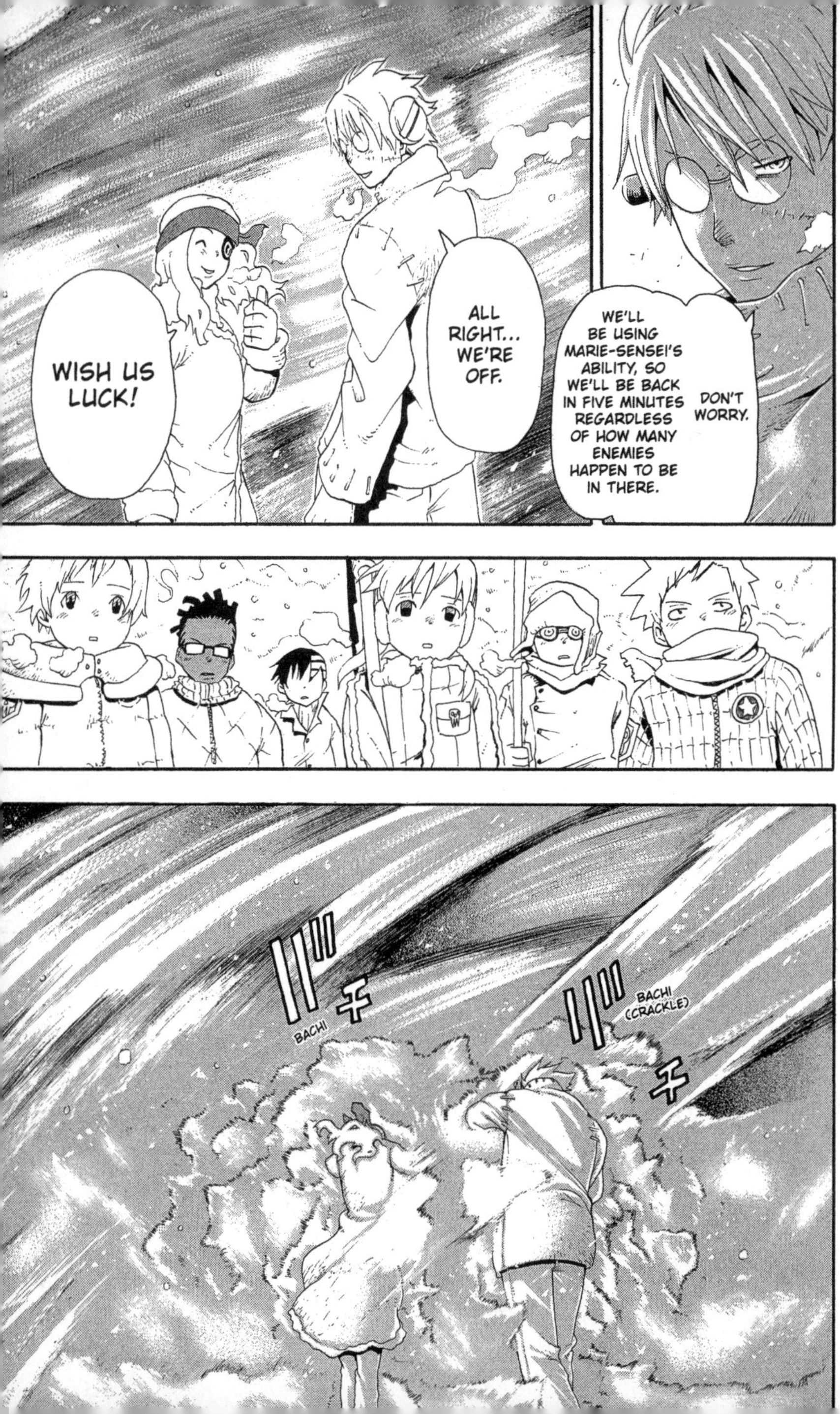
DON'T WORRY.
WE'LL BE USING MARIE-SENSEI'S ABILITY, SO WE'LL BE BACK IN FIVE MINUTES REGARDLESS OF HOW MANY ENEMIES HAPPEN TO BE IN THERE.
ALL RIGHT... WE'RE OFF.
WISH US LUCK!
BACHI (CRACKLE)
BACHI

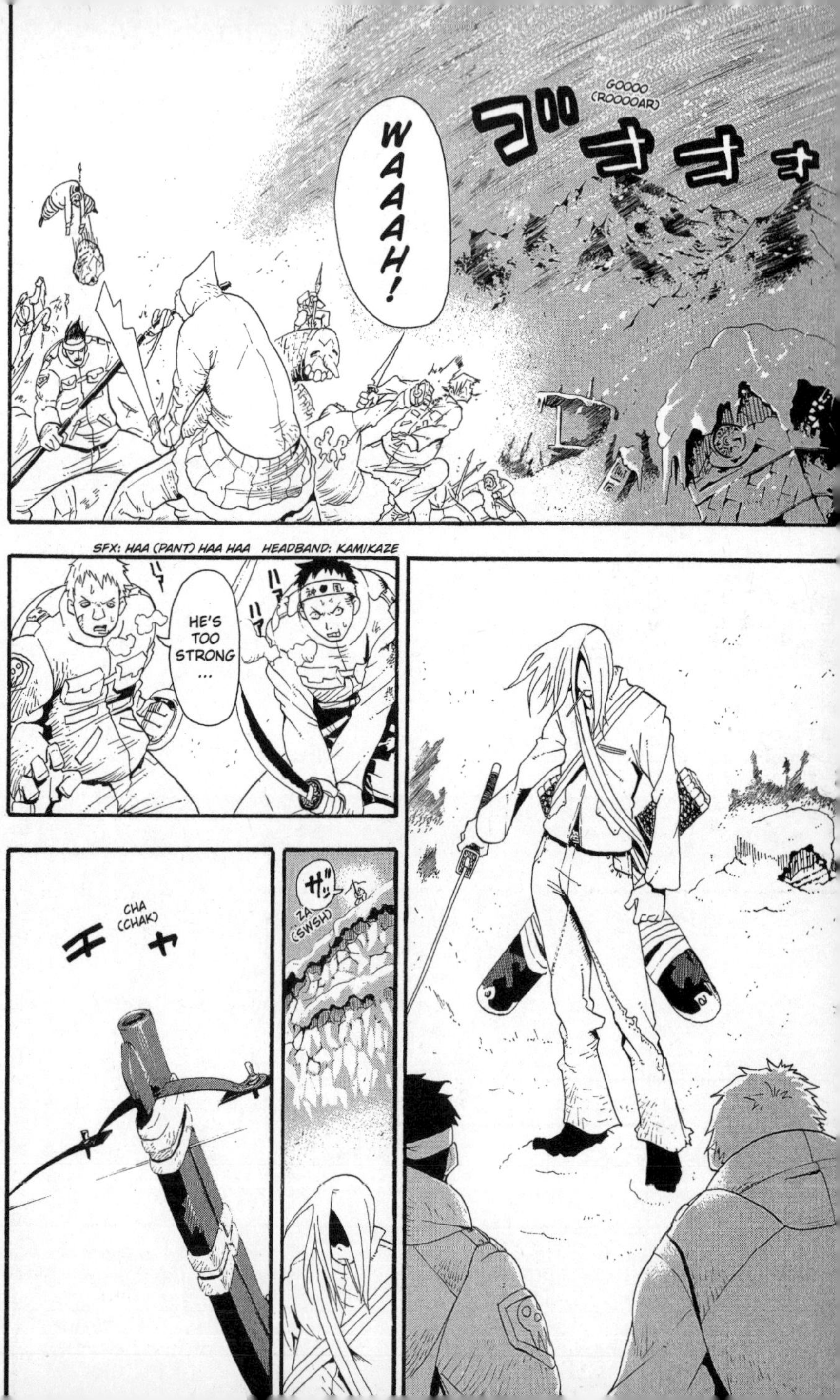
ゴオオォ
GOOOO (ROOOOAR)
WAAAAH!
SFX: HAA (PANT) HAA HAA HEADBAND: KAMIKAZE
HE'S TOO STRONG ...
ザッ
ZA (SWSH)
チャ
CHA (CHAK)

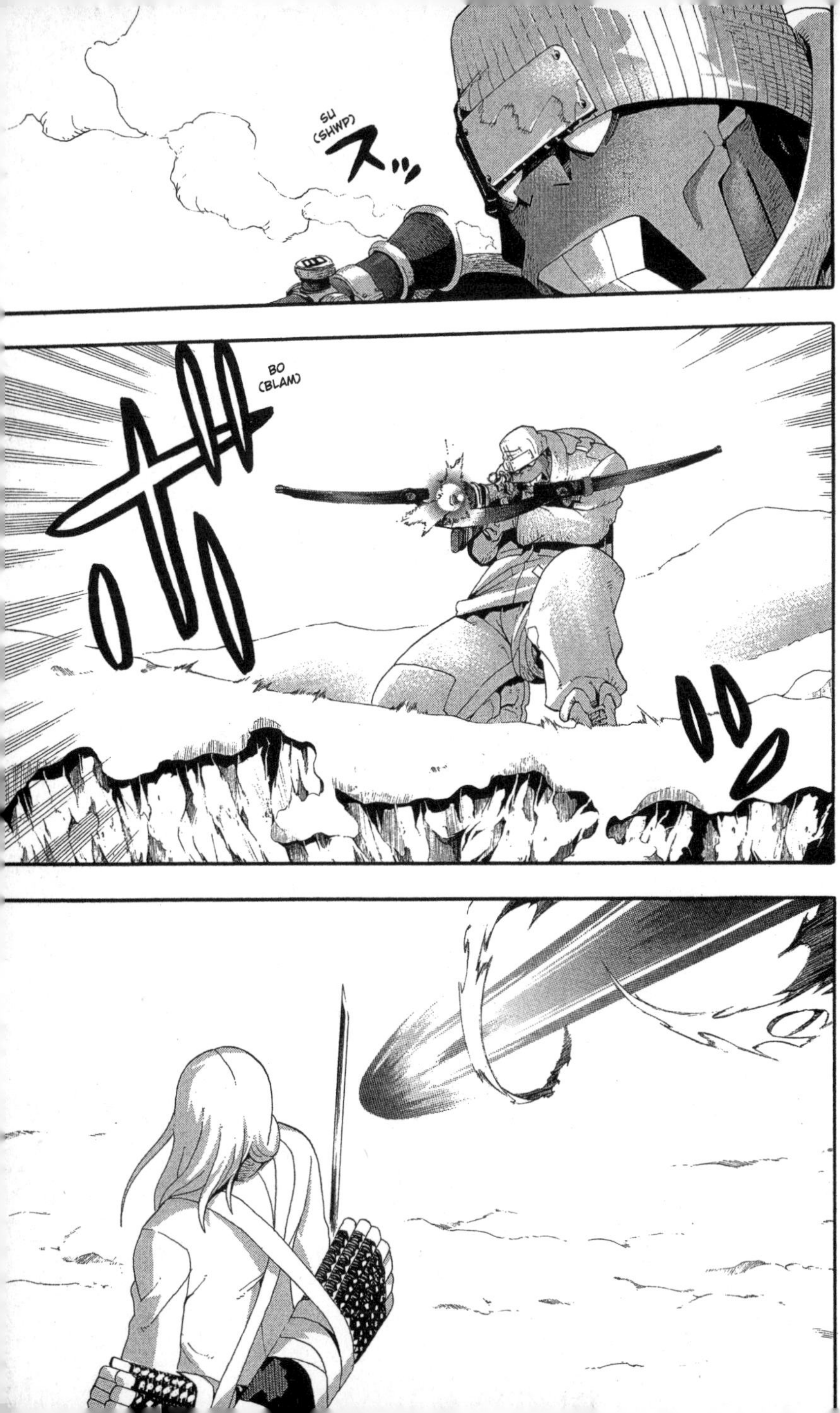
SU (SHWP)
スッ
BO (BLAM)

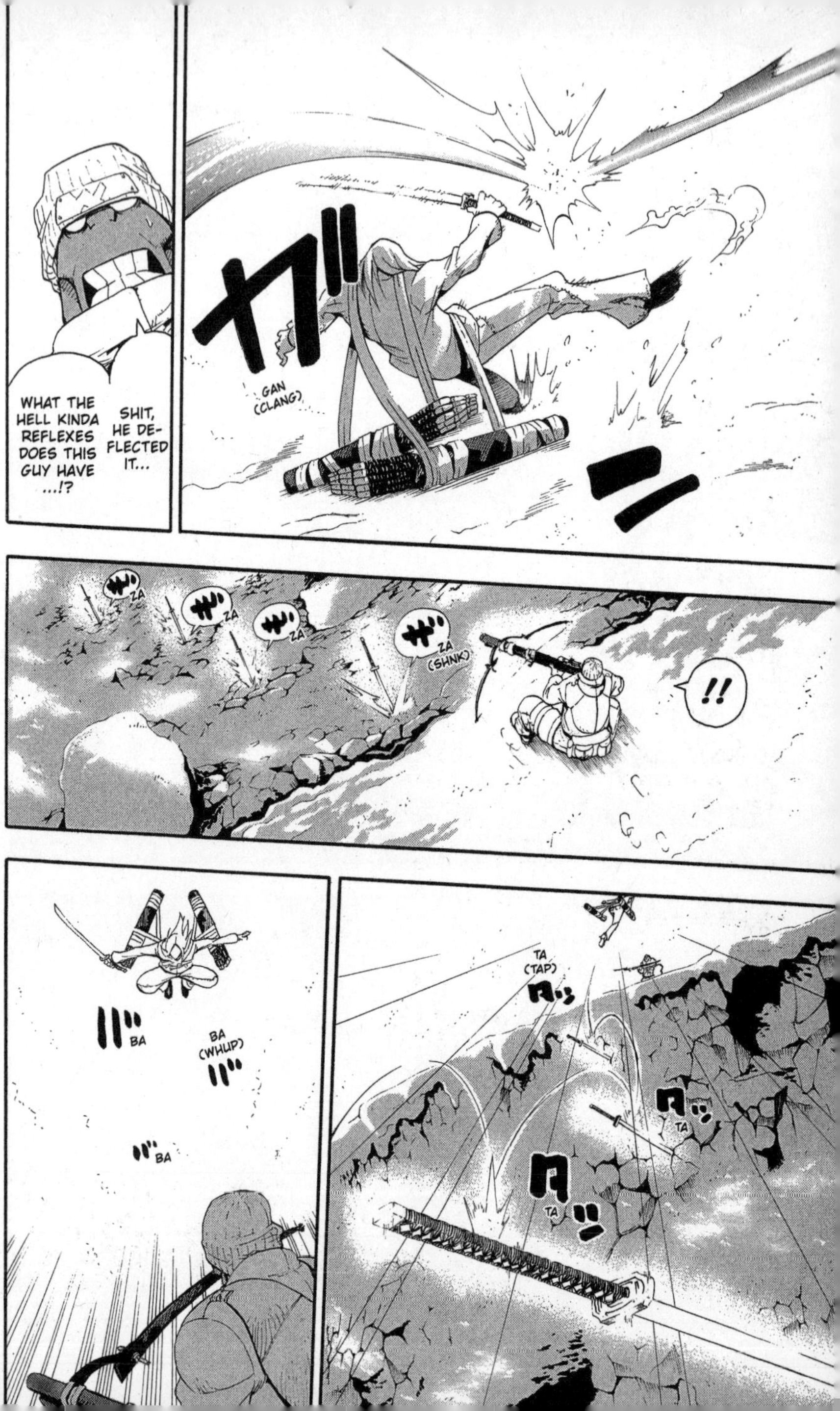
GAN
(CLANG)
SHIT, HE DEFLECTED IT...
WHAT THE HELL KINDA REFLEXES DOES THIS GUY HAVE ...!?
!!
ZA
(SHNK)
ZA
ZA
ZA
TA
(TAP)
TA
TA
BA
(WHUP)
BA
BA

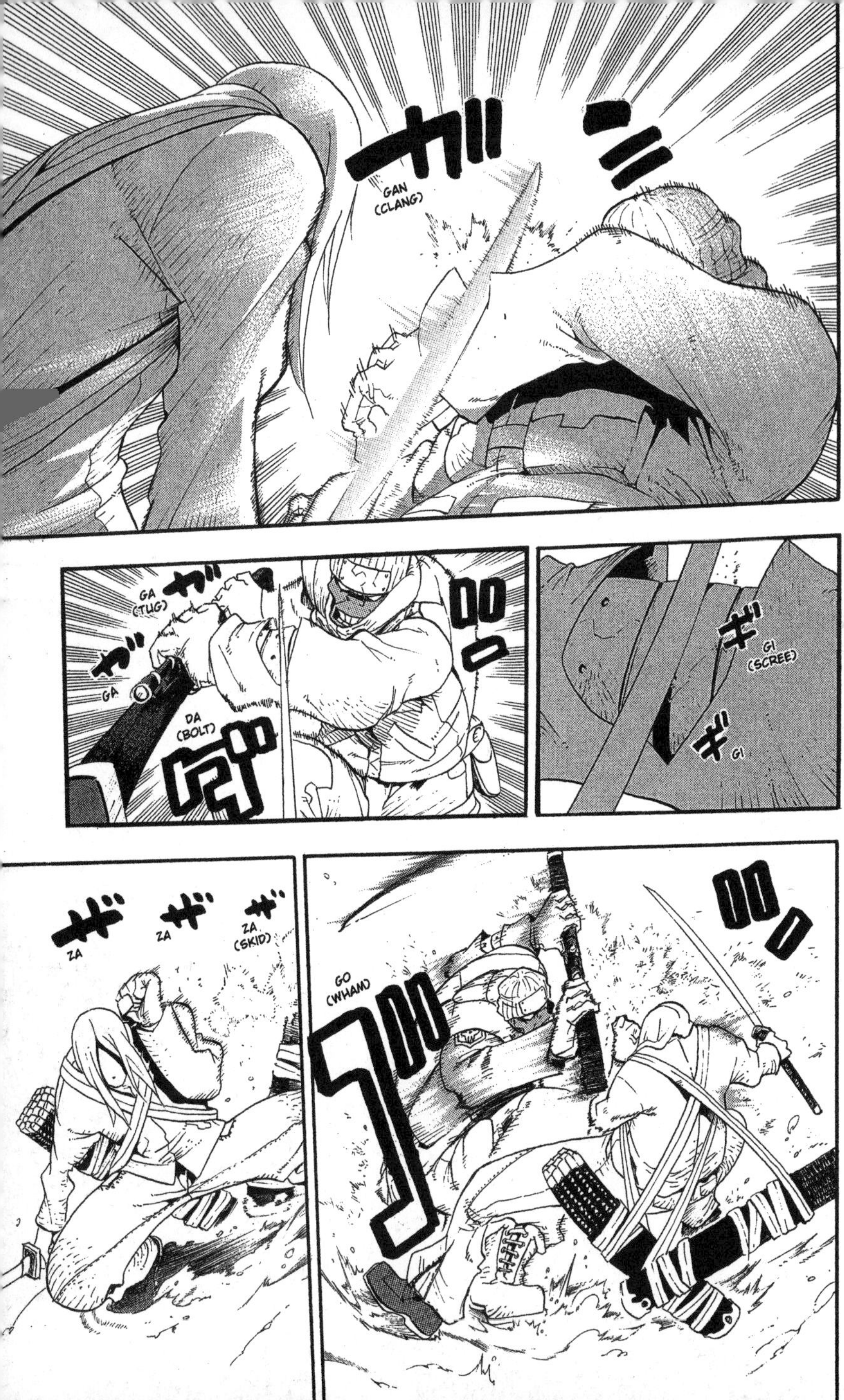
GAN
(CLANG)
GI
(SCREE)
GI
GA
(TUG)
GA
DA
(BOLT)
GO
(WHAM)
ZA
(SKID)
ZA
ZA

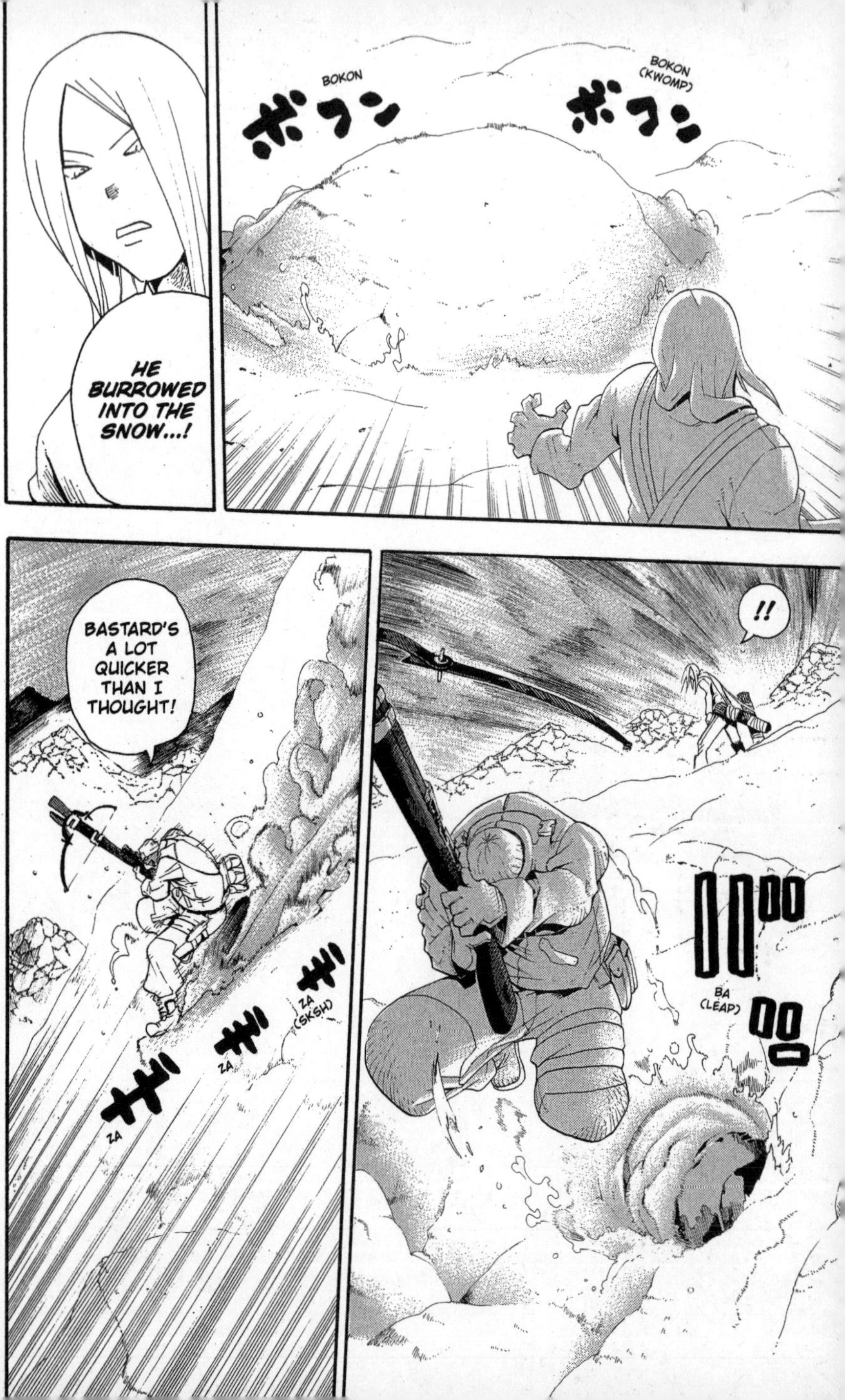
ボコン
BOKON (KWOMP)
ボコン
BOKON
HE BURROWED INTO THE SNOW...!
!!
BA (LEAP)
BASTARD'S A LOT QUICKER THAN I THOUGHT!
ZA (SKSH)
ZA
ZA

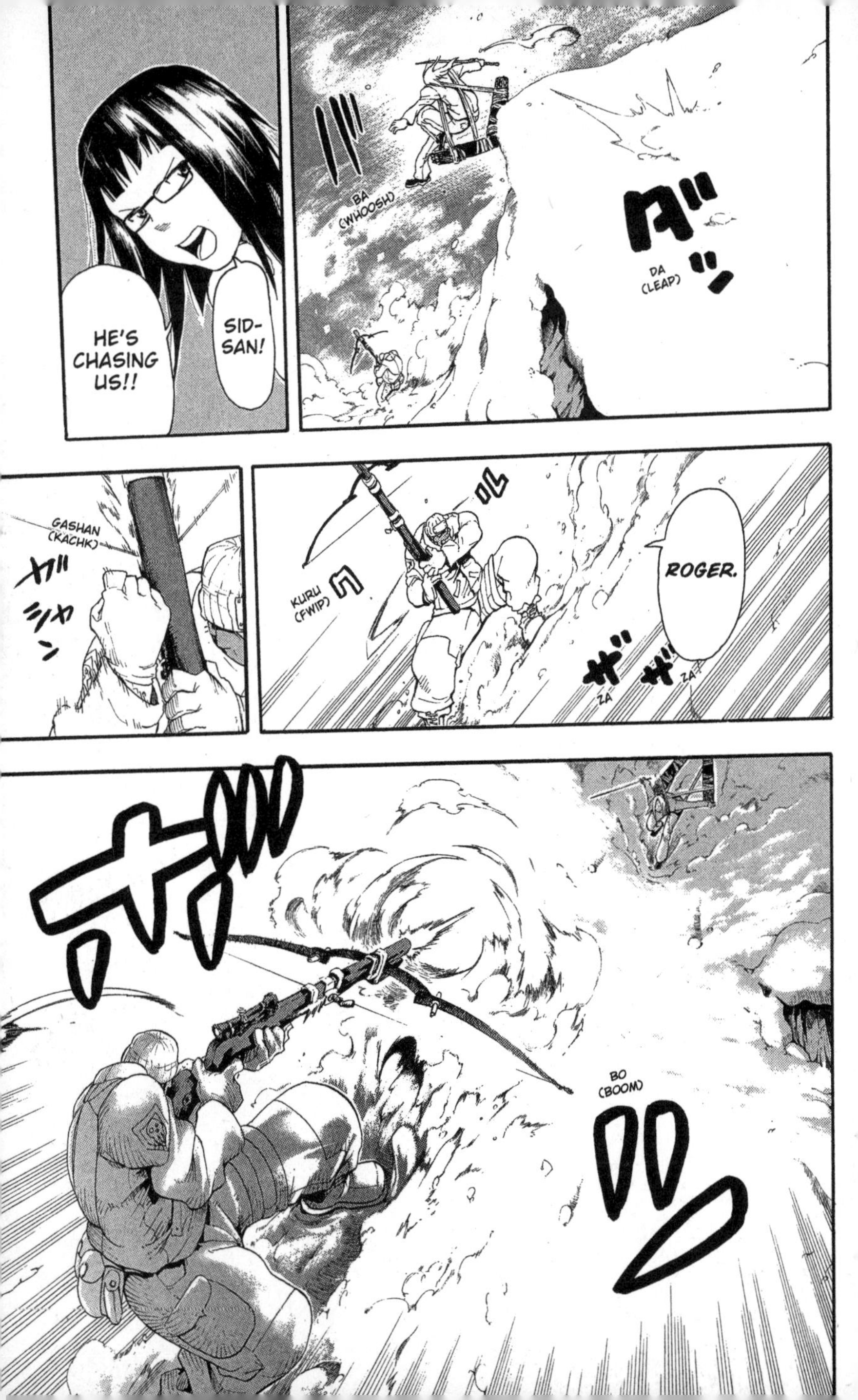
BA (WHOOSH)
DA (LEAP)
SID-SAN!
HE'S CHASING US!!
ROGER.
KURU (FWIP)
ZA
ZA
GASHAN (KACHK)
BO (BOOM)

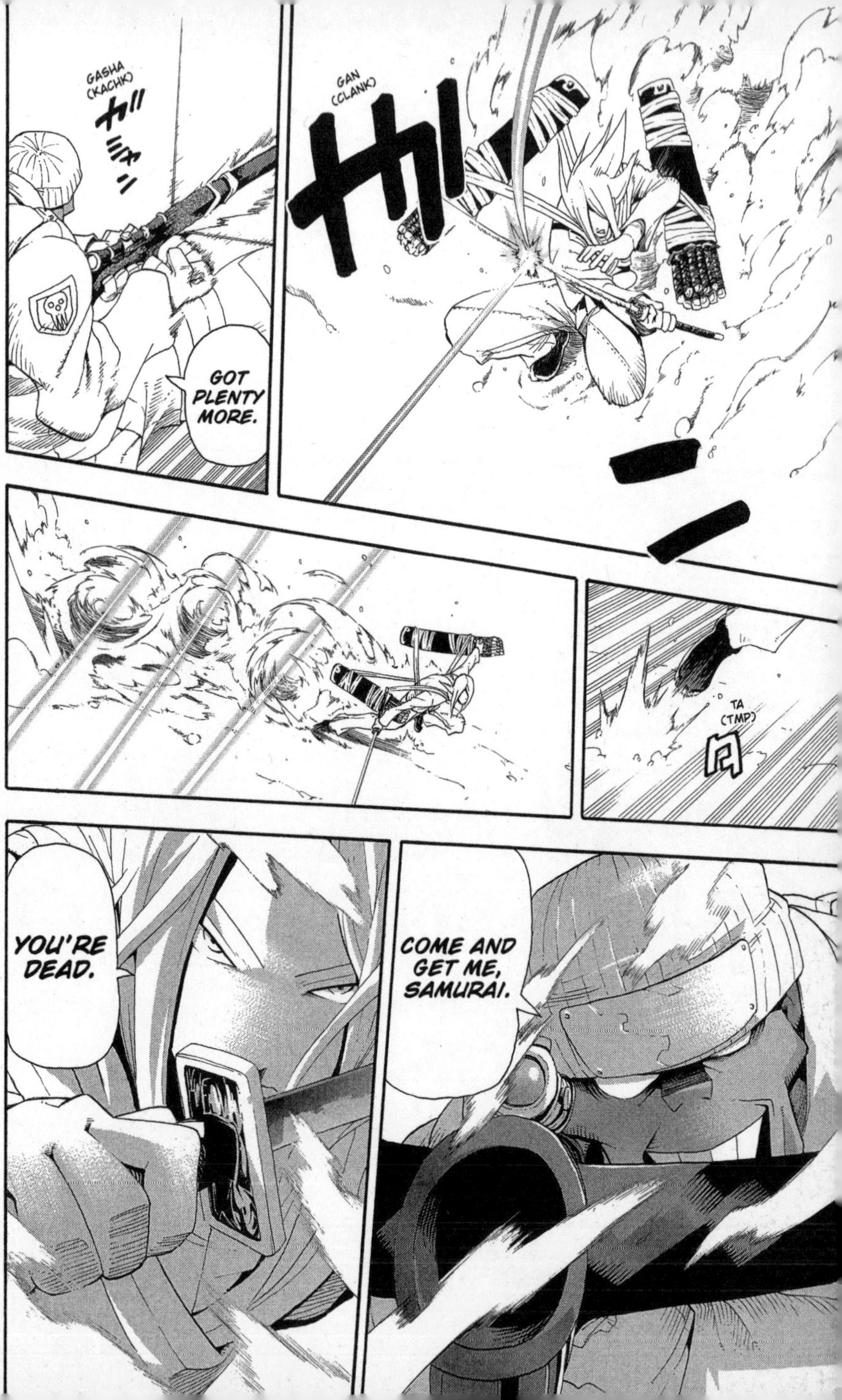
GAN (CLANK)
GASHA (KACHK)
GOT PLENTY MORE.
TA (TMP)
COME AND GET ME, SAMURAI.
YOU'RE DEAD.

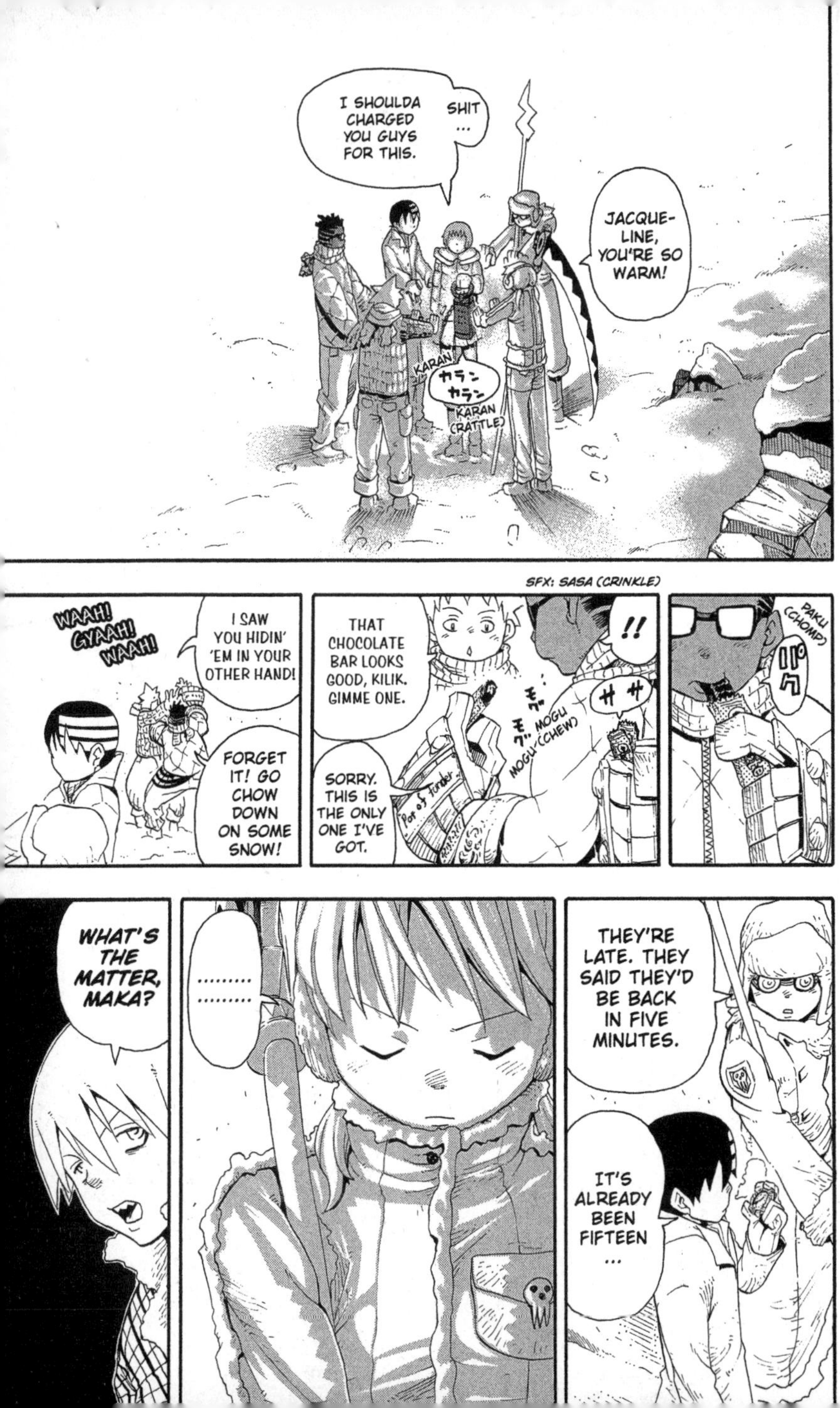
JACQUE-LINE, YOU'RE SO WARM!
SHIT ...
I SHOULDA CHARGED YOU GUYS FOR THIS.
KARAN カラン カラン KARAN (RATTLE)
SFX: SASA (CRINKLE)
パク PAKU (CHOMP)
!!
ササ
THAT CHOCOLATE BAR LOOKS GOOD, KILIK. GIMME ONE.
モグ モグ MOGU MOGU (CHEW)
SORRY. THIS IS THE ONLY ONE I'VE GOT.
I SAW YOU HIDIN' 'EM IN YOUR OTHER HAND!
WAAH! GYAAH! WAAH!
FORGET IT! GO CHOW DOWN ON SOME SNOW!
THEY'RE LATE. THEY SAID THEY'D BE BACK IN FIVE MINUTES.
IT'S ALREADY BEEN FIFTEEN ...
....
WHAT'S THE MATTER, MAKA?

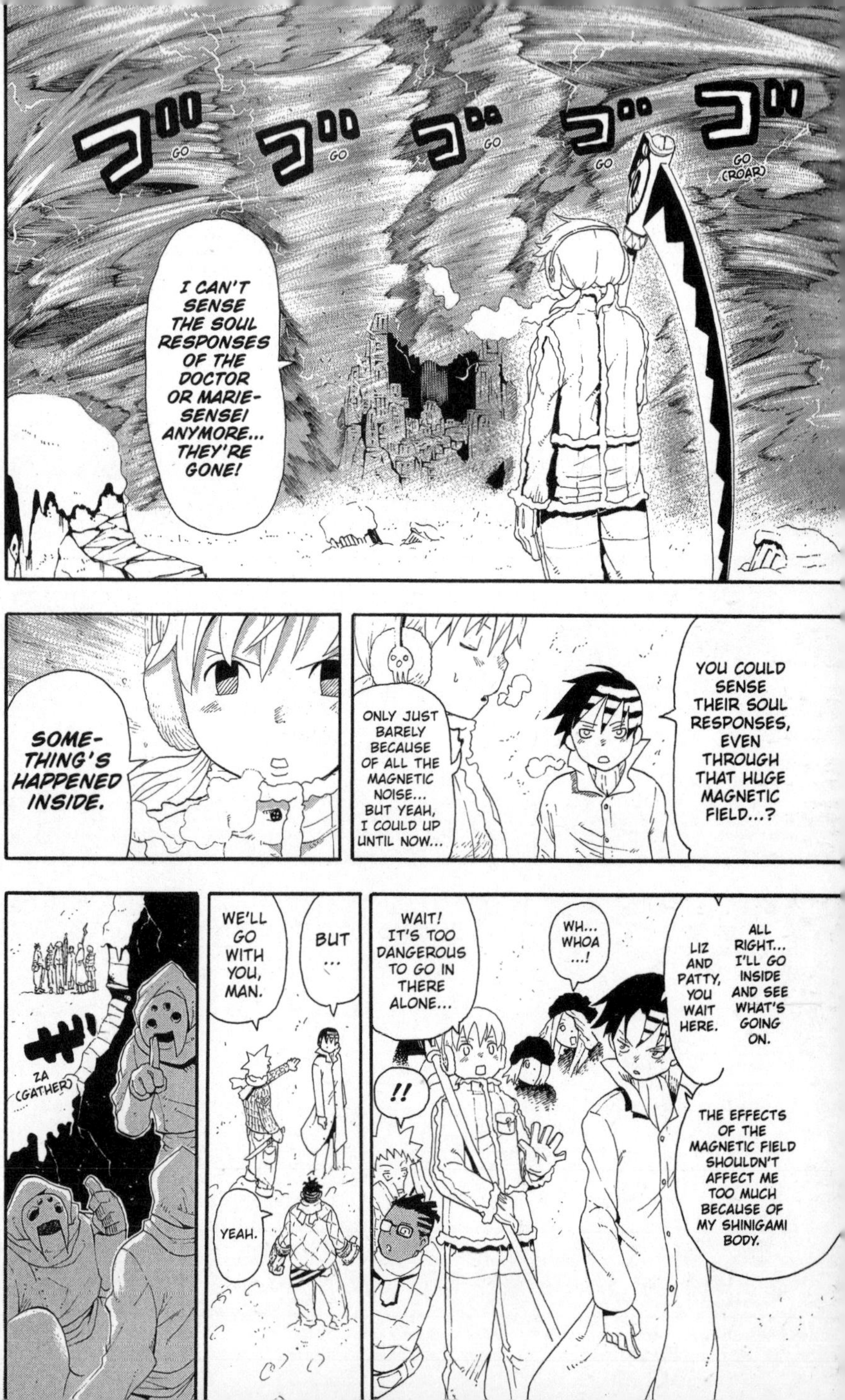

GO (ROAR)
GO
GO
GO
GO
I CAN'T SENSE THE SOUL RESPONSES OF THE DOCTOR OR MARIE-SENSEI ANYMORE... THEY'RE GONE!
YOU COULD SENSE THEIR SOUL RESPONSES, EVEN THROUGH THAT HUGE MAGNETIC FIELD...?
ONLY JUST BARELY BECAUSE OF ALL THE MAGNETIC NOISE... BUT YEAH, I COULD UP UNTIL NOW...
SOME-THING'S HAPPENED INSIDE.
ALL RIGHT... I'LL GO INSIDE AND SEE WHAT'S GOING ON.
LIZ AND PATTY, YOU WAIT HERE.
WH... WHOA...!
WAIT! IT'S TOO DANGEROUS TO GO IN THERE ALONE...
!!
THE EFFECTS OF THE MAGNETIC FIELD SHOULDN'T AFFECT ME TOO MUCH BECAUSE OF MY SHINIGAMI BODY.
BUT...
WE'LL GO WITH YOU, MAN.
YEAH.
ZA (GATHER)

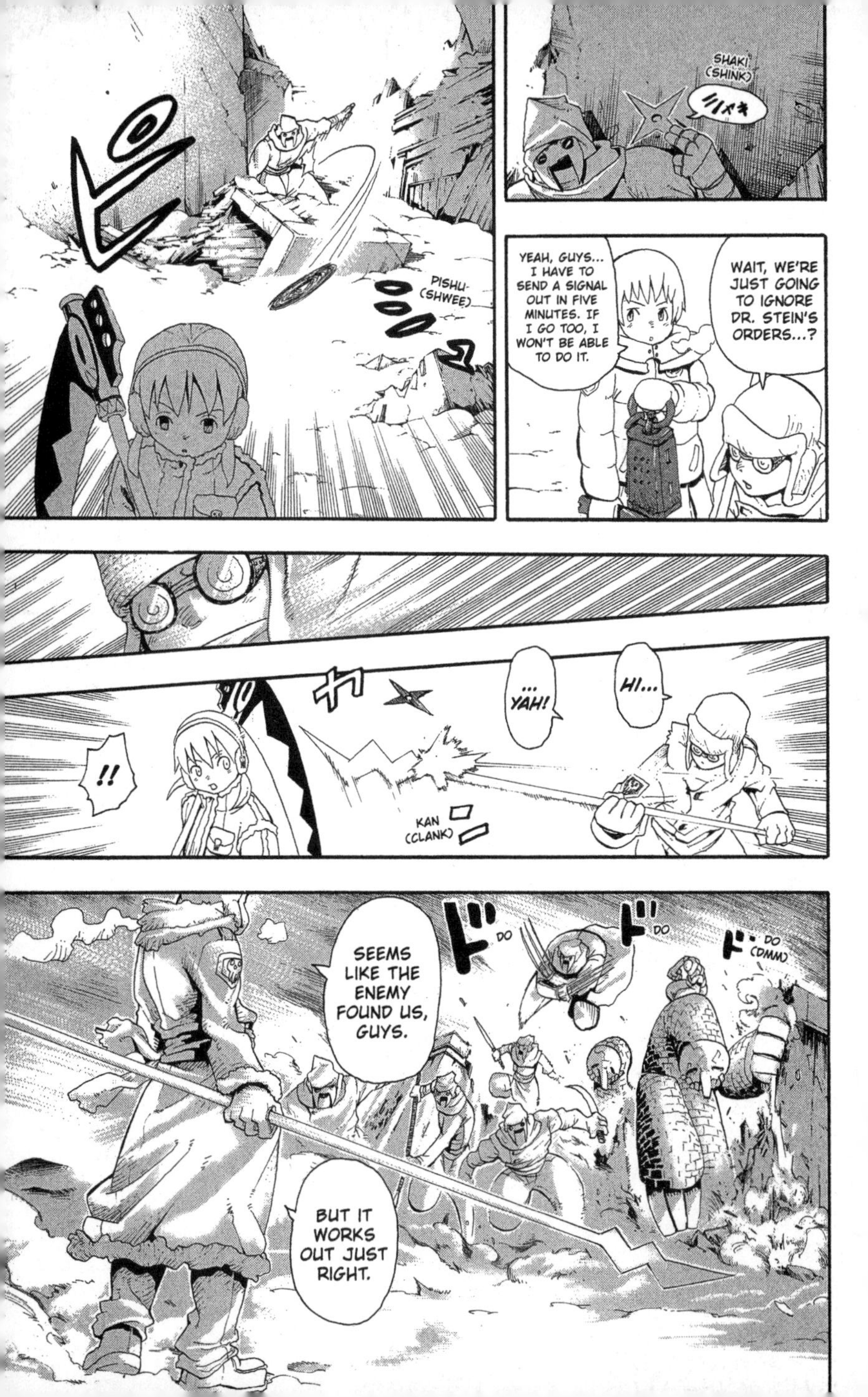

SHAKI (SHINK)
WAIT, WE'RE JUST GOING TO IGNORE DR. STEIN'S ORDERS...?
YEAH, GUYS... I HAVE TO SEND A SIGNAL OUT IN FIVE MINUTES. IF I GO TOO, I WON'T BE ABLE TO DO IT.
PISHU- (SHWEE)
HI...
...YAH!
!!
KAN (CLANK)
DO (DMM)
DO
DO
SEEMS LIKE THE ENEMY FOUND US, GUYS.
BUT IT WORKS OUT JUST RIGHT.

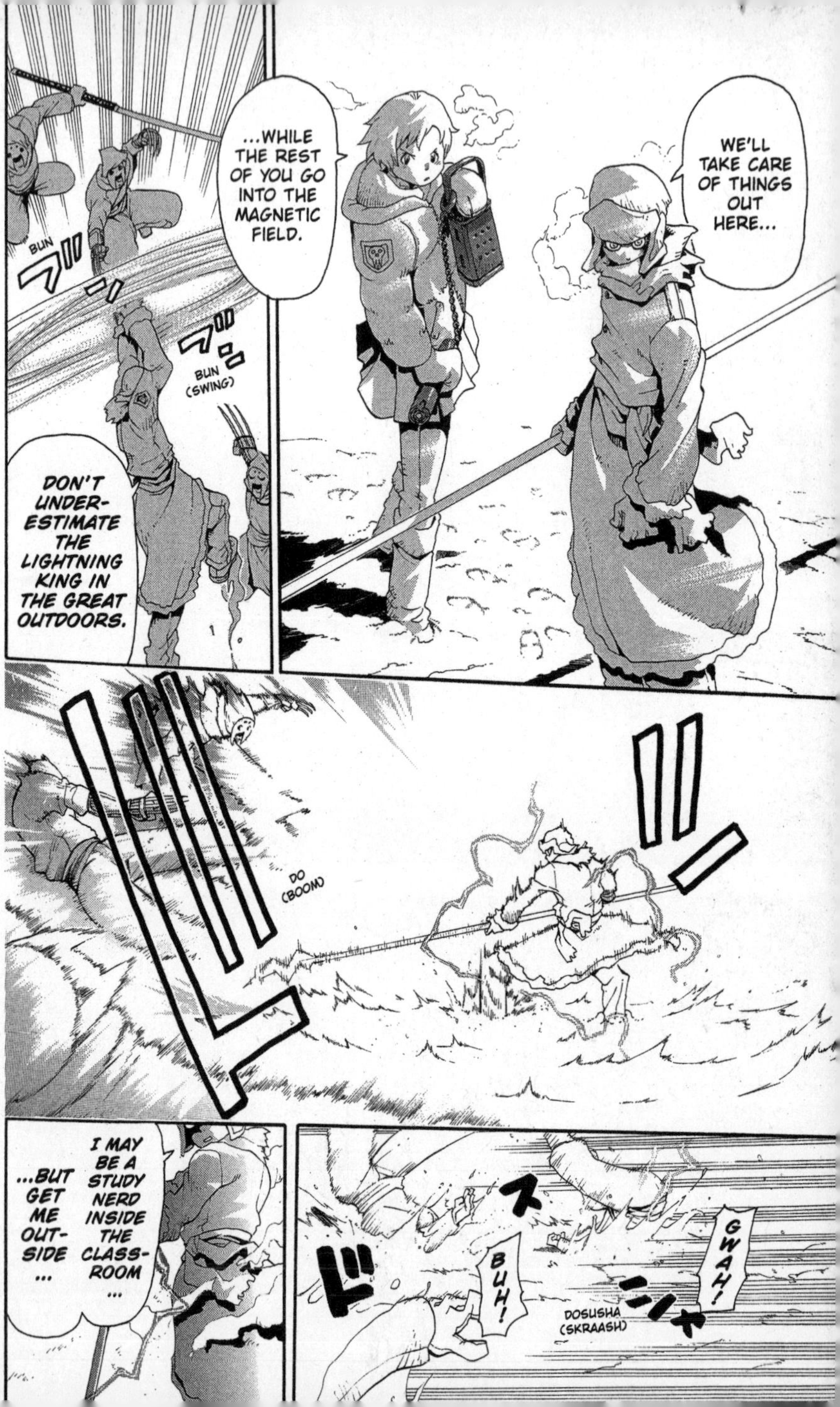
WE'LL TAKE CARE OF THINGS OUT HERE...
...WHILE THE REST OF YOU GO INTO THE MAGNETIC FIELD.
BUN
BUN (SWING)
DON'T UNDER-ESTIMATE THE LIGHTNING KING IN THE GREAT OUTDOORS.
DO (BOOM)
GWAH!
BUH!
DOSUSHA (SKRAASH)
I MAY BE A STUDY NERD INSIDE THE CLASS-ROOM...
...BUT GET ME OUT-SIDE...

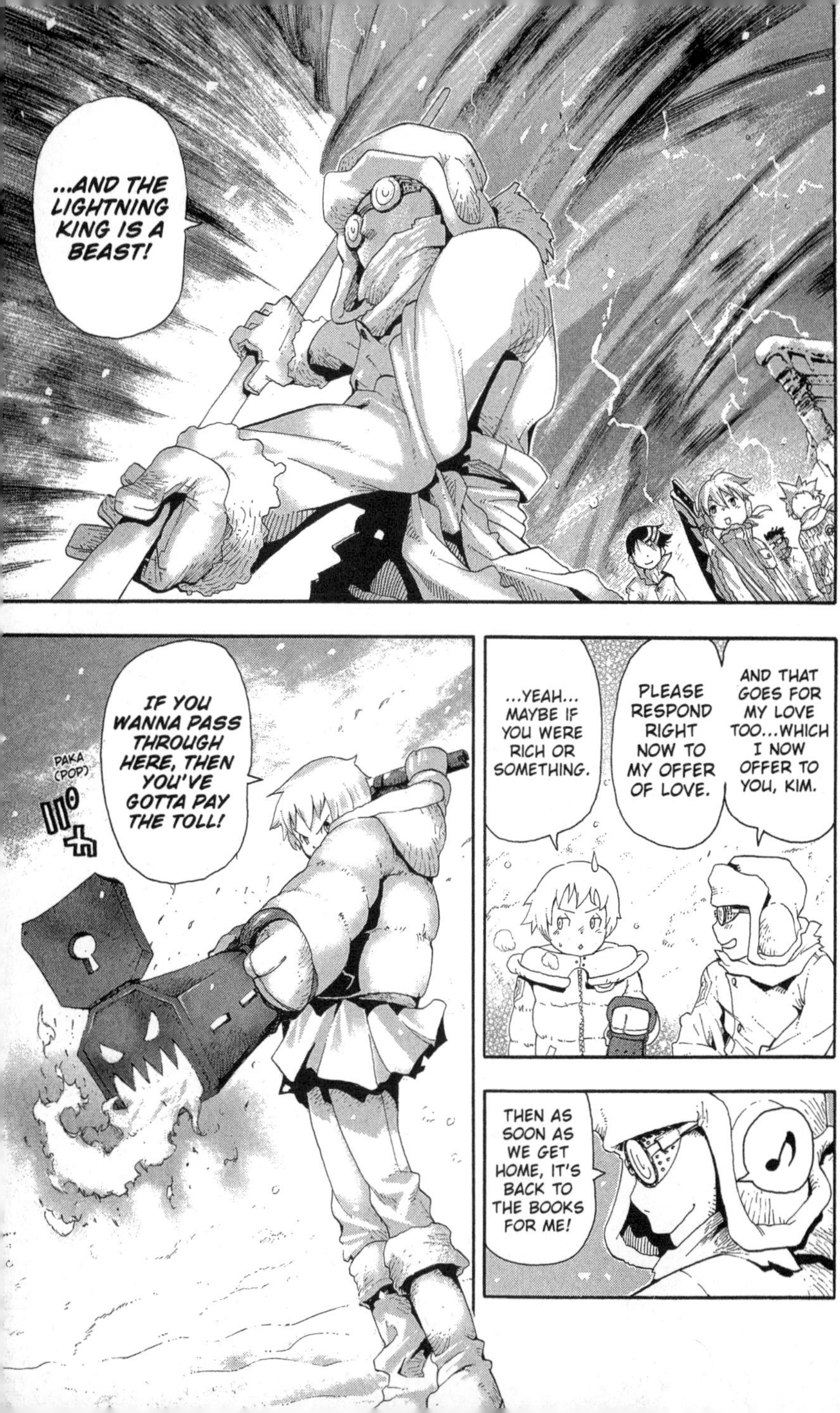
...AND THE LIGHTNING KING IS A BEAST!
AND THAT GOES FOR MY LOVE TOO...WHICH I NOW OFFER TO YOU, KIM.
PLEASE RESPOND RIGHT NOW TO MY OFFER OF LOVE.
...YEAH... MAYBE IF YOU WERE RICH OR SOMETHING.
THEN AS SOON AS WE GET HOME, IT'S BACK TO THE BOOKS FOR ME!
IF YOU WANNA PASS THROUGH HERE, THEN YOU'VE GOTTA PAY THE TOLL!
PAKA (POP)

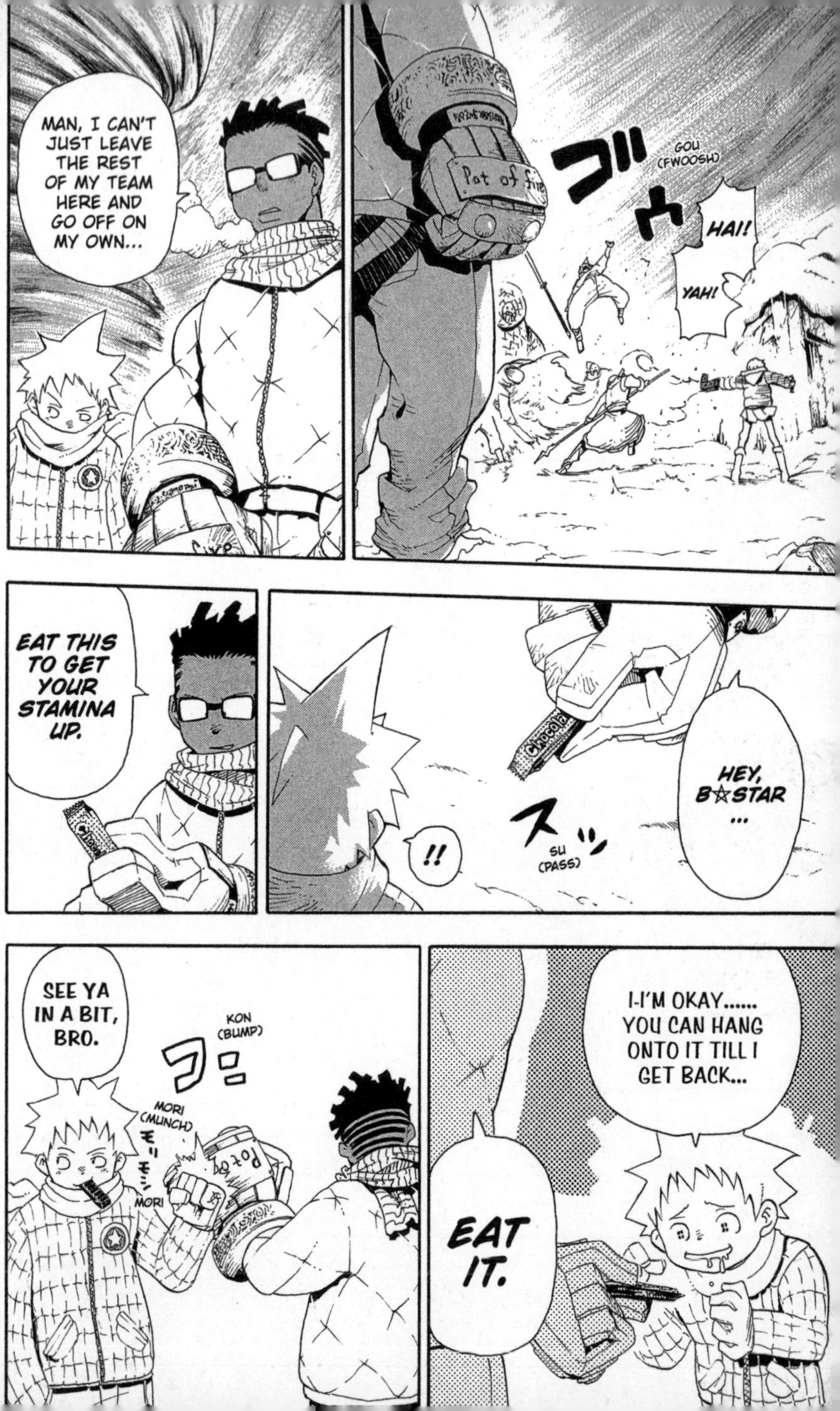
Pot of fire
GOU (FWOOSH)
HAI!
YAH!
MAN, I CAN'T JUST LEAVE THE REST OF MY TEAM HERE AND GO OFF ON MY OWN...
HEY, B☆STAR...
Chocola
SU (PASS)
!!
EAT THIS TO GET YOUR STAMINA UP.
I-I'M OKAY...... YOU CAN HANG ONTO IT TILL I GET BACK...
EAT IT.
SEE YA IN A BIT, BRO.
KON (BUMP)
MORI (MUNCH)
MORI

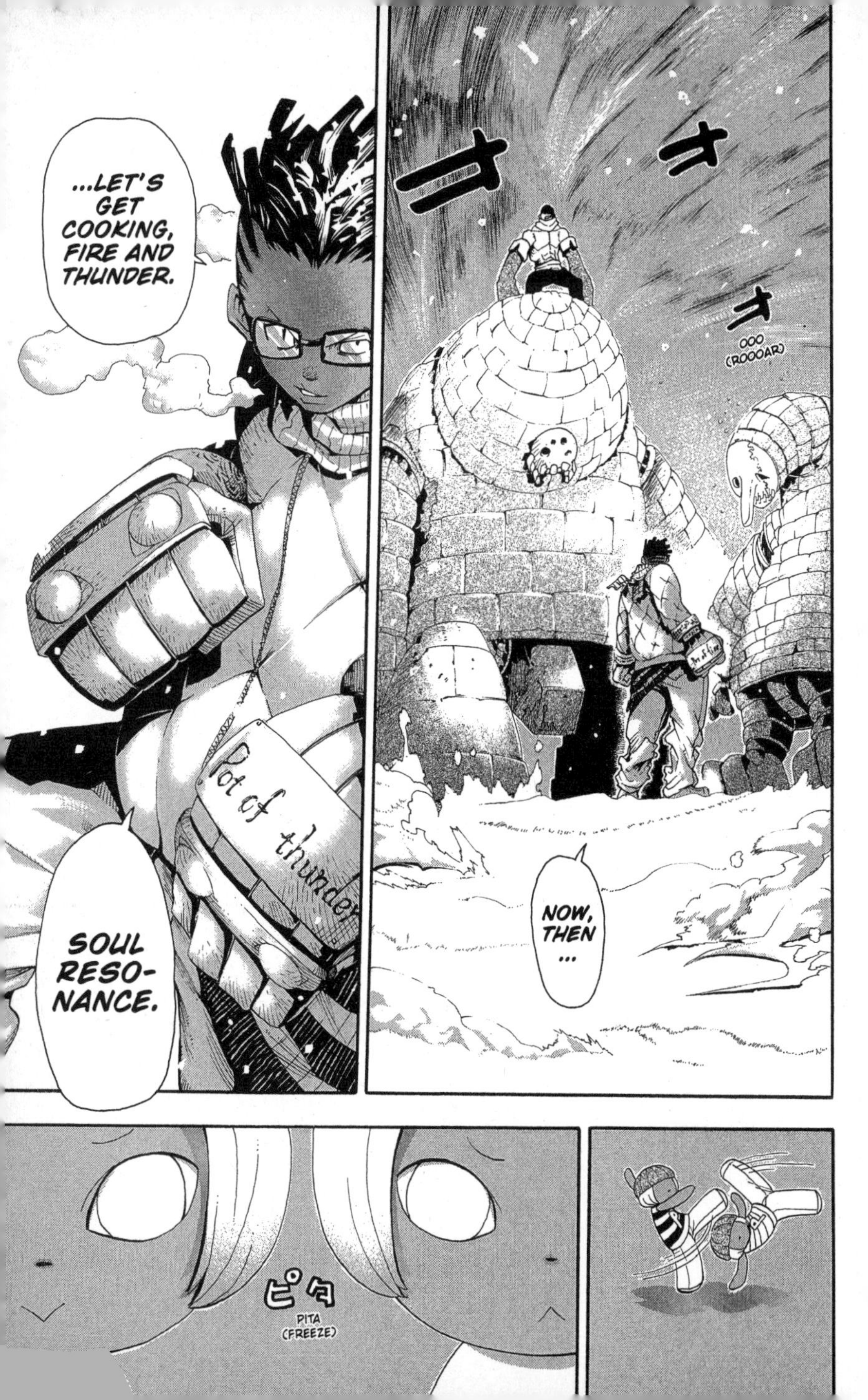
オオオ
OOO (ROOOAR)
NOW, THEN...
...LET'S GET COOKING, FIRE AND THUNDER.
SOUL RESONANCE.
Pot of thunder
ピタ
PITA (FREEZE)

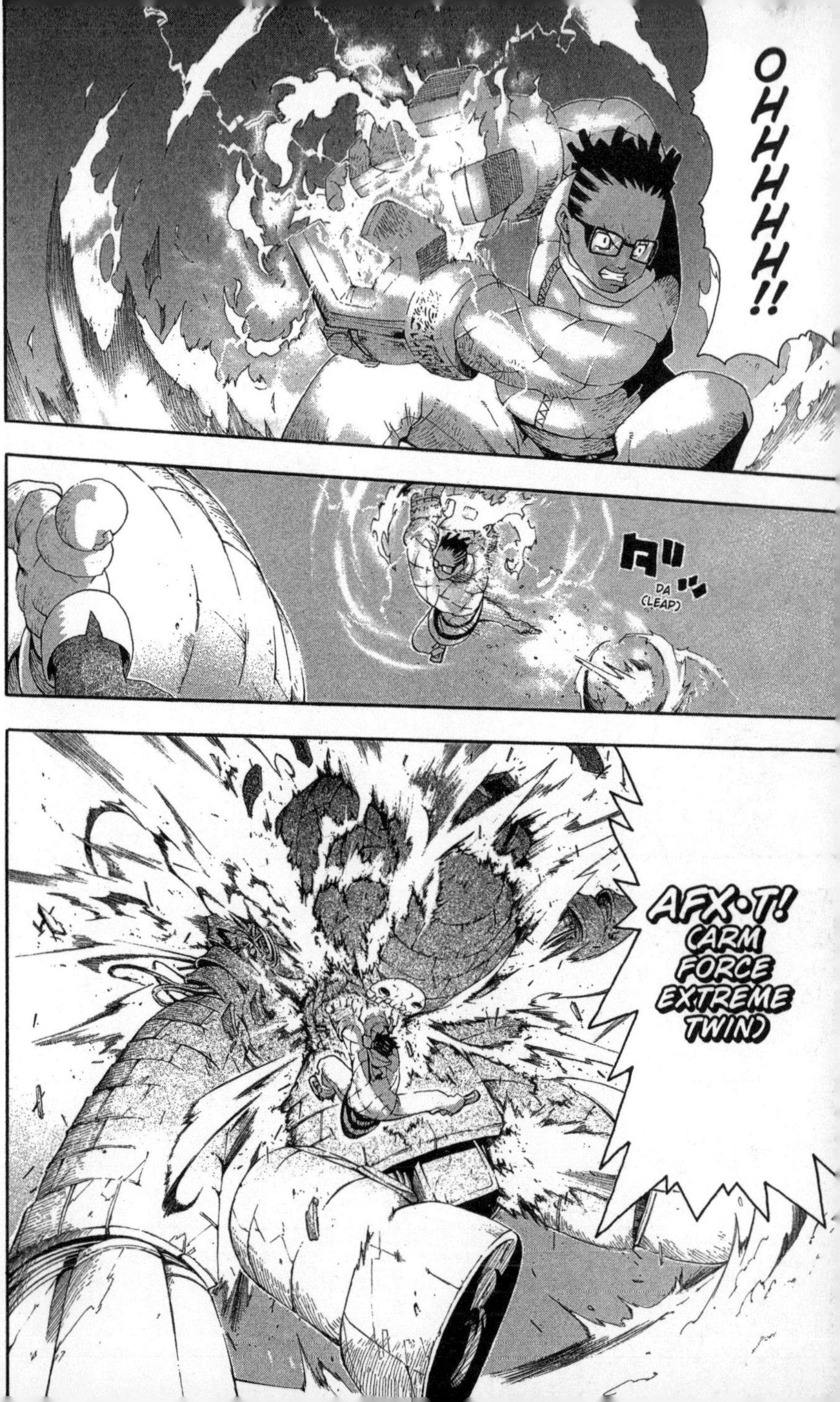
OHHHHHH!!
ダッ
DA
(LEAP)
AFX・T!
(ARM
FORCE
EXTREME
TWIN)

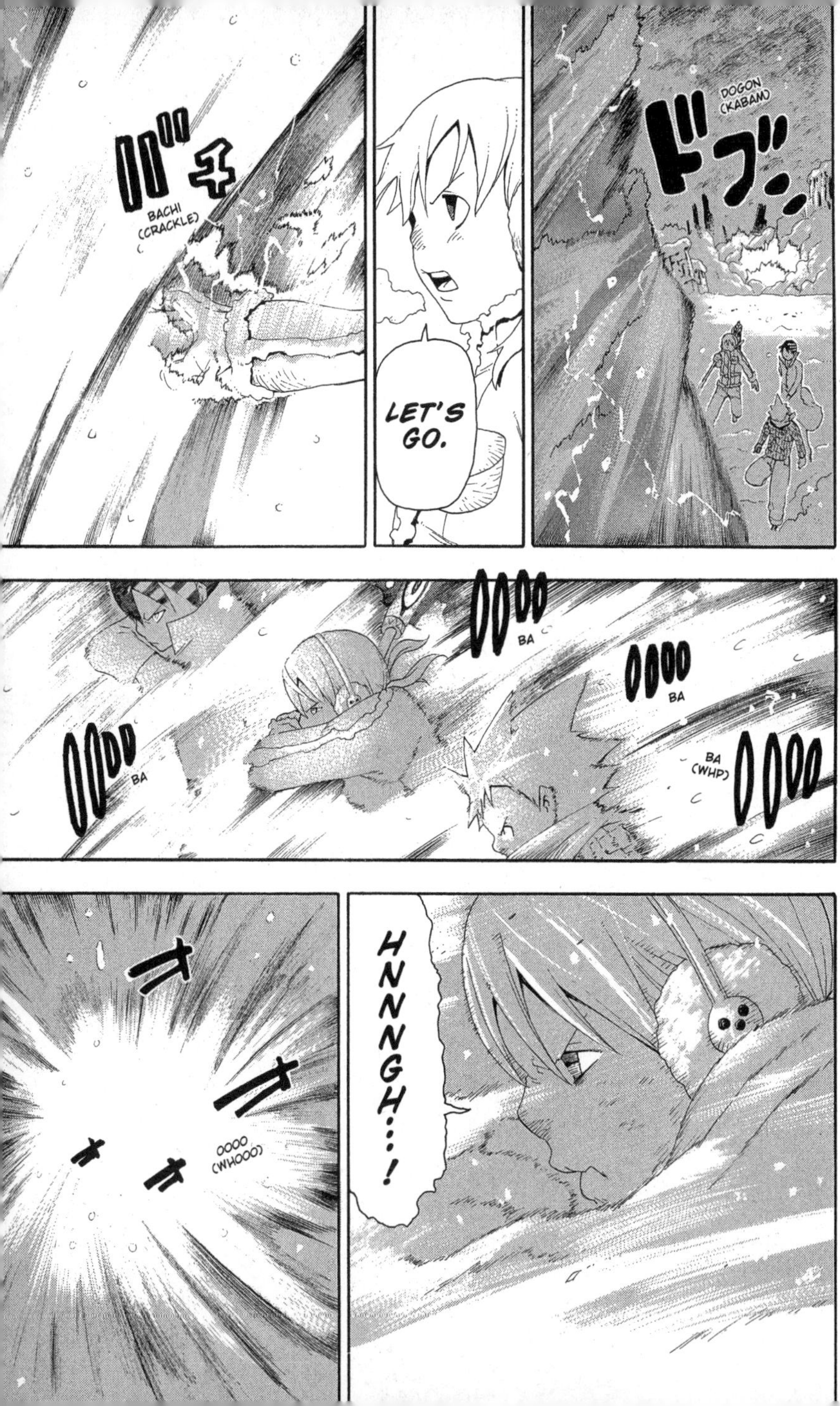
DOGON (KABAM)
LET'S GO.
BACHI (CRACKLE)
BA (WHP)
BA
BA
BA
HNNNGH...!
OOOO (WHOOO)

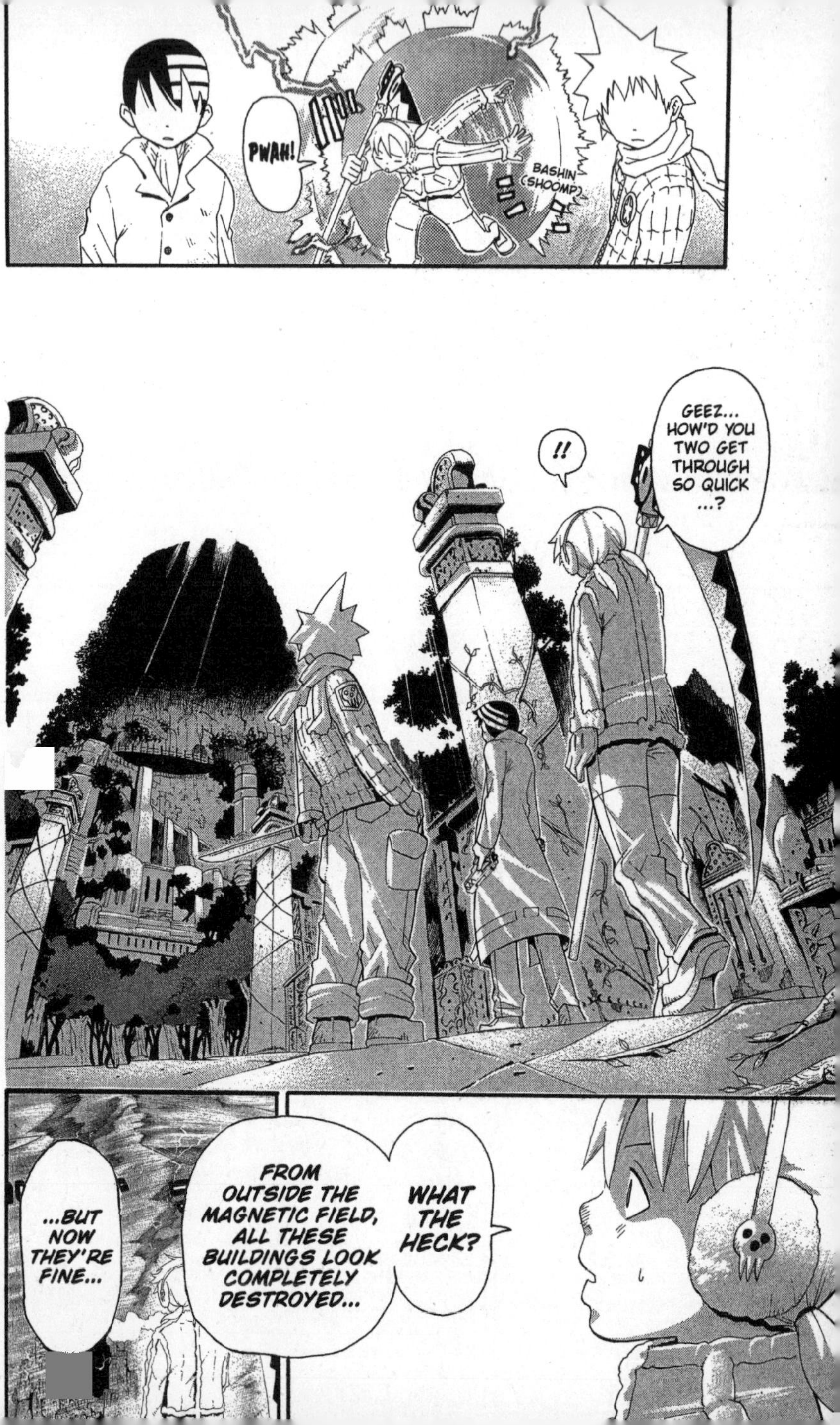
BASHIN (SHOOMP)
PWAH!
GEEZ... HOW'D YOU TWO GET THROUGH SO QUICK ...?
!!
WHAT THE HECK?
FROM OUTSIDE THE MAGNETIC FIELD, ALL THESE BUILDINGS LOOK COMPLETELY DESTROYED...
...BUT NOW THEY'RE FINE...

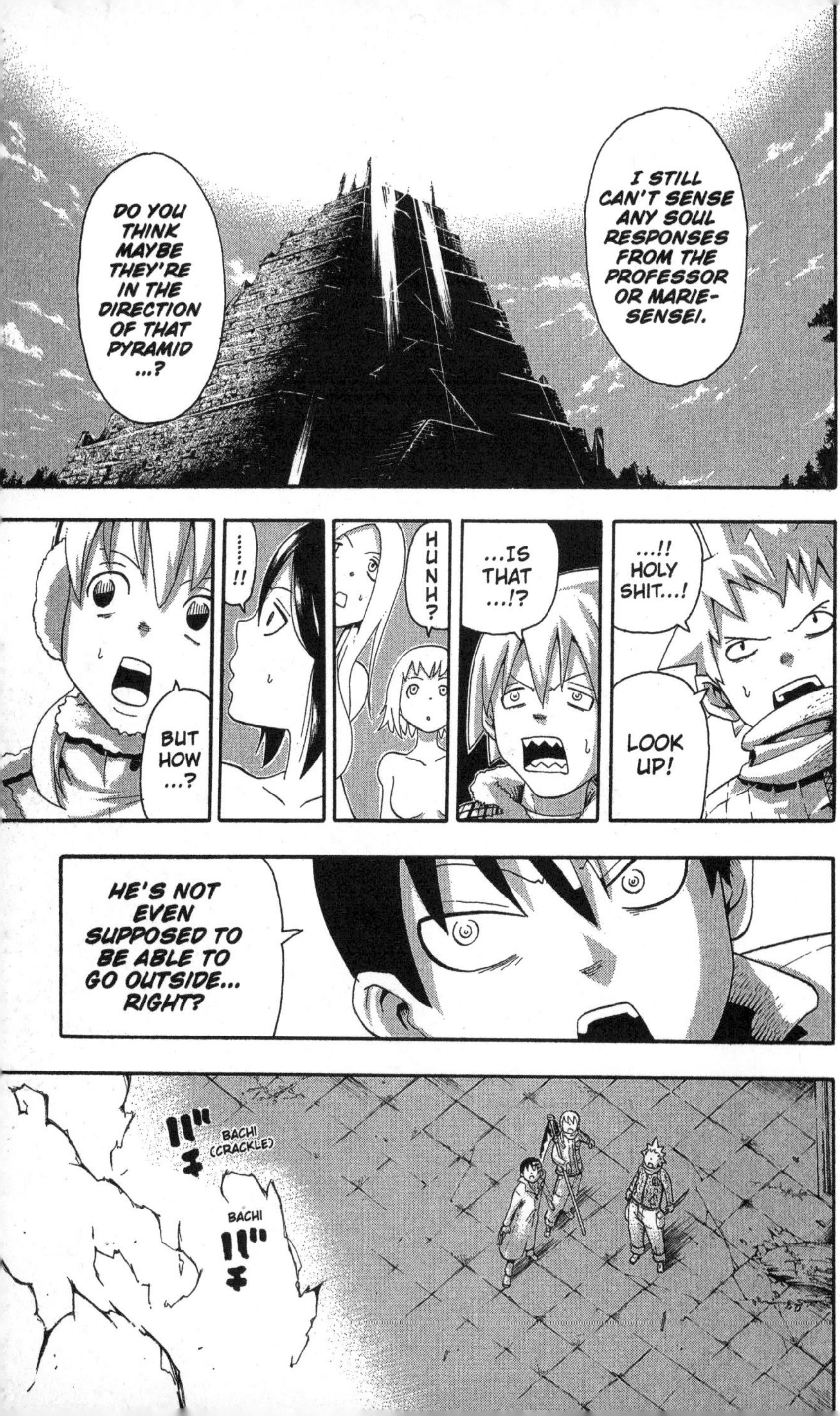
I STILL CAN'T SENSE ANY SOUL RESPONSES FROM THE PROFESSOR OR MARIE-SENSEI.
DO YOU THINK MAYBE THEY'RE IN THE DIRECTION OF THAT PYRAMID ...?
...!! HOLY SHIT...!
LOOK UP!
...IS THAT ...!?
HUNH?
......!!
BUT HOW ...?
HE'S NOT EVEN SUPPOSED TO BE ABLE TO GO OUTSIDE... RIGHT?
バチ
BACHI (CRACKLE)
バチ
BACHI

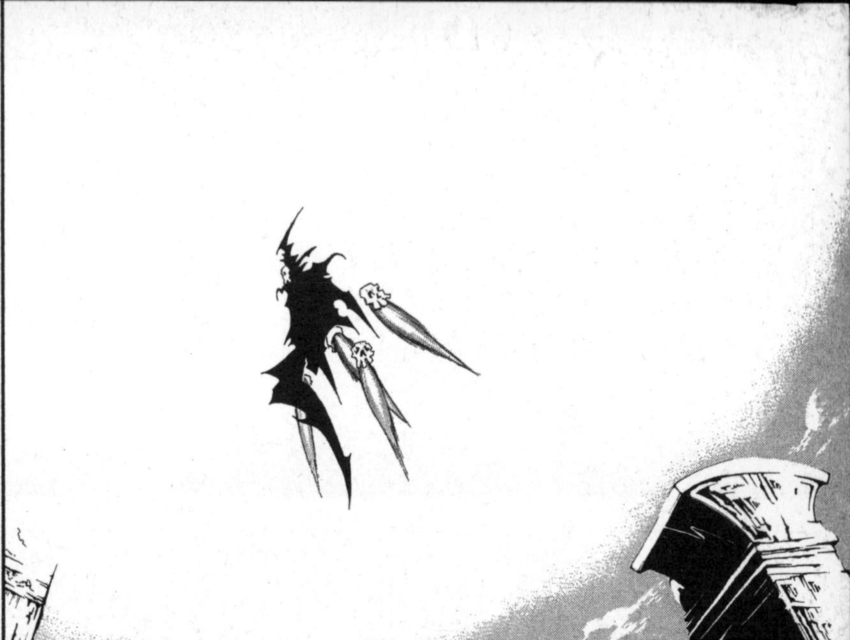

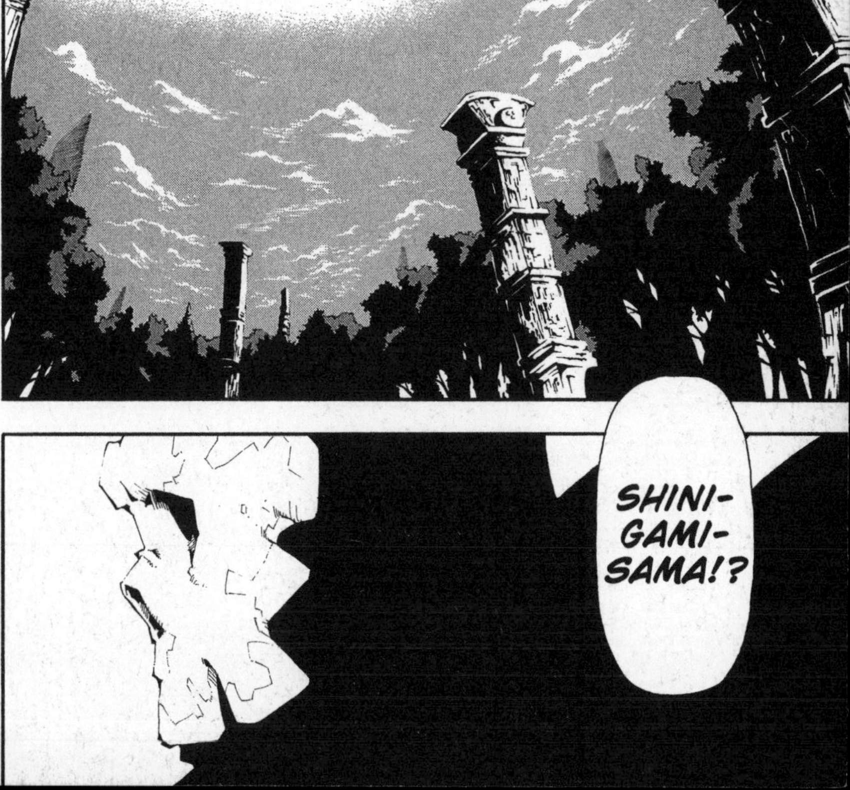
SHINI-GAMI-SAMA!?

SOUL EATER

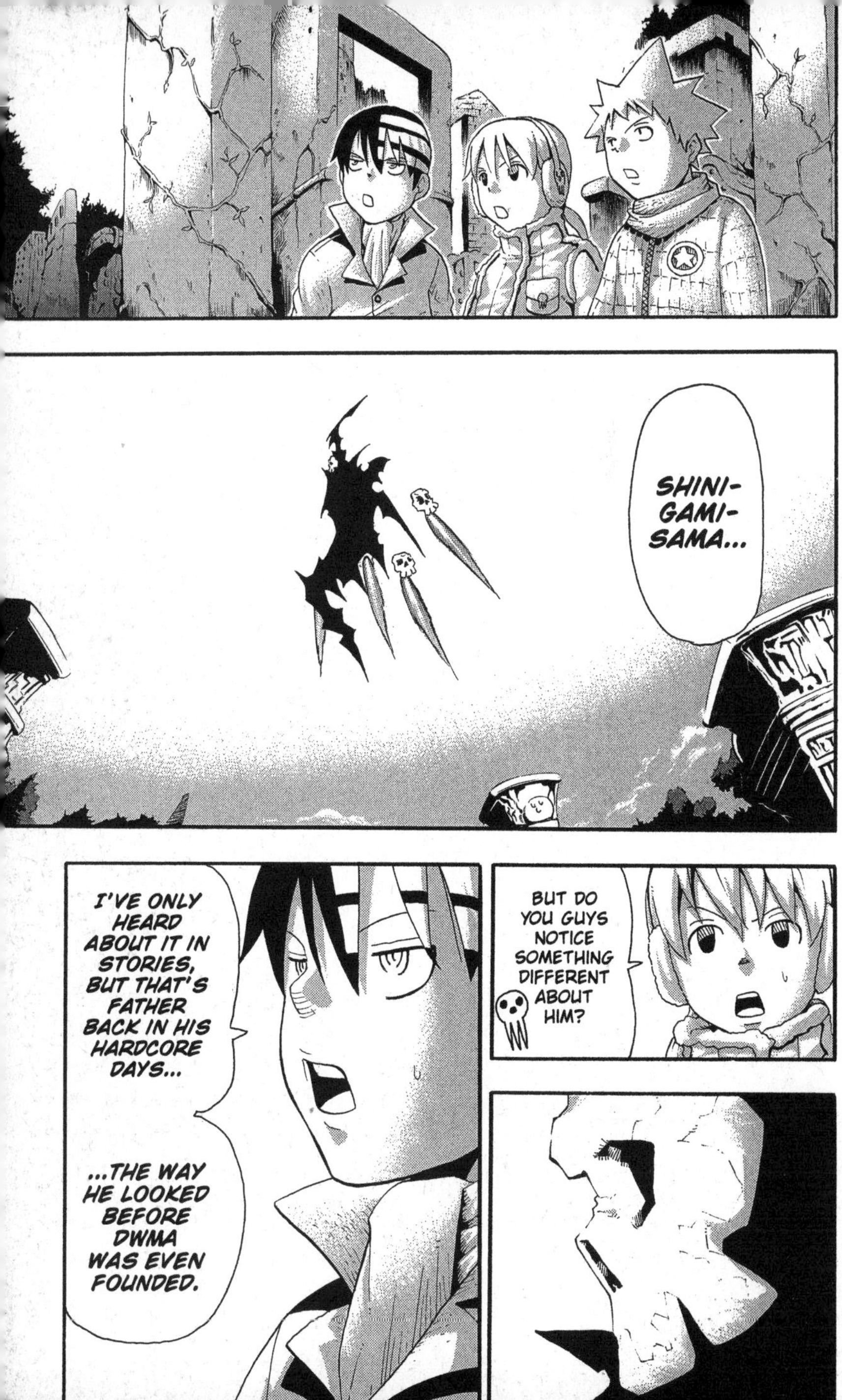
SHINI-GAMI-SAMA...
BUT DO YOU GUYS NOTICE SOMETHING DIFFERENT ABOUT HIM?
I'VE ONLY HEARD ABOUT IT IN STORIES, BUT THAT'S FATHER BACK IN HIS HARDCORE DAYS...
...THE WAY HE LOOKED BEFORE DWMA WAS EVEN FOUNDED.

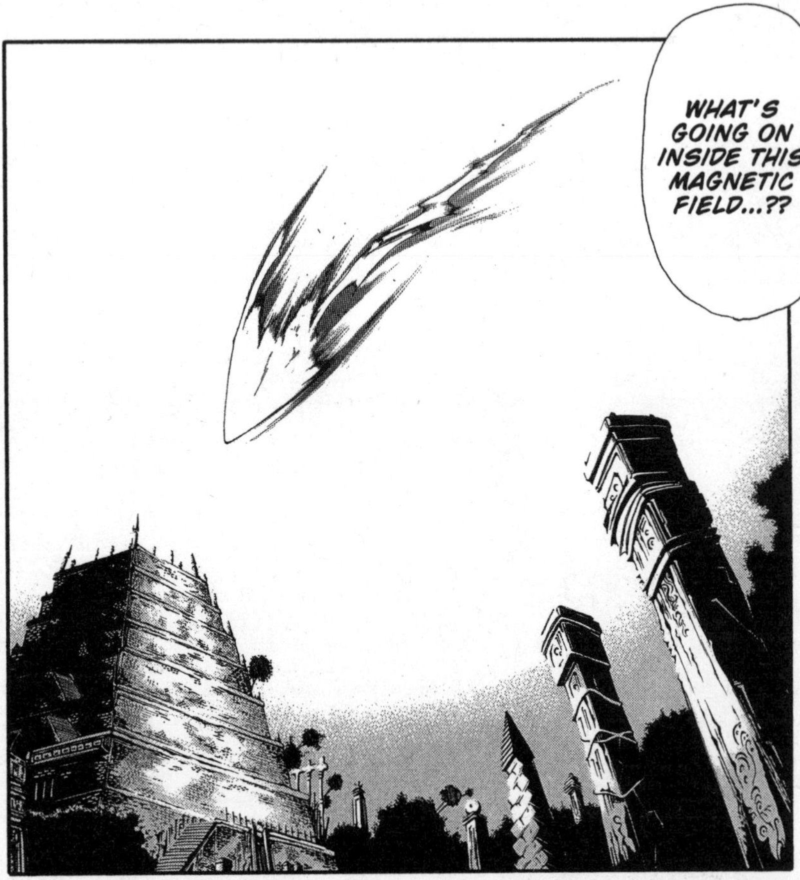
WHAT'S GOING ON INSIDE THIS MAGNETIC FIELD...??

SOUL EATER

CHAPTER 35: "BREW"—THE TEMPEST (PART 2)

TE
TE
TE
TE
(SCAMPER)

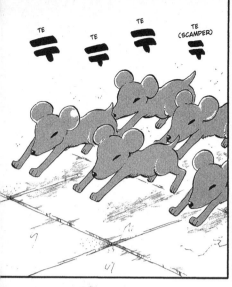

WE SHOULD HEAD FOR THAT PYRAMID TOO, AS QUICKLY AS WE CAN.

ヒ。キ
PIKIIIN
(GLIIINT)

オオオオ
(WHOOO)

GOOD LUCK! MIZUNE!

パカ
PAKA
(POP)

IN THE MEANTIME, WE'LL LET DWMA AND ARACHNOPHOBIA POINTLESSLY DUKE IT OUT AMONGST THEMSELVES.

HUFF! HUFF! HUFF! HUFF!

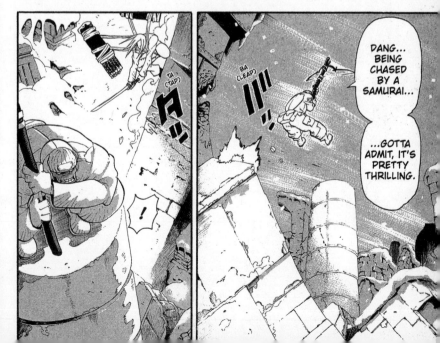

TA (TAP)

!

BA (LEAP)

DANG... BEING CHASED BY A SAMURAI...

...GOTTA ADMIT, IT'S PRETTY THRILLING.

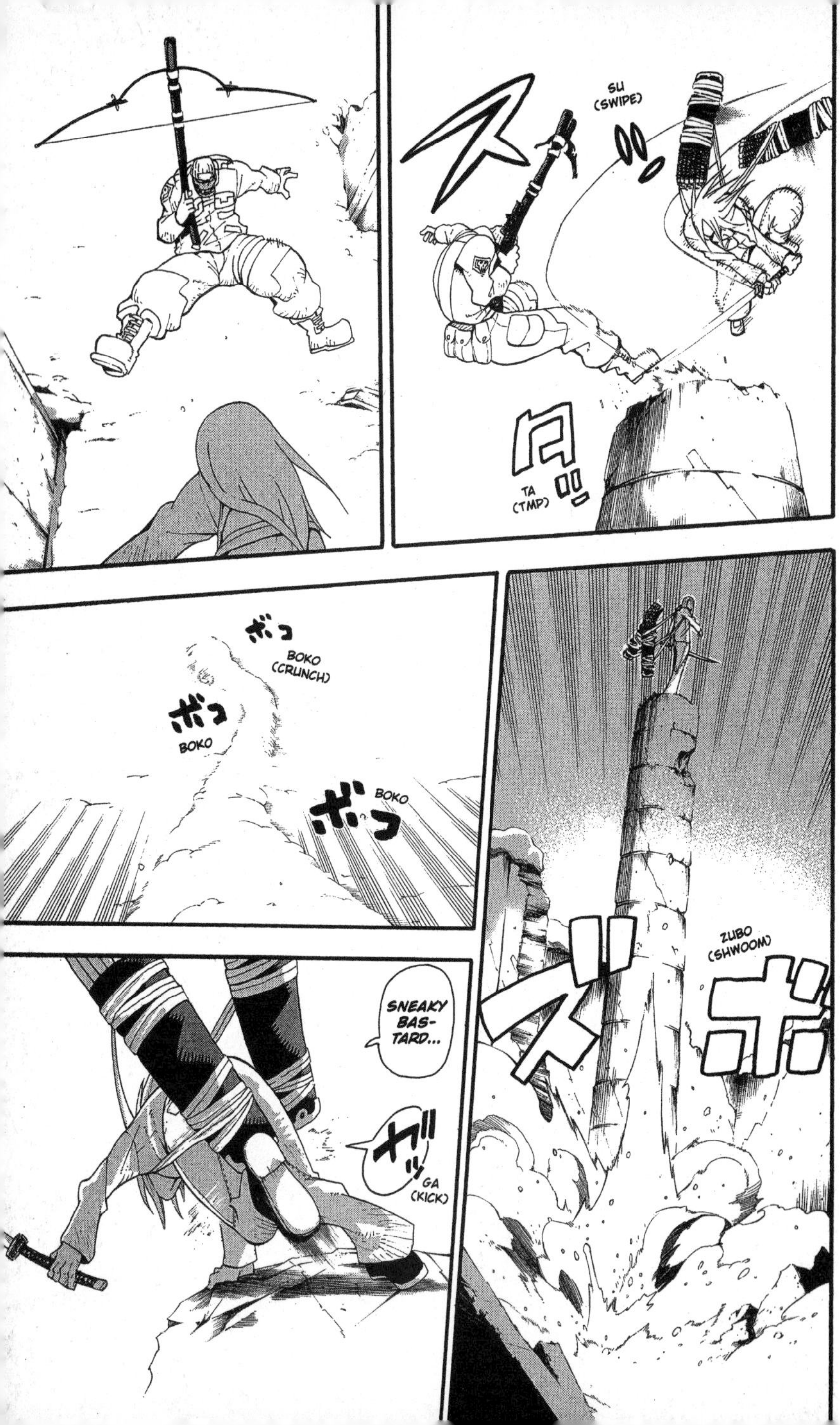
SU (SWIPE)
TA (TMP)
ZUBO (SHWOOM)
ボッ
BOKO (CRUNCH)
ボッ
BOKO
ボッ
BOKO
SNEAKY BASTARD...
GA (KICK)

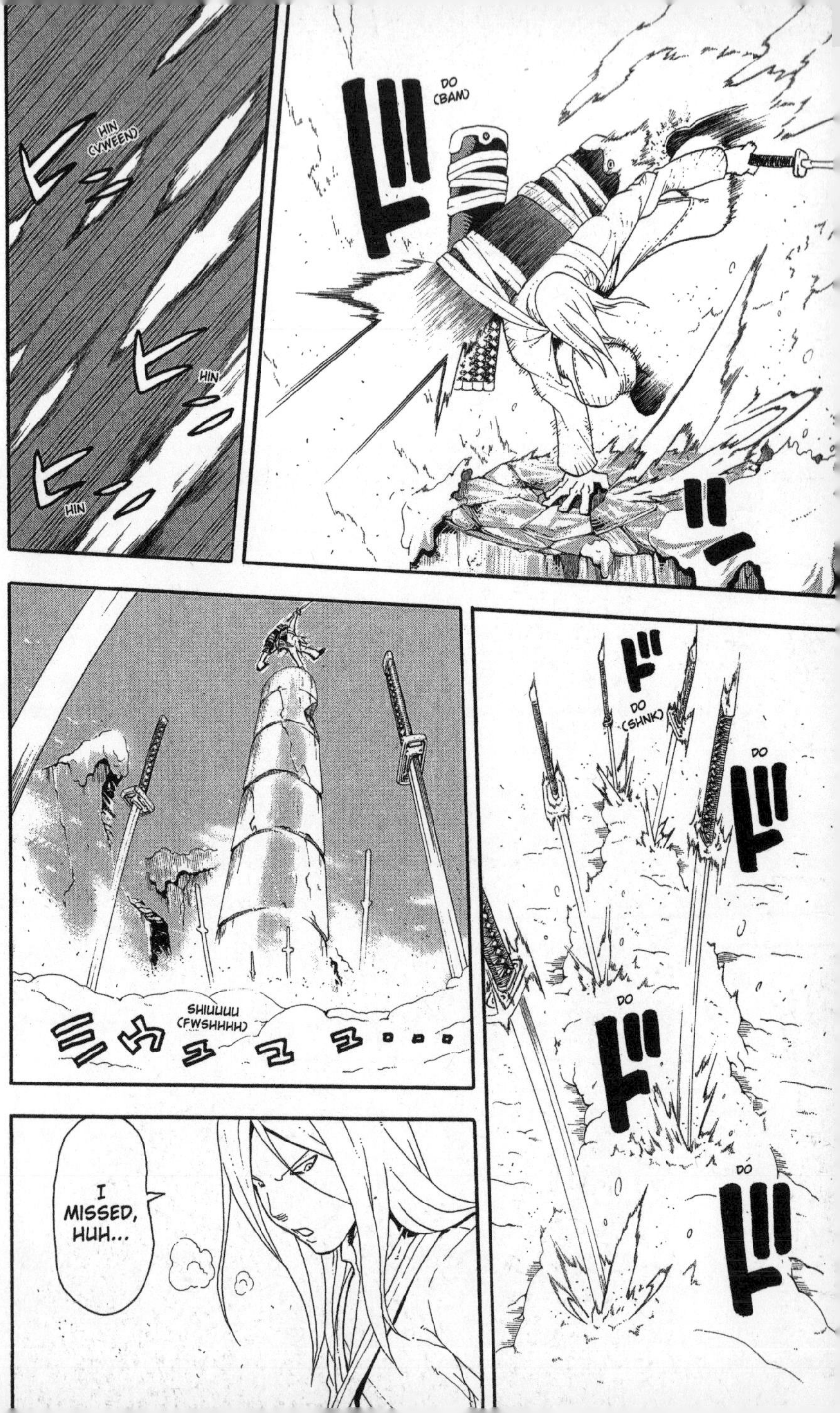
DO (BAM)
HIN (VWEEN)
HIN
HIN
DO (SHNK)
DO
DO
DO
SHIUUUU (FWSHHHH)
I MISSED, HUH...

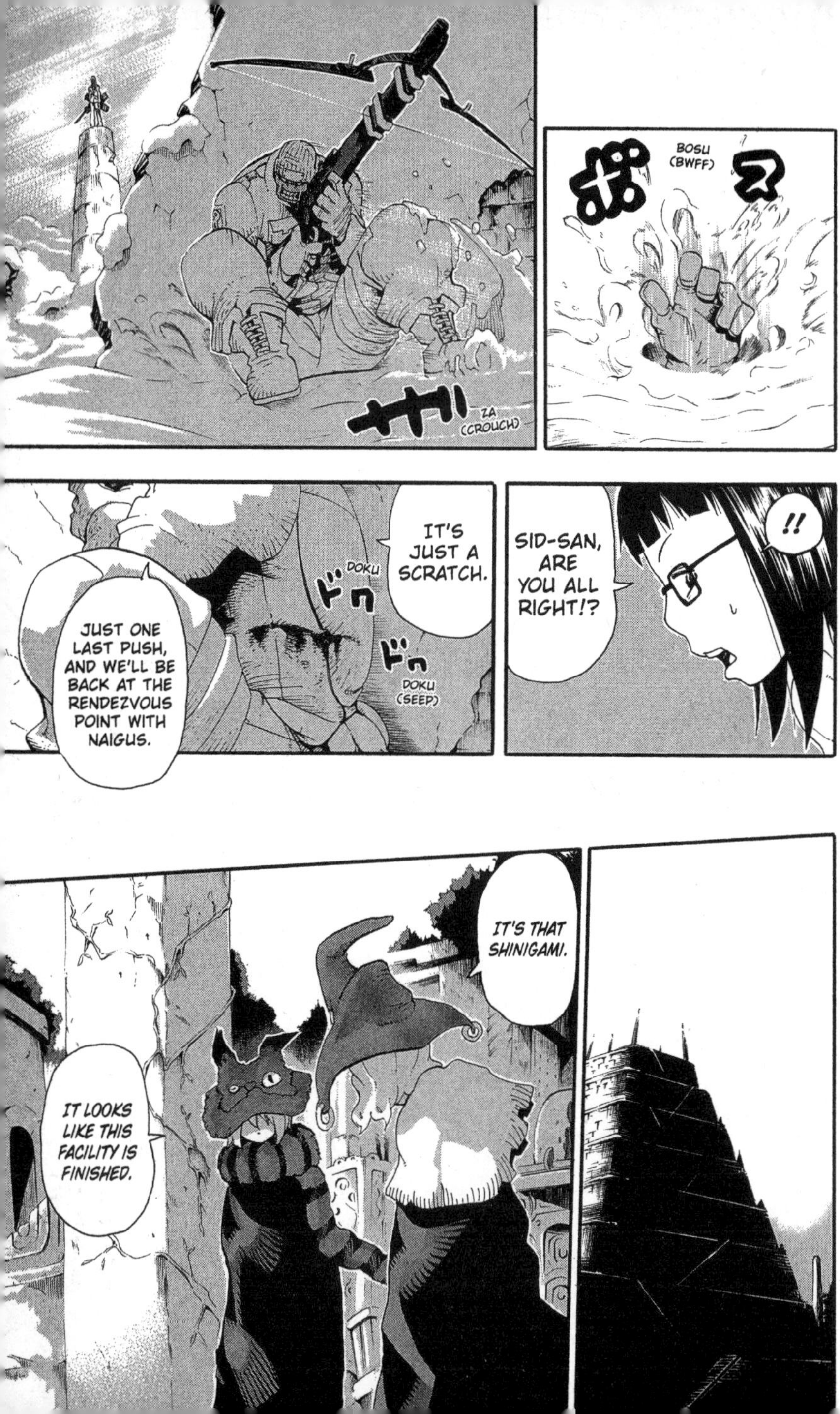
BOSU (BWFF)
ZA (CROUCH)
!!
SID-SAN, ARE YOU ALL RIGHT!?
IT'S JUST A SCRATCH.
DOKU
DOKU (SEEP)
JUST ONE LAST PUSH, AND WE'LL BE BACK AT THE RENDEZVOUS POINT WITH NAIGUS.
IT'S THAT SHINIGAMI.
IT LOOKS LIKE THIS FACILITY IS FINISHED.

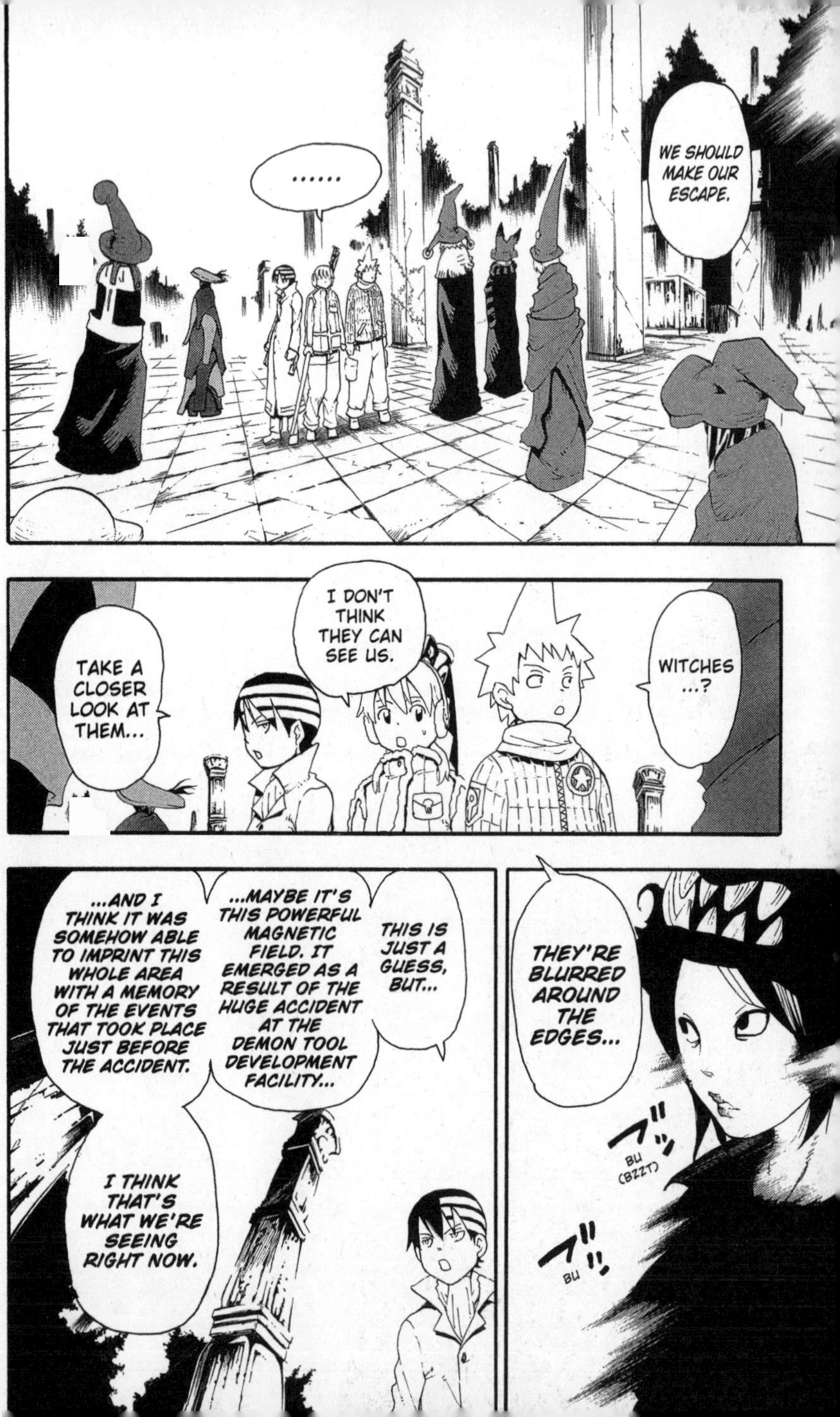
WE SHOULD MAKE OUR ESCAPE.
......
WITCHES ...?
I DON'T THINK THEY CAN SEE US.
TAKE A CLOSER LOOK AT THEM...
THEY'RE BLURRED AROUND THE EDGES...
BU (BZZT)
BU
THIS IS JUST A GUESS, BUT...
...MAYBE IT'S THIS POWERFUL MAGNETIC FIELD. IT EMERGED AS A RESULT OF THE HUGE ACCIDENT AT THE DEMON TOOL DEVELOPMENT FACILITY...
...AND I THINK IT WAS SOMEHOW ABLE TO IMPRINT THIS WHOLE AREA WITH A MEMORY OF THE EVENTS THAT TOOK PLACE JUST BEFORE THE ACCIDENT.
I THINK THAT'S WHAT WE'RE SEEING RIGHT NOW.

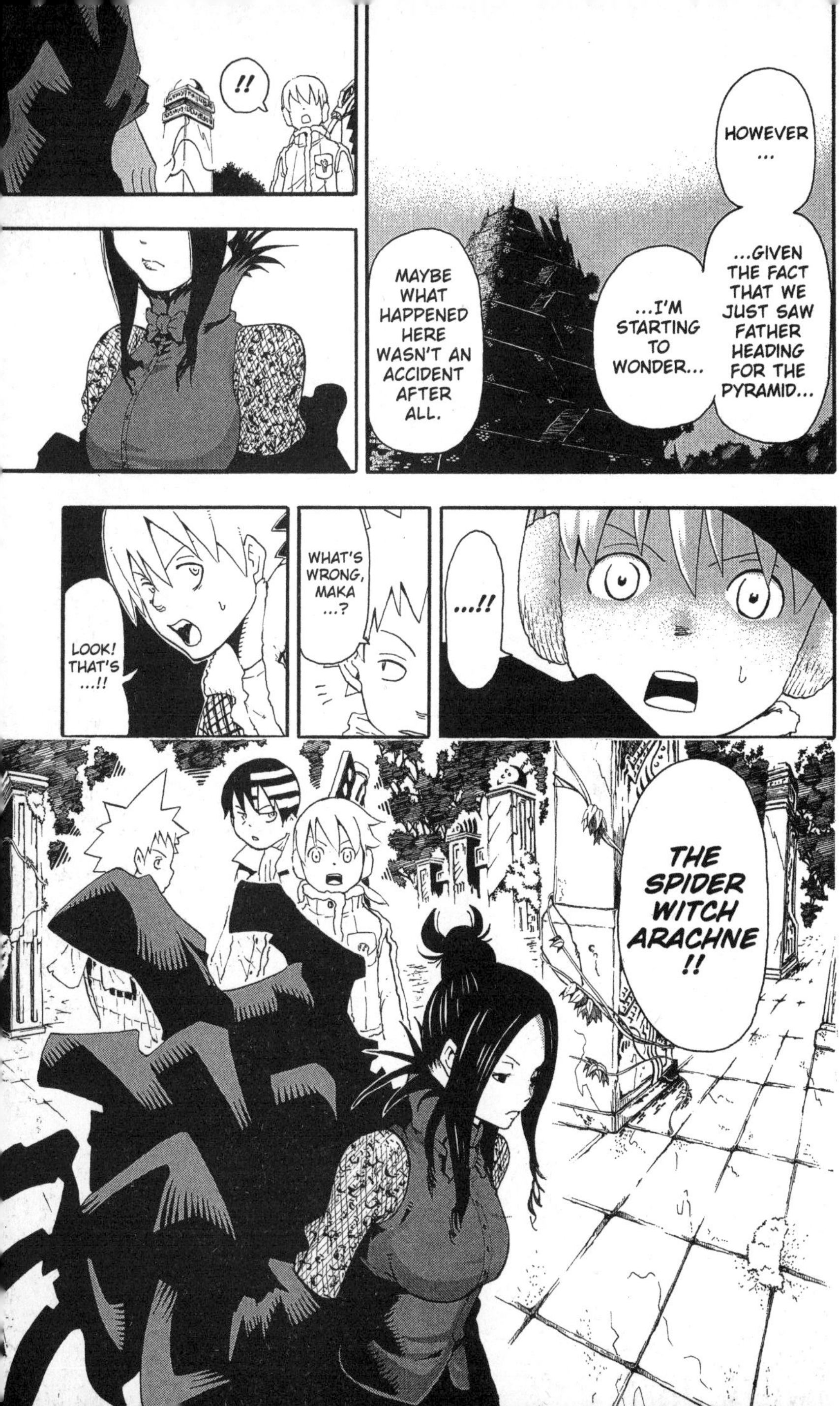
HOWEVER ...
...GIVEN THE FACT THAT WE JUST SAW FATHER HEADING FOR THE PYRAMID...
...I'M STARTING TO WONDER...
MAYBE WHAT HAPPENED HERE WASN'T AN ACCIDENT AFTER ALL.
!!
...!!
WHAT'S WRONG, MAKA ...?
LOOK! THAT'S ...!!
THE SPIDER WITCH ARACHNE !!

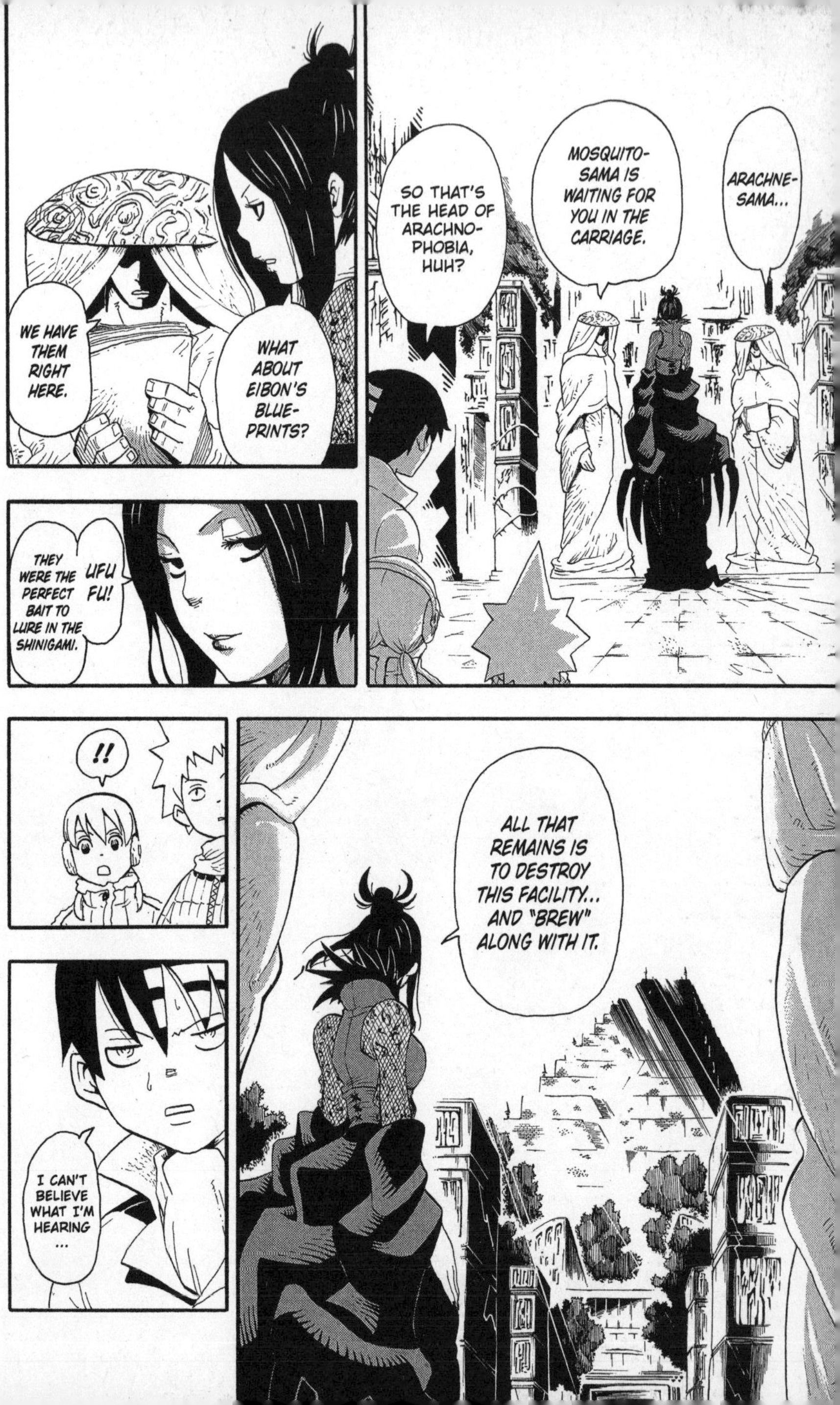
ARACHNE-SAMA...
MOSQUITO-SAMA IS WAITING FOR YOU IN THE CARRIAGE.
SO THAT'S THE HEAD OF ARACHNOPHOBIA, HUH?
WHAT ABOUT EIBON'S BLUEPRINTS?
WE HAVE THEM RIGHT HERE.
UFU FU!
THEY WERE THE PERFECT BAIT TO LURE IN THE SHINIGAMI.
ALL THAT REMAINS IS TO DESTROY THIS FACILITY... AND "BREW" ALONG WITH IT.
!!
I CAN'T BELIEVE WHAT I'M HEARING...

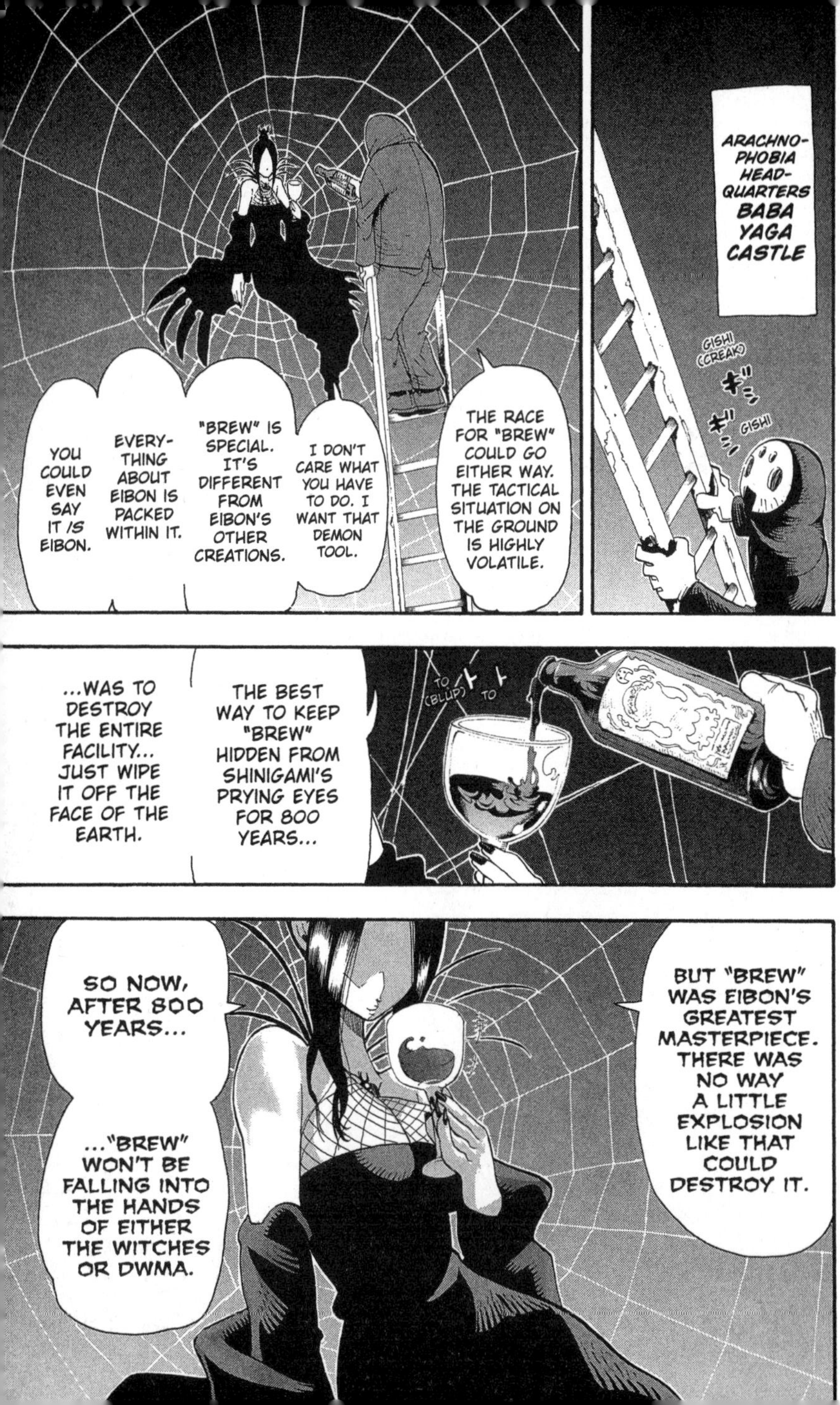

ARACHNOPHOBIA HEADQUARTERS BABA YAGA CASTLE
GISHI (CREAK)
GISHI
THE RACE FOR "BREW" COULD GO EITHER WAY. THE TACTICAL SITUATION ON THE GROUND IS HIGHLY VOLATILE.
I DON'T CARE WHAT YOU HAVE TO DO. I WANT THAT DEMON TOOL.
"BREW" IS SPECIAL. IT'S DIFFERENT FROM EIBON'S OTHER CREATIONS.
EVERYTHING ABOUT EIBON IS PACKED WITHIN IT.
YOU COULD EVEN SAY IT *IS* EIBON.
TO (BLUP) TO
THE BEST WAY TO KEEP "BREW" HIDDEN FROM SHINIGAMI'S PRYING EYES FOR 800 YEARS...
...WAS TO DESTROY THE ENTIRE FACILITY... JUST WIPE IT OFF THE FACE OF THE EARTH.
BUT "BREW" WAS EIBON'S GREATEST MASTERPIECE. THERE WAS NO WAY A LITTLE EXPLOSION LIKE THAT COULD DESTROY IT.
SO NOW, AFTER 800 YEARS...
..."BREW" WON'T BE FALLING INTO THE HANDS OF EITHER THE WITCHES OR DWMA.

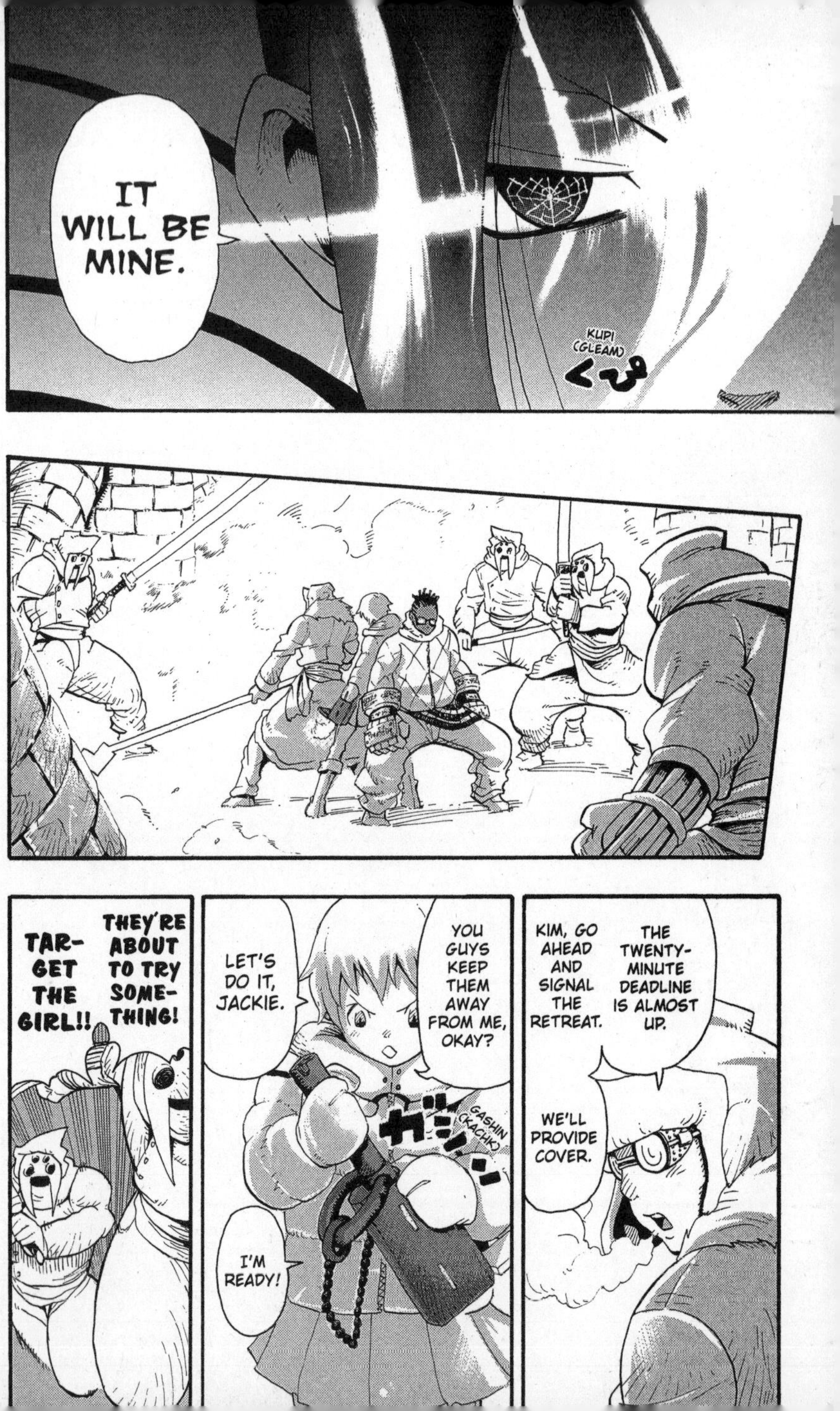
IT WILL BE MINE.
KUPI (GLEAM)
THE TWENTY-MINUTE DEADLINE IS ALMOST UP.
KIM, GO AHEAD AND SIGNAL THE RETREAT.
WE'LL PROVIDE COVER.
YOU GUYS KEEP THEM AWAY FROM ME, OKAY?
LET'S DO IT, JACKIE.
GASHIN (KACHK)
I'M READY!
THEY'RE ABOUT TO TRY SOMETHING!
TAR-GET THE GIRL!!

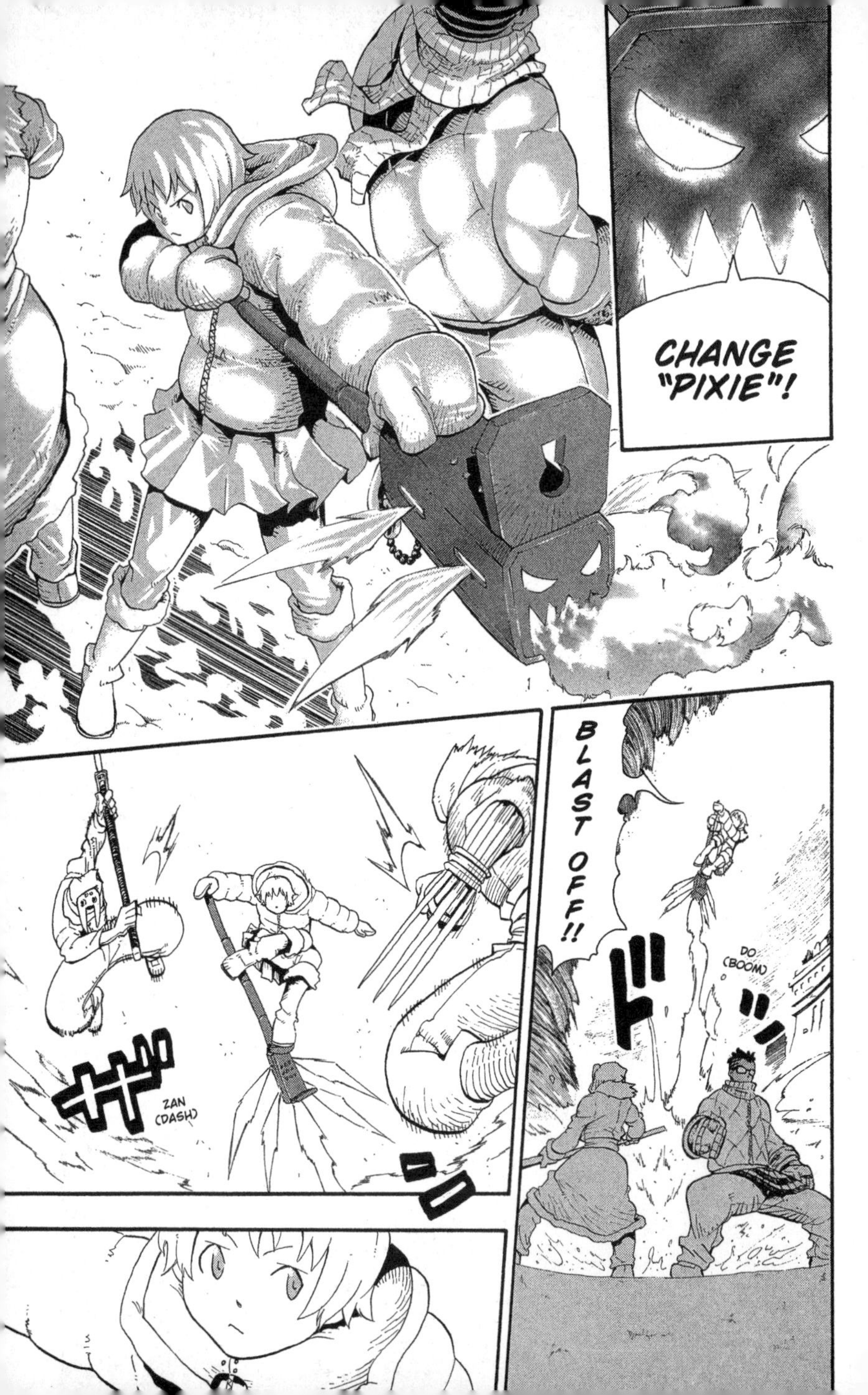
CHANGE "PIXIE"!
BLAST OFF!!
DO (BOOM)
ZAN (DASH)

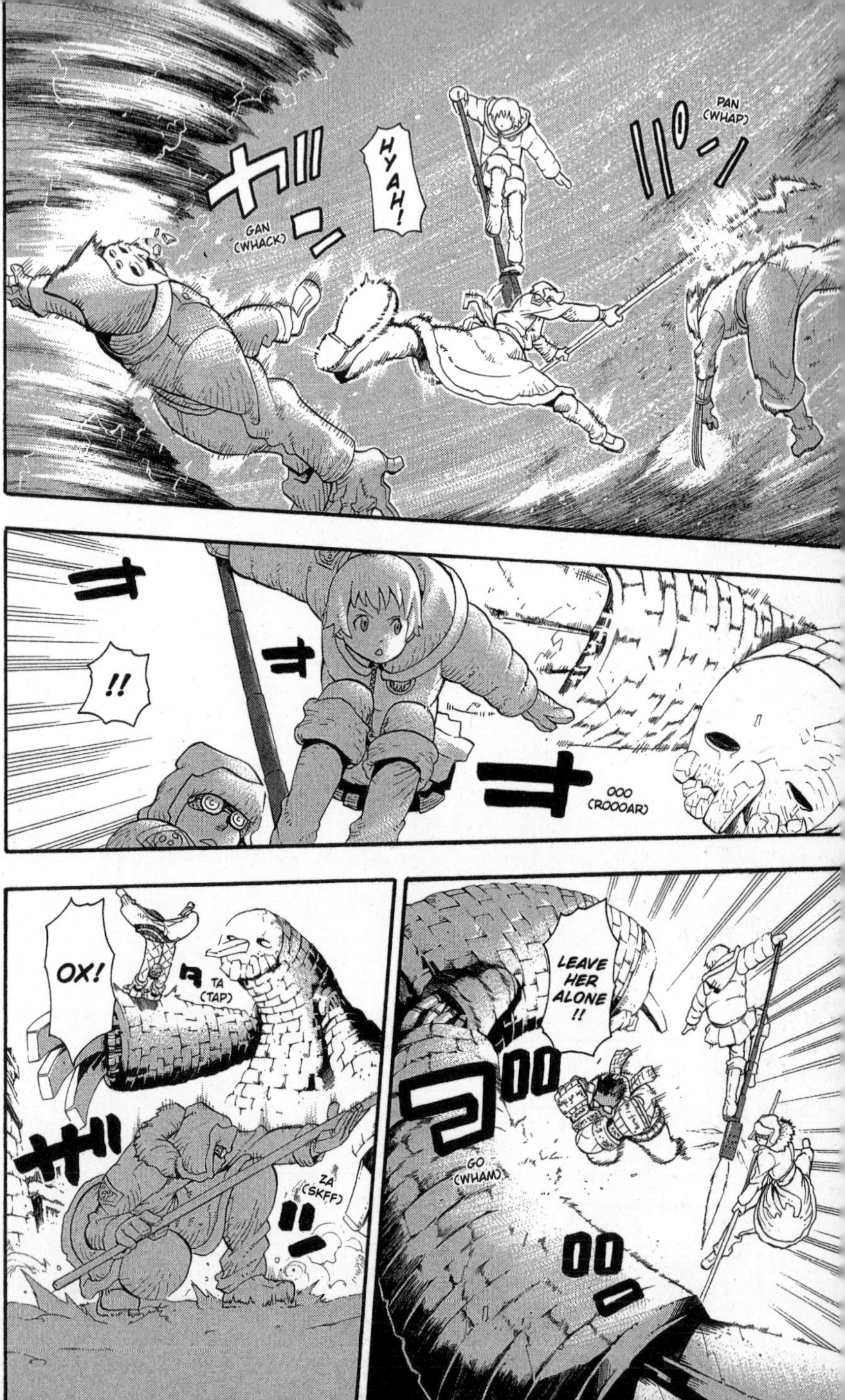
PAN
(WHAP)
HYAH!
GAN
(WHACK)
OOO
(ROOOAR)
!!
LEAVE HER ALONE!!
GO
(WHAM)
OX!
TA
(TAP)
ZA
(SKFF)

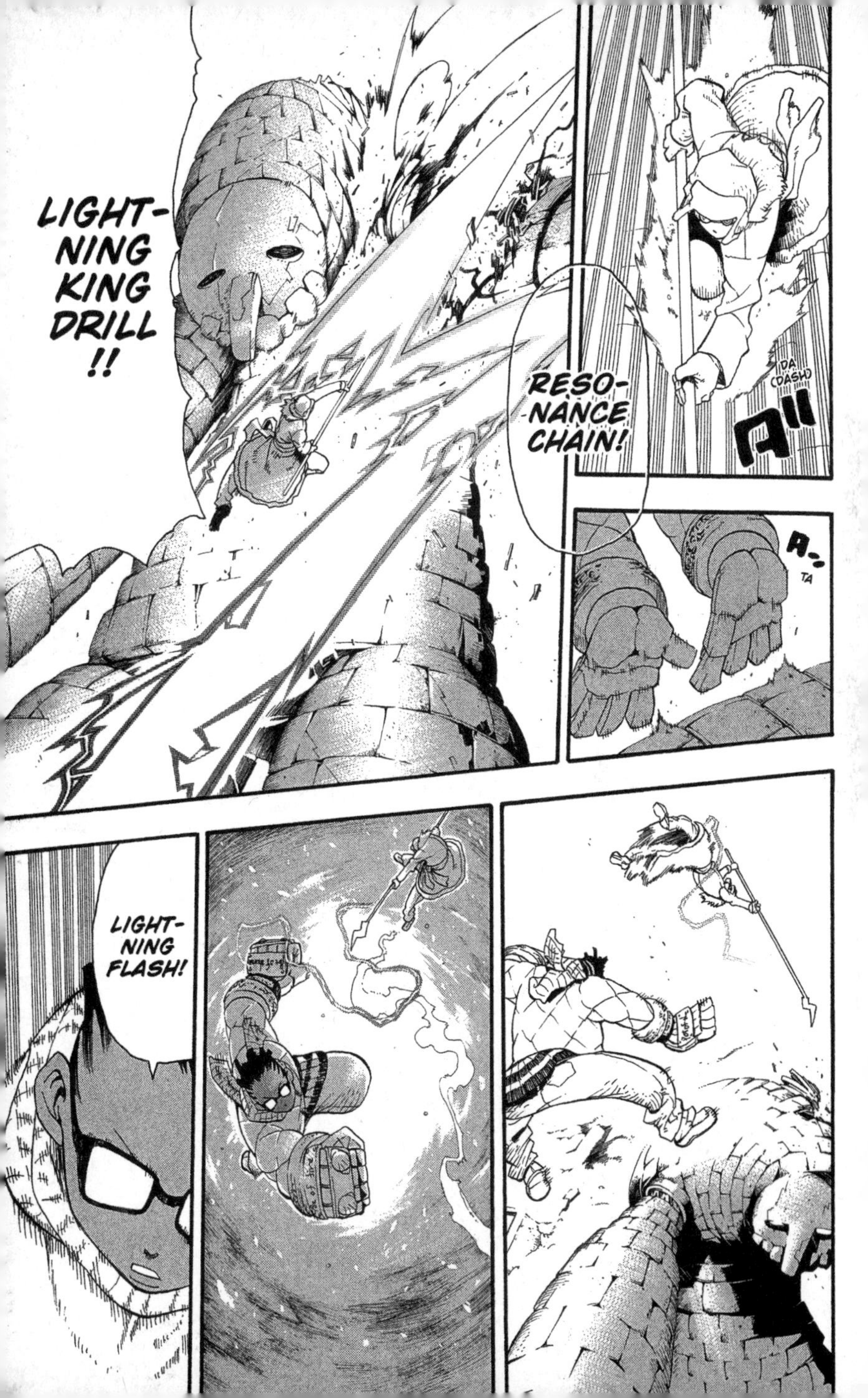
RESO-NANCE CHAIN!
DA (DASH)
TA
LIGHT-NING KING DRILL!!
LIGHT-NING FLASH!

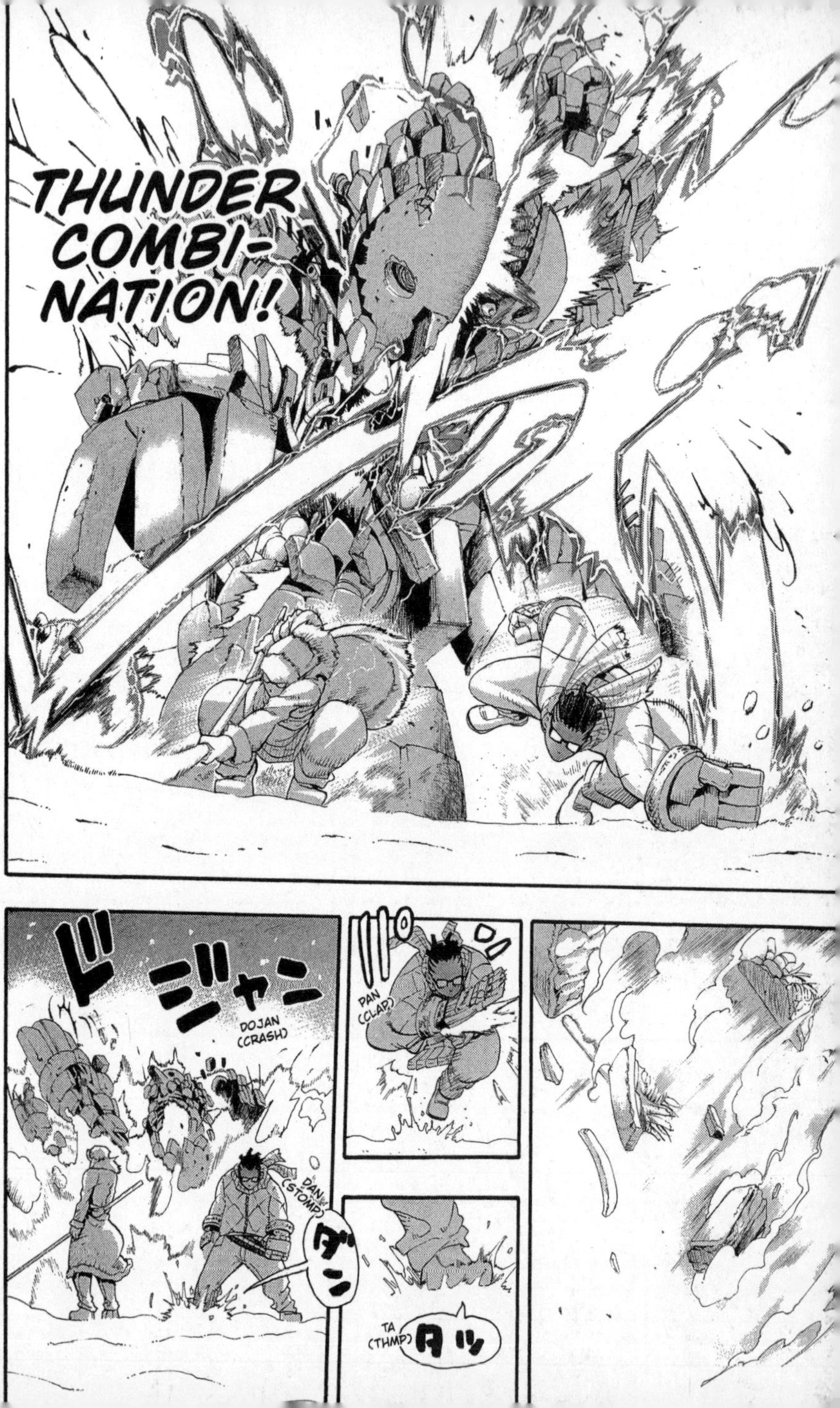
THUNDER COMBI-NATION!
PAN (CLAP)
TA (THMP)
タッ
DOJAN (CRASH)
DAN (STOMP)
ダン

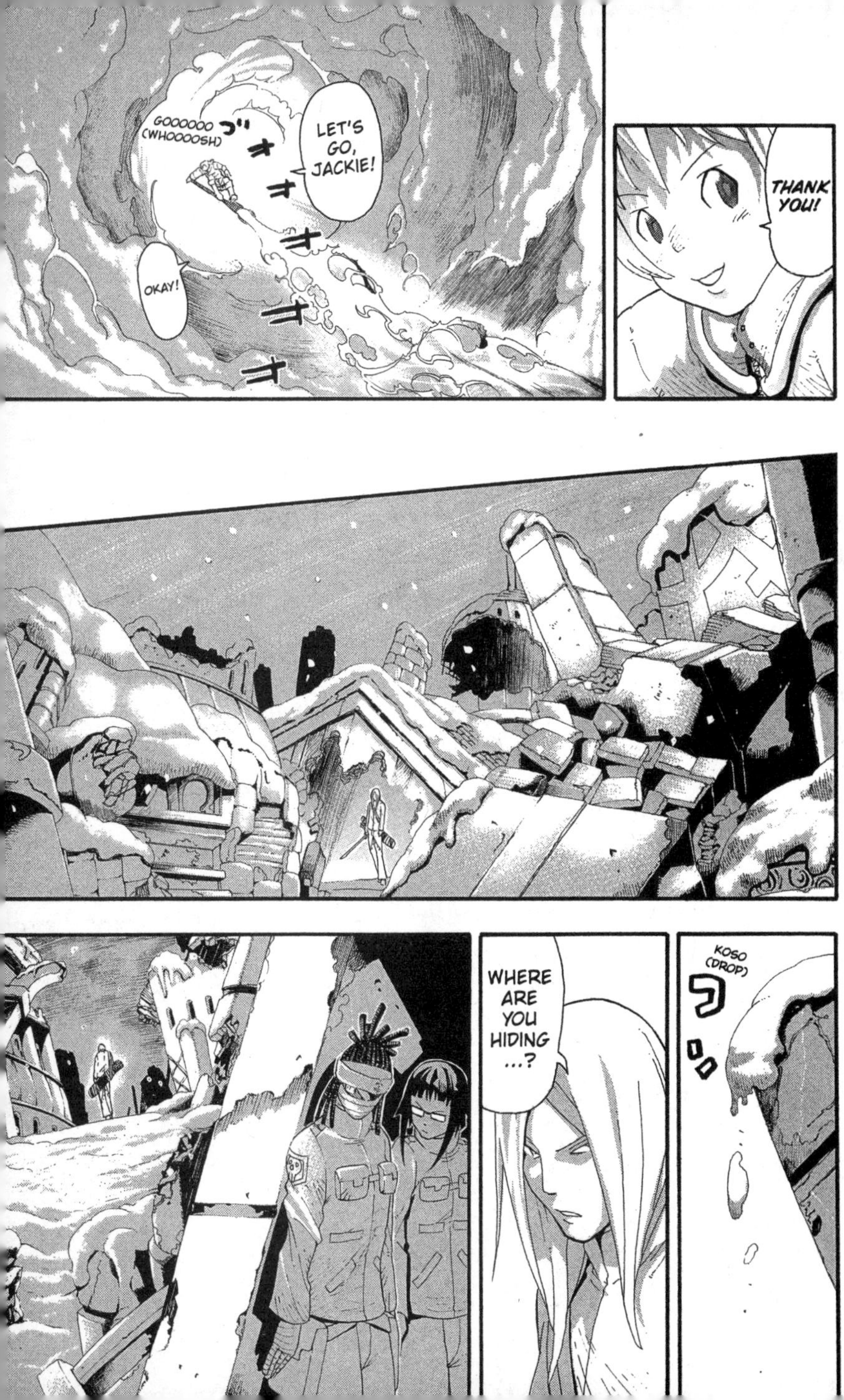
THANK YOU!
LET'S GO, JACKIE!
GOOOOOO (WHOOOOSH)
OKAY!
KOSO (DROP)
WHERE ARE YOU HIDING ...?

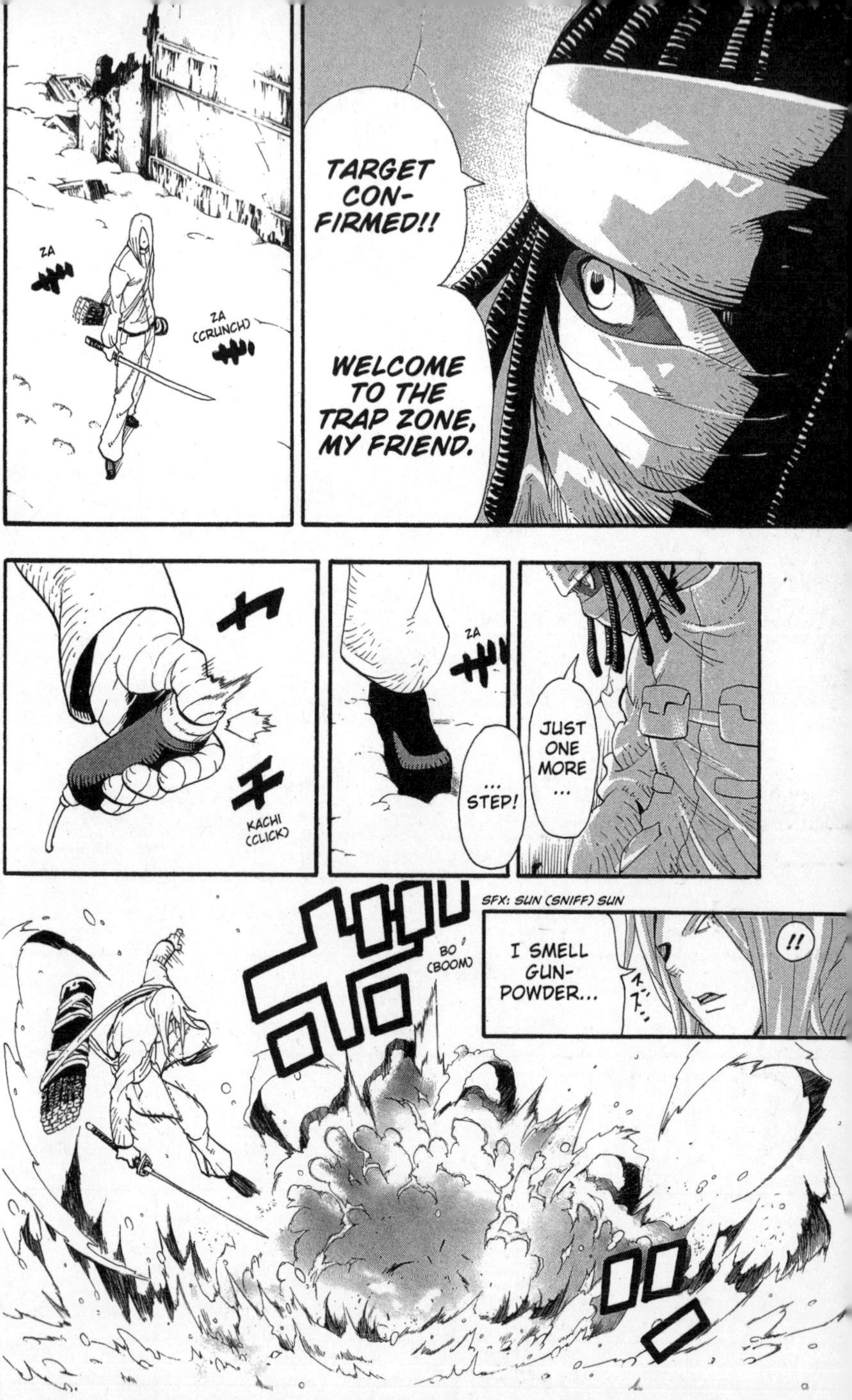
TARGET CON-FIRMED!!
WELCOME TO THE TRAP ZONE, MY FRIEND.
ZA
ZA (CRUNCH)
JUST ONE MORE ...
... STEP!
ZA
KACHI (CLICK)
SFX: SUN (SNIFF) SUN
!!
I SMELL GUN-POWDER...
BO (BOOM)

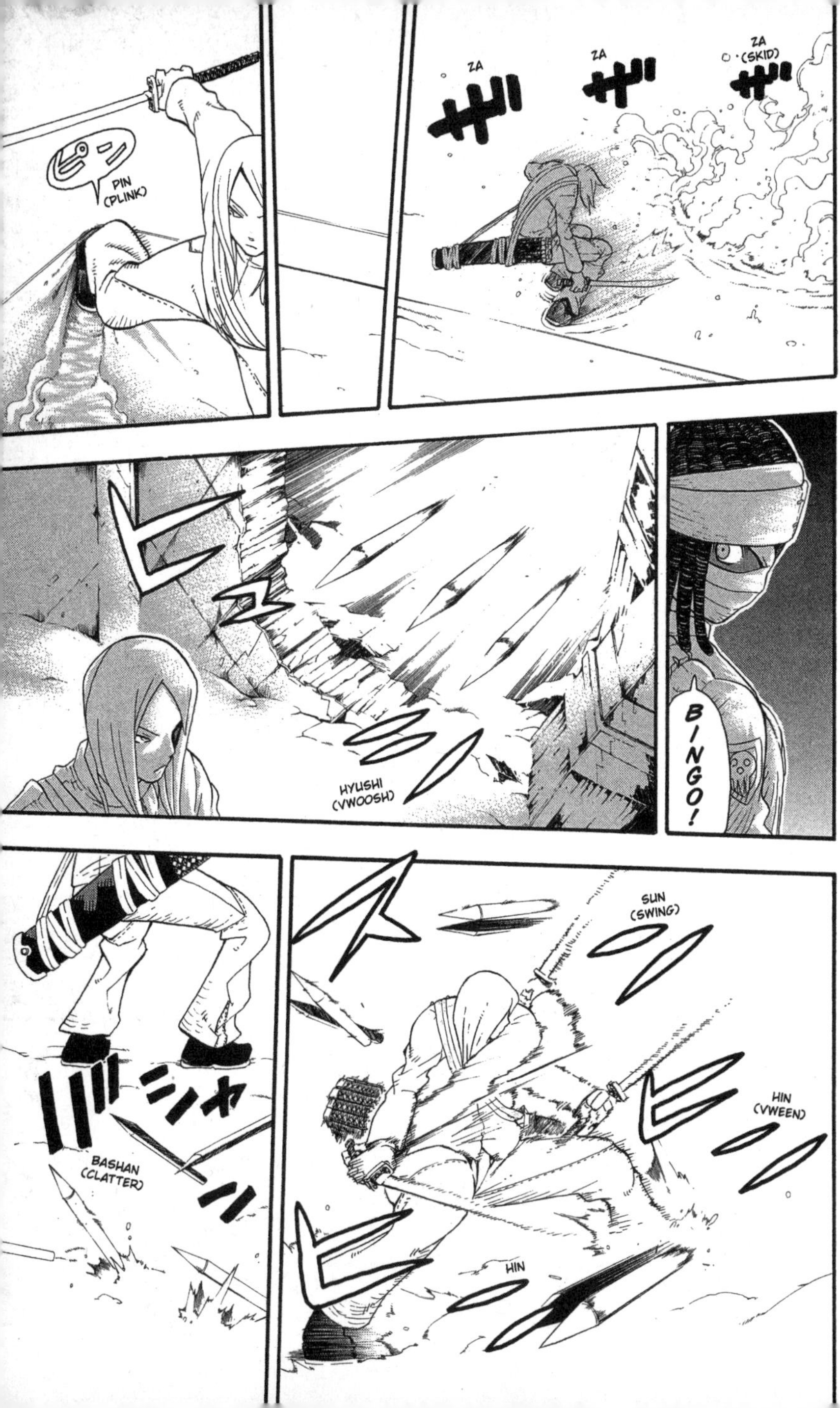
ZA
ZA
ZA (SKID)
ピン
PIN (PLINK)
BINGO!
HYUSHI (VWOOSH)
SUN (SWING)
HIN (VWEEN)
HIN
BASHAN (CLATTER)

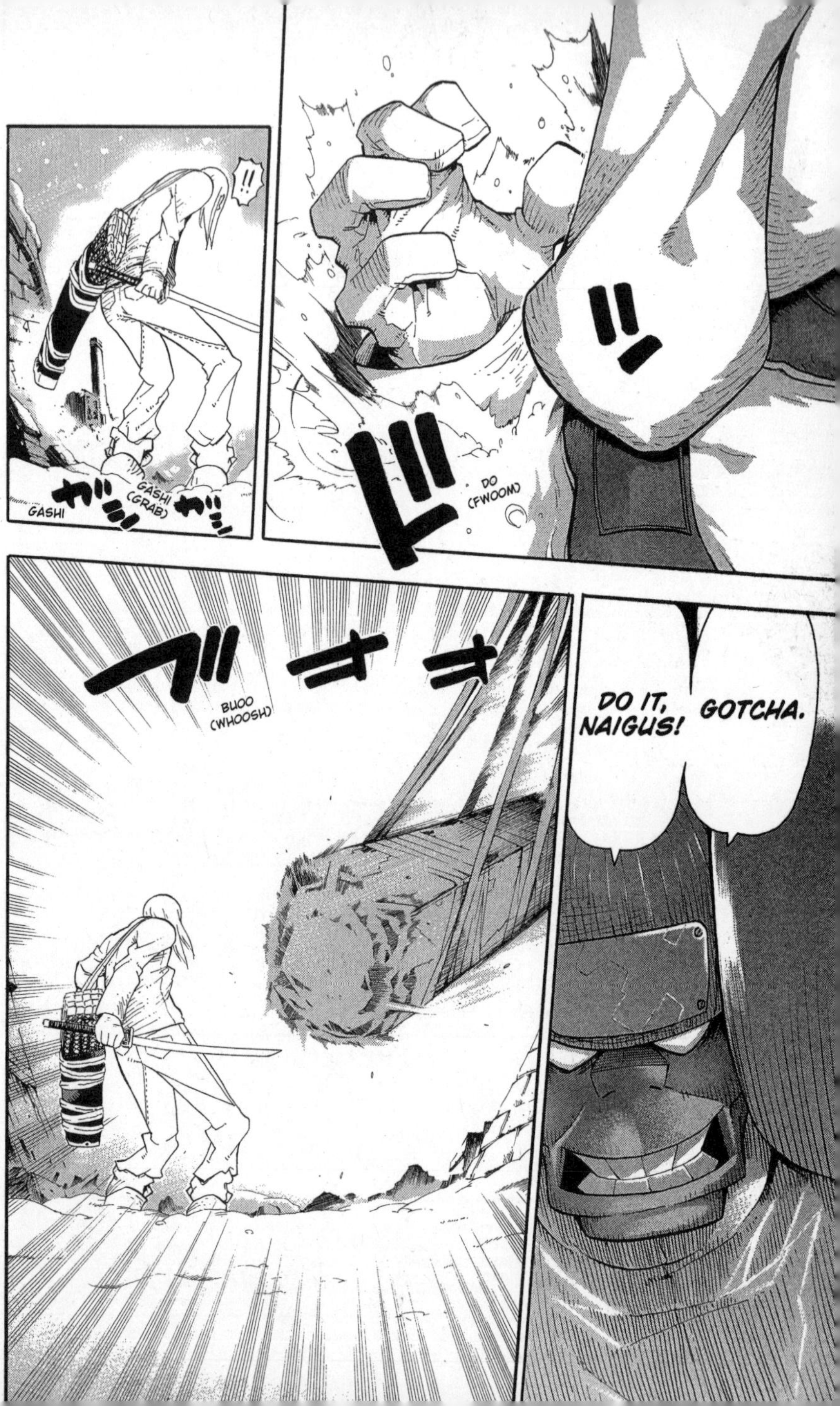
DO
(FWOOM)
!!
GASHI
(GRAB)
GASHI
GOTCHA.
DO IT,
NAIGUS!
BUOO
(WHOOSH)

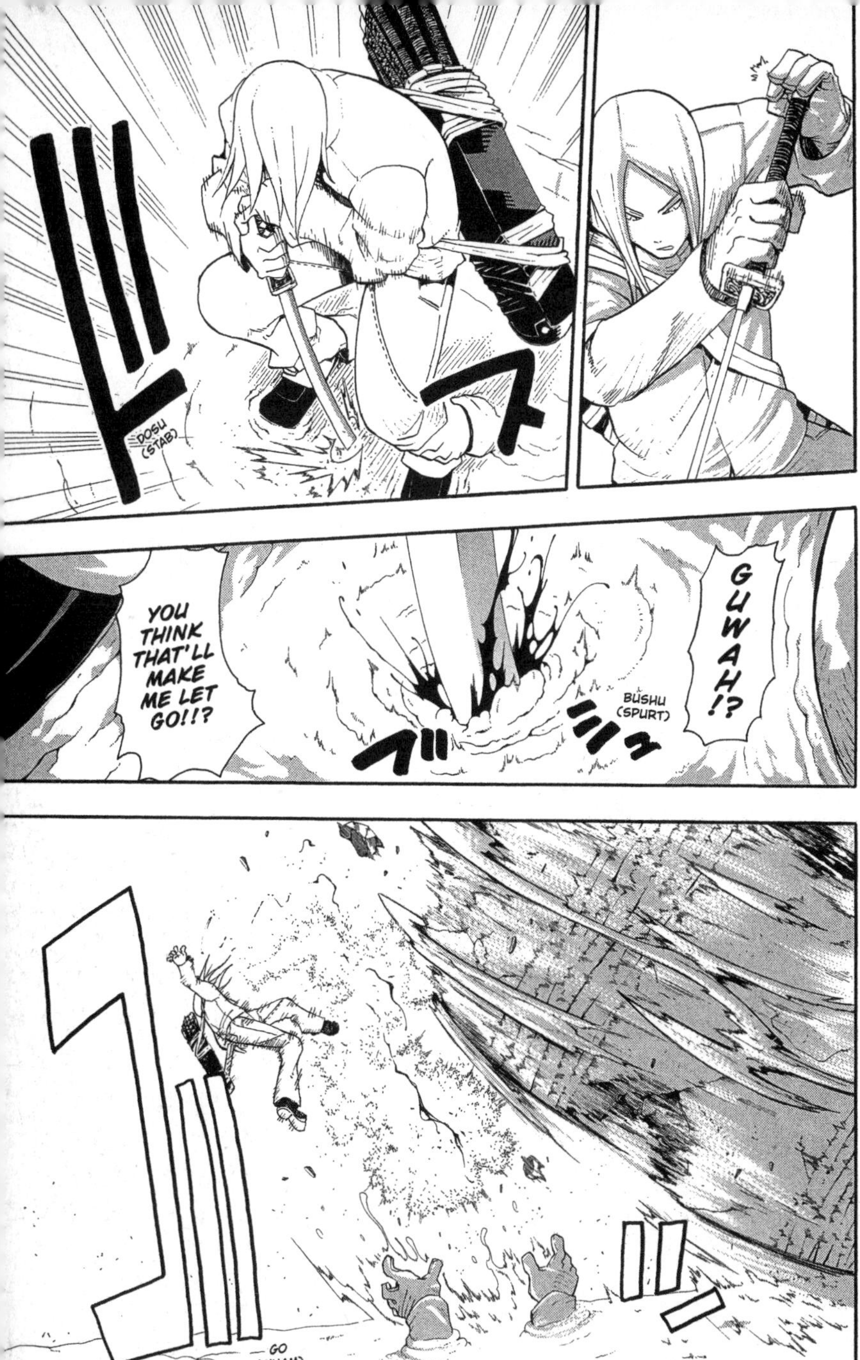
DOSU (STAB)
GUWAH!?
BUSHU (SPURT)
YOU THINK THAT'LL MAKE ME LET GO!!?
GO (WHAM)

GA
GA
GA (WHUMP)
GA

ZA (SHFF)

NAI-GUS.

DOPA (SPLOOSH)

BUSHU (SPURT)

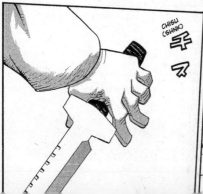

CHISU (SHNK)

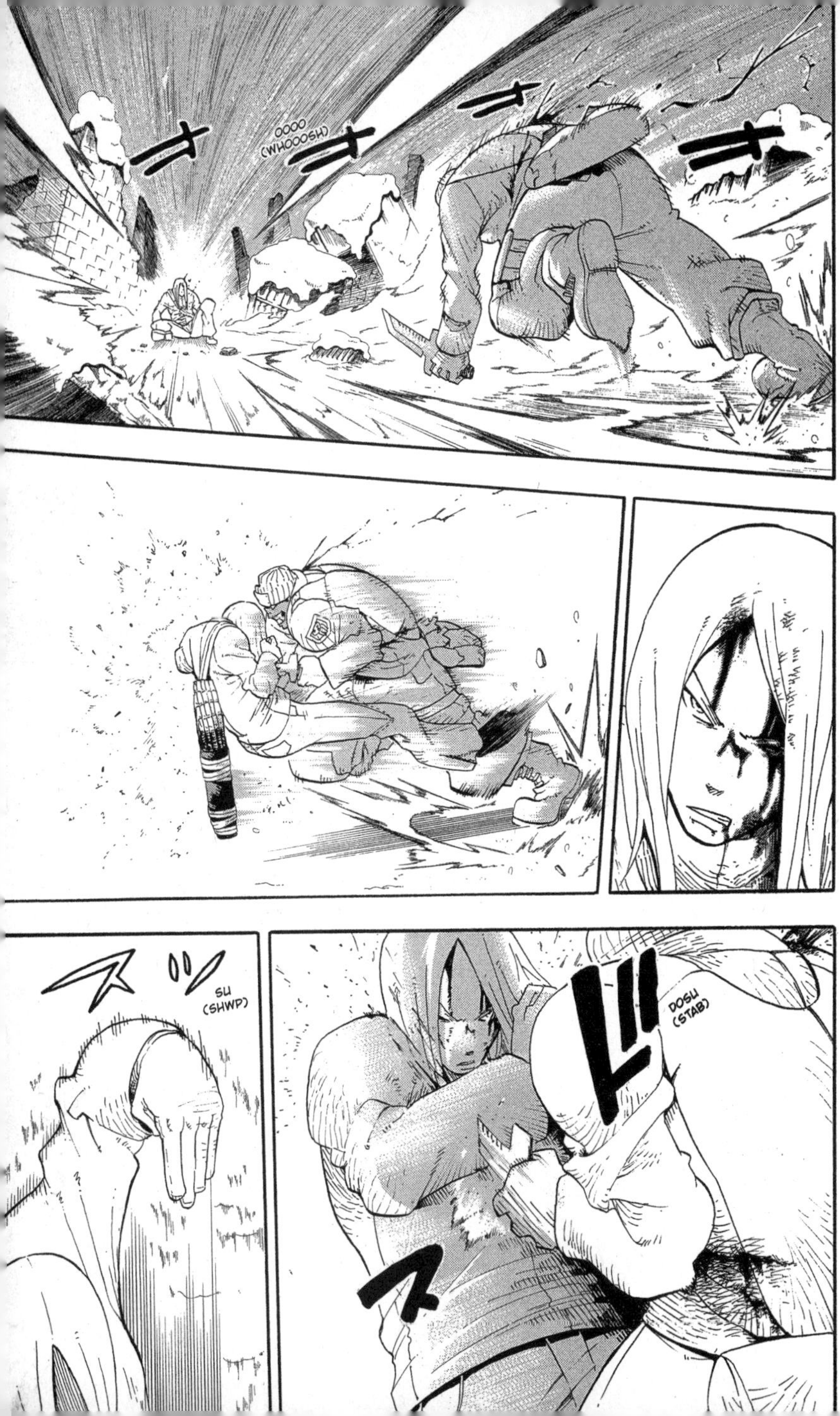
OOOO
(WHOOOSH)
DOSU
(STAB)
SU
(SHWP)

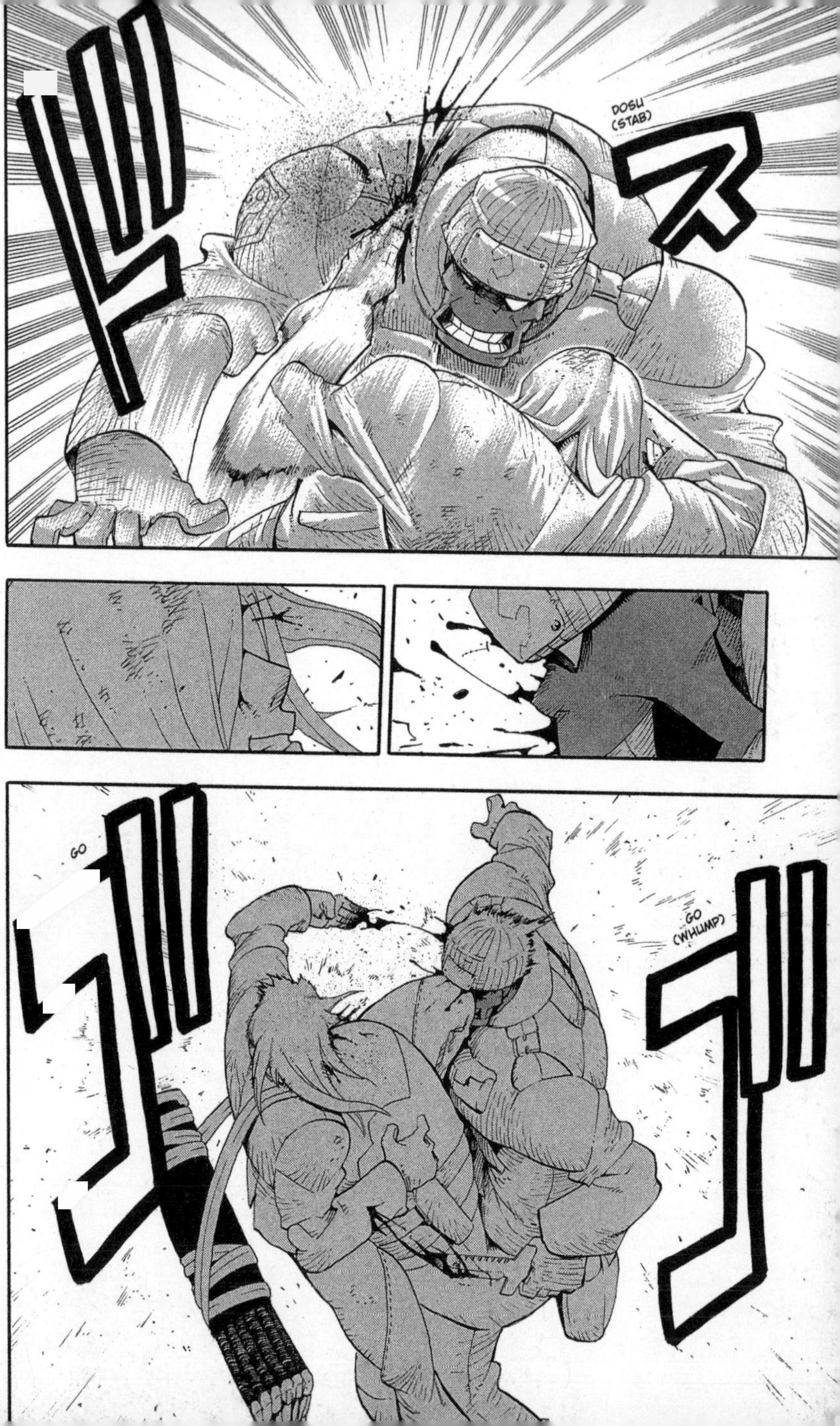
DOSU
(STAB)
GO
(WHUMP)
GO

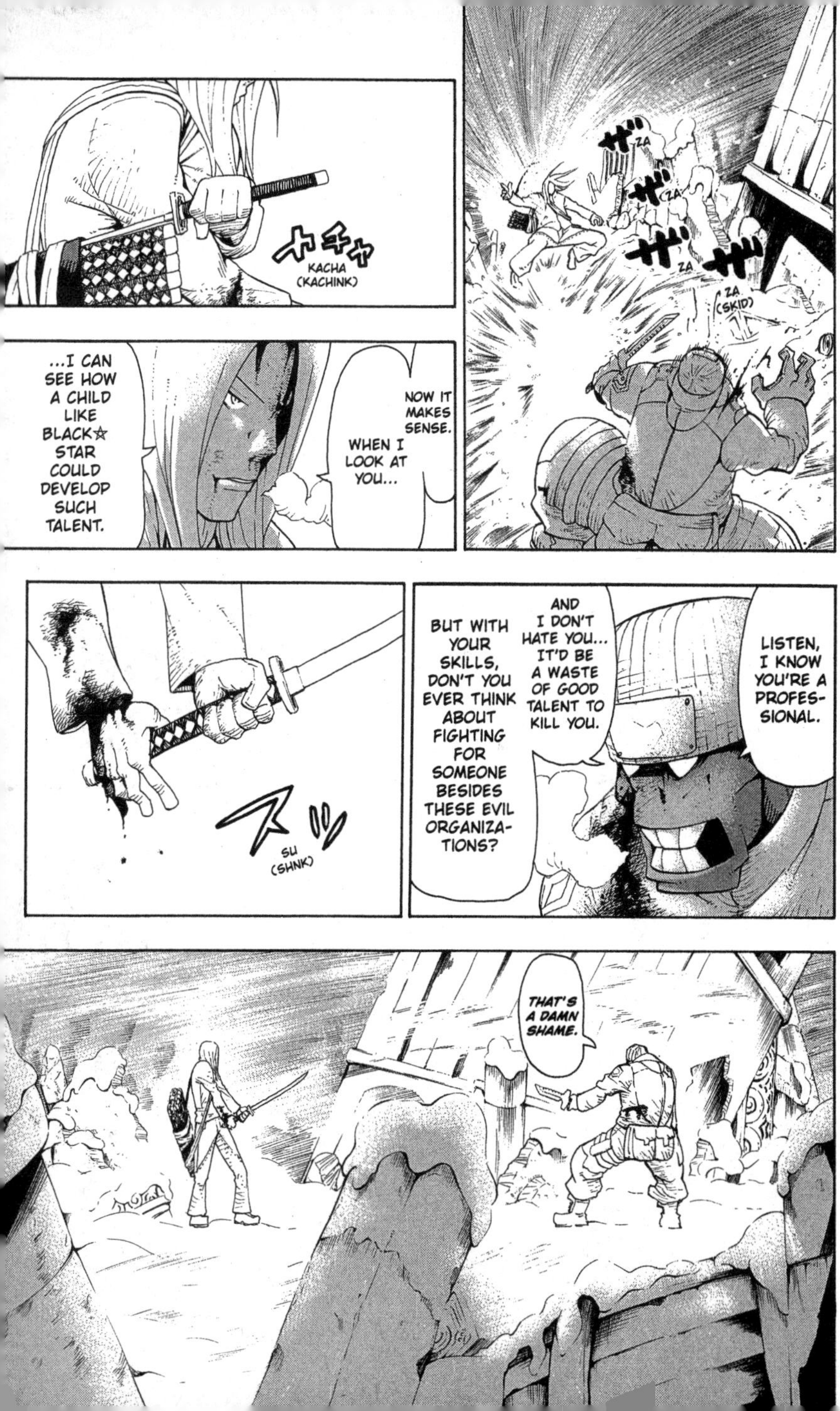
ZA
ZA
ZA
ZA (SKID)
KACHA (KACHINK)
NOW IT MAKES SENSE.
WHEN I LOOK AT YOU...
...I CAN SEE HOW A CHILD LIKE BLACK☆STAR COULD DEVELOP SUCH TALENT.
LISTEN, I KNOW YOU'RE A PROFES-SIONAL.
AND I DON'T HATE YOU... IT'D BE A WASTE OF GOOD TALENT TO KILL YOU.
BUT WITH YOUR SKILLS, DON'T YOU EVER THINK ABOUT FIGHTING FOR SOMEONE BESIDES THESE EVIL ORGANIZA-TIONS?
SU (SHNK)
THAT'S A DAMN SHAME.

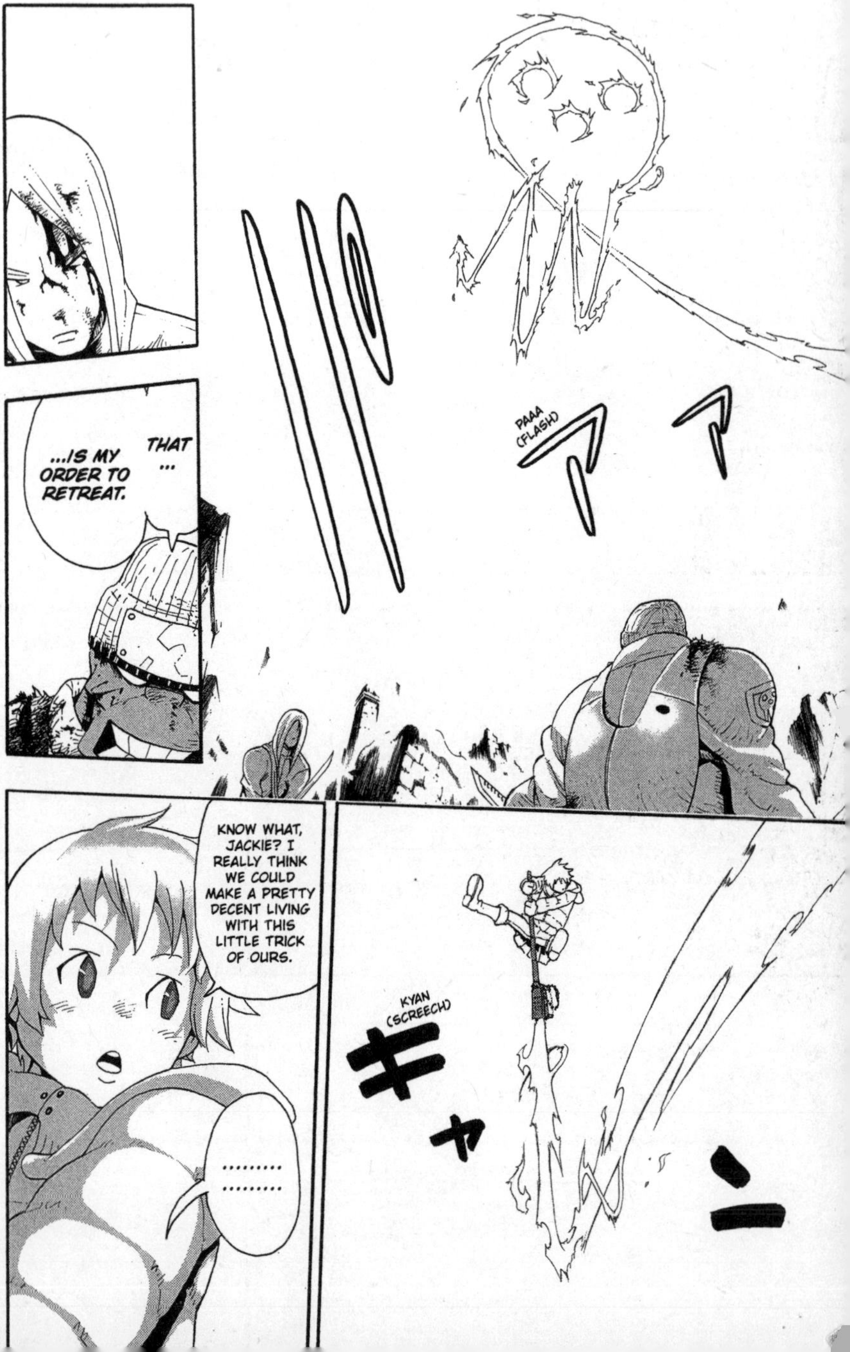
PAAA (FLASH)
THAT ...
...IS MY ORDER TO RETREAT.
KYAN (SCREECH)
KNOW WHAT, JACKIE? I REALLY THINK WE COULD MAKE A PRETTY DECENT LIVING WITH THIS LITTLE TRICK OF OURS.
....
....

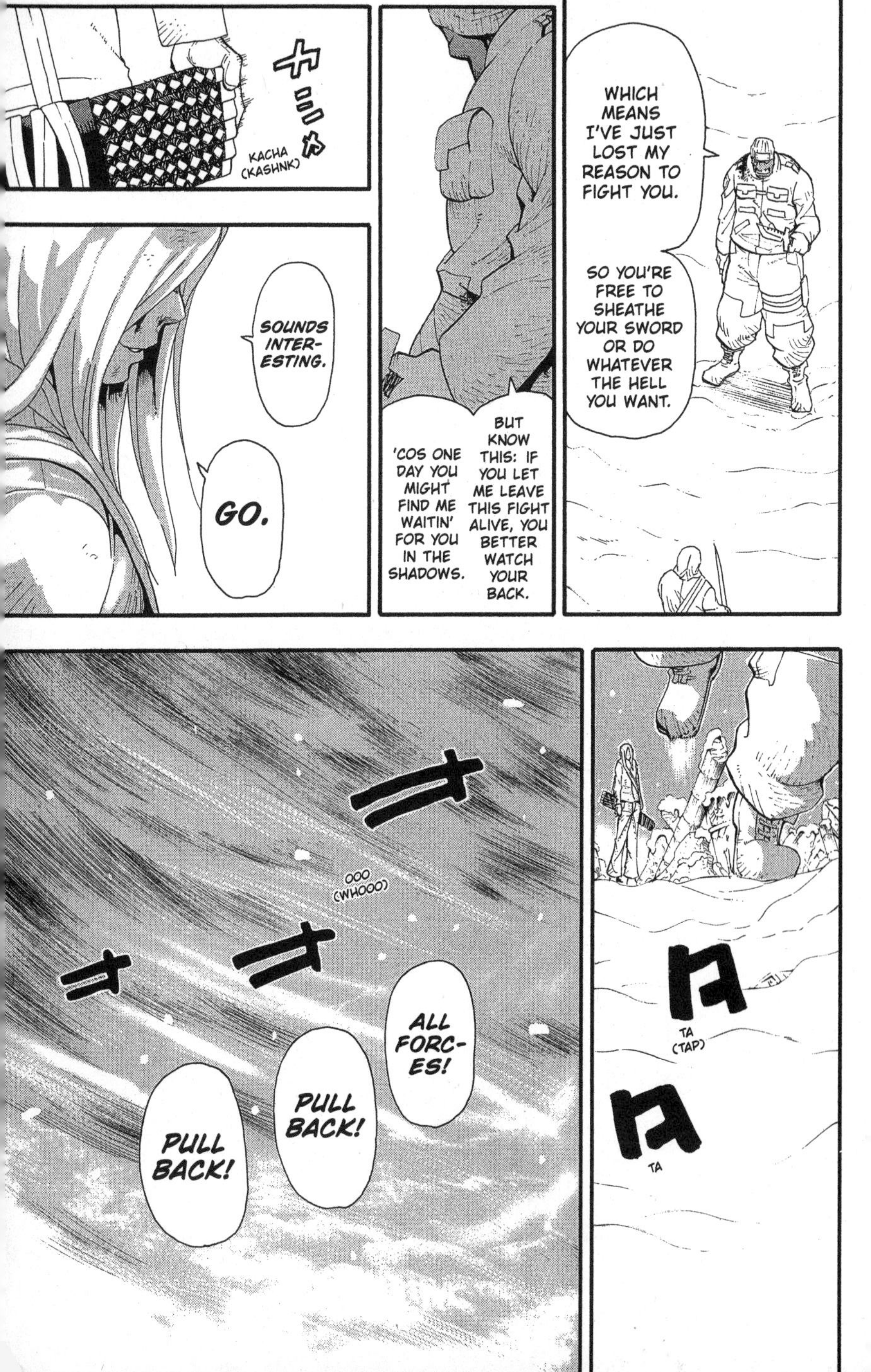
WHICH MEANS I'VE JUST LOST MY REASON TO FIGHT YOU.
SO YOU'RE FREE TO SHEATHE YOUR SWORD OR DO WHATEVER THE HELL YOU WANT.
BUT KNOW THIS: IF YOU LET ME LEAVE THIS FIGHT ALIVE, YOU BETTER WATCH YOUR BACK.
'COS ONE DAY YOU MIGHT FIND ME WAITIN' FOR YOU IN THE SHADOWS.
KACHA (KASHNK)
SOUNDS INTER-ESTING.
GO.
TA (TAP)
TA
OOO (WHOOO)
ALL FORC-ES!
PULL BACK!
PULL BACK!

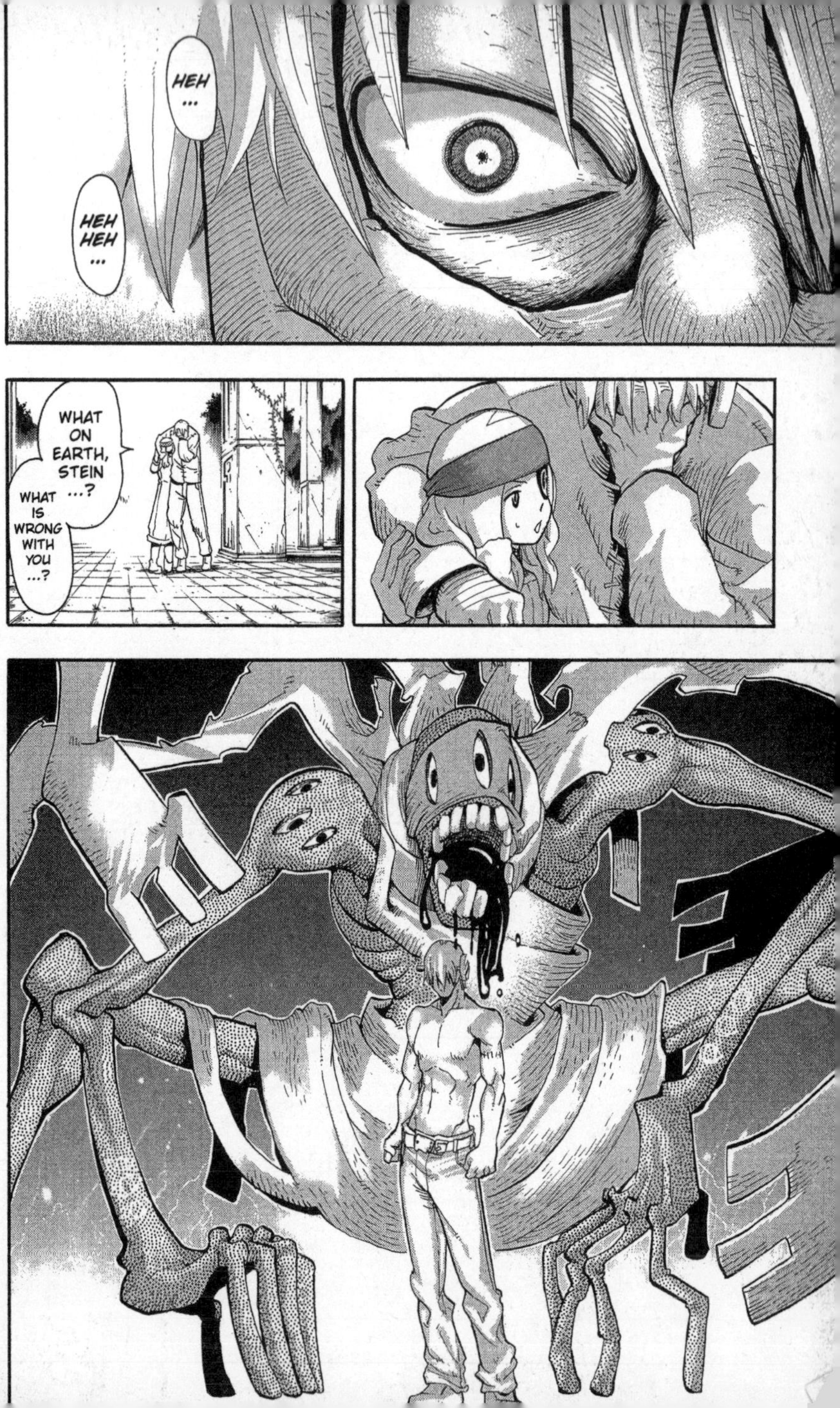
HEH ...
HEH HEH ...
WHAT ON EARTH, STEIN ...?
WHAT IS WRONG WITH YOU ...?

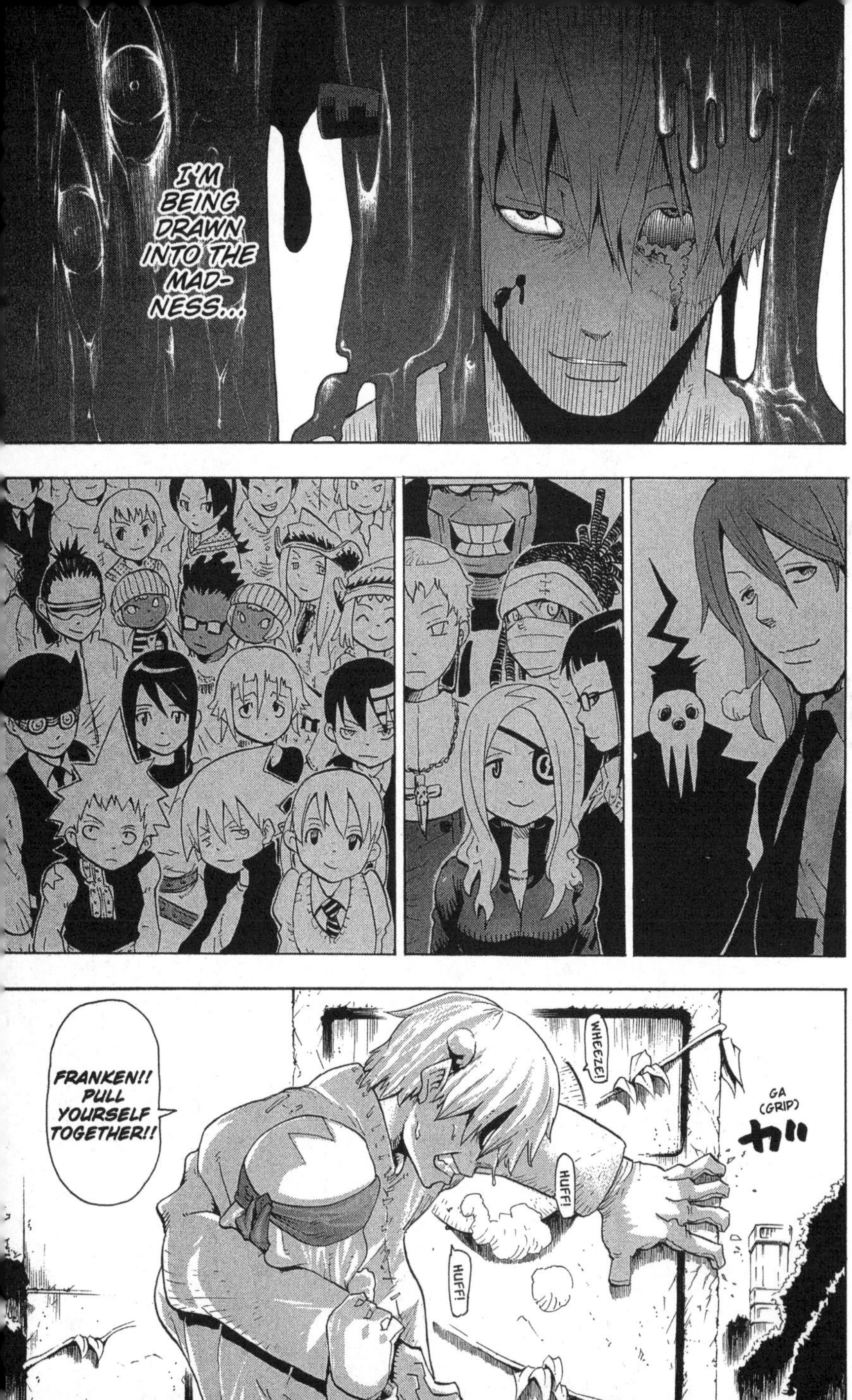

I'M BEING DRAWN INTO THE MAD-NESS...
GA (GRIP)
カッ
WHEEZE!
HUFF!
HUFF!
FRANKEN!! PULL YOURSELF TOGETHER!!

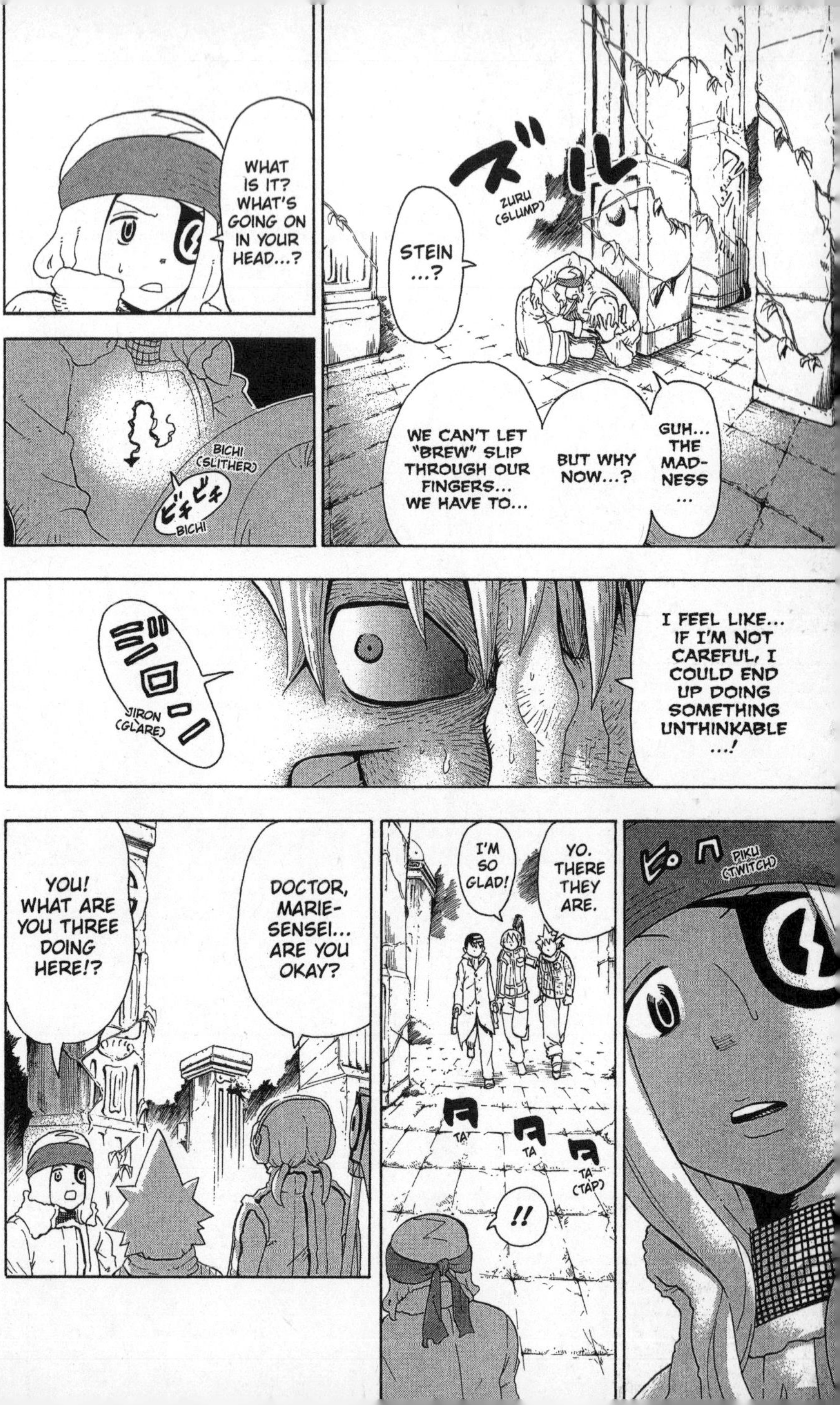
ズル
ZURU (SLUMP)
STEIN ...?
GUH... THE MAD-NESS ...
BUT WHY NOW...?
WE CAN'T LET "BREW" SLIP THROUGH OUR FINGERS... WE HAVE TO...
WHAT IS IT? WHAT'S GOING ON IN YOUR HEAD...?
BICHI (SLITHER)
ビチビチ
BICHI
I FEEL LIKE... IF I'M NOT CAREFUL, I COULD END UP DOING SOMETHING UNTHINKABLE ...!
JIRON (GLARE)
PIKU (TWITCH)
YO. THERE THEY ARE.
I'M SO GLAD!
TA
TA
TA (TAP)
!!
DOCTOR, MARIE-SENSEI... ARE YOU OKAY?
YOU! WHAT ARE YOU THREE DOING HERE!?

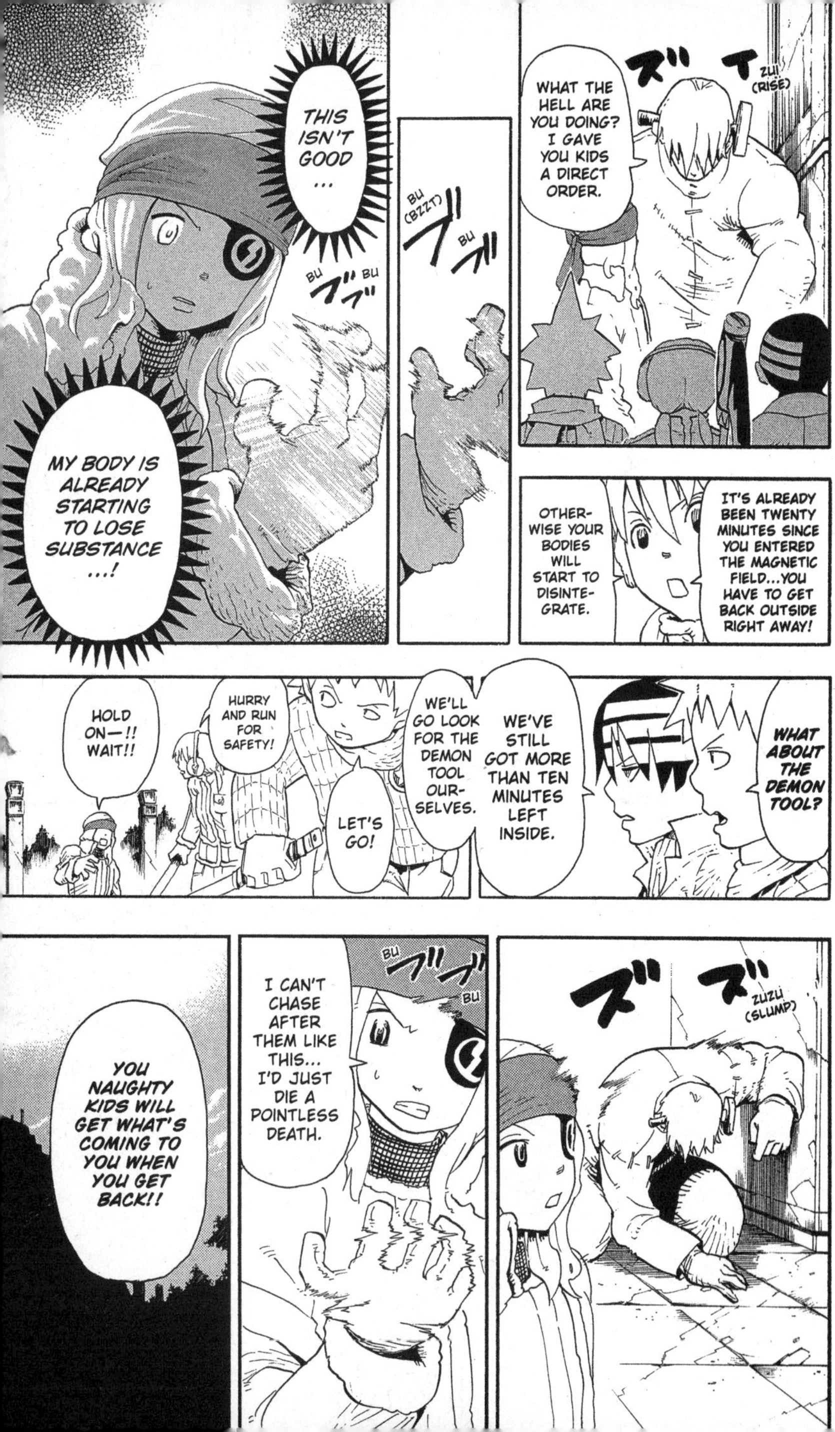
ZUI (RISE)
WHAT THE HELL ARE YOU DOING? I GAVE YOU KIDS A DIRECT ORDER.
IT'S ALREADY BEEN TWENTY MINUTES SINCE YOU ENTERED THE MAGNETIC FIELD...YOU HAVE TO GET BACK OUTSIDE RIGHT AWAY!
OTHER-WISE YOUR BODIES WILL START TO DISINTE-GRATE.
BU (BZZT)
BU
THIS ISN'T GOOD...
BU BU
MY BODY IS ALREADY STARTING TO LOSE SUBSTANCE...!
WHAT ABOUT THE DEMON TOOL?
WE'VE STILL GOT MORE THAN TEN MINUTES LEFT INSIDE.
WE'LL GO LOOK FOR THE DEMON TOOL OURSELVES.
LET'S GO!
HURRY AND RUN FOR SAFETY!
HOLD ON—!! WAIT!!
ZUZU (SLUMP)
BU
BU
I CAN'T CHASE AFTER THEM LIKE THIS... I'D JUST DIE A POINTLESS DEATH.
YOU NAUGHTY KIDS WILL GET WHAT'S COMING TO YOU WHEN YOU GET BACK!!

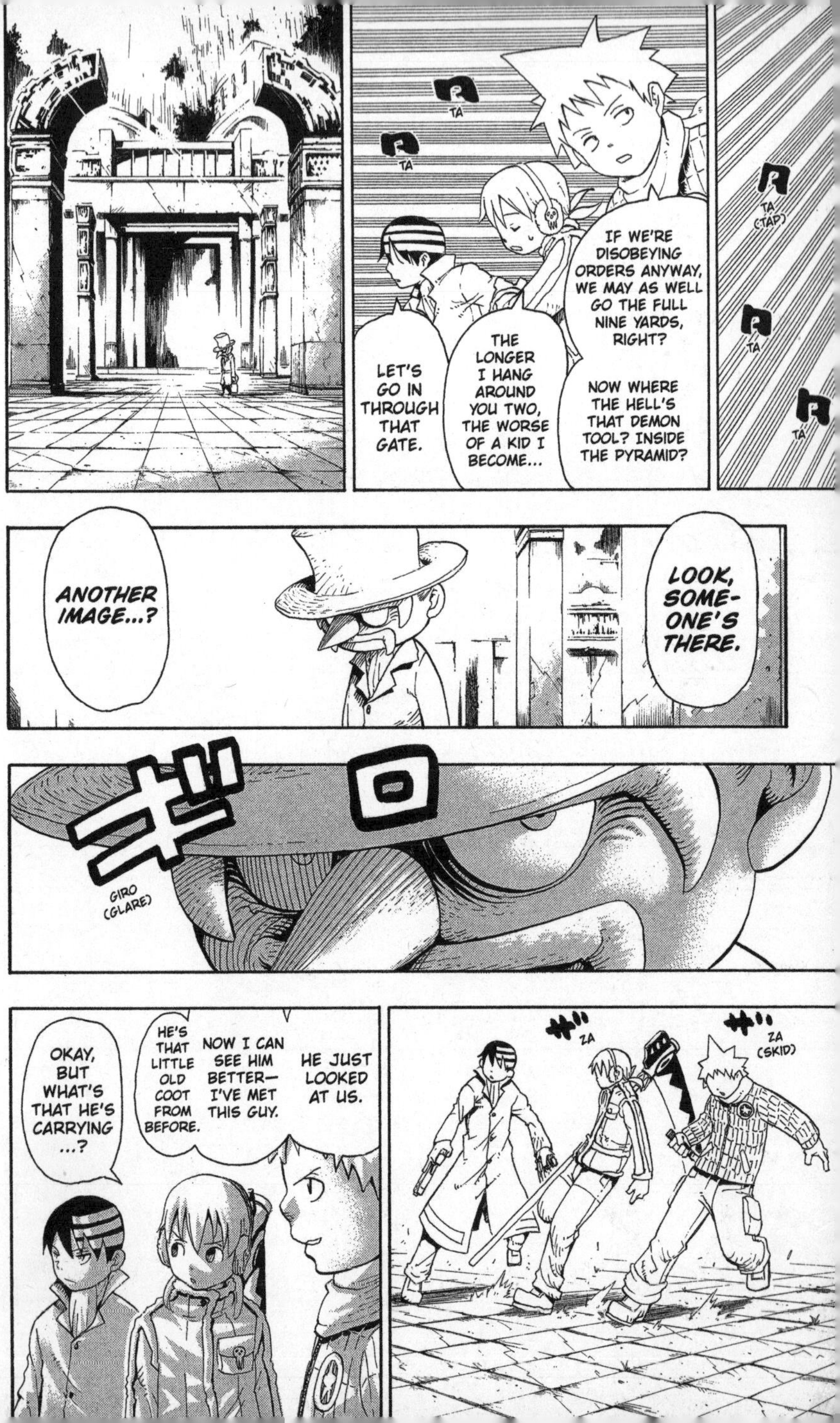
TA (TAP)
TA
TA
TA
TA
IF WE'RE DISOBEYING ORDERS ANYWAY, WE MAY AS WELL GO THE FULL NINE YARDS, RIGHT?
NOW WHERE THE HELL'S THAT DEMON TOOL? INSIDE THE PYRAMID?
THE LONGER I HANG AROUND YOU TWO, THE WORSE OF A KID I BECOME...
LET'S GO IN THROUGH THAT GATE.
LOOK, SOME-ONE'S THERE.
ANOTHER IMAGE...?
GIRO (GLARE)
ZA (SKID)
ZA
HE JUST LOOKED AT US.
NOW I CAN SEE HIM BETTER— I'VE MET THIS GUY.
HE'S THAT LITTLE OLD COOT FROM BEFORE.
OKAY, BUT WHAT'S THAT HE'S CARRYING...?

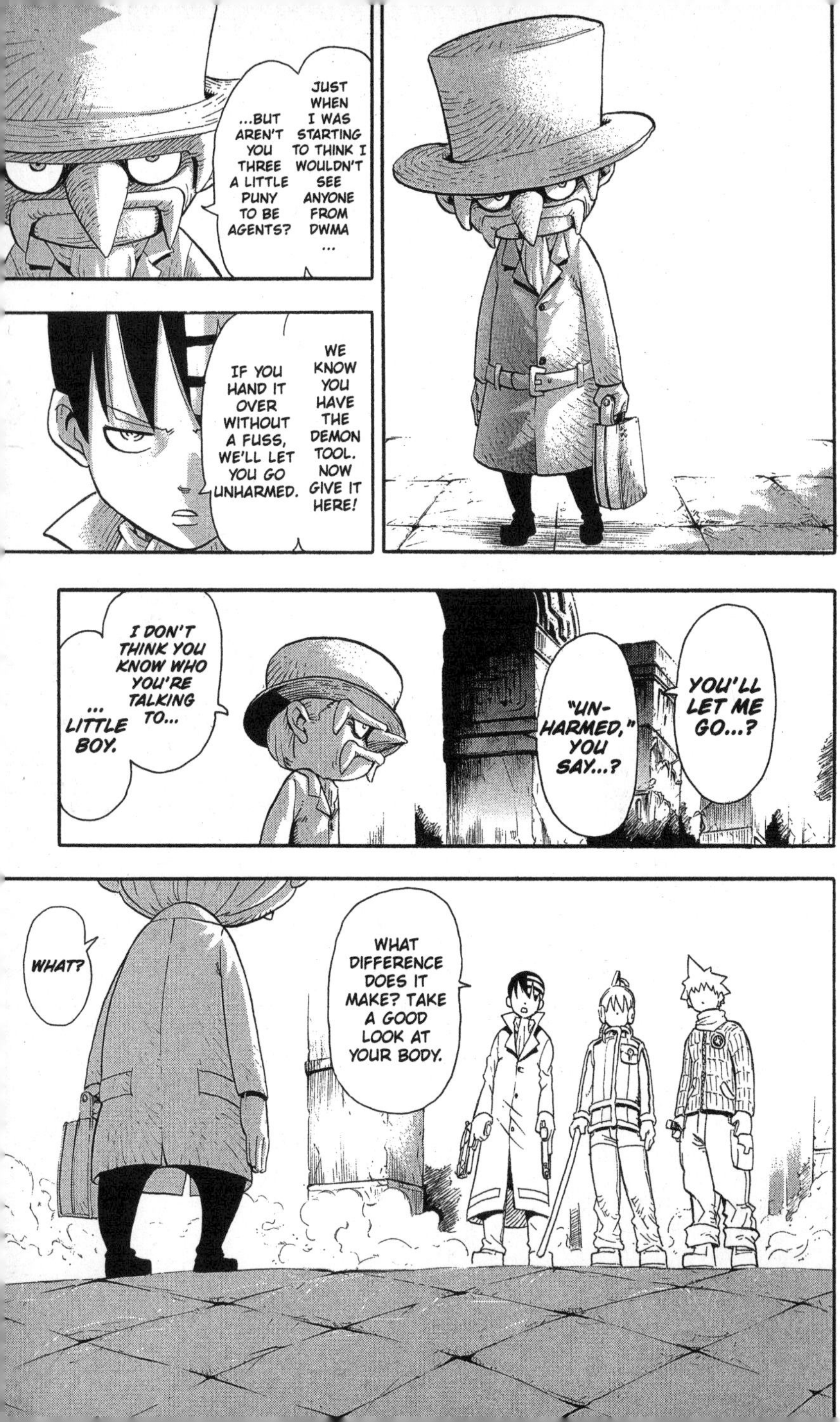
JUST WHEN I WAS STARTING TO THINK I WOULDN'T SEE ANYONE FROM DWMA ...
...BUT AREN'T YOU THREE A LITTLE PUNY TO BE AGENTS?
WE KNOW YOU HAVE THE DEMON TOOL. NOW GIVE IT HERE!
IF YOU HAND IT OVER WITHOUT A FUSS, WE'LL LET YOU GO UNHARMED.
YOU'LL LET ME GO...?
"UN-HARMED," YOU SAY...?
I DON'T THINK YOU KNOW WHO YOU'RE TALKING TO...
... LITTLE BOY.
WHAT DIFFERENCE DOES IT MAKE? TAKE A GOOD LOOK AT YOUR BODY.
WHAT?

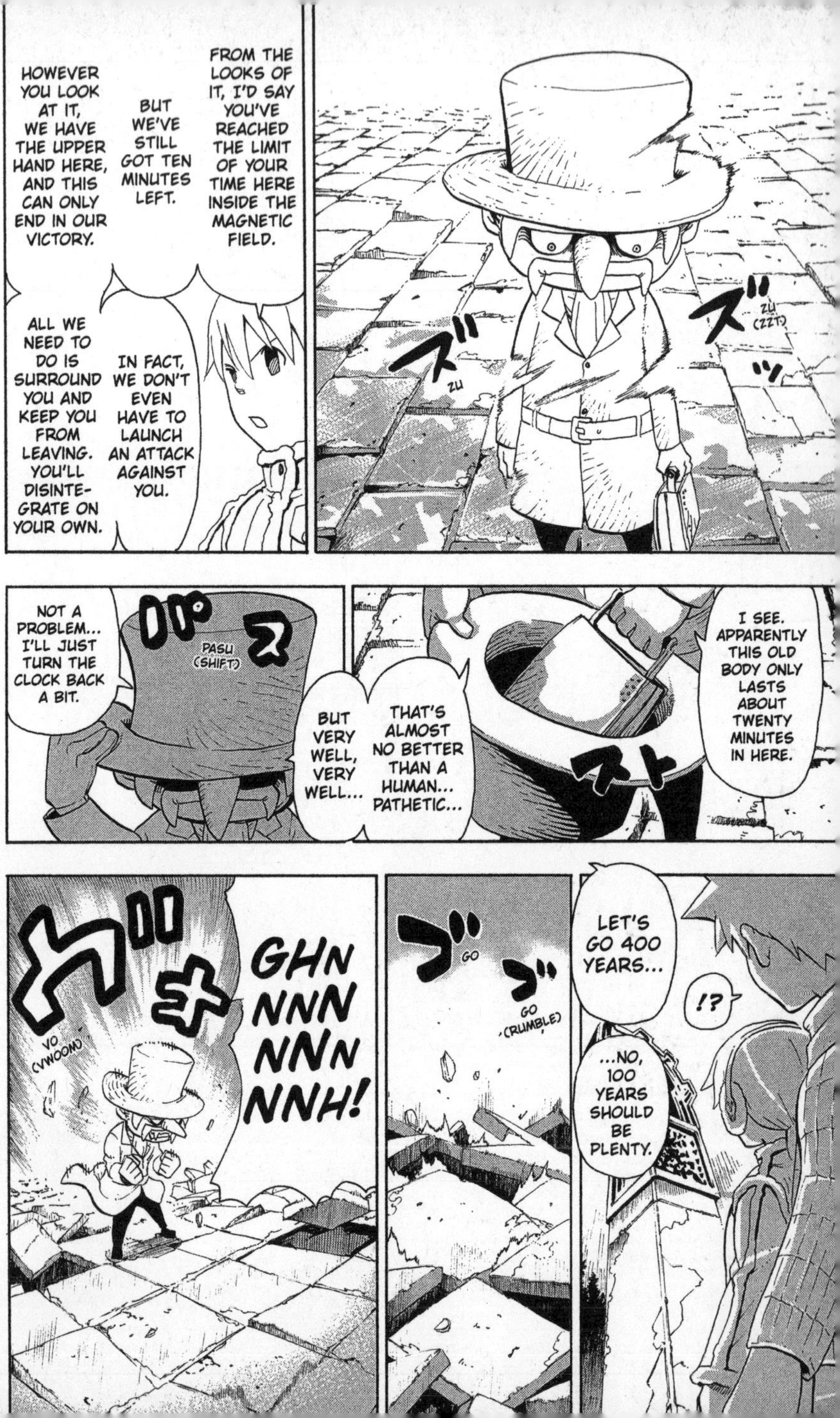
ZU (ZZT)
ZU
FROM THE LOOKS OF IT, I'D SAY YOU'VE REACHED THE LIMIT OF YOUR TIME HERE INSIDE THE MAGNETIC FIELD.
BUT WE'VE STILL GOT TEN MINUTES LEFT.
HOWEVER YOU LOOK AT IT, WE HAVE THE UPPER HAND HERE, AND THIS CAN ONLY END IN OUR VICTORY.
IN FACT, WE DON'T EVEN HAVE TO LAUNCH AN ATTACK AGAINST YOU.
ALL WE NEED TO DO IS SURROUND YOU AND KEEP YOU FROM LEAVING. YOU'LL DISINTE-GRATE ON YOUR OWN.
I SEE. APPARENTLY THIS OLD BODY ONLY LASTS ABOUT TWENTY MINUTES IN HERE.
THAT'S ALMOST NO BETTER THAN A HUMAN... PATHETIC...
BUT VERY WELL, VERY WELL...
PASU (SHIFT)
NOT A PROBLEM... I'LL JUST TURN THE CLOCK BACK A BIT.
LET'S GO 400 YEARS...
!?
...NO, 100 YEARS SHOULD BE PLENTY.
GO
GO (RUMBLE)
GHNNNNNNNNNNH!
VO (VWOOM)

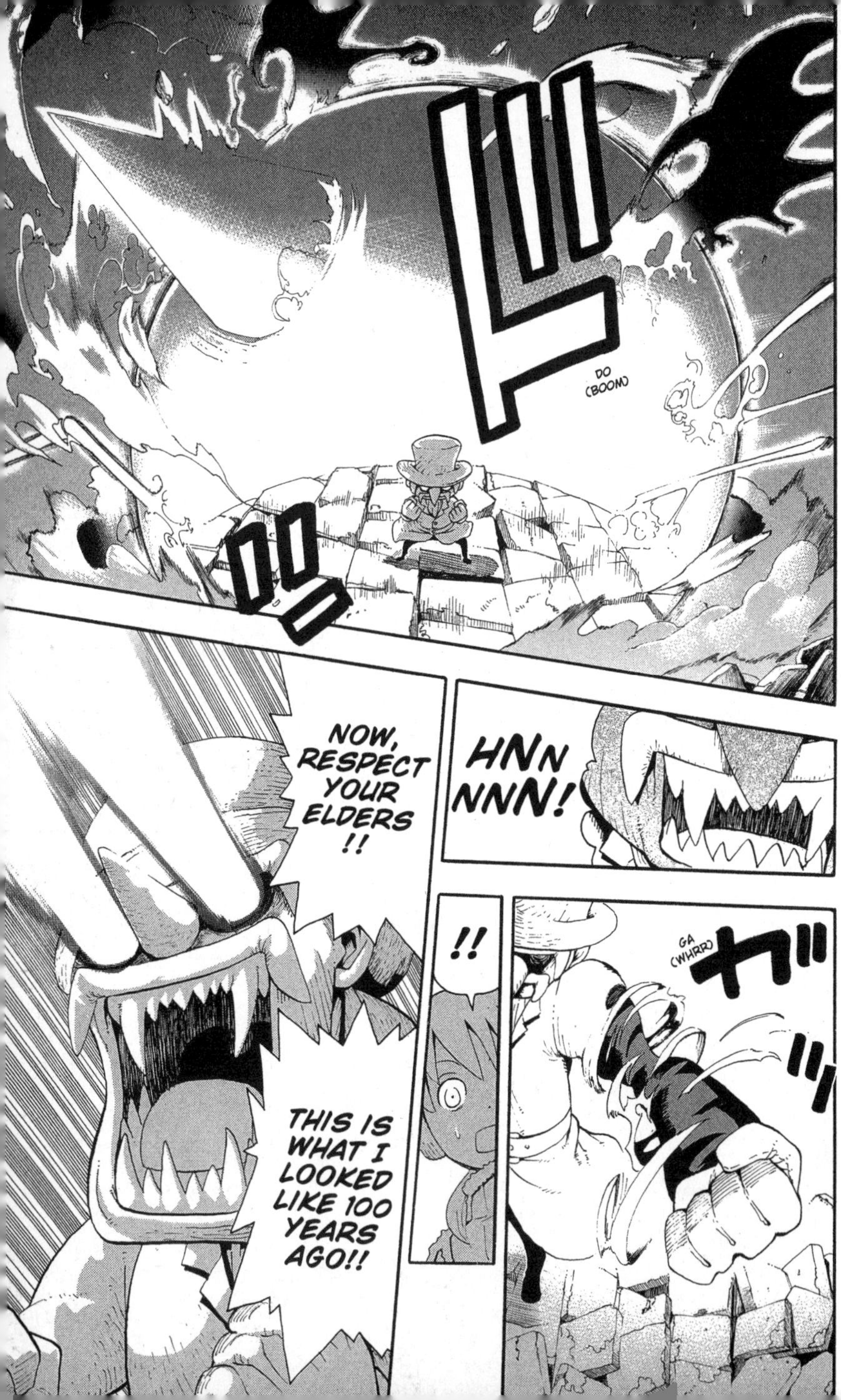
DO
(BOOM)
HNN NNN!
GA
(WHRR)
!!
NOW, RESPECT YOUR ELDERS!!
THIS IS WHAT I LOOKED LIKE 100 YEARS AGO!!

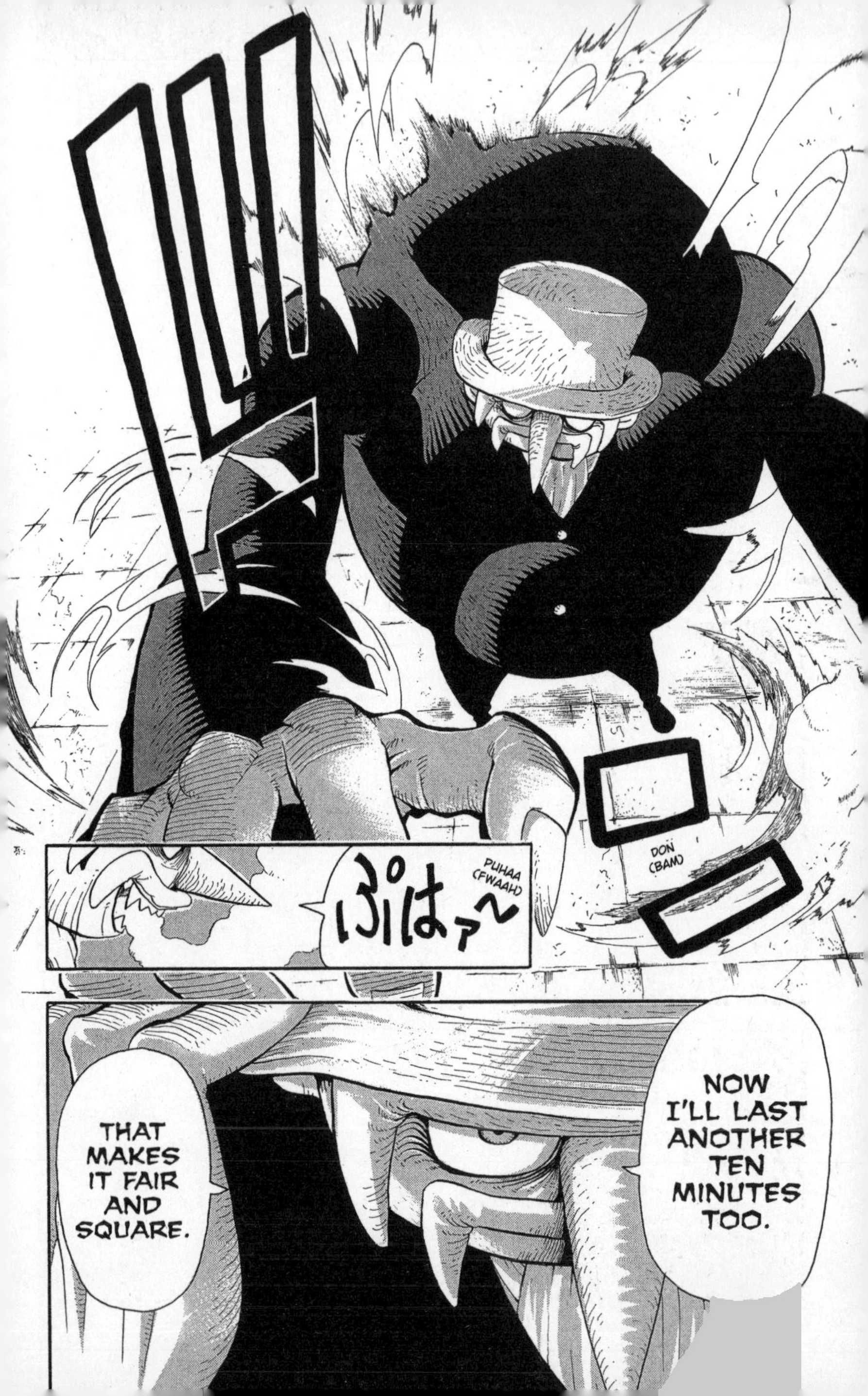
DON (BAM)
ぷはァ~
PUHAA (FWAAH)
NOW I'LL LAST ANOTHER TEN MINUTES TOO.
THAT MAKES IT FAIR AND SQUARE.

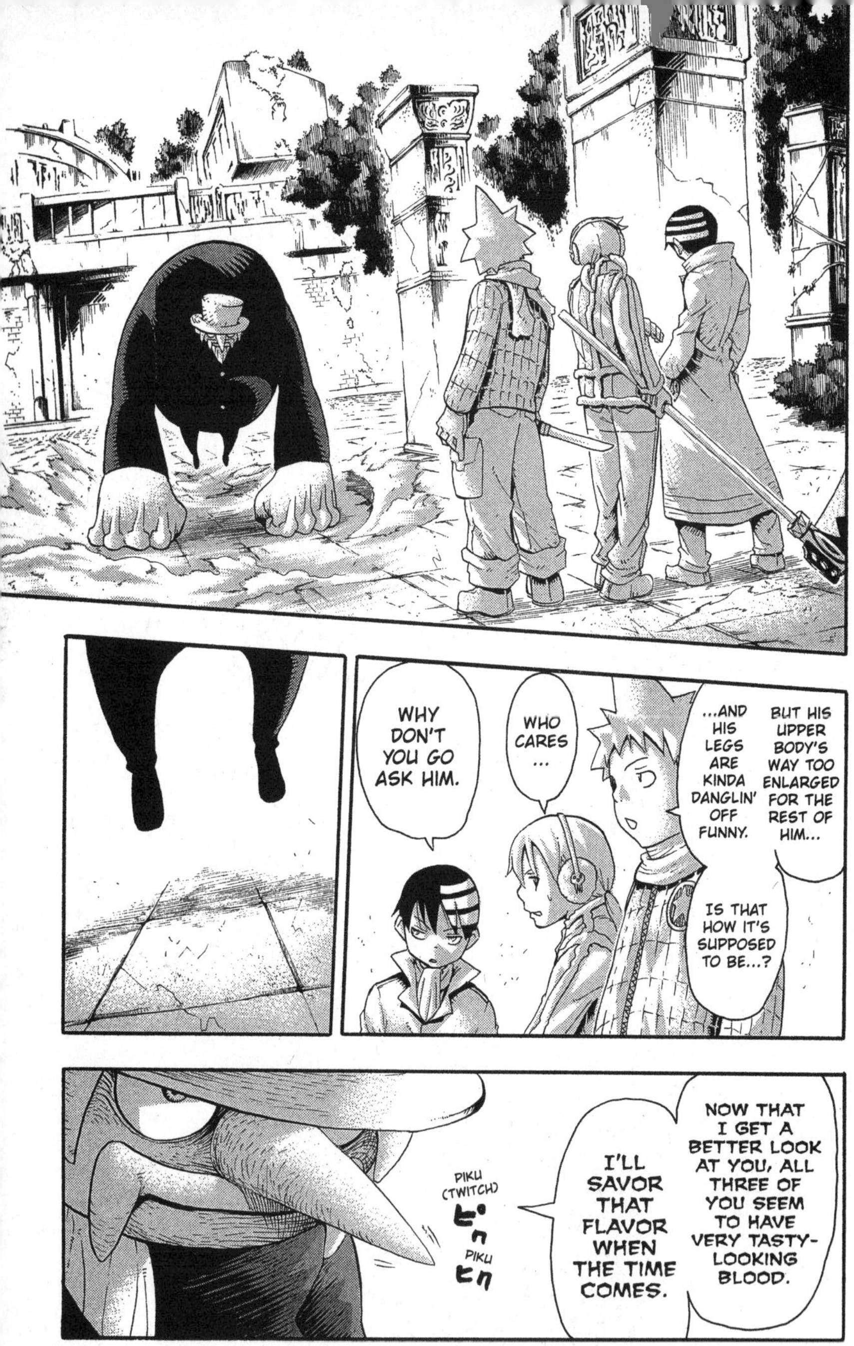
BUT HIS UPPER BODY'S WAY TOO ENLARGED FOR THE REST OF HIM...
...AND HIS LEGS ARE KINDA DANGLIN' OFF FUNNY.
IS THAT HOW IT'S SUPPOSED TO BE...?
WHO CARES...
WHY DON'T YOU GO ASK HIM.
NOW THAT I GET A BETTER LOOK AT YOU, ALL THREE OF YOU SEEM TO HAVE VERY TASTY-LOOKING BLOOD.
I'LL SAVOR THAT FLAVOR WHEN THE TIME COMES.
PIKU (TWITCH)
ピク
PIKU
ピク

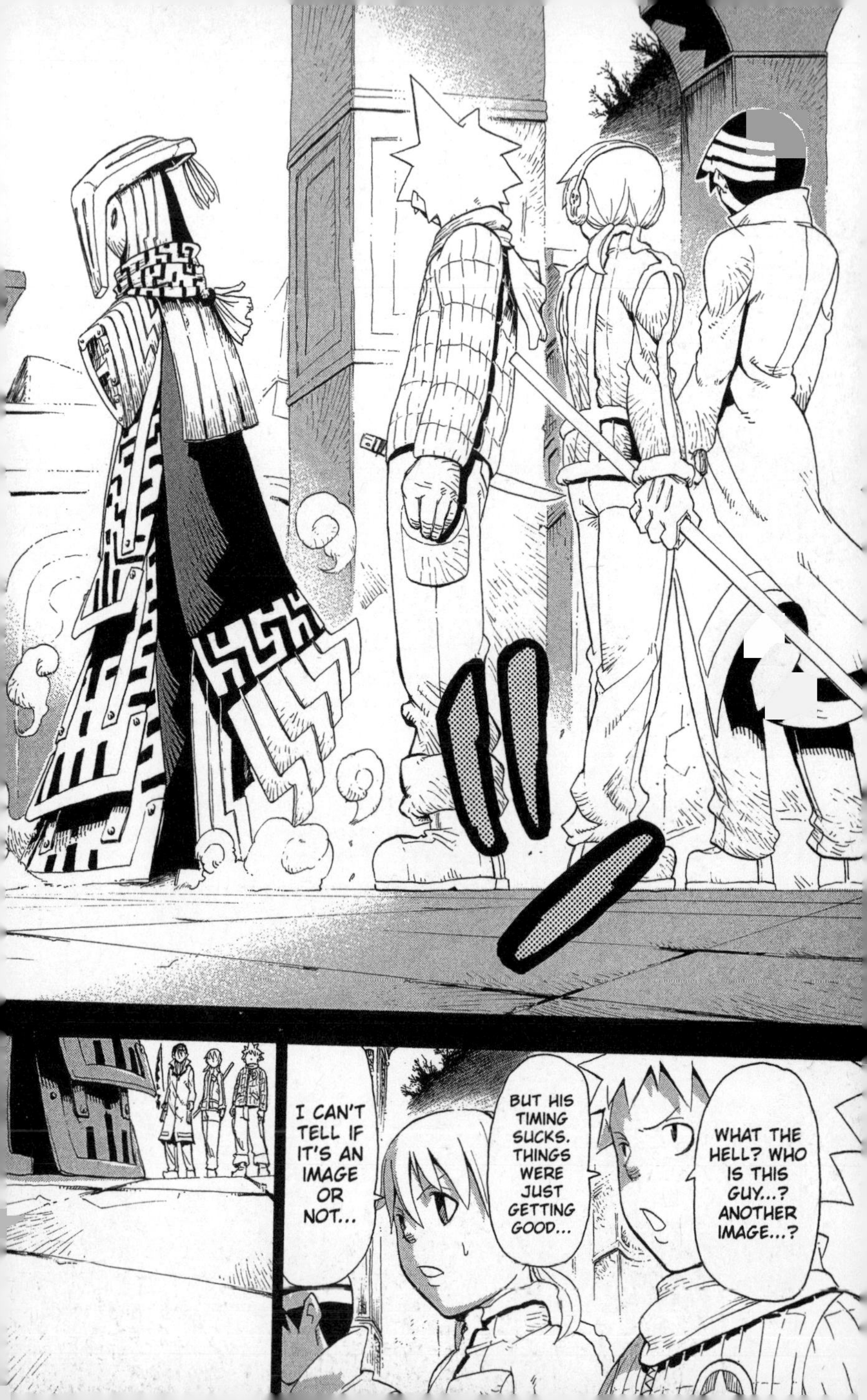
WHAT THE HELL? WHO IS THIS GUY...? ANOTHER IMAGE...?
BUT HIS TIMING SUCKS. THINGS WERE JUST GETTING GOOD...
I CAN'T TELL IF IT'S AN IMAGE OR NOT...

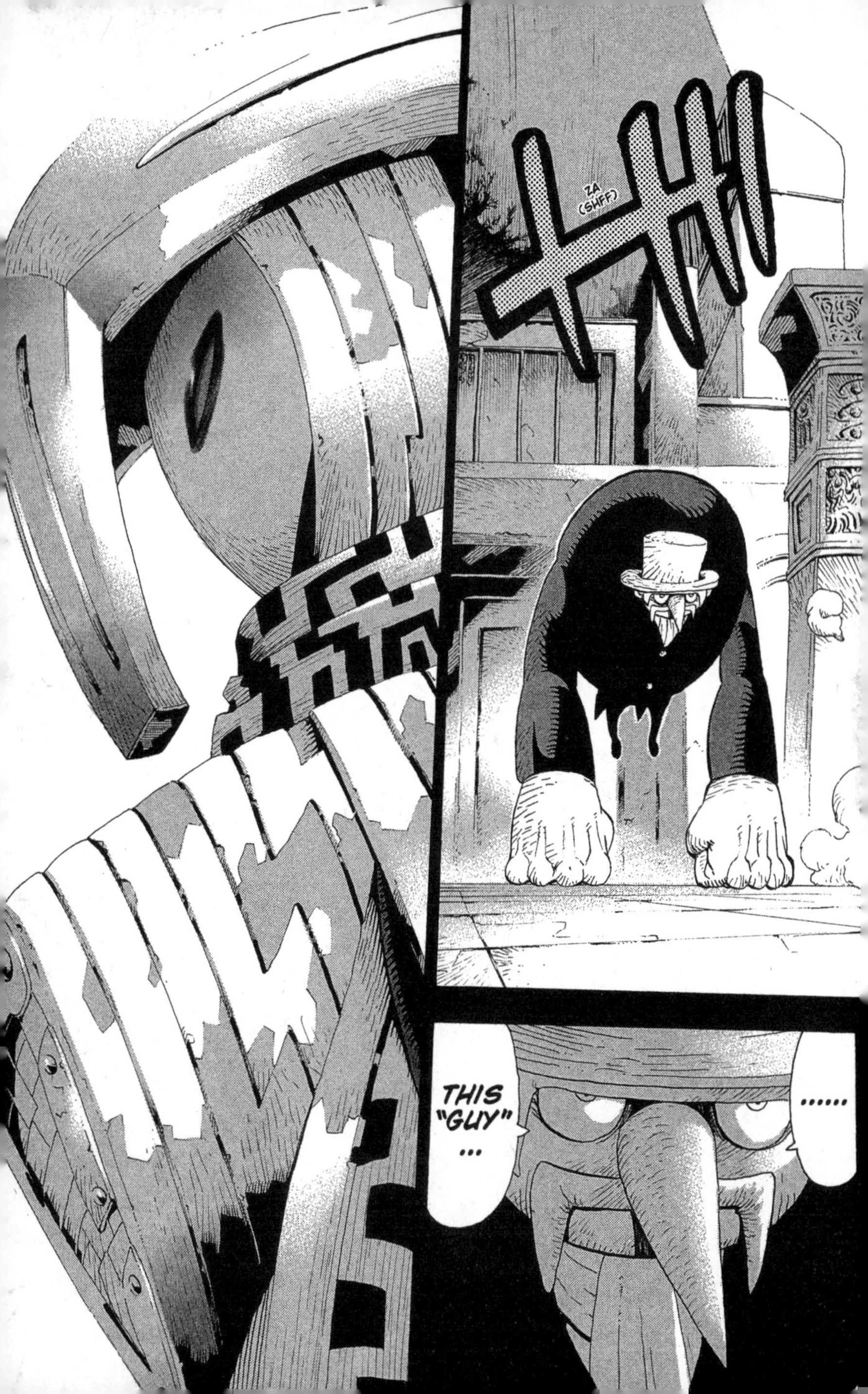
ZA
(SHFF)
......
THIS "GUY" ...

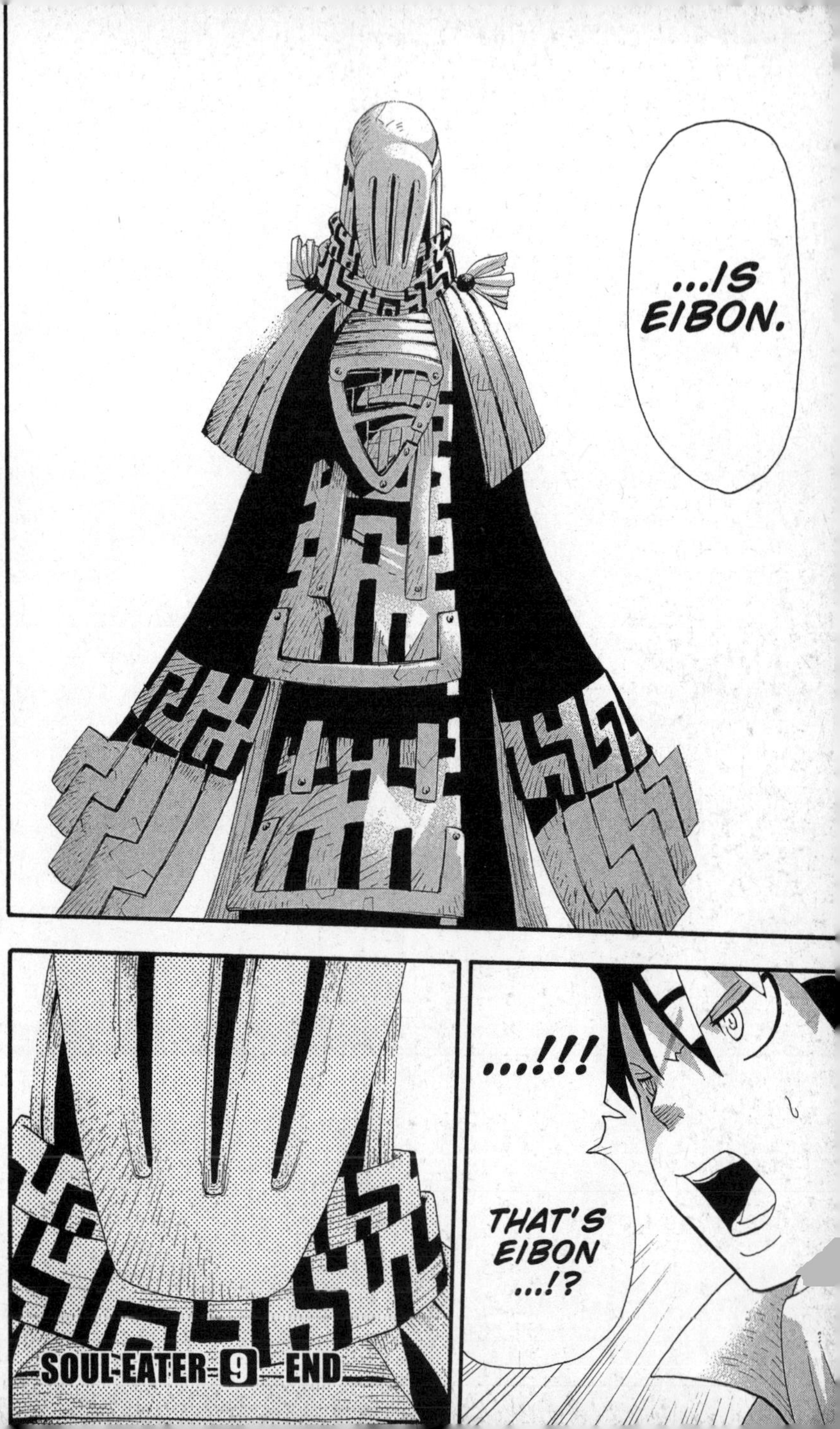
...IS EIBON.
...!!!
THAT'S EIBON ...!?
SOUL EATER 9 END

SOUL EATER

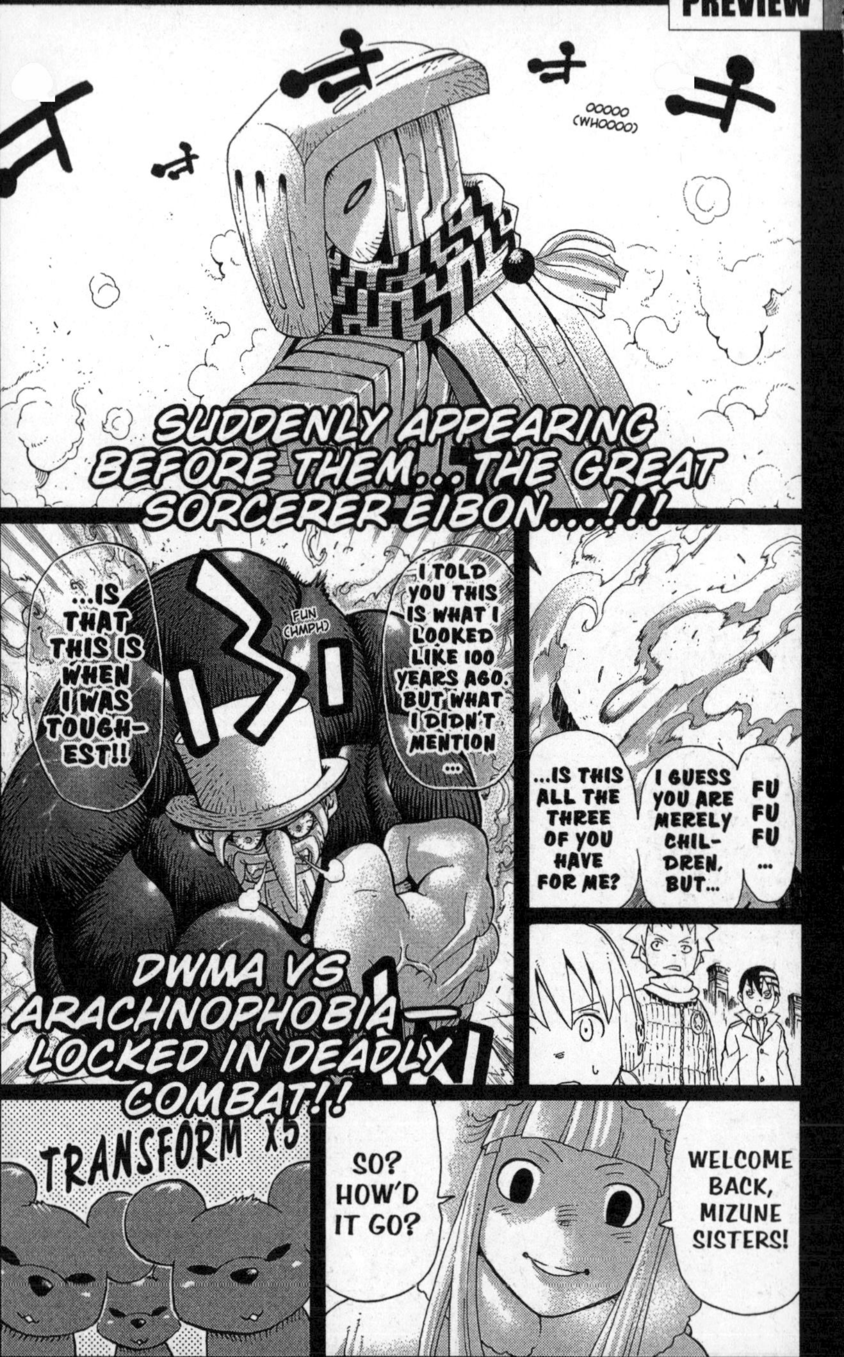
OOOOO (WHOOOO)
SUDDENLY APPEARING BEFORE THEM... THE GREAT SORCERER EIBON...!!!
FU FU FU...
I GUESS YOU ARE MERELY CHIL-DREN, BUT...
...IS THIS ALL THE THREE OF YOU HAVE FOR ME?
I TOLD YOU THIS IS WHAT I LOOKED LIKE 100 YEARS AGO. BUT WHAT I DIDN'T MENTION...
FUN (HMPH)
...IS THAT THIS IS WHEN I WAS TOUGH-EST!!
DWMA VS ARACHNOPHOBIA—LOCKED IN DEADLY COMBAT!!
WELCOME BACK, MIZUNE SISTERS!
SO? HOW'D IT GO?
TRANSFORM X5

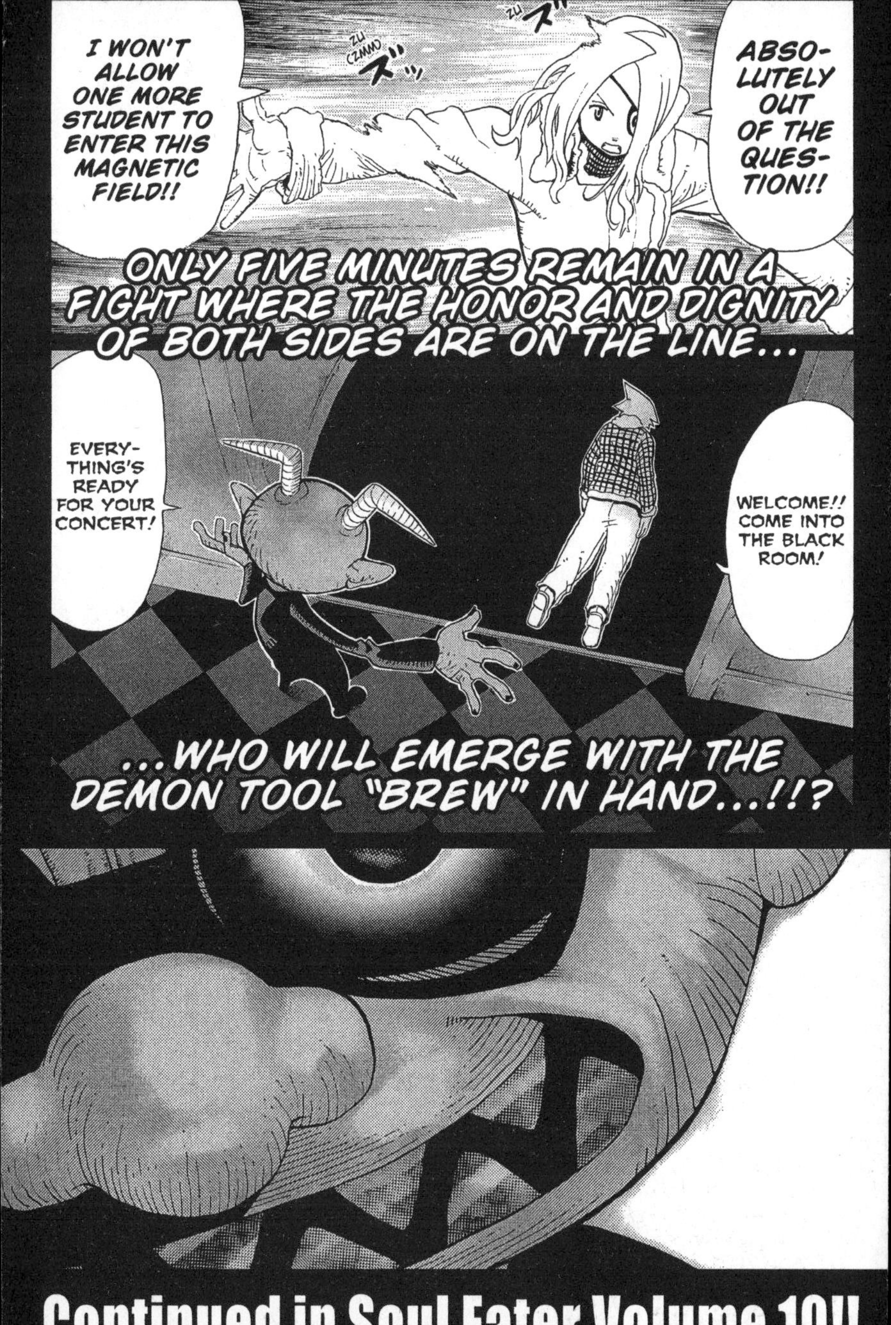
ZU
ZU (ZWMM)
ABSO-LUTELY OUT OF THE QUES-TION!!
I WON'T ALLOW ONE MORE STUDENT TO ENTER THIS MAGNETIC FIELD!!
ONLY FIVE MINUTES REMAIN IN A FIGHT WHERE THE HONOR AND DIGNITY OF BOTH SIDES ARE ON THE LINE...
WELCOME!! COME INTO THE BLACK ROOM!
EVERY-THING'S READY FOR YOUR CONCERT!
...WHO WILL EMERGE WITH THE DEMON TOOL "BREW" IN HAND...!!?

Continued in Soul Eater Volume 10!!

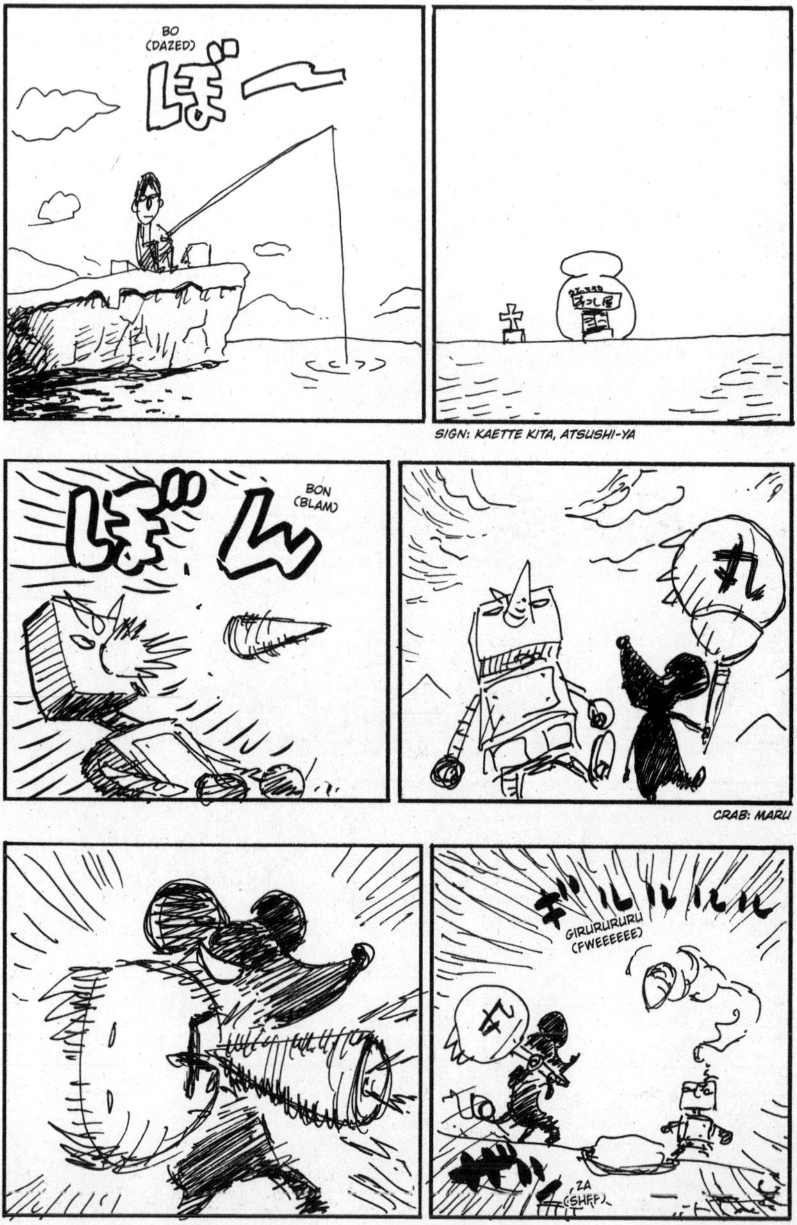
SIGN: KAETTE KITA, ATSUSHI-YA
BO
(DAZED)
ぼー
CRAB: MARU
BON
(BLAM)
ぼん
GIRURURURU
(FWEEEEEE)
ZA
(SHFF)

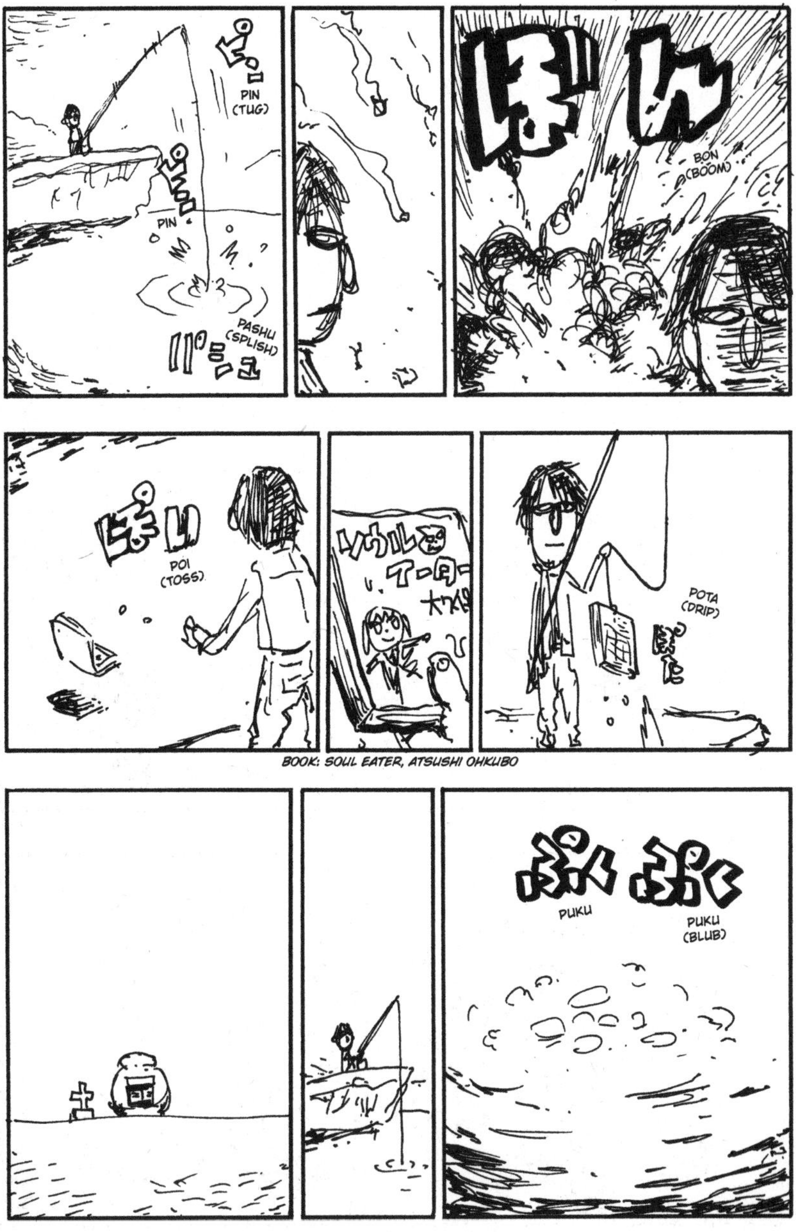
BON (BOOM)
PIN (TUG)
PIN
PASHU (SPLISH)
POTA (DRIP)
POI (TOSS)
BOOK: SOUL EATER, ATSUSHI OHKUBO
PUKU
PUKU (BLUB)

Translation Notes

Common Honorifics

no honorific: Indicates familiarity or closeness; if used without permission or reason, addressing someone in this manner would constitute an insult.

-san: The Japanese equivalent of Mr./Mrs./Miss. If a situation calls for politeness, this is the fail-safe honorific.

-sama: Conveys great respect; may also indicate that the social status of the speaker is lower than that of the addressee.

-kun: Used most often when referring to boys, this indicates affection or familiarity. Occasionally used by older men among their peers, but it may also be used by anyone referring to a person of lower standing.

-chan: An affectionate honorific indicating familiarity used mostly in reference to girls; also used in reference to cute persons or animals of either gender.

-senpai: A suffix used to address upperclassmen or more experienced coworkers.

-sensei: A respectful term for teachers, artists, or high-level professionals.

Page 59
Sanzu River
In Japanese Buddhist mythology, the **Sanzu River** (literally "river of three crossings") is the river that separates the land of the living from the land of the dead. Thus, it plays a role similar to that of the River Styx in beliefs about the afterlife. According to the myth, a person's soul crosses in one of three ways depending on the weight of their sins (i.e., their karma): the good cross over a bridge, the neither good nor bad cross through a shallows, and the bad cross through deep waters where vicious snakes swim.

Page 62
Excalibur's poem is actually a tanka—that is, a traditional Japanese short poetic form similar to a haiku, but with a syllabic meter of 5-7-5-7-7 instead of 5-7-5. It makes him seem like a blowhard (which he is).

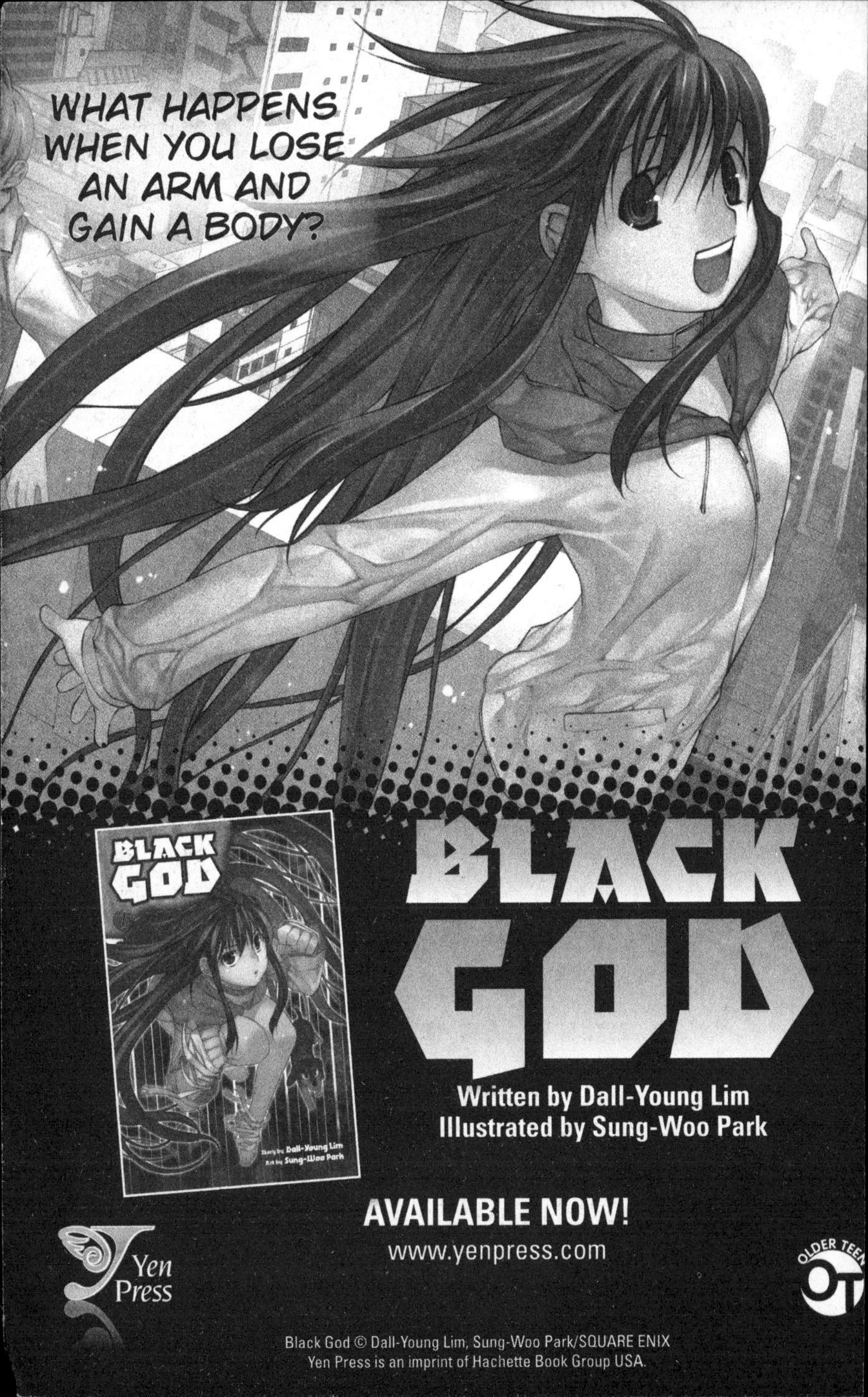

The Phantomhive family has a butler who's almost too good to be true...

...or maybe he's just too good to be human.

Black Butler

YANA TOBOSO

VOLUME 1-9 IN STORES NOW!

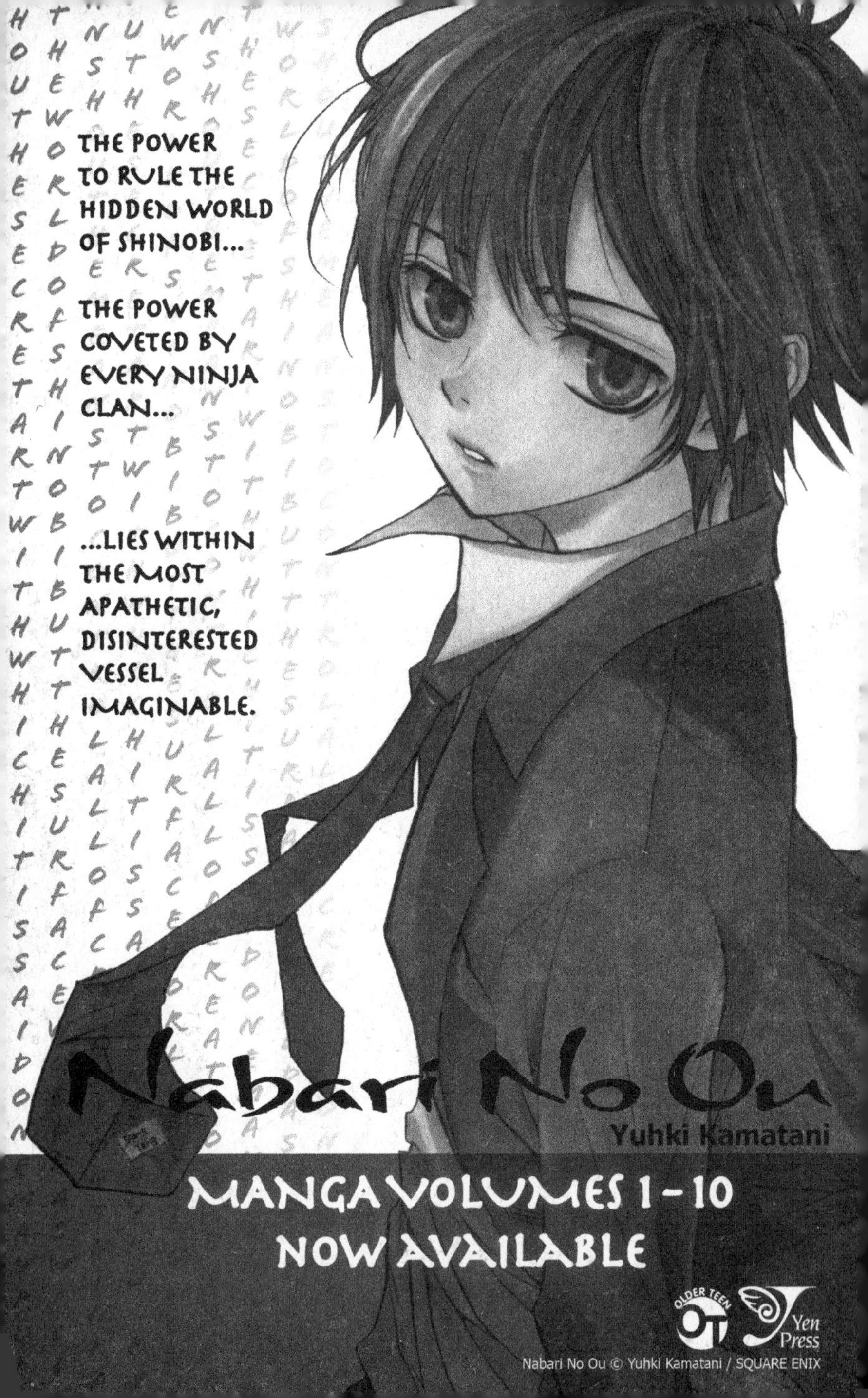
THE POWER TO RULE THE HIDDEN WORLD OF SHINOBI...
THE POWER COVETED BY EVERY NINJA CLAN...
...LIES WITHIN THE MOST APATHETIC, DISINTERESTED VESSEL IMAGINABLE.
Nabari No Ou
Yuhki Kamatani
MANGA VOLUMES 1-10
NOW AVAILABLE
OLDER TEEN OT
Yen Press
Nabari No Ou © Yuhki Kamatani / SQUARE ENIX

SOUL EATER ⑨

ATSUSHI OHKUBO

Translation: Jack Wiedrick

Lettering: Alexis Eckerman

SOUL EATER Vol. 9 © 2007 Atsushi Ohkubo / SQUARE ENIX. All rights reserved. First published in Japan in 2007 by SQUARE ENIX CO., LTD. English translation rights arranged with SQUARE ENIX CO., LTD. and Hachette Book Group through Tuttle-Mori Agency, Inc.

Translation © 2012 by SQUARE ENIX CO., LTD.

Yen Press
Hachette Book Group
1290 Avenue of the Americas, New York, NY 10104

www.HachetteBookGroup.com
www.YenPress.com

Yen Press is an imprint of Hachette Book Group, Inc. The Yen Press name and logo are trademarks of Hachette Book Group, Inc.

First Yen Press Edition: May 2012

ISBN: 978-0-316-07113-0

10 9 8 7

BVG

Printed in the United States of America